I0016847

LEARN FROM SCRATCH
VISUAL C# .NET
WITH SQL SERVER

To Develop Database-Driven Desktop Applications

First Edition

VIVIAN SIAHAAN

First published: October 2020
Production reference: 06102020
Published by BALIGE Publishing Ltd.
BALIGE, North Sumatera

ABOUT THE AUTHOR

 Vivian Siahaan is a fast-learner who likes to do new things. She was born, raised in Hinalang Bagasan, Balige, on the banks of Lake Toba, and completed high school education from SMAN 1 Balige. She started herself learning Java, Android, JavaScript, CSS, C ++, Python, R, Visual Basic, Visual C #, MATLAB, Mathematica, PHP, JSP, MySQL, SQL Server, Oracle, Access, and other programming languages. She studied programming from scratch, starting with the most basic syntax and logic, by building several simple and applicable GUI applications. Animation and games are fields of programming that are interests that she always wants to develop. Besides studying mathematical logic and programming, the author also has the pleasure of reading novels. Vivian Siahaan has written dozens of ebooks that have been published on Sparta Publisher: Data Structure with Java; Java Programming: Cookbook; C ++ Programming: Cookbook; C Programming For High Schools / Vocational Schools and Students; Java Programming for SMA / SMK; Java Tutorial: GUI, Graphics and Animation; Visual Basic Programming: From A to Z; Java Programming for Animation and Games; C # Programming for SMA / SMK and Students; MATLAB For Students and Researchers; Graphics in JavaScript: Quick Learning Series; JavaScript Image Processing Methods: From A to Z; Java GUI Case Study: AWT & Swing; Basic CSS and JavaScript; PHP / MySQL Programming: Cookbook; Visual Basic: Cookbook; C ++ Programming for High Schools / Vocational Schools and Students; Concepts and Practices of C ++; PHP / MySQL For Students; C # Programming: From A to Z; Visual Basic for SMA / SMK and Students; C # .NET and SQL Server for High School / Vocational School and Students. At the ANDI Yogyakarta publisher, Vivian Siahaan also wrote a number of books including: Python Programming Theory and Practice; Python GUI Programming; Python GUI and Database; Build From Zero School Database Management System In Python / MySQL; Database Management System in Python / MySQL; Python / MySQL For Management Systems of Criminal Track Record Database; Java / MySQL For Management Systems of Criminal Track Records Database; Database and Critptography Using Java / MySQL; Build From Zero School Database Management System With Java / MySQL.

ABOUT THE BOOK

In Tutorial 1, you will start building a Visual C# interface for database management system project with SQL Server. The database, named DBMS, is created. The designed interface in this tutorial will used as the main terminal in accessing other forms. This tutorial will also discuss how to create login form and login table.

In Tutorial 2, you will build a project, as part of database management system, where you can store information about valuables in school. In Tutorial 3 up to Tutorial 4, you will perform the steps necessary to add 6 tables into DBMS database. You will build each table and add the associated fields as needed. In this tutorials, you will create a library database project, as part of database management system, where you can store all information about library including author, title, and publisher.

In Tutorial 5 up to Tutorial 7, you will perform the steps necessary to add 6 more tables into DBMS database. You will build each table and add the associated fields as needed. In this tutorials, you will create a high school database project, as part of database management system, where you can store all information about school including parent, teacher, student, subject, and, title, and grade.

CONTENTS

TUTORIAL 1
MAIN AND LOGIN FORMS

In this tutorial, you will build a Visual C# interface for the database. This interface will used as the main terminal in accessing other forms. This tutorial will also discuss how to create login form and login table.

1.1 Tutorial Steps of Creating Main Form

Step 1   You will start this project by creating a main form. This form is useful as a central place to access a number of forms.

Place on the form nine control labels, three picture box controls, and seven control buttons. Set the following properties:

Form1 Control	
Name	FormMain
FormBorderStyle	FixedSingle
StartPosition	CenterScreen
Text	BALIGE HIGH SCHOOL DATABASE MANAGEMENT SYSTEM
BackColor	MediumBlue

Label1 Control	
Font	Jokerman
ForeColor	Yellow
Text	BALIGE HIGH SCHOOL DATABASE MANAGEMENT SYSTEM

PictureBox1 Control	
Image	school.jpg
SizeMode	StretchImage

PictureBox2 Control	
Image	crown1.jpg
SizeMode	StretchImage

PictureBox2 Control	
Image	crown2.jpg
SizeMode	StretchImage

Button1 Control	
BackColor	Red
FlatStyle	Standard
Name	btnLibrary
Image	library.jpg

Button2 Control	
BackColor	Red
FlatStyle	Standard
Name	btnInventory
Image	inventory.jpg

Button3 Control	
BackColor	Red
FlatStyle	Standard
Name	btnAcademy
Image	academy.jpg

Button4 Control	
BackColor	Red
FlatStyle	Standard
Name	btnTuition
Image	tuition.jpg

Button5 Control	
BackColor	Red
FlatStyle	Standard
Name	btnLogin
Image	login.jpg

Button6 Control	
BackColor	Red
FlatStyle	Standard
Name	btnSeting
Image	setting.jpg

Button7 Control	
BackColor	Red
FlatStyle	Standard
Name	btnExit
Image	exit.jpg

Button7 Control	
BackColor	Red
FlatStyle	Standard
Name	btnExit
Image	exit.jpg

Label2 Control	
Font	Buxton Sketch
ForeColor	White
Text	Library DBMS

Label3 Control	
Font	Buxton Sketch
ForeColor	White
Text	Inventory DBMS

Label4 Control	
Font	Buxton Sketch
ForeColor	White
Text	Academy DBMS

Label5 Control	
Font	Buxton Sketch
ForeColor	White
Text	Tuition Fee DBMS

Label6 Control	
Font	Buxton Sketch
ForeColor	White
Text	Login

Label7 Control	
Font	Buxton Sketch
ForeColor	White
Text	Setting

Label8 Control	
Font	Buxton Sketch
ForeColor	White
Text	Exit

Step 2   Run the application. You will see what is shown in Figure 1.1.

Figure 1.1 Main form when it first runs

Step 3   Define **Load** event of the form to specify that only the login button is active when the main form is first run. This is done by making use of each button's **Enabled** property.

```
1   private void FormMain_Load(object sender, EventArgs e)
2   {
3       btnLibrary.Enabled = false;
```

```
4        btnInventory.Enabled = false;
5        btnAcademy.Enabled = false;
6        btnTuition.Enabled = false;
7        btnSetting.Enabled = false;
8        btnExit.Enabled = true;
9    }
```

Step 4 Define the **Click** event of **btnExit** to exit the application:

```
1    private void btnExit_Click(object sender, EventArgs e)
2    {
3        Application.Exit();
4    }
```

Step 5 Run the application. Note that all buttons except **Login** button are disabled as shown
        in Figure 1.2.

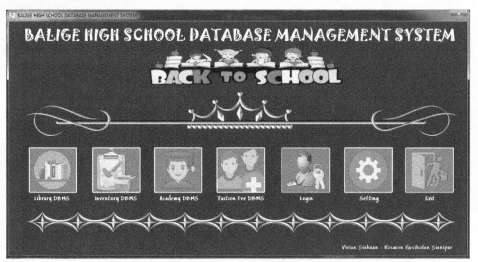

Figure 1.2 All buttons except Login button are disabled when applications first runs

1.2 Tutorial Steps of Creating Login Table

Step 1 In this tutorial, you will perform the necessary steps to build a version of SQL Server
        (**DBMS.mdf**) and **Login** table using Microsoft Visual Studio 2019. You will build the
        table and add the corresponding fields as needed (along with the necessary keys and
        indexes).

        Start Visual Studio. Open **Server Explorer** by selecting the **View** menu option and
        then **Server Explorer**, as shown in the figure below:

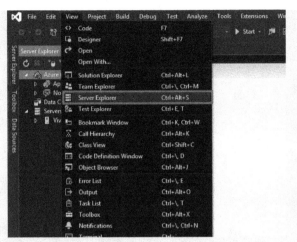

Figure 1.3 Server Explorer option on the **View** menu

You will then find:

Figure 1.4 Server Explorer window

Step 2   Right click on **Data Connections** and select **Create New SQL Server Database**. This window will be displayed as shown in Figure 1.5.

Figure 1.5 The **Create New SQL Server Database** window

Provide your server name (your computer name followed by backslash and SQLEXPRESS). Enter **DBMS** for New database name as shown in Figure 1.6.

Figure 1.6 The **Create New SQL Server Database** window: Server name and New database name

The new database will appear in the **Server Explorer** window under **Data Connections** as shown in Figure 1.7.

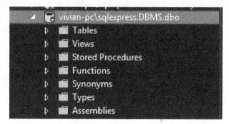

Figure 1.7 The new database that has been created

For each table you want to create, right click on the **Tables** folder and **select Add New Table**. Once you do this, the design window will open so you can enter fields in the table.

You do this for each table in the **DBMS** database.

Step 3   Create a new table in the design window. You will see as shown in Figure 1.8.

There is a grid for each field (also known as a column). You provide the column name with its data type. You also need to decide whether the field can be null. For each field or column, you assign properties using the **Properties** Window. To the right of the grid is where keys and indexes are defined. Below is the Design window, where the actual scripting language for creating the tables is written. Name the table **Login** by changing the first row of the script to: **CREATE TABLE [dbo]. [Login]**.

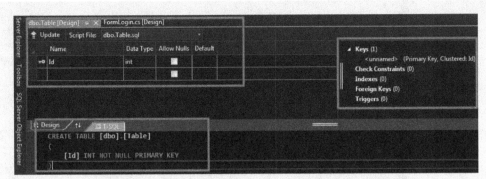

Figure 1.8 The design window for the table to add

Step 4   The first field in the **Login** table is **ID**. Enter that name for the column name, use **bigint**
data type and set the **Is Identity** property to **True**:

Figure 1.9 The first field (**ID**) is appended with the **Is Identity** property set to **True**

Step 5   Set other fields using the following options:

Name	Data Type
User	varchar(50)
Password	varchar (50)

Make sure all fields don't allow **Null** values (because you want a complete address).
At this point, your design grid should look as shown in Figure 1.10.

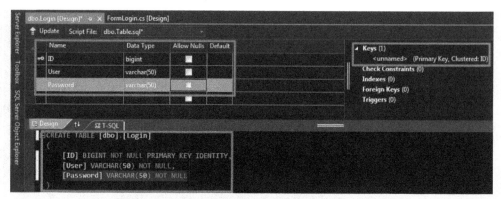

Figure 1.10 Grid design for the **Login** table

Now, you define primary key and indexes to allow fast searching. **ID** is a primary field.
If a small key doesn't appear in the field, you need to place it there. Right click on the
ID row and select **Set Primary Key**. A small key will be displayed next to the entry,
indicating that it is a primary key.

You need to set **User** as the index. Right click on **Indexes** and select **Add New**, then
Index. You will see an added index (**IX_Login_Column**):

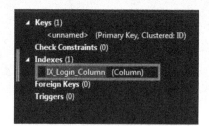

Figure 1.11 The panel with the newly added index

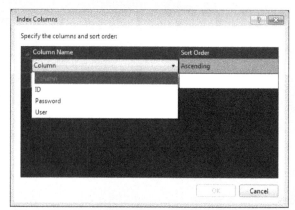

Figure 1.12 The **Index Columns** window to determine which column will be used
as index

Highlight the index displayed and look at the **Properties** window on the bottom right. Select the **Columns** property and click the ellipsis to see as shown in Figure 1.12.

Select the **User** and **Ascending** columns for the sort order:

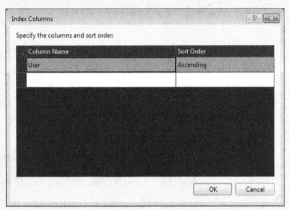

Figure 1.12 The **Index Columns** window after **User** is selected as the index

Then click OK. Here is the final table design panel as shown in Figure 1.13.

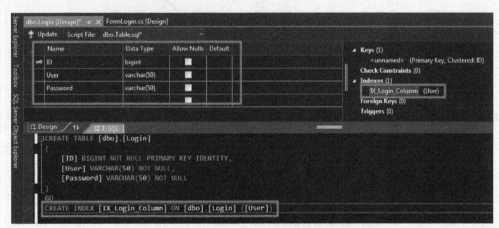

Figure 1.13 The final panel for the **Login** table

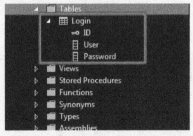

Figure 1.14 Server Explorer window after **Login** table created

Click **Update** in right corner to create **Login** table. The created table is shown in **Server Explorer** window as shown in Figure 1.14.

Step 6   Insert some rows into **Login** table by right clicking on **Login** table and **Show Table Data** in **Server Explorer** window as shown in Figure 1.15. Now, **Login** table has three rows as shown in Figure 1.16.

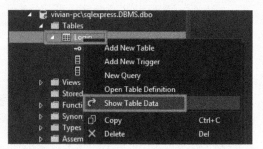

Figure 1.15 Insert some rows into **Login** table

Figure 1.16 The **Login** table now has three rows of data

1.3 Tutorial Steps of Creating Login Form

Step 1   You will create login form. Place on the form one picture box, two labels, one combo box, one text box, and two buttons.

Set the following properties:

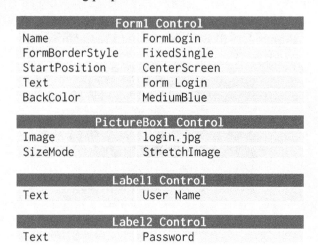

Form1 Control	
Name	FormLogin
FormBorderStyle	FixedSingle
StartPosition	CenterScreen
Text	Form Login
BackColor	MediumBlue

PictureBox1 Control	
Image	login.jpg
SizeMode	StretchImage

Label1 Control	
Text	User Name

Label2 Control	
Text	Password

ComboBox1 Control	
DropDownStyle	DropDownList
Name	cboUser

TextBox1 Control	
Name	txtPassword
PasswordChar	*

Button1 Control	
Name	btnLogin
Text	LOGIN

Button2 Control	
Name	btnCancel
Text	CANCEL

Step 2   Run the application. Click **Login** button and you will see what is shown in Figure 1.17.

Figure 1.17 Login form

Step 3   Next, you need to open **DBMS** database and **Login** table and bind its controls to related fields. Put this line of code at the top of the code window to use the data objects:

```
1  using System.Data.SqlClient;
```

Step 4   Place these lines of code on the form level declaration:

```
1  SqlConnection loginConn;
2  SqlCommand loginCommand;
3  SqlDataReader loginDataReader;
```

Step 5   Copy **DBMS.mdf** into **D:\Database** folder. Place this code in **Click** event of **btnLogin** to connect to database and verify username and its password:

```
1  private void btnLogin_Click(object sender, EventArgs e)
2  {
3      loginConn = new SqlConnection("Data Source=.\\SQLEXPRESS;
```

```
4    AttachDbFilename=D:\\Database\\DBMS.mdf;
5    Integrated Security = True; Connect Timeout = 30;
6    User Instance = True");
7
8    loginCommand = new SqlCommand();
9    loginConn.Open();
10   loginCommand.Connection = loginConn;
11
12   if (cboUser.SelectedItem.ToString() == "admin")
13   {
14       loginCommand.CommandText =
15           "SELECT * FROM Login WHERE Password='" +
16           txtPassword.Text + "'";
17       loginDataReader = loginCommand.ExecuteReader();
18
19       if (loginDataReader.Read())
20       {
21           FormMain f2 = new FormMain();
22           f2.Show();
23           this.Dispose();
24       }
25       else
26       {
27           MessageBox.Show("Username or password is wrong");
28           this.Close();
29       }
30   }
31   else if (cboUser.SelectedItem.ToString() == "user")
32   {
33       loginCommand.CommandText =
34           "SELECT * FROM Login WHERE Password='" +
35           txtPassword.Text + "'";
36       loginDataReader = loginCommand.ExecuteReader();
37
38       if (loginDataReader.Read())
39       {
40           FormMain f2 = new FormMain();
41           f2.Show();
42           this.Dispose();
43       }
44       else
45       {
46           MessageBox.Show("Username or password is wrong");
47           this.Close();
48       }
49   }
50   else if (cboUser.SelectedItem.ToString() == "boss")
51   {
52       loginCommand.CommandText =
53           "SELECT * FROM Login WHERE Password='" +
54
```

```
55              txtPassword.Text + "'";
56          loginDataReader = loginCommand.ExecuteReader();
57
58          if (loginDataReader.Read())
59          {
60              FormMain f2 = new FormMain();
61              f2.Show();
62              this.Dispose();
63          }
64          else
65          {
66              MessageBox.Show("Username or password is wrong");
67              this.Close();
68          }
69      }
70
71      else
72      {
73          MessageBox.Show("Username or password is wrong");
74          this.Close();
75      }
76
77      loginConn.Close();
78  }
```

Step 6   Define **FormClosing** event of form as follows:

```
1   private void FormLogin_FormClosing(object sender, FormClosingEventArgs e)
2   {
3       FormMain f2 = new FormMain();
4       f2.Show();
5   }
```

This code says that if form is closed, application will return to main form.

Step 7   Define **Click** event of **btnCancel** as follows:

```
1   private void btnCancel_Click(object sender, EventArgs e)
2   {
3       this.Close();
4   }
```

Step 8   Define **KeyDown** event of **btnLogin** as follows:

```
1   private void btnLogin_KeyDown(object sender, KeyEventArgs e)
2   {
3       if (e.KeyCode == Keys.Enter)
4       {
5           btnLogin.PerformClick();
6       }
7   }
```

The code says that if the user presses Enter while **btnLogin** has focus it will trigger the **Click** event of **btnLogin**.

Step 9   Define **KeyDown** event of **txtPassword** as follows:

```
private void txtPassword_KeyDown(object sender, KeyEventArgs e)
{
    if (e.KeyCode == Keys.Enter)
    {
        btnLogin.PerformClick();
    }
}
```

The code says that if the user presses Enter while **txtPassword** has focus it will trigger the **Click** event of **btnLogin**.

Step 10   Run application. Click on **Login** button. Login form will show up. Choose one of usernames available and give the correct password as shown in Figure 1.18.

Figure 1.18 User chooses usernam and fills password

You then will return to main form. Notice that nothing happens in main form. All buttons except **Login** and **Exit** buttons are disabled. In the next step, you will fix this.

Step 12   Modify **FormMain** and adds six public properties as follows:

Figure 1.19 After user chooses one of usernames available and give the correct password. It then will return to main form. Notice that all buttons except **Login** and **Exit** buttons are now enabled.

```
1   public Button showButtonLibrary
2   {
3       get { return btnLibrary; }
4       set { btnLibrary = value; }
5    }
6
7   public Button showButtonInventory
8   {
9       get { return btnInventory; }
10      set { btnInventory = value; }
11  }
12
13  public Button showButtonAcademy
14  {
15      get { return btnAcademy; }
16      set { btnAcademy = value; }
17  }
18
19  public Button showButtonLogin
20  {
21      get { return btnLogin; }
22      set { btnLogin = value; }
23  }
24
25  public Button showButtonTuition
26  {
27      get { return btnTuition; }
28      set { btnTuition = value; }
29  }
30
```

```
31   public Button showButtonSetting
32   {
33       get { return btnSetting; }
34       set { btnSetting = value; }
35   }
```

Step 13   Modify **Click** event of **btnLogin** so that if user gives correct username and password
then all buttons except **Login** button will be enabled:

```
1    private void btnLogin_Click(object sender, EventArgs e)
2    {
3        loginConn = new SqlConnection("Data Source=.\\SQLEXPRESS;
4            AttachDbFilename=D:\\Database\\DBMS.mdf;
5            Integrated Security = True; Connect Timeout = 30;
6            User Instance = True");
7
8        loginCommand = new SqlCommand();
9        loginConn.Open();
10       loginCommand.Connection = loginConn;
11
12       if (cboUser.SelectedItem.ToString() == "admin")
13       {
14           loginCommand.CommandText =
15               "SELECT * FROM Login WHERE Password='" +
16               txtPassword.Text + "'";
17           loginDataReader = loginCommand.ExecuteReader();
18
19           if (loginDataReader.Read())
20           {
21               FormMain f2 = new FormMain();
22               f2.Show();
23               f2.showButtonLibrary.Enabled = true;
24               f2.showButtonInventory.Enabled = true;
25               f2.showButtonAcademy.Enabled = true;
26               f2.showButtonLogin.Enabled = false;
27               f2.showButtonSetting.Enabled = true;
28               f2.showButtonTuition.Enabled = true;
29               this.Dispose();
30           }
31           else
32           {
33               MessageBox.Show("Username or password is wrong");
34               this.Close();
35           }
36       }
37       else if (cboUser.SelectedItem.ToString() == "user")
38       {
39           loginCommand.CommandText =
40               "SELECT * FROM Login WHERE Password='" +
41               txtPassword.Text + "'";
```

```
42      loginDataReader = loginCommand.ExecuteReader();
43
44          if (loginDataReader.Read())
45          {
46              FormMain f2 = new FormMain();
47              f2.Show();
48              f2.showButtonLibrary.Enabled = true;
49              f2.showButtonInventory.Enabled = true;
50              f2.showButtonAcademy.Enabled = true;
51              f2.showButtonLogin.Enabled = false;
52              f2.showButtonSetting.Enabled = false;
53              f2.showButtonTuition.Enabled = true;
54              this.Dispose();
55          }
56          else
57          {
58              MessageBox.Show("Username or password is wrong");
59              this.Close();
60          }
61      }
62      else if (cboUser.SelectedItem.ToString() == "boss")
63      {
64          loginCommand.CommandText =
65              "SELECT * FROM Login WHERE Password='" +
66              txtPassword.Text + "'";
67          loginDataReader = loginCommand.ExecuteReader();
68
69          if (loginDataReader.Read())
70          {
71              FormMain f2 = new FormMain();
72              f2.Show();
73              f2.showButtonLibrary.Enabled = true;
74              f2.showButtonInventory.Enabled = true;
75              f2.showButtonAcademy.Enabled = true;
76              f2.showButtonLogin.Enabled = false;
77              f2.showButtonSetting.Enabled = true;
78              f2.showButtonTuition.Enabled = true;
79              this.Dispose();
80          }
81          else
82          {
83              MessageBox.Show("Username or password is wrong");
84              this.Close();
85          }
86      }
87
88      else
89      {
90          MessageBox.Show("Username or password is wrong");
91          this.Close();
92      }
```

```
93
94      loginConn.Close();
95  }
```

Step 14   Run application. Click on **Login** button. Login form will show up. Choose one of usernames available and give the correct password. You then will return to main form. Notice that all buttons except **Login** and **Exit** buttons are now enabled as shown in Figure 1.19.

BALIGE HIGH SCHOOL INVENTORY

In this project, you will build a database management system where you can store information about valuables in school.

Description

The table will have seven fields: **Item** (description of the item), **Location** (where the item was placed), **Shop** (where the item was purchased), **DatePurchased** (when the item was purchased), **Cost** (how much the item cost), **SerialNumber** (serial number of the item), **PhotoFile** (path of the photo file of the item), and **Fragile** (indicates whether a particular item is fragile or not).

The development of this **School Inventory Project** will be performed, as usual, in a step-by-step manner. You will first create the database. Furthermore, the interface will be built so that the user can view, edit, add, or add data records from the database. Finally, you add code to create a printable list of information from the database.

2.1 Tutorial Steps of Creating SQL Server Database of Warehouse Inventory

Step 1   Use **Server Explorer** to create a new table and name the table as **Warehouse**. Add nine fields (columns) to the database. The information required for the database is:

Name	Data Type
Item	varchar(50)
Quantity	int
Location	varchar(50)
Shop	varchar(50)
DatePurchased	datetime
Cost	money
SerialNumber	varchar(50)
PhotoFile	varchar(200)
Fragile	bit

Only the **Item** field cannot allow null values.

Step 2   Make the **Item** field the primary key. When finished, the table structure will be displayed as shown in Figure 2.1.

Step 3   Write SQL query below to add table and nine fields:

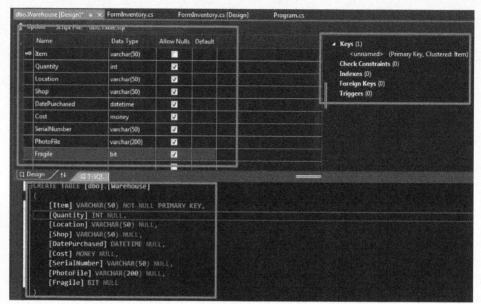

Figure 2.1 The table structure of **Warehouse** table

```
1   CREATE TABLE [dbo].[Warehouse]
2   (
3       [Item] VARCHAR(50) NOT NULL PRIMARY KEY,
4   [Quantity] INT NULL,
5   [Location] VARCHAR(50) NULL,
6   [Shop] VARCHAR(50) NULL,
7   [DatePurchased] DATETIME NULL,
8   [Cost] MONEY NULL,
9   [SerialNumber] VARCHAR(50) NULL,
10  [PhotoFile] VARCHAR(200) NULL,
11  [Fragile] BIT NULL
12  )
```

Step 4   The created table is now can been seen in Server Explorer windows as shown in Figure 2.2.

Figure 2.2 Warehouse table has been created

Step 4 Insert some rows into **Warehouse** table as shown in Figure 2.3.

Figure 2.3 Inserting two rows of data into **Warehouse** table

2.2 Tutorial Steps of Designing Warehouse Inventory Interface

Step 1 Start a new project in Visual C#. The warehouse inventory interface will be used by the user to view, edit, delete, or add records to the database. Each field will be displayed on the form interface.

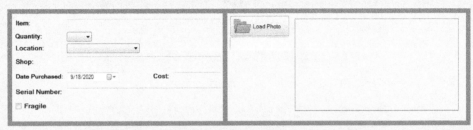

Figure 2.4 School Inventory form designed

Step 2 Set the properties of each control as follows:

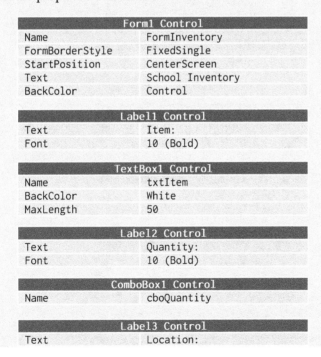

Form1 Control	
Name	FormInventory
FormBorderStyle	FixedSingle
StartPosition	CenterScreen
Text	School Inventory
BackColor	Control

Label1 Control	
Text	Item:
Font	10 (Bold)

TextBox1 Control	
Name	txtItem
BackColor	White
MaxLength	50

Label2 Control	
Text	Quantity:
Font	10 (Bold)

ComboBox1 Control	
Name	cboQuantity

Label3 Control	
Text	Location:

Font   10 (Bold)

ComboBox2 Control	
Name	cboLocation

Label4 Control	
Text	Shop:
Font	10 (Bold)

TextBox2 Control	
Name	txtShop
BackColor	White
MaxLength	50

Label5 Control	
Text	Date Purchased:
Font	10 (Bold)

dateTimePicker1 Control	
Name	dtpDatePurchased
Format	short

Label6 Control	
Text	Cost:
Font	10 (Bold)

TextBox3 Control	
Name	txtCost
BackColor	White

Label7 Control	
Text	Serial Number:
Font	10 (Bold)

TextBox4 Control	
Name	txtSerialNumber
BackColor	White
MaxLength	50

CheckBox1 Control	
Name	chkFragile
Text	Fragile
Font	10 (Bold)

PictureBox1 Control	
Name	picItem
BorderStyle	FixedSingle
SizeMode	Zoom

Label8 Control	
Name	lblPhotoFile
AutoSize	False
BackColor	Gold
BorderStyle	Fixed3D
Text	[Empty]

Button1 Control	

Name	btnLoadPhoto
Text	Load Photo

2.3 Tutorial Steps of Connecting to SQL Server Database

Step 1   You need to open **DBMS** database, read **Warehouse** table, and bind its controls to related fields. Put this line of code at the top of the code window to use the data objects:

```
1  using System.Data.SqlClient;
2  using System.IO;
```

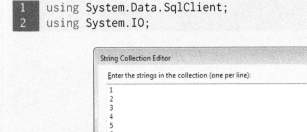

Figure 2.5 Items property for **cboQuantity**

Step 2   Put the following code in the form-level declaration to create the data objects:

```
1  SqlConnection inventoryConn;
2  SqlCommand inventoryCommand;
3  SqlDataAdapter inventoryAdapter;
4  DataTable warehouseTable;
5  CurrencyManager inventoryManager;
```

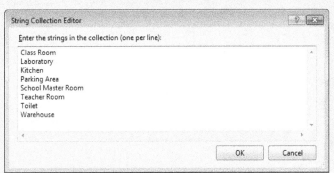

Figure 2.6 Items property for **cboLocation**

Step 3   Populate two comboboxes, **cboQuantity** and **cboLocation**, using Items property in Properties windows as shown in Figure 2.5 and Figure 2.6.

Step 4   Put this code in the **FormInventory_Load** event method:

```
1   private void FormInventory_Load(object sender, EventArgs e)
2   {
3       // Connects to database
4       inventoryConn = new SqlConnection("Data Source=.\\SQLEXPRESS;
5           AttachDbFilename=D:\\Database\\DBMS.mdf;
6           Integrated Security = True; Connect Timeout = 30;
7           User Instance = True");
8
9       inventoryConn.Open();
10
11      // Sets inventory command
12      inventoryCommand = new SqlCommand(
13          "SELECT * FROM Warehouse ORDER BY Item", inventoryConn);
14
15      // Sets warehouse data table
16      inventoryAdapter = new SqlDataAdapter();
17      inventoryAdapter.SelectCommand = inventoryCommand;
18      warehouseTable = new DataTable();
19      inventoryAdapter.Fill(warehouseTable);
20
21      // Binds controls
22      txtItem.DataBindings.Add("Text", warehouseTable, "Item");
23      cboQuantity.DataBindings.Add("Text", warehouseTable,
24          "Quantity");
25      cboLocation.DataBindings.Add("Text", warehouseTable,
26          "Location");
27      txtShop.DataBindings.Add("Text", warehouseTable, "Shop");
28      dtpDatePurchased.DataBindings.Add("Text",
29          warehouseTable, "DatePurchased");
30      txtCost.DataBindings.Add("Text", warehouseTable, "Cost");
31      txtSerialNumber.DataBindings.Add("Text",
32          warehouseTable, "SerialNumber");
33      chkFragile.DataBindings.Add("Checked",
34          warehouseTable, "Fragile");
35      lblPhotoFile.DataBindings.Add("Text",
36          warehouseTable, "PhotoFile");
37
38      // Sets currency manager kekinian to read current items from table
39      inventoryManager =
40          (CurrencyManager)this.BindingContext[warehouseTable];
41
42      DisplayPhoto();
43  }
```

The code above connects to **DBMS** database file and creates the required data objects to view the data table. The code above also binds controls to table fields. Pay particular attention to the date time picker control and check boxes.

Figure 2.7 Form displays the first entry in the **Warehouse** table

Define **DisplayPhoto** method to display photo in **picItem**:

```
1   private void DisplayPhoto()
2   {
3       // Displays photo
4       if (!lblPhotoFile.Text.Equals(""))
5       {
6           try
7           {
8               picItem.Image = Image.FromFile(lblPhotoFile.Text);
9           }
10          catch (Exception ex)
11          {
12              MessageBox.Show(ex.Message, "Error Loading photo",
13                  MessageBoxButtons.OK, MessageBoxIcon.Error);
14          }
15      }
16      else
17      {
18          string dir =
19              Path.GetDirectoryName(Application.ExecutablePath);
20          string namafile = Path.Combine(dir, @"user.png");
21          picItem.Image = Image.FromFile(namafile);
22      }
23  }
```

Step 5   Put the following code in the **FormInventory_FormClosing** event method to save all changes to the database and delete all objects:

```
1   private void FormInventory_FormClosing(object sender,
2   FormClosingEventArgs e)
3   {
4       try
5       {
6           // Saves updates into Warehouse table
7           SqlCommandBuilder commandAdapterInventori = new
8               SqlCommandBuilder (inventoryAdapter);
9           inventoryAdapter.Update(warehouseTable);
10      }
11      catch (Exception ex)
```

```
12    {
13          MessageBox.Show(ex.Message, "Error in Saving into Database",
14              MessageBoxButtons.OK, MessageBoxIcon.Error);
15    }
16
17    // Close connetion
18    inventoryConn.Close();
19
20    // Deletes objects
21    inventoryCommand.Dispose();
22    inventoryAdapter.Dispose();
23    warehouseTable.Dispose();
24 }
```

Step 6   Save the application and run. The results are shown in Figure 2.7.

2.4 Tutorial Steps of Navigating Database

Step 1   As a first step, you need the ability to move from one record to another in this inventory database.

Add four buttons to the form. Set the properties:

button1 Control	
Name	btnFirst
Text	|< First
FontSize	10
TabStop	False

button2 Control	
Name	btnPrev
Text	< Prev
FontSize	10
TabStop	False

button3 Control	
Name	btnNext
Text	Next >
FontSize	10
TabStop	False

button4 Control	
Name	btnLast
Text	Last >|
FontSize	10
TabStop	False

Figure 2.8 Interface design after four new buttons are added

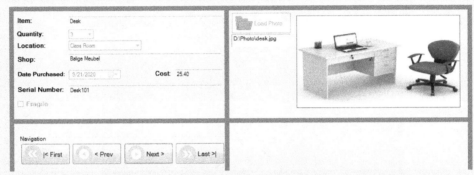

Figure 2.9 User now can navigates row by row

Step 2   Add this code to the **Click** event method of each new button:

```
1   private void btnFirst_Click(object sender, EventArgs e)
2   {
3       inventoryManager.Position = 0;
4       DisplayPhoto();
5   }
6
7   private void btnPrev_Click(object sender, EventArgs e)
8   {
9       inventoryManager.Position--;
10      DisplayPhoto();
11  }
12
13  private void btnNext_Click(object sender, EventArgs e)
14  {
15      inventoryManager.Position++;
16      DisplayPhoto();
17  }
18
19  private void btnLast_Click(object sender, EventArgs e)
20  {
21      inventoryManager.Position = inventoryManager.Count - 1;
22      DisplayPhoto();
```

`23` `}`

Step 3   Save and run the application. Make sure the navigation buttons work properly, as shown in Figure 2.9.

2.5 Tutorial Steps of Editing Records

Step 1   You now will add the ability to edit records in the warehouse inventory database. Lock all text boxes (**Readonly** is **True**) on the form. You will decide when editing is allowed. Also, disable the date time picker control and the button for loading photo files (**Enabled = False**).

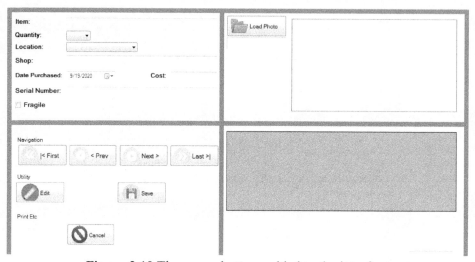

Figure 2.10 Three new buttons added to the interface

Step 2   Add three buttons to the form. Set the properties:

button1 Control	
Name	btnEdit
Text	Edit
TabStop	False

button2 Control	
Name	btnSave
Text	Save
Enabled	False
TabStop	False

button3 Control	
Name	btnCancel
Text	Cancel
Enabled	False

TabStop	False

Now, the form looks as shown in Figure 2.10.

Step 3   Add a variable to the form-level declaration to keep track of the system state:

```
1   string myState;
```

Step 4   Add a method named **SetState** to specify the state of the application:

```
1    private void SetState(string appSate)
2    {
3        myState = appSate;
4        switch (myState)
5        {
6            case "View":
7                btnFirst.Enabled = true;
8                btnPrev.Enabled = true;
9                btnNext.Enabled = true;
10               btnLast.Enabled = true;
11               btnEdit.Enabled = true;
12               btnSave.Enabled = false;
13               btnCancel.Enabled = false;
14               txtItem.ReadOnly = true;
15               txtLocation.ReadOnly = true;
16               txtShop.ReadOnly = true;
17               dtpDatePurchased.Enabled = false;
18               txtCost.ReadOnly = true;
19               txtSerialNumber.ReadOnly = true;
20               chkFragile.Enabled = false;
21               btnLoadPhoto.Enabled = false;
22               break;
23
24           default: // "Edit", "Add"
25               btnFirst.Enabled = false;
26               btnPrev.Enabled = false;
27               btnNext.Enabled = false;
28               btnLast.Enabled = false;
29               btnEdit.Enabled = false;
30               btnSave.Enabled = true;
31               btnCancel.Enabled = true;
32               txtItem.ReadOnly = false;
33               txtLocation.ReadOnly = false;
34               txtShop.ReadOnly = false;
35               dtpDatePurchased.Enabled = true;
36               txtCost.ReadOnly = false;
37               txtSerialNumber.ReadOnly = false;
38               chkFragile.Enabled = true;
39               btnLoadPhoto.Enabled = true;
40               break;
41       }
```

```
42      txtItem.Focus();
43 }
```

This method has two modes: **View** and **Edit**. In **View** mode (the mode when the form is loaded), you can only view data. In **Edit** mode, data can be changed, and then saved (or the edit operation is canceled).

Step 5   Put the following code in line 41 to **FormInventory_Load** event method:

```
1  private void FormInventory_Load(object sender, EventArgs e)
2  {
3      // Connects to database
4      inventoryConn = new SqlConnection("Data Source=.\\SQLEXPRESS;
5          AttachDbFilename=D:\\Database\\DBMS.mdf;
6          Integrated Security = True; Connect Timeout = 30;
7          User Instance = True");
8
9      inventoryConn.Open();
10
11     // Sets inventory command
12     inventoryCommand = new SqlCommand(
13         "SELECT * FROM Warehouse ORDER BY Item", inventoryConn);
14
15     // Sets warehouse data table
16     inventoryAdapter = new SqlDataAdapter();
17     inventoryAdapter.SelectCommand = inventoryCommand;
18     warehouseTable = new DataTable();
19     inventoryAdapter.Fill(warehouseTable);
20
21     // Binds controls
22     txtItem.DataBindings.Add("Text", warehouseTable, "Item");
23     cboQuantity.DataBindings.Add("Text", warehouseTable,
24         "Quantity");
25     cboLocation.DataBindings.Add("Text", warehouseTable,
26         "Location");
27     txtShop.DataBindings.Add("Text", warehouseTable, "Shop");
28     dtpDatePurchased.DataBindings.Add("Text",
29         warehouseTable, "DatePurchased");
30     txtCost.DataBindings.Add("Text", warehouseTable, "Cost");
31     txtSerialNumber.DataBindings.Add("Text",
32         warehouseTable, "SerialNumber");
33     chkFragile.DataBindings.Add("Checked",
34         warehouseTable, "Fragile");
35     lblPhotoFile.DataBindings.Add("Text",
36         warehouseTable, "PhotoFile");
37
38     // Sets currency manager kekinian to read current items from table
39     inventoryManager =
40         (CurrencyManager)this.BindingContext[warehouseTable];
41
```

```
42      DisplayPhoto();
43      SetState("View");
44  }
```

Step 6   Place the following line of code in the **btnEdit_Click** event method:

```
1   private void btnEdit_Click(object sender, EventArgs e)
2   {
3       SetState("Edit");
4   }
```

The code above will put the form in **Edit** mode and allow the data table to be edited.

Step 7   Place the following code in the **buttonSave_Click** event method:

```
1   private void btnSave_Click(object sender, EventArgs e)
2   {
3       string itemSaved = txtItem.Text;
4       int rowSaved;
5       inventoryManager.EndCurrentEdit();
6
7       warehouseTable.DefaultView.Sort = "Item";
8       rowSaved = warehouseTable.DefaultView.Find(itemSaved);
9       inventoryManager.Position = rowSaved;
10      SetState("View");
11  }
```

The code above will save all changes and return to **View** mode. The code assigns the current manager position to the saved record when finished.

Step 8   Put the following code in the **btnCancel_Click** method:

```
1   private void btnCancel_Click(object sender, EventArgs e)
2   {
3       inventoryManager.CancelCurrentEdit();
4       DisplayPhoto();
5       SetState("View");
6   }
```

Step 9   Save and run the application. Make sure that **Edit** button is working properly. Additionally, test the **Save** and **Cancel** buttons:

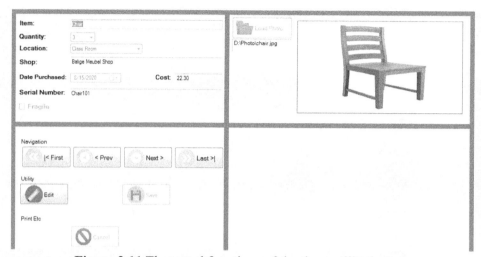

Figure 2.11 The tested functions of the three utility buttons

2.6 Tutorial Steps of Loading Photo File

Step 1   You can edit all fields on the form except the photo. You will add this capability. Add
         a file open dialog control to the project. Use the following properties:

openFileDialog1 Control	
Name	dlgOpen
DefaultExtension	png
FileName	[empty]
Filter	Photo (*.jpg)|*.jpg

Step 2   When user clicks **Load Photo** button, a photo dialog box will be opened, allowing the
         user to select a specific photo. Add the following code to **btnLoadPhoto_Click** event
         method:

```
1  private void btnLoadPhoto_Click(object sender, EventArgs e)
2  {
3      try {
4          if (dlgOpen.ShowDialog() == DialogResult.OK) {
5              lblPhotoFile.Text = dlgOpen.FileName;
6              DisplayPhoto();
7          }
8      }
9      catch (Exception ex) {
10         MessageBox.Show(ex.Message, "Error Opening Photo File",
11             MessageBoxButtons.OK, MessageBoxIcon.Error);
12     }
13 }
```

Step 3   Save and run the application. Click **Edit** button. Then, click the **Load Photo** button. A file open dialog box displays. Next, you can select a photo of the appropriate item. In this example, you have successfully replaced the chair photo as shown in Figure 2.12.

Figure 2.12 The bicycle photo has been successfully replaced with another photo

2.7 Tutorial Steps of Adding New Records

Step 1   Now, you are adding the capability to add new records to the warehouse inventory database. Add a button to the form below the **Edit** button. Use the following properties:

Button1 Control	
Name	btnAdd
Text	Add
TabStop	False

The form now looks as shown in Figure 2.13.

Step 2   Add this line of code to the form-level declaration to save the current record (in anticipation of the **Add** operation being canceled):

```
1    int recordPos;
```

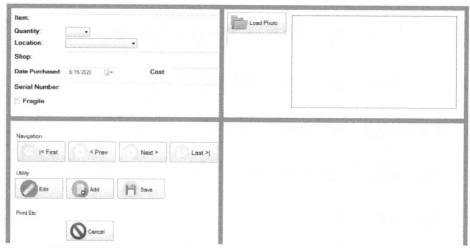

Figure 2.13 Another button added to the form to add new records to the database

Step 3   Put the following code in the **btnAdd_Click** event method:

```
1  private void btnAdd_Click(object sender, EventArgs e)
2  {
3      recordPos = inventoryManager.Position;
4
5      // Set default photo
6      picItem.Image = Image.FromFile("D:\\Photo\\dummy.ico");
7
8      SetState("Add");
9      inventoryManager.AddNew();
10 }
```

The code above first saves the current record position, which then sets default photo, puts the application in **Add** mode, and adds a new recording.

Step 4   Modify the **btnCancel_Click** event method to distinguish cancellation on editing from cancellation when adding a new record:

```
1  private void btnCancel_Click(object sender, EventArgs e)
2  {
3      inventoryManager.CancelCurrentEdit();
4
5      if (myState.Equals("Add"))
6      {
7          inventoryManager.Position = recordPos;
8      }
9
10     DisplayPhoto();
11     SetState("View");
12 }
```

Stp 5   Modify **SetState** event method to involve the new **Add** mode (identical to **Edit** mode, in line 22 and line 41):

```
private void SetState(string appSate)
{
    myState = appSate;
    switch (myState)
    {
        case "View":
            btnFirst.Enabled = true;
            btnPrev.Enabled = true;
            btnNext.Enabled = true;
            btnLast.Enabled = true;
            btnEdit.Enabled = true;
            btnSave.Enabled = false;
            btnCancel.Enabled = false;
            txtItem.ReadOnly = true;
            txtLocation.ReadOnly = true;
            txtShop.ReadOnly = true;
            dtpDatePurchased.Enabled = false;
            txtCost.ReadOnly = true;
            txtSerialNumber.ReadOnly = true;
            chkFragile.Enabled = false;
            btnLoadPhoto.Enabled = false;
            btnAdd.Enabled = true;
            break;

        default: // "Edit", "Add"
            btnFirst.Enabled = false;
            btnPrev.Enabled = false;
            btnNext.Enabled = false;
            btnLast.Enabled = false;
            btnEdit.Enabled = false;
            btnSave.Enabled = true;
            btnCancel.Enabled = true;
            txtItem.ReadOnly = false;
            txtLocation.ReadOnly = false;
            txtShop.ReadOnly = false;
            dtpDatePurchased.Enabled = true;
            txtCost.ReadOnly = false;
            txtSerialNumber.ReadOnly = false;
            chkFragile.Enabled = true;
            btnLoadPhoto.Enabled = true;
            btnAdd.Enabled = false;
            break;
    }
    txtItem.Focus();
}
```

Step 6   Save the application and run. Click the **Add** button. You will see:

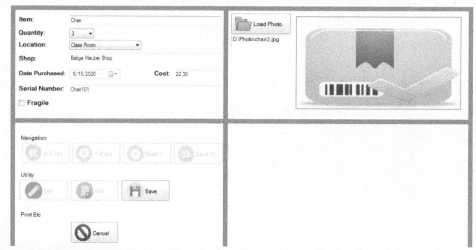

Figure 2.14 Add button added to the form to add a new record to the database

Note that the fields are not cleared when the user adds a new record to the database.
What is wrong? This is a bug in Visual C#, which occurs when binding a checkbox to
an update manager.

You need to fix this bug. Since the problem lies with the binding of the checkbox, you
need to remove the binding when adding a record, then bind it again after the new add
operation is saved.

Step 7   Add the following code in line 9-10 to the **btnAdd_Click** event method (removes the
binding from the checkbox and unchecks):

```
1   private void btnAdd_Click(object sender, EventArgs e)
2   {
3       recordPos = inventoryManager.Position;
4
5       // Sets default photo
6       picItem.Image = Image.FromFile("D:\\Photo\\dummy.ico");
7
8       // Deletes binding from check box
9       chkFragile.DataBindings.Clear();
10      chkFragile.Checked = false;
11
12      SetState("Add");
13      inventoryManager.AddNew();
14  }
```

Step 8   Add the following code in line 7 -13 to the **bnSave_Click** event method (manually set
database fields and set data binding):

```
1  private void btnSave_Click(object sender, EventArgs e)
2  {
3      string itemSaved = txtItem.Text;
4      int rowSaved;
5      inventoryManager.EndCurrentEdit();
6
7      if (myState.Equals("Add"))
8      {
9          warehouseTable.Rows[inventoryManager.Count - 1]["Fragile"] =
10             chkFragile.Checked;
11         chkFragile.DataBindings.Add("Checked", warehouseTable,
12             "Fragile");
13     }
14
15     warehouseTable.DefaultView.Sort = "Item";
16     rowSaved = warehouseTable.DefaultView.Find(itemSaved);
17     inventoryManager.Position = rowSaved;
18     SetState("View");
19 }
```

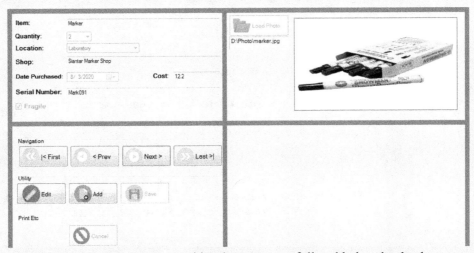

Figure 2.15 The new record has been successfully added to the database

Step 9   Finally, add the following code in line 8-9 to **btnCancel_Click** event method (bind
the data if it was canceled while adding the record):

```
1  private void btnCancel_Click(object sender, EventArgs e)
2  {
3      inventoryManager.CancelCurrentEdit();
4
5      if (myState.Equals("Add"))
6      {
7          inventoryManager.Position = recordPos;
8          chkFragile.DataBindings.Add("Checked",
9              warehouseTable, "Fragile");
```

```
10          }
11
12          DisplayPhoto();
13          SetState("View");
14      }
```

Step 10   Save and run the application again. The fields are now blank as desired. Type in new
          values. Click on the **Save** button. The new record will be saved into the database. This
          is illustrated in Figure 2.15.

2.8 Tutorial Steps of Deleting Records

Step 1   The last functionality required is deleting records from the warehouse inventory
          database. Add a button to the form next to the **Add** button. Use the following
          properties:

Button1 Control	
Name	btnDelete
Text	Delete
TabStop	False

          The form will be as shown in Figure 2.16.

Step 2   Add the following code to **btnDelete_Click** event method:

```
1    private void btnDelete_Click(object sender, EventArgs e)
2    {
3        if (MessageBox.Show("Do you sure want to delete this record?",
4            "Delete", MessageBoxButtons.YesNo, MessageBoxIcon.Question,
5            MessageBoxDefaultButton.Button2) == DialogResult.Yes) {
6            inventoryManager.RemoveAt(inventoryManager.Position);
7            DisplayPhoto();
8        }
9
10       SetState("View");
11   }
```

          The code above confirms deletion of the record. If **Yes** is pressed, deletion of the record
          is performed and controls are bound to another record, which requires loading the
          associated photo. If **No** is pressed, nothing happens.

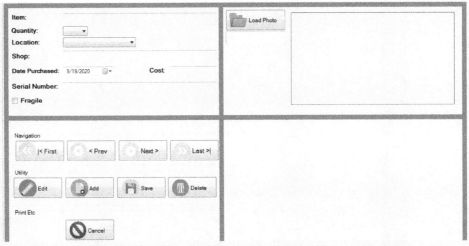

Figure 2.16 One more button added to the interface

Step 3   Add the following code in line 23 and line 43 to the **SetState** method to set the
Enabled property of the **Delete** button to **true** in **View** mode and **false** in **Edit/Add**
mode:

```
1   private void SetState(string appSate)
2   {
3       myState = appSate;
4       switch (myState)
5       {
6           case "View":
7               btnFirst.Enabled = true;
8               btnPrev.Enabled = true;
9               btnNext.Enabled = true;
10              btnLast.Enabled = true;
11              btnEdit.Enabled = true;
12              btnSave.Enabled = false;
13              btnCancel.Enabled = false;
14              txtItem.ReadOnly = true;
15              txtLocation.ReadOnly = true;
16              txtShop.ReadOnly = true;
17              dtpDatePurchased.Enabled = false;
18              txtCost.ReadOnly = true;
19              txtSerialNumber.ReadOnly = true;
20              chkFragile.Enabled = false;
21              btnLoadPhoto.Enabled = false;
22              btnAdd.Enabled = true;
23              btnDelete.Enabled = true;
24              break;
25
26          default: // "Edit", "Add"
27              btnFirst.Enabled = false;
28              btnPrev.Enabled = false;
                btnNext.Enabled = false;
```

```
29          btnLast.Enabled = false;
30          btnEdit.Enabled = false;
31          btnSave.Enabled = true;
32          btnCancel.Enabled = true;
33          txtItem.ReadOnly = false;
34          txtLocation.ReadOnly = false;
35          txtShop.ReadOnly = false;
36          dtpDatePurchased.Enabled = true;
37          txtCost.ReadOnly = false;
38          txtSerialNumber.ReadOnly = false;
39          chkFragile.Enabled = true;
40          btnLoadPhoto.Enabled = true;
41          btnAdd.Enabled = false;
42          btnDelete.Enabled = false;
43          break;
44      }
45      txtItem.Focus();
46  }
47
```

Figure 2.17 A message box to ask if you are serious about deleting record in the database

Step 4   Save the application and run. Click **Add** button to add a new record. Click **Save** button. Now, try to delete one of the records in the database.

Test your application, by responding to **Yes** and **No** in the message box displayed.

2.9 Tutorial Steps of Validating Entry

Step 1   Entry validation is intended to check for the correct characters in a data field. In this database, almost any field can contain any character. There is only one exception, which is the **Cost** field, which can only accept numeric characters and a decimal point.

Here, you will implement this restriction. And, you will also implement the ability to let the user press <Enter> to move from one field to the next.

Add the following code to **Item_KeyPress** event text:

```
1  private void txtItem_KeyPress(object sender, KeyPressEventArgs e)
2  {
```

```
3    if ((int)e.KeyChar == 13)
4        txtLocation.Focus();
5  }
```

When the user presses **<Enter>**, the focus will be shifted to the next text box control
(**txtLocation**).

Step 2   Add the following code to **txtLocation_KeyPress** event method:

```
1  private void txtLocation_KeyPress(object sender, KeyPressEventArgs e)
2  {
3      if ((int)e.KeyChar == 13)
4          txtShop.Focus();
5  }
```

When the user presses <Enter>, the focus will be shifted to the next text box control
(**txtShop**).

Step 3   Add the following code to **txtShop_KeyPress** event method:

```
1  private void txtShop_KeyPress(object sender, KeyPressEventArgs e)
2  {
3      if ((int)e.KeyChar == 13) {
4          if (dtpDatePurchased.Enabled)
5              dtpDatePurchased.Focus();
6          else
7              txtCost.Focus();
8      }
9  }
```

When the user presses <Enter>, focus will be shifted to the date time picker control
(**dtpDatePurchased**), if the control is active (**Enabled** property is **true**). Otherwise,
the focus will shift to the next text box control (**txtCost**).

Step 4   Add the following code to **dtpDatePurchased_KeyPress** event method:

```
1  private void dtpDatePurchased_KeyPress(object sender,
2  KeyPressEventArgs e)
3  {
4      if ((int)e.KeyChar == 13)
5          txtCost.Focus();
6  }
```

When the user presses **<Enter>**, the focus will be shifted to the next text box control
(**txtCost**).

Step 5   Add the following code to **txtCost_KeyPress** event method:

```
1   private void txtCost_KeyPress(object sender, KeyPressEventArgs e)
2   {
3       if ((e.KeyChar >= '0' && e.KeyChar <= '9') || (int)e.KeyChar == 8)
4           e.Handled = false;
5       else if ((int)e.KeyChar == 13) {
6           txtSerialNumber.Focus(); e.Handled = false;
7       }
8       else if (e.KeyChar == '.')
9       {
10          if (txtCost.Text.IndexOf(".") == -1)
11              e.Handled = false;
12          else
13              e.Handled = true;
14      }
15      else
16      {
17          e.Handled = true;
18      }
19  }
```

When the user presses <Enter>, the focus will be shifted to the next text box control
(**txtSerialNumber**). The code above also limits input to only numeric characters,
backspace, and decimal point.

Step 6   Add the following code to **txtSerialNumber_KeyPress** event method:

```
1   private void txtSerialNumber_KeyPress(object sender,
2   KeyPressEventArgs e)
3   {
4       if ((int)e.KeyChar == 13)
5       {
6           if (btnLoadPhoto.Enabled)
7               btnLoadPhoto.Focus();
8           else
9               txtItem.Focus();
10      }
11  }
```

When the user presses <Enter>, focus will be given to **btnLoadPhoto**, if the button is
active (**Enabled** property is **true**). If that button is inactive, focus returns to **txtItem**
control.

Step 7   Save and run the application. Try to move from field to field with the <Enter> key in
View mode and **Edit** mode. Key entrapment test implemented in **Cost** field.

2.10 Tutorial Steps of Validating Input

Step 1   There is only one validation rule required: The **Item** field cannot be left blank, because it is the primary key.

Add the following code in line 4-10 to **btnSave_Click** method to check if a value for the **Item** field was entered:

```
1   private void btnSave_Click(object sender, EventArgs e)
2   {
3       // Checks Item field
4       if (txtItem.Text.Trim().Equals("")) {
5           MessageBox.Show("You should enter item name.",
6               "Input Error", MessageBoxButtons.OK,
7               MessageBoxIcon.Information);
8           txtItem.Focus();
9           return;
10      }
11
12      string itemSaved = txtItem.Text;
13      int rowSaved;
14      inventoryManager.EndCurrentEdit();
15
16      if (myState.Equals("Add"))
17      {
18          warehouseTable.Rows[inventoryManager.Count - 1]["Fragile"] =
19              chkFragile.Checked;
20          chkFragile.DataBindings.Add("Checked", warehouseTable,
21              "Fragile");
22      }
23
24      warehouseTable.DefaultView.Sort = "Item";
25      rowSaved = warehouseTable.DefaultView.Find(itemSaved);
26      inventoryManager.Position = rowSaved;
27      SetState("View");
28  }
```

If the **Item** field is left blank, the user will be given a message to remind her.

Step 2   Save and run the application. Click **Add** button. Then click **Save**. A message box will remind the user:

Figure 2.18 A message box to remind you not to leave the **Item** field blank

2.11 Tutorial Steps of Reporting Inventory

Step 1   Now, you will add a feature to read all the data in the database. You need a database report. The report is quite simple. For each record, the data from each field will be displayed.

Add a button and a print preview dialog control to the project. Use the following properties:

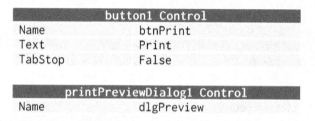

button1 Control	
Name	btnPrint
Text	Print
TabStop	False

printPreviewDialog1 Control	
Name	dlgPreview

The form will look as shown in Figure 2.19.

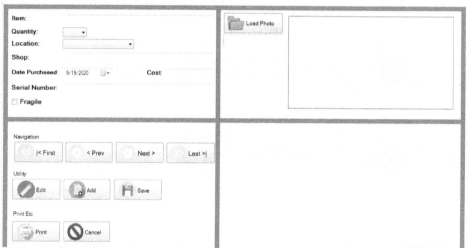

Figure 2.19 Another button, **Print**, and a **printPreviewDialog1** control added to the form

Step 2   Add this line of code at the top of the code window:

```
1    using System.Drawing.Printing;
```

Step 3   Add the page number variable to the form level declaration:

```
1    int pageNumber;
```

Step 4   Add code in line 25 and line 47 to the **SetState** method to set **Enabled** property of **btnPrint** to **true** in **View** mode and **false** in **Add/Edit** mode.

```csharp
private void SetState(string appSate)
{
    myState = appSate;
    switch (myState)
    {
        case "View":
            btnFirst.Enabled = true;
            btnPrev.Enabled = true;
            btnNext.Enabled = true;
            btnLast.Enabled = true;
            btnEdit.Enabled = true;
            btnSave.Enabled = false;
            btnCancel.Enabled = false;
            txtItem.ReadOnly = true;
            txtLocation.ReadOnly = true;
            txtShop.ReadOnly = true;
            dtpDatePurchased.Enabled = false;
            txtCost.ReadOnly = true;
            txtSerialNumber.ReadOnly = true;
            chkFragile.Enabled = false;
            btnLoadPhoto.Enabled = false;
            btnAdd.Enabled = true;
            btnDelete.Enabled = true;
            grpSearchInventory.Enabled = true;
            btnPrint.Enabled = true;
            break;

        default: // "Edit", "Add"
            btnFirst.Enabled = false;
            btnPrev.Enabled = false;
            btnNext.Enabled = false;
            btnLast.Enabled = false;
            btnEdit.Enabled = false;
            btnSave.Enabled = true;
            btnCancel.Enabled = true;
            txtItem.ReadOnly = false;
            txtLocation.ReadOnly = false;
            txtShop.ReadOnly = false;
            dtpDatePurchased.Enabled = true;
            txtCost.ReadOnly = false;
            txtSerialNumber.ReadOnly = false;
            chkFragile.Enabled = true;
            btnLoadPhoto.Enabled = true;
            btnAdd.Enabled = false;
            btnDelete.Enabled = false;
            grpSearchInventory.Enabled = false;
            btnPrint.Enabled = false;
            break;
    }
    txtItem.Focus();
}
```

Step 5   Add the following code to **btnPrint_Click** event method:

```
1   private void btnPrint_Click(object sender, EventArgs e)
2   {
3       // Declares document
4       PrintDocument docInventory;
5
6       // Creates document and gives it a name
7       docInventory = new PrintDocument();
8       docInventory.DocumentName = "School Inventory";
9
10      // Adds code handler
11      docInventory.PrintPage += new
12          PrintPageEventHandler(this.PrintInventory);
13
14      // Prints document in preview control
15      pageNumber = 1;
16      int positionSaved = inventoryManager.Position;
17      dlgPreview.Document = docInventory;
18      dlgPreview.ShowDialog();
19
20      // Deletes document when finished printing
21      docInventory.Dispose();
22      inventoryManager.Position = positionSaved;
23
24      DisplayPhoto();
25  }
```

Step 6   Add the following code to **PrintInventory** method:

```
1   private void PrintInventory(object sender, PrintPageEventArgs e)
2   {
3       // Tracks every record, prints every record
4       inventoryManager.Position = pageNumber - 1;
5       DisplayPhoto();
6
7       // Prints header
8       Font myFont = new Font("Arial", 14, FontStyle.Bold);
9       int y = e.MarginBounds.Top + 50;
10      e.Graphics.DrawString("Warehouse Inventory (" +
11          DateTime.Now.ToShortDateString() + ") - Page " +
12          pageNumber.ToString(), myFont, Brushes.Black,
13          e.MarginBounds.Left, y);
14      y += 2 * Convert.ToInt32(myFont.GetHeight(e.Graphics));
15
16      // Prints text information
17      myFont = new Font("Arial", 12, FontStyle.Regular);
18      e.Graphics.DrawString("Item:", myFont, Brushes.Black,
19          e.MarginBounds.X, y);
20      e.Graphics.DrawString(txtItem.Text, myFont, Brushes.Black,
```

```
21          e.MarginBounds.X + 150, y);
22      y += Convert.ToInt32(myFont.GetHeight(e.Graphics));
23
24      e.Graphics.DrawString("Quantity:", myFont, Brushes.Black,
25          e.MarginBounds.X, y);
26      e.Graphics.DrawString(cboQuantity.Text, myFont,
27          Brushes.Black, e.MarginBounds.X + 150, y);
28      y += Convert.ToInt32(myFont.GetHeight(e.Graphics));
29
30      e.Graphics.DrawString("Location:", myFont, Brushes.Black,
31          e.MarginBounds.X, y);
32      e.Graphics.DrawString(txtLocation.Text, myFont, Brushes.Black,
33          e.MarginBounds.X + 150, y);
34      y += Convert.ToInt32(myFont.GetHeight(e.Graphics));
35
36      e.Graphics.DrawString("Shop:", myFont, Brushes.Black,
37          e.MarginBounds.X, y);
38      e.Graphics.DrawString(txtShop.Text, myFont, Brushes.Black,
39          e.MarginBounds.X + 150, y);
40      y += Convert.ToInt32(myFont.GetHeight(e.Graphics));
41
42      e.Graphics.DrawString("Date Purchased:", myFont, Brushes.Black,
43          e.MarginBounds.X, y);
44      e.Graphics.DrawString(dtpDatePurchased.Text, myFont,
45          Brushes.Black, e.MarginBounds.X + 150, y);
46      y += Convert.ToInt32(myFont.GetHeight(e.Graphics));
47
48      e.Graphics.DrawString("Cost:", myFont, Brushes.Black,
49          e.MarginBounds.X, y);
50      e.Graphics.DrawString("$ " + String.Format("{0:f2}",
51          txtCost.Text), myFont,
52              Brushes.Black, e.MarginBounds.X + 150, y);
53          y += Convert.ToInt32(myFont.GetHeight(e.Graphics));
54
55      e.Graphics.DrawString("Serial Number:", myFont, Brushes.Black,
56          e.MarginBounds.X, y);
57      e.Graphics.DrawString(txtSerialNumber.Text, myFont,
58          Brushes.Black, e.MarginBounds.X + 150, y);
59      y += 50;
60
61      // Prints photo (width 4 inci, height depends on
62      // height/width ratio of photo)
63      int h = Convert.ToInt32(
64          400 * picItem.Image.Height / picItem.Image.Width);
65      e.Graphics.DrawImage(picItem.Image,
66          e.MarginBounds.X, y, 400, h);
67
68      pageNumber++;
69      if (pageNumber <= inventoryManager.Count)
70          e.HasMorePages = true;
71      else
```

```
72    {
73        e.HasMorePages = false;
74        pageNumber = 1;
75    }
76 }
```

On each page, a header is printed along with the data fields and item photo.

Step 7   Save and run the application. Click on the **Print** button. The print preview control will be displayed on all inventory pages, as shown in Figure 2.20.

Figure 2.20 Each record in the table can now be printed

2.12 Tutorial Steps of Searching Capability

Step 1   Add a group box in the top-right corner of the form. Place a label, a text box, and a button on the group box. Set the properties as follows:

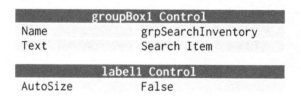

groupBox1 Control	
Name	grpSearchInventory
Text	Search Item

label1 Control	
AutoSize	False

Text	Type the first few letters of the item
TextAlign	TopCenter

textBox1 Control	
Name	txtSearch
TabStop	False

button1 Control	
Name	btnSearch
Text	Search
TabStop	False

When finished, the modified form will look like in Figure 2.21.

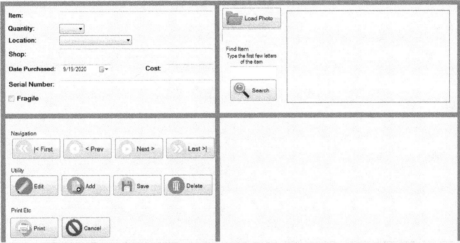

Figure 2.21 Inventory form when group box and controls are added

Step 2   In the **SetState** method, enable group box control in **View** mode and disable it in **Add** and **Edit** mode. Use its **Enabled** property.

Step 3   Add the following code to **btnSearch_Click** event method:

```
1   private void btnSearch_Click(object sender, EventArgs e)
2   {
3       if (txtSearch.Text.Equals(""))
4       {
5           return;
6       }
7
8       int rowSaved = inventoryManager.Position;
9       DataRow[] rowFound;
10      warehouseTable.DefaultView.Sort = "Item";
11      rowFound = warehouseTable.Select("Item LIKE '" +
12          txtSearch.Text + "*'");
13
```

```
14    if (rowFound.Length == 0)
15    {
16        inventoryManager.Position = rowSaved;
17    }
18    else
19    {
20        inventoryManager.Position =
21            warehouseTable.DefaultView.Find(rowFound[0]["Item"]);
22        DisplayPhoto();
23    }
24 }
```

Step 4   Save and run the application. Try searching by providing the first letter or two of the
item's name, as shown in Figure 2.22.

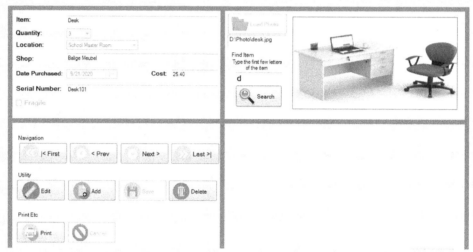

Figure 2.22 Item's name search feature added

2.13 Tutorial Steps of Adding Search Buttons

Step 1   Add a button control on the form. Set its **Name** property as **btnAll** and its **Text** poperty
as **Show All Items**. You add another **DataGridView** control and set its **Name** property
as **grdItem**. You alse need to add a label and set its **Text** property as **Number of
Records:**. Then add a textbox on the form. Set its **Name** property as
txtNumberRecord. The resulting form is shown in Figure 2.24.

Step 2   Add the following form-level declarations:

```
1  String SQLAll = "SELECT * FROM Warehouse";
2  Button[] buttonArr = new Button[26];
```

SQLAll is a variable that contains the default SQL statements, while **buttonArr** is an array containing the search buttons.

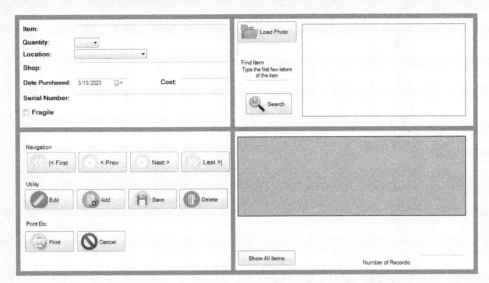

Figure 2.23 Form after a number of controls added

Step 3   Define a new method named **createSearchButton()** as follows:

```
1   private void createSearchButton()
2   {
3       // Creates search buttons
4       int w, lStart, l, t;
5       int btnHeight = 35; // by trial and error
6
7       // Search buttons
8       // Button width - 13 buttons in a row
9       w = Convert.ToInt32(grdItem.Width / 13);
10
11      // Aligns buttons
12      lStart = Convert.ToInt32((grdItem.Width)) + 18;
13      l = lStart; t = grdItem.Top + grdItem.Height + 10;
14
15      // Creates and positions 26 buttons
16      for (int i = 0; i < 26; i++)
17      {
18          // Creates push button
19          buttonArr[i] = new Button();
20          buttonArr[i].TabStop = false;
21
22          // Sets Text property
23          buttonArr[i].Text = ((char)(65 + i)).ToString();
24          buttonArr[i].Font = new Font(buttonArr[i].Font.FontFamily,
25              9, FontStyle.Bold);
26
```

```
27    // Positions buttons
28    buttonArr[i].Width = w;
29    buttonArr[i].Height = btnHeight;
30    buttonArr[i].Left = l;
31    buttonArr[i].Top = t;
32
33    // Gives color
34    buttonArr[i].BackColor = Color.Red;
35    buttonArr[i].ForeColor = Color.White;
36
37    // Adds each button on form
38    this.Controls.Add(buttonArr[i]);
39
40    // Adds event handler
41    buttonArr[i].Click +=
42        new System.EventHandler(this.btnSQL_Click);
43    l += w+1;
44
45    if (i == 12)
46    {
47        // Next row
48        l = lStart; t += btnHeight;
49    }
50    }
51 }
```

This method creates search buttons A through Z using **buttonArrr** array. The code above then specifies the width of the button and places it on the form. Finally, the resulting records are displayed by programmatically clicking **btnSQL** button.

Step 4   Write the code for **btnSQL_Click** event method (handle **Click** event for all search buttons) as follows:

```
1  private void btnSQL_Click(object sender, EventArgs e)
2  {
3      MySqlCommand commResult = null;
4      MySqlDataAdapter adapterResult = new MySqlDataAdapter();
5      DataTable tableResult = new DataTable();
6      String StatemenSQL;
7
8      // Determines which button is clicked and creates SQL statement
9      Button buttonClicked = (Button)sender;
10     switch (buttonClicked.Text)
11     {
12         case "Show All Items":
13             StatemenSQL = SQLAll;
14             break;
15         case "Z":
16             // Z button is clicked
```

```
17          // Appends at SQLAll to limit records upto for item Z
18          StatemenSQL = SQLAll + " WHERE Item > 'Z' ";
19          break;
20      default:
21          // Letter keys except Z
22          // Appends at SQLAll to limit records
23          // for letter that is clicked
24          int idx = (int)(Convert.ToChar(buttonClicked.Text)) - 65;
25          StatemenSQL = SQLAll + " WHERE Item > '" +
26          buttonArr[idx].Text + " ' ";
27          StatemenSQL += " AND Item < '" +
28                  buttonArr[idx + 1].Text + " ' ";
29
30          // Binds to controls
31          int rowSaved = inventoryManager.Position;
32          DataRow[] rowFound;
33          warehouseTable.DefaultView.Sort = "Item";
34          rowFound = warehouseTable.Select("Item LIKE '" +
35              buttonArr[idx].Text + "*'");
36
37          if (rowFound.Length == 0)
38          {
39              inventoryManager.Position = rowSaved;
40          }
41          else
42          {
43              inventoryManager.Position =
44                  warehouseTable.DefaultView.Find(
45                      rowFound[0]["Item"]);
46              DisplayPhoto();
47          }
48          break;
49      }
50  StatemenSQL += " ORDER BY Item";
51
52  // Applies SQL statement
53  try
54  {
55      // Creates Command and DataAdapater objects
56      commResult = new MySqlCommand(StatemenSQL, inventoryConn);
57      adapterResult.SelectCommand = commResult;
58      adapterResult.Fill(tableResult);
59
60      // Binds DataGridView with data table
61      grdItem.DataSource = tableResult;
62      txtNumberRecord.Text = tableResult.Rows.Count.ToString();
63  }
64
65  catch (Exception ex)
66  {
67      MessageBox.Show(ex.Message, "Error Processing SQL",
```

```
68              MessageBoxButtons.OK, MessageBoxIcon.Error);
69      }
70      commResult.Dispose();
71      adapterResult.Dispose();
72      tableResult.Dispose();
73  }
```

This method determines which button is clicked and forms an SQL statement. If the button with the **Text** property of the button is **"Show All Items"** is clicked, then all records will be displayed. When a key letter is clicked, the code determines which letter the user clicks on and attaches an additional test (using **AND**) to the **WHERE** field in the default SQL statement.

Step 5   Add the following code in line 43-48 to **FormInventory_Load** event method. The code creates search buttons and perform **Click** event of **btnAll** programmatically:

```
1   private void FormInventory_Load(object sender, EventArgs e)
2   {
3       // Connects to database
4       inventoryConn = new SqlConnection("Data Source=.\\SQLEXPRESS;
5           AttachDbFilename=D:\\Database\\DBMS.mdf;
6           Integrated Security = True; Connect Timeout = 30;
7           User Instance = True");
8
9       inventoryConn.Open();
10
11      // Sets inventory command
12      inventoryCommand = new SqlCommand(
13          "SELECT * FROM Warehouse ORDER BY Item", inventoryConn);
14
15      // Sets warehouse data table
16      inventoryAdapter = new SqlDataAdapter();
17      inventoryAdapter.SelectCommand = inventoryCommand;
18      warehouseTable = new DataTable();
19      inventoryAdapter.Fill(warehouseTable);
20
21      // Binds controls
22      txtItem.DataBindings.Add("Text", warehouseTable, "Item");
23      cboQuantity.DataBindings.Add("Text", warehouseTable,
24          "Quantity");
25      cboLocation.DataBindings.Add("Text", warehouseTable,
26          "Location");
27      txtShop.DataBindings.Add("Text", warehouseTable, "Shop");
28      dtpDatePurchased.DataBindings.Add("Text",
29          warehouseTable, "DatePurchased");
30      txtCost.DataBindings.Add("Text", warehouseTable, "Cost");
31      txtSerialNumber.DataBindings.Add("Text",
32          warehouseTable, "SerialNumber");
33      chkFragile.DataBindings.Add("Checked",
```

```
34        warehouseTable, "Fragile");
35    lblPhotoFile.DataBindings.Add("Text",
36        warehouseTable, "PhotoFile");
37
38    // Sets currency manager kekinian to read current items from table
39    inventoryManager =
40        (CurrencyManager)this.BindingContext[warehouseTable];
41
42    DisplayPhoto();
43    SetState("View");
44
45    //Creates 26 search buttons
46    createSearchButton();
47
48    // Clicks all records when form starts
49    btnAll.Click += new System.EventHandler(this.btnSQL_Click);
50    btnAll.PerformClick();
51 }
```

Step 6   Define **RowPostPaint** event of **grdItem** control to give it a row numbering:

```
1    private void grdItem_RowPostPaint(object sender,
2    DataGridViewRowPostPaintEventArgs e)
3    {
4        var grid = sender as DataGridView;
5        var rowIdx = (e.RowIndex + 1).ToString();
6
7        var centerFormat = new StringFormat()
8        {
9            // Aligns to middle
10            Alignment = StringAlignment.Center,
11            LineAlignment = StringAlignment.Center
12        };
13
14        var headerBounds = new Rectangle(e.RowBounds.Left,
15            e.RowBounds.Top, grid.RowHeadersWidth, e.RowBounds.Height);
16        e.Graphics.DrawString(rowIdx, this.Font,
17            SystemBrushes.ControlText, headerBounds, centerFormat);
18 }
```

Step 7   Save and run the application. The result is shown in Figure 2.24. Notice how the search
buttons are created. Also note that all records are displayed initially. Click on one of
the search buttons. Only records with the item's initial matching the letter in the clicked
button will be displayed. Figure 2.25 is the query result when the 'S' button is clicked.

Figure 2.24 The application when it first runs

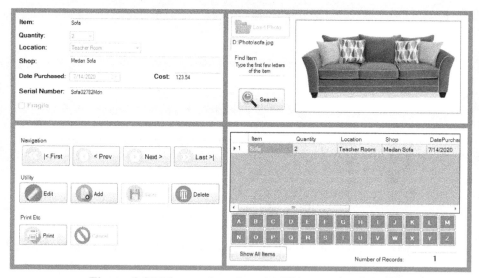

Figure 2.25 The results when the 'S' button is clicked

2.14 Tutorial Steps of Stopping Application and Refresh DataGridView Control

Step 1   You will add a button to stop the application. Add a button next to the **Print** button. Use the following properties:

button1 Control	
Name	btnExit
Text	Exit
TabStop	False

Step 2   Add the following code in line 26 and 49 to **SetState** method to set the **Enabled**
property of the **btnExit** to **true** in **View** mode and **false** in **Add/Edit** mode.

```
1    private void SetState(string appSate)
2    {
3        myState = appSate;
4        switch (myState)
5        {
6            case "View":
7                btnFirst.Enabled = true;
8                btnPrev.Enabled = true;
9                btnNext.Enabled = true;
10               btnLast.Enabled = true;
11               btnEdit.Enabled = true;
12               btnSave.Enabled = false;
13               btnCancel.Enabled = false;
14               txtItem.ReadOnly = true;
15               txtLocation.ReadOnly = true;
16               txtShop.ReadOnly = true;
17               dtpDatePurchased.Enabled = false;
18               txtCost.ReadOnly = true;
19               txtSerialNumber.ReadOnly = true;
20               chkFragile.Enabled = false;
21               btnLoadPhoto.Enabled = false;
22               btnAdd.Enabled = true;
23               btnDelete.Enabled = true;
24               grpSearchInventory.Enabled = true;
25               btnPrint.Enabled = true;
26               btnExit.Enabled = true;
27               break;
28
29           default: // "Edit", "Add"
30               btnFirst.Enabled = false;
31               btnPrev.Enabled = false;
32               btnNext.Enabled = false;
33               btnLast.Enabled = false;
34               btnEdit.Enabled = false;
35               btnSave.Enabled = true;
36               btnCancel.Enabled = true;
37               txtItem.ReadOnly = false;
38               txtLocation.ReadOnly = false;
39               txtShop.ReadOnly = false;
40               dtpDatePurchased.Enabled = true;
41               txtCost.ReadOnly = false;
42               txtSerialNumber.ReadOnly = false;
43               chkFragile.Enabled = true;
44               btnLoadPhoto.Enabled = true;
45               btnAdd.Enabled = false;
46               btnDelete.Enabled = false;
47               grpSearchInventory.Enabled = false;
```

```
48          btnPrint.Enabled = false;
49          btnExit.Enabled = true;
50          break;
51      }
52      txtItem.Focus();
53  }
```

Step 3   Add the following code to **btnExit_Click** event method:

```
1  private void btnExit_Click(object sender, EventArgs e)
2  {
3      this.Close();
4  }
```

Step 4   Add the following code in line 4-9 to **formWarehouse_FormClosing** event method
(the application will not be terminated while record editing is in progress):

```
1  private void formWarehouse_FormClosing(object sender,
2  FormClosingEventArgs e)
3  {
4      if (myState.Equals("Edit") || myState.Equals("Add"))
5      {
6          MessageBox.Show("You should finish editing before quit.",
7              "", MessageBoxButtons.OK, MessageBoxIcon.Information);
8          e.Cancel = true;
9      }
10     else
11     {
12       try
13         {
14             // Saves updates into Warehouse table
15             SqlCommandBuilder commandAdapterInventori =
16                 new SqlCommandBuilder (inventoryAdapter);
17             inventoryAdapter.Update(warehouseTable);
18         }
19         catch (Exception ex)
20         {
21             MessageBox.Show(ex.Message,
22                 "Error in Saving into Database",
23                 MessageBoxButtons.OK, MessageBoxIcon.Error);
24         }
25
26         // Close connetion
27         inventoryConn.Close();
28
29         // Deletes objects
30         inventoryCommand.Dispose();
31         inventoryAdapter.Dispose();
32         warehouseTable.Dispose();
33     }
```

34 }

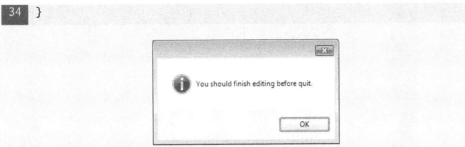

Figure 2.26 The application cannot be stopped when the user is editing or adding new recording

Step 5   Save and run the application. Try exiting the program by clicking the X in the upper-right corner of the form while you are editing or adding recording. Figure 2.26 will be displayed.

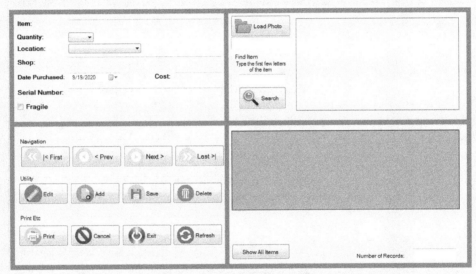

Figure 2.27 Exit and **Refresh** buttons added to the form

Step 5   You will add a button to stop the application. Add a button next to the **Exit** button as shown in Figure 2.27. Use the following properties:

button1 Control	
Name	btnRefresh
Text	Refresh
TabStop	False

Step 6   In **SetState** method, set the **Enabled** property of the **btnRefresh** to **true** in **View** mode and **false** in **Add/Edit** mode.

Step 7   Add the following code to **btnRefresh_Click** event method:

```
1   private void btnRefresh_Click(object sender, EventArgs e)
2   {
```

```
3      // Connects to database
4      inventoryConn = new SqlConnection("Data Source=.\\SQLEXPRESS;
5          AttachDbFilename=D:\\Database\\DBMS.mdf;
6          Integrated Security = True; Connect Timeout = 30;
7          User Instance = True");
8
9      inventoryConn.Open();
10
11     // Save changes to database
12     SqlCommandBuilder invtDBAdapterCommand = new
13         SqlCommandBuilder(inventoryAdapter);
14     inventoryAdapter.Update(warehouseTable);
15
16     SqlCommand commandResult = null;
17     SqlDataAdapter adapterResult = new SqlDataAdapter();
18     DataTable tableResult = new DataTable();
19     string StatemenSQL = "SELECT * FROM Warehouse ORDER BY Item";
20
21     try
22     {
23         // Creates Command and DataAdapter objects
24         commandResult = new
25             SqlCommand(StatemenSQL, inventoryConn);
26         adapterResult.SelectCommand = commandResult;
27         tableResult.Clear();
28         adapterResult.Fill(tableResult);
29
30         // Binds grid view to data table
31         grdItem.DataSource = tableResult;
32         txtNumberRecord.Text = tableResult.Rows.Count.ToString();
33         setRowColor(grdItem);
34         grdItem.Rows[0].Selected = true;
35         grdItem.MultiSelect = false;
36     }
37     catch (Exception ex)
38     {
39         MessageBox.Show(ex.Message, "Error Pemrosesan SQL",
40             MessageBoxButtons.OK, MessageBoxIcon.Error);
41     }
42
43     commandResult.Dispose();
44     adapterResult.Dispose();
45     tableResult.Dispose();
46 }
```

Step 8   Save and run the application. Click one of search buttons and then click Refresh button
          to refresh datagridview control.

2.15 Tutorial Steps of Modifying Main Form and Global Variable LoginState

Step 1   Back in the main form, define the click event of **btnLogin** in line 68-73.

```csharp
FormMain.cs
1    using System;
2    using System.Collections.Generic;
3    using System.ComponentModel;
4    using System.Data;
5    using System.Drawing;
6    using System.Linq;
7    using System.Text;
8    using System.Threading.Tasks;
9    using System.Windows.Forms;
10   using System.Threading;
11
12   namespace Balige_HighSchool_DMBS
13   {
14       public partial class FormMain : Form
15       {
16
17           public FormMain()
18           {
19               InitializeComponent();
20           }
21
22           public Button showButtonLibrary
23           {
24               get { return btnLibrary; }
25               set { btnLibrary = value; }
26           }
27
28           public Button showButtonInventory
29           {
30               get { return btnInventory; }
31               set { btnInventory = value; }
32           }
33
34           public Button showButtonAcademy
35           {
36               get { return btnAcademy; }
37               set { btnAcademy = value; }
38           }
39
40           public Button showButtonLogin
41           {
42               get { return btnLogin; }
43               set { btnLogin = value; }
44           }
45
46           public Button showButtonTuition
```

```
47      {
48          get { return btnTuition; }
49          set { btnTuition = value; }
50      }
51
52      public Button showButtonSetting
53      {
54          get { return btnSetting; }
55          set { btnSetting = value; }
56      }
57
58      private void FormMain_Load(object sender, EventArgs e)
59      {
60          btnLibrary.Enabled = false;
61          btnInventory.Enabled = false;
62          btnAcademy.Enabled = false;
63          btnTuition.Enabled = false;
64          btnSetting.Enabled = false;
65          btnExit.Enabled = true;
66      }
67
68      private void btnLogin_Click(object sender, EventArgs e)
69      {
70          FormLogin formlogin = new FormLogin();
71          formlogin.Show();
72          this.Hide();
73      }
74
75      private void btnExit_Click(object sender, EventArgs e)
76      {
77          //this.Close();
78          Application.Exit();
79      }
80      }
81  }
```

Step 2   Add a new .cs file in project and set its name as **Global_Var.cs**:

```
1   using System;
2   using System.Collections.Generic;
3   using System.Linq;
4   using System.Text;
5   using System.Threading.Tasks;
6
7   namespace Balige_HighSchool_DMBS
8   {
9       public class Global_Var
10      {
11          public static int LoginState = 0;
12      }
```

```
13  }
```

Step 3   In **FormInventory.cs**, define **LoginState** method to disable a number of buttons if user logins:

```
 1  private void LoginState()
 2  {
 3      // If user logins
 4      if (Balige_HighSchool_DMBS.Global_Var.LoginState == 1)
 5      {
 6          btnEdit.Enabled = false;
 7          btnAdd.Enabled = false;
 8          btnSave.Enabled = false;
 9          btnCancel.Enabled = false;
10          btnDelete.Enabled = false;
11      }
12  }
```

Step 4   Call **LoginState** method in **Load** event of **FormInventory** in line 49 as follows:

```
 1  private void FormInventory_Load(object sender, EventArgs e)
 2  {
 3      // Connects to database
 4      inventoryConn = new SqlConnection("Data Source=.\\SQLEXPRESS;
 5          AttachDbFilename=D:\\Database\\DBMS.mdf;
 6          Integrated Security = True; Connect Timeout = 30;
 7          User Instance = True");
 8
 9      inventoryConn.Open();
10
11      // Sets inventory command
12      inventoryCommand = new SqlCommand(
13          "SELECT * FROM Warehouse ORDER BY Item", inventoryConn);
14
15      // Sets warehouse data table
16      inventoryAdapter = new SqlDataAdapter();
17      inventoryAdapter.SelectCommand = inventoryCommand;
18      warehouseTable = new DataTable();
19      inventoryAdapter.Fill(warehouseTable);
20
21      // Binds controls
22      txtItem.DataBindings.Add("Text", warehouseTable, "Item");
23      cboQuantity.DataBindings.Add("Text", warehouseTable,
24          "Quantity");
25      cboLocation.DataBindings.Add("Text", warehouseTable,
26          "Location");
27      txtShop.DataBindings.Add("Text", warehouseTable, "Shop");
28      dtpDatePurchased.DataBindings.Add("Text",
29          warehouseTable, "DatePurchased");
30      txtCost.DataBindings.Add("Text", warehouseTable, "Cost");
```

```
31    txtSerialNumber.DataBindings.Add("Text",
32        warehouseTable, "SerialNumber");
33    chkFragile.DataBindings.Add("Checked",
34        warehouseTable, "Fragile");
35    lblPhotoFile.DataBindings.Add("Text",
36        warehouseTable, "PhotoFile");
37
38    // Sets currency manager kekinian to read current items from table
39    inventoryManager =
40        (CurrencyManager)this.BindingContext[warehouseTable];
41
42    DisplayPhoto();
43    SetState("View");
44
45    //Creates 26 search buttons
46    createSearchButton();
47
48    // Clicks all records when form starts
49    btnAll.Click += new System.EventHandler(this.btnSQL_Click);
50    btnAll.PerformClick();
51
52    LoginState();
53  }
```

Step 5   Run application. Try to login as user. Then click on **Inventory DBMS** and you will
see a number of button controls are disabled as shown in Figure 2.28.

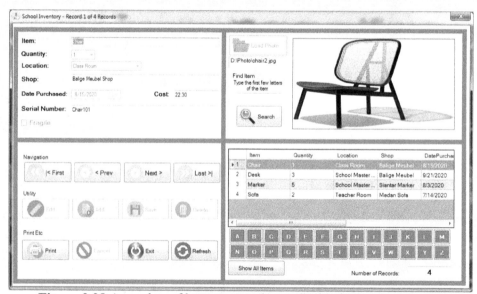

Figure 2.28 A number of button controls are disabled when user logins

TUTORIAL 3
LIBRARY DATABASE PROJECT: PART 1

Description

In this tutorial, you will perform the steps necessary to add 6 tables using Visual C# into **DBMS** database. You will build each table and add the associated fields as needed.

3.1 Tutorial Steps of Creating Author Table

Step 1   Create a new table in the design window. You will see something like the one shown in Figure 3.1. There is a grid for each field (also known as a column). You provide the following column names with their data types. You also need to decide whether the field can be null. For each field or column, you assign properties using the **Properties Window**. To the right of the grid is where keys and indexes are defined. Figure 3.1 is the Design window, where the actual scripting language for creating the tables is written. Name the table as **Author** by changing the first row of the script to: **CREATE TABLE [dbo]. [Author]**.

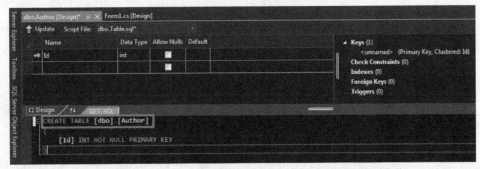

Figure 3.1 The design window for the table to be added

Step 2   The first field in the **Author** table is **AuthorID**. Enter that name for the column name, use **bigint** data type and set the **Is Identity** property to **True** as shown in Figure 3.2.

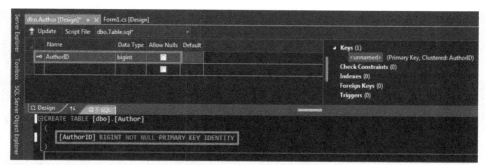

Figure 3.2 The first field (**AuthorID**) is added to table with the **Is Identity** property
set to **True**

Step 3   Continue to other fields using the following options:

Name	Data Type
Name	varchar(50)
BirthDate	datetime
PhotoFile	varchar(200)

Make sure all fields do not allow **Null** values (as a full author name is desired), except
PhotoFile. At this point, your design grid should look as shown in Figure 3.3.

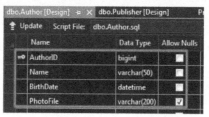

Figure 3.3 The design grid for **Author** table

Step 4   The table definition is now complete. In the top-left corner of the **Table Designer**,
select the **Update** button. In the **Preview Database Updates** dialog box, select the
Update Database button. The changes are now saved to the local database file.

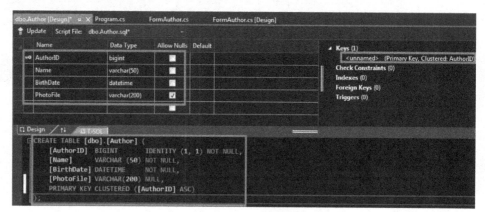

Figure 3.4 Panel for **Author** table

Step 5   Return to the **Server Explorer** window. Right-click on the window and select **Refresh**. You will see what is shown in Figure 3.5.

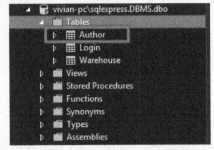

Figure 3.5 Server Explorer window after **Author** table was created

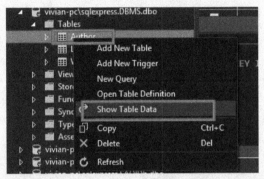

Figure 3.6 Menu items for filling in the data in the **Author** table

Step 6   To fill in the table data, you right-click on the table name, then select **Show Table Data**, as shown in Figure 3.6.

Step 7   Fill in the data in the **Author** table, as shown in Figure 3.7.

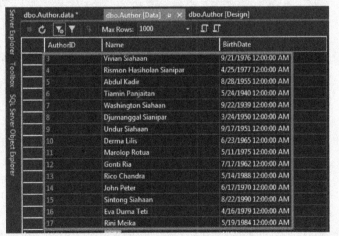

Figure 3.7 Author table filled with a number of rows of data

3.2 Tutorial Steps of Creating Publisher Table

Step 1　Create a new table in the **Server Explorer** window. Follow the same steps as for the **Author** table to create this **Publisher** table. Add the following fields:

Name	Data Type
PublisherID	bigint
Name	varchar(50)
OwnerName	varchar(50)
Address	varchar(100)
City	varchar(50)
Province	varchar(50)
ZIPCode	varchar(10)
Phone	varchar(20)
Fax	varchar(20)
Comment	varchar(50)
PhotoFile	varchar(200)

Set **Allow Nulls** to **Yes** for all fields except **PublisherID**, **Name**, and **OwnerName**. Also set **PublisherID** as the primary key. For **PublisherID**, set **Is Identity** property to **True** in Property Window. Make **Name** and **OwnerName** fields as indexes as shown in Figure 3.8.

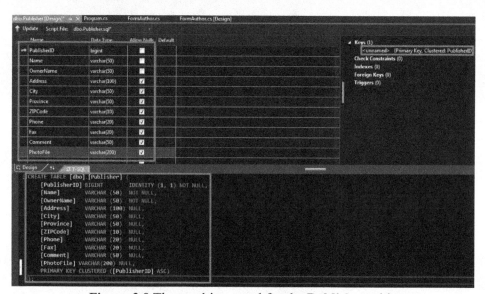

Figure 3.8 The resulting panel for the **Publisher** table

Step 2　Save the table and name it as **Publisher**. In the top-left corner of the **Table Designer**, select the **Update** button. In the **Preview Database Updates** dialog box, select the **Update Database** button. The changes are now saved to the local database file, as shown in Figure 3.9.

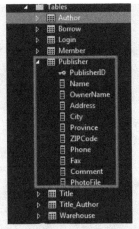

Figure 3.9 Publisher table has been saved in the database

Step 3   Fill in the **Publisher** table with a number of data:

PublisherID	Name	OwnerName	Address	City	Province	ZIPCode	Phone	Fax	Commen
1	SPARTA Publisher	Washington Siahaan	Jalan Balige No. 1	Balige	SUMUT	55281	089536892362	0632-6383934	Great!
2	Balige Publishing	Poltak Sianipar	Jalan Tarabunga	Balige	SUMUT	55287	081182937345	0632-7637383	Good!
3	Siantar Publishing	Tonggam Panjaitan	Dolok Ulu	Siantar	SUMUT	56382	081364748332	0622-3673832	Great!
4	Medan Publisher	Jonathan Sianturi	Medan Area	Medan	SUMUT	56323	081763726223	021-82936282	Great!
5	Minang Publishing	Pulanglah Udo	Padang	Padang	SUMBAR	45342	081927363844	022-37383643	Mantap!
6	Riau Publisher	Anak Riau	Pekan Baru	Pekan Baru	RIAU	63732	081625362534	025-92927283	Super!
7	Palembang Publishing	Uwong Kito	Palembang	Palembang	SUMSEL	62436	081632722322	026-82826232	Great!
8	Lampung Publishing	Anak Lampung	Lampung	Bandar Lampung	LAMPUNG	72823	082526373849	027-28292738	Sip!
NULL	NULL	NULL	NULL	NULL	NULL	NULL	NULL	NULL	NULL

Figure 3.10 Publisher table filled with a number of data

3.3 Tutorial Steps of Creating Title Table

Step 1   This table contains information about each book title in the database. This table has eight fields: **BookTitle**, **PublishYear**, **ISBN**, **PublisherID**, **Description**, **Note**, **Subject**, and **Comment**. Add the following fields:

Name	Data Type
BookTitle	varchar(50)
PublishYear	datetime
ISBN	varchar(50)
PublisherID	bigint
Description	varchar(50)
Note	varchar(50)
Subject	varchar(50)
Comment	varchar(50)

The **ISBN** is the identity number for each book. Only **Title**, **PublishYear**, **ISBN** and **PublisherID** fields cannot accept **NULL** values.

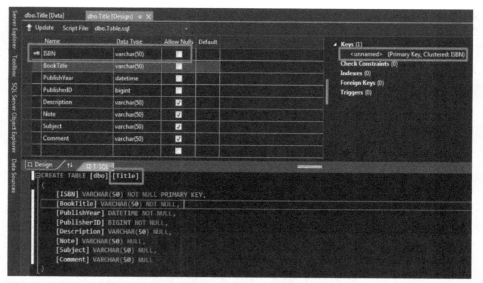

Figure 3.11 The resulting panel for **Title** table

Step 2   Make **ISBN** as the primary key. The final design panel for this table (set table's name as **Title**) is shown in Figure 3.11.

Step 3   Populate **Title** table with some data:

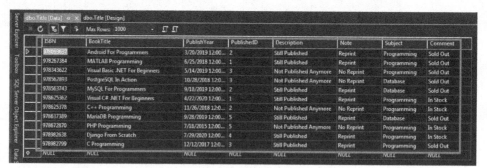

Figure 3.12 The **Title** table is filled with a number of data

3.4 Tutorial Steps of Creating Title_Author Table

Step 1   The **Title_Author** table contains information that relates the title to the author in the database. This table has only two fields: **ISBN** and **AuthorID**:

Name	Data Type
ISBN	varchar(50)
AuthorID	bigint

Step 2   Make **ISBN** as the primary key. The final design panel for this table (set table's name as **Title**) is shown in Figure 3.13.

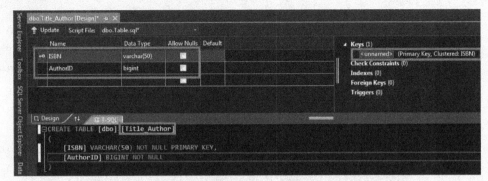

Figure 3.13 The resulting panel for **Title_Author** table

Step 3   Fill in **Title_ Author** with a number of data:

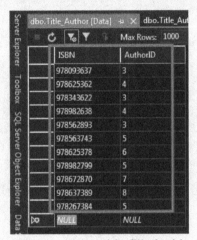

Figure 3.14 The **Title_Author** table filled with a number of data

3.5 Tutorial Steps of Creating Member Table

Step 1   Create a fifth table named **Member**. Add the following fields:

Name	Data Type
MemberID	bigint
FirstName	varchar(50)
LastName	varchar(50)
BirthDate	datetime
Status	bit
Ethnicity	varchar(100)
Nationality	varchar(100)
Mobile	varchar(20)

```
Phone         varchar(20)
Religion      varchar(50)
Gender        varchar(10)
PhotoFile     varchar(200)
```

Set **Allow Nulls** to **Yes** for all fields except **MemberID**, **FirstName**, and **LastName**.
Also set **MemberID** as the primary key. For **MemberID**, set its **Is Identity** as **True**.
Make **FirstName** and **LastName** fields as indexes.

Step 2   The final design panel for this table is shown in Figure 3.15.

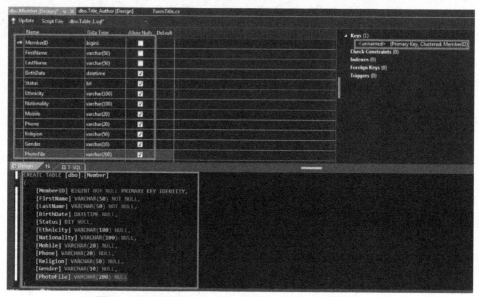

Figure 3.15 The resulting panel for **Member** table

3.6 Tutorial Steps of Creating Borrow Table

Step 1   Create a sixth table named **Borrow**. Add the following fields:

Name	Data Type
BorrowID	bigint
MemberID	bigint
BorrowCode	varchar(50)
ISBN	varchar(50)
BorrowDate	datetime
ReturnDate	datetime
Penalty	money

Set **BorrowID** as primary key and set **NOT NULL** for all fields except **Penalty**.

Step 2   The final design panel for this table is shown in Figure 3.16.

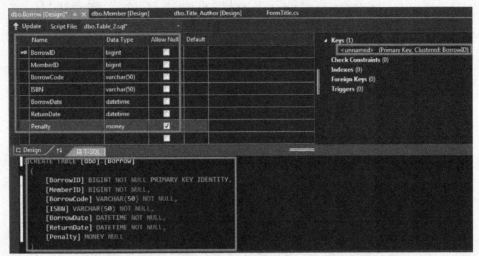

Figure 3.16 The resulting panel for **Borrow** table

3.7 Tutorial Steps of Defining Relationship

Step 1   You now have new six tables in your **DBMS** database, but each table is an independent entity. The final step is to define the relationship between the primary key and foreign key. You need to be careful because a relationship can only be defined between two fields when they have the same data type.

To do so, you need to modify the script code in the table design.

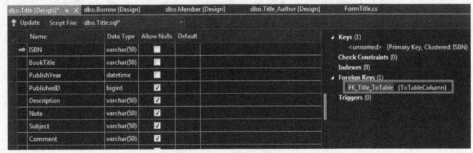

Figure 3.17 Panel for adding foreign key

To associate a foreign key from one table with a primary key in another table, you right-click the table containing the foreign key and select **Open Table Definition**. For example, you want to associate **PublisherID** (foreign key) field in the **BookTitle** table with **PublisherID** (primary key) in the **Publisher** table. To do so, right-click on the **Title** table in the **Server Explorer** window and select **Open Table Definition**. On the right-hand side of the design panel, right-click on **Foreign Keys** then select **Add New Foreign Key**. A default key will be created. You will see as shown in Figure 3.17.

Step 2   Click on the scripts pane (**Design** tab) under table definition, and replace the default definitions of foreign key references with the following:

```
1    CONSTRAINT [FK_Title_Publisher] FOREIGN KEY ([PublisherID])
2    REFERENCES [Publisher]([PublisherID])
```

This says that you have a relationship named **FK_Title_Publisher** that associates the **PublisherID** field in the **Title** table with the **PublisherID** field in the **Publisher** table.

The script pane for **Title** table is shown in Figure 3.18. You still need four other relationships.

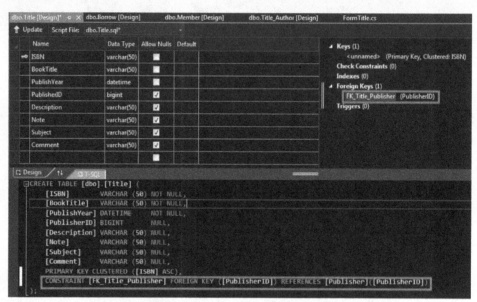

Figure 3.18 Script pane for **Title** table

Click **Update** to update the **Title** table definition.

Step 3   Click on the scripts pane (**Design** tab) under **Auhor_Table** table definition, and replace the default definitions of foreign key references with the following:

```
1    CONSTRAINT [FK_Title_Author_Author] FOREIGN KEY ([AuthorID])
2    REFERENCES [Author]([AuthorID])
```

The scripts pane for **Title_Author** table is shown in Figure 3.19.

Next, you need to associate the **ISBN** (foreign key) field in **Title_Author** table with **ISBN** (primary key) in the **Title** table. To do this, right-click on **Title_Author** table in

Server Explorer and select **Open Table Definition**. On the right side of the design panel, right-click on **Foreign Keys** then select **Add New Foreign Key**. A default key will be created.

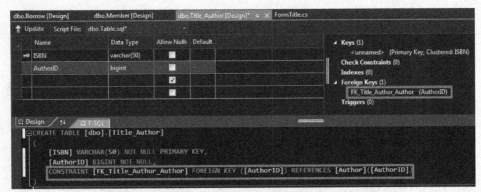

Figure 3.19 Script pane for **Title_Author** table

Click on the scripts pane (**Design** tab) under table definitions, and replace the default definitions of foreign key references with the following:

```
1    CONSTRAINT [FK_Title_Author_Author2] FOREIGN KEY ([ISBN]) REFERENCES
2    [Title]([ISBN])
```

The scripts pane for **Title_Author** table is shown in Figure 3.20.

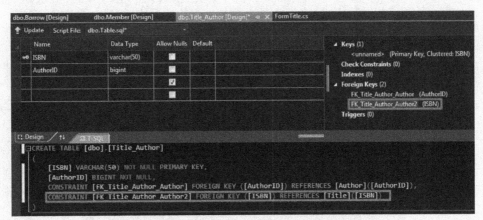

Figure 3.20 Script pane for **Title_Author** table

Click **Update** to update the **Title_Author** table definition.

Step 4   Then, you need to associate the **ISBN** (foreign key) field in **Borrow** table with **ISBN** (primary key) in the **Title** table.

Click on the scripts pane (**Design** tab) under **Borrow** table definitions, and replace the default definitions of foreign key references with the following:

```
1   CONSTRAINT [FK_Borrow_Title] FOREIGN KEY ([ISBN]) REFERENCES
2   [Title]([ISBN])
```

The scripts pane for **Borrow** table is shown in Figure 3.21.

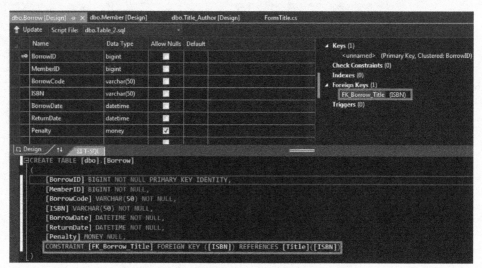

Figure 3.21 Script pane for **Borrow** table

Click **Update** to update the **Borrow** table definition.

Step 5   Finally, you need to associate the **MemberID** (foreign key) field in **Borrow** table with **MemberID** (primary key) in the **Member** table.

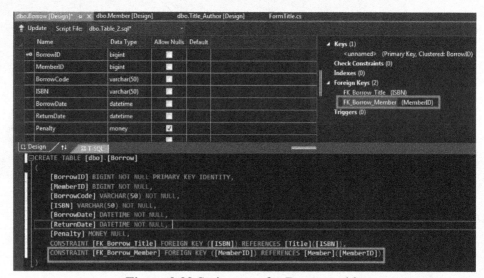

Figure 3.22 Script pane for **Borrow** table

Click on the scripts pane (**Design** tab) under **Borrow** table definition, and replace the default definitions of foreign key references with the following:

```
1  CONSTRAINT [FK_Borrow_Member] FOREIGN KEY ([MemberID]) REFERENCES
2  [Member]([MemberID])
```

The scripts pane for **Borrow** table is shown in Figure 3.22.

Click **Update** to update the **Borrow** table definition.

3.8 Tutorial Steps of Creating Form for Author Table: Interface

Step 1   You will build a complete database management system for this book inventory database. Every table in the database will need input form. In this tutorial, you will build such a form for **Author** table. Although this table is quite simple (only four fields: **AuthorID**, **Name**, **BirthDate**, and **PhotoFile**), it provides a basis for illustrating the many steps in interface design. SQL statement is required by the **Command** object to read fields (sorted by **Name**).

You need an input form so that user can edit existing records, delete records, or add new records. The form will also have the capability of navigating from one record to another. The steps that need to be done are as follows:

Start a new Visual C# application. You need three label controls, one picture box, three text boxes and one date time picker control to display the fields. You also need four buttons for navigation, six buttons for controlling editing features, and one button to upload author's photo. Apart from that, you also need one button for the user to stop editing. Place these controls on the form. The complete form looks as shown in Figure 3.23.

Step 2   Set the properties of each control as follows:

Form1 Control	
Name	FormAuthor
BackColor	Control
FormBorderStyle	FixedSingle
StartPosition	CenterScreen
Text	Form Author

label1 Control	
Text	Author ID

textBox1 Control	
Name	txtAuthorID
ReadOnly	True

label2 Control	
ForeColor	White
Text	Author Name

textBox2 Control	
Name	txtAuthorName
ReadOnly	True

label3 Control	
Text	Birth Date

dateTimePicker1 Control	
Name	dtpBirthDate
Format	short

textBox3 Control	
Name	txtPhoto
ReadOnly	True

pictureBox1 Control	
Name	picAuthor
SizeMode	StretchImage

button1 Control	
Name	btnPrev
Text	<= Prev

button2 Control	
Name	btnNext
Text	Next =>

button3 Control	
Name	btnEdit
Text	&Edit

button4 Control	
Name	btnSave
Text	&Save

button5 Control	
Name	btnCancel
Text	&Cancel

button6 Control	
Name	btnAddNew
Text	&Add New

button7 Control	
Name	btnDelete
Text	&Delete

button8 Control	
Name	btnDone
Text	D&one

button9 Control	
Name	btnUpload
Text	&Upload

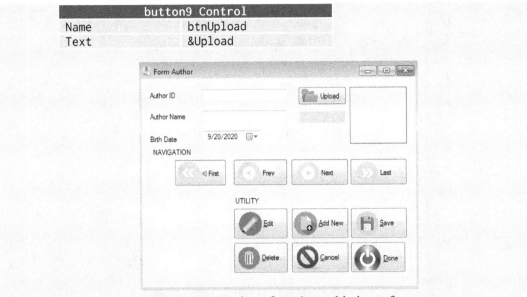

Figure 3.23 Design of **Author** table input form

Step 3   You will add features to this author form gradually. At this point, you will add code to construct the data table and to navigate the records in the **Author** table. Add this line of code at the top of the window:

```
1  using System.Data.SqlClient;
```

Step 4   Write the following form-level declarations for creating data objects:

```
1  SqlConnection connBook;
2  SqlCommand commandAuthor;
3  SqlDataAdapter adapterAuthor;
4  DataTable tableAuthor;
5  CurrencyManager managerAuthor;
```

Step 5   Add the following code to the **FormAuthor_Load** event method:

```
1   private void FormAuthor_Load(object sender, EventArgs e)
2   {
3       try
4       {
5           // Connects to database
6           connBook = new SqlConnection("Data Source=.\\SQLEXPRESS;
7           AttachDbFilename=D:\\Database\\DBMS.mdf;
8           Integrated Security = True; Connect Timeout = 30;
9           User Instance = True");
10
11          connBook.Open();
12
13          // Creates Command object
```

```
14    commandAuthor = new
15        SqlCommand("SELECT * FROM Author ORDER BY Name",
16        connBook);
17
18    // Creates DataAdapter/DataTable objects
19    adapterAuthor = new SqlDataAdapter();
20    adapterAuthor.SelectCommand = commandAuthor;
21    tableAuthor = new DataTable();
22    adapterAuthor.Fill(tableAuthor);
23
24    // Binds controls to data table
25    txtAuthorID.DataBindings.Add("Text",
26        tableAuthor, "AuthorID");
27    txtAuthorName.DataBindings.Add("Text", tableAuthor, "Name");
28    dtpBirthDate.DataBindings.Add("Text",
29        tableAuthor, "BirthDate");
30    txtPhoto.DataBindings.Add("Text", tableAuthor, "PhotoFile");
31
32    // Creates data update
33    managerAuthor =
34        (CurrencyManager)this.BindingContext[tableAuthor];
35    }
36    catch (Exception ex)
37    {
38        MessageBox.Show(ex.Message,
39            "Error in reading Author table.",
40            MessageBoxButtons.OK, MessageBoxIcon.Error);
41        return;
42    }
43
44    this.Show();
      DisplayPhoto();
    }
```

The code above creates the data objects needed to open the database and construct the **Author** table (includes all fields). The code above then binds the controls with the update manager object (**CurrencyManager**).

Step 6   Define **DisplayPhoto** to display author photo in **picAuthor**:

```
1    private void DisplayPhoto()
2    {
3        // Displays photo
4        if (!txtPhoto.Text.Equals(""))
5        {
6            try
7            {
8                picAuthor.Image = Image.FromFile(txtPhoto.Text);
9            }
10           catch (Exception ex)
```

```
11          {
12              MessageBox.Show(ex.Message, "Error Loading Photo",
13                  MessageBoxButtons.OK, MessageBoxIcon.Error);
14          }
15      }
16      else
17      {
18          string dir =
19              Path.GetDirectoryName(Application.ExecutablePath);
20          string filename = Path.Combine(dir, @"author.png");
21          picAuthor.Image = Image.FromFile(filename);
22      }
23  }
```

Step 7   Add the following code to **FormAuthor_FormClosing** event method to close the
database connection:

```
1   private void FormAuthor_FormClosing(object sender,
2   FormClosingEventArgs e)
3   {
4       // Closes connection to database
5       connBook.Close();
6
7       // Deletes objects
8       connBook.Dispose();
9       commandAuthor.Dispose();
10      adapterAuthor.Dispose();
11  }
```

Step 8   Write the following code for the **Click** event of the four navigation buttons:

```
1   private void btnPrev_Click(object sender, EventArgs e)
2   {
3       if (managerAuthor.Position == 0)
4       {
5           Console.Beep();
6       }
7       managerAuthor.Position--;
8   }
9
10  private void btnNext_Click(object sender, EventArgs e)
11  {
12      if (managerAuthor.Position == managerAuthor.Count - 1)
13      {
14          Console.Beep();
15      }
16      managerAuthor.Position++;
17  }
18
19  private void btnFirst_Click(object sender, EventArgs e)
```

```
20  {
21      managerAuthor.Position = 0;
22  }
23
24  private void btnLast_Click(object sender, EventArgs e)
25  {
26      managerAuthor.Position = managerAuthor.Count - 1;
27  }
```

Step 9   Save and run the application. What is displayed first is the first record in **Author** table.
Click on four navigation buttons to prove the result.

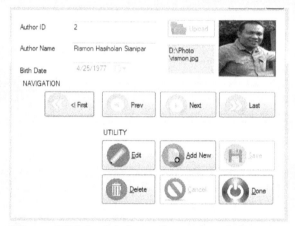

Figure 3.24 Author input form when it first runs

Figure 3.25 The result when user clicks **Last >|** button

3.9 Tutorial Steps of Creating Form for Author Table: Message Box

Step 1   There are two places where you can use the message box in **Author** table input form. One message box is provided after saving updates to let the user know that the save was successful and another message box is related to record deletion.

Use the following code in **btnSave_Click** event method:

```
1   private void btnSave_Click(object sender, EventArgs e)
2   {
3       MessageBox.Show("Records successfully saved", "Save",
4           MessageBoxButtons.OK, MessageBoxIcon.Information);
5   }
```

There will be more code in this event. The code implements only message box.

Step 2   Use this code on **btnDelete_Click** event method:

```
1   private void btnDelete_Click(object sender, EventArgs e)
2   {
3       DialogResult response;
4       response = MessageBox.Show("Dou you really want to delete this record?",
5           "Delete", MessageBoxButtons.YesNo, MessageBoxIcon.Question,
6           MessageBoxDefaultButton.Button2);
7   }
```

Step 3   Save the application and run it. Click on **Delete** button to see as shown in Figure 3.12.

Figure 3.26 Message box is displayed when user clicks **Delete** button

3.10 Tutorial Steps of Creating Form for Author Table: Application State

Step 1   The **Author** table input form operates in one of three states: **View** state, **Add** state, or **Edit** state. In the **View** state, user can navigate one record to another, user can switch to **Edit** state, user can add and/or delete records, or user can exit the application.

In **Add** and **Edit** state, no navigation is made possible, data can be updated, and user can have access to **Save** and **Cancel** operations. Each of these steps can be implemented using the **Enabled** property of the button and the **ReadOnly** property of the text box. You use **TabIndex** (and **TabOrder**) to shift focus on the text box controls. You will use a method of moving from one state to another.

Clear all tab ordering for the ten buttons by setting the **TabStop** property to **False**. Additionally, set the **TabStop** property to **False** for the **Author ID** text box.

Step 2   Add a method named **SetState** as follows:

```
1   private void SetState(string stateStr) {
2       switch (stateStr)
3       {
4           case "View":
5               txtAuthorID.BackColor = Color.White;
6               txtAuthorID.ForeColor = Color.Black;
7               txtAuthorName.ReadOnly = true;
8               dtpBirthDate.Enabled = false;
9               btnPrev.Enabled = true;
10              btnNext.Enabled = true;
11              btnAddNew.Enabled = true;
12              btnSave.Enabled = false;
13              btnCancel.Enabled = false;
14              btnEdit.Enabled = true;
15              btnDelete.Enabled = true;
16              btnFinish.Enabled = true;
17              btnFirst.Enabled = true;
18              btnLast.Enabled = true;
19              btnUpload.Enabled = false;
20              txtAuthorName.Focus();
21              break;
22
23          default: // Add or Edit state
24              txtAuthorID.BackColor = Color.Red;
25              txtAuthorID.ForeColor = Color.White;
26              txtAuthorName.ReadOnly = false;
27              dtpBirthDate.Enabled = true;
28              btnPrev.Enabled = false;
29              btnNext.Enabled = false;
30              btnAddNew.Enabled = false;
31              btnSave.Enabled = true;
32              btnCancel.Enabled = true;
```

```
33          btnEdit.Enabled = false;
34          btnDelete.Enabled = false;
35          btnFinish.Enabled = false;
36          btnFirst.Enabled = false;
37          btnLast.Enabled = false;
38          btnUpload.Enabled = true;
39          txtAuthorName.Focus();
40          break;
41      }
42 }
```

The code above specifies **View**, **Add**, or **Edit** state for the application. Pay attention to which buttons are available and which are not. Note that **Author ID** text box is given red back color if it is in **Add** or **Edit** state to indicate that it cannot be changed.

Step 3   Set the **View** state when the application first runs. Add the following code in line 44 to **FormAuthor_Load** event method:

```
1  private void FormAuthor_Load(object sender, EventArgs e)
2  {
3      try
4      {
5          // Connects to database
6          connBook = new SqlConnection("Data Source=.\\SQLEXPRESS;
7          AttachDbFilename=D:\\Database\\DBMS.mdf;
8          Integrated Security = True; Connect Timeout = 30;
9          User Instance = True");
10
11         connBook.Open();
12
13         // Creates Command object
14         commandAuthor = new
15             SqlCommand("SELECT * FROM Author ORDER BY Name",
16             connBook);
17
18         // Creates DataAdapter/DataTable objects
19         adapterAuthor = new SqlDataAdapter();
20         adapterAuthor.SelectCommand = commandAuthor;
21         tableAuthor = new DataTable();
22         adapterAuthor.Fill(tableAuthor);
23
24         // Binds controls to data table
25         txtAuthorID.DataBindings.Add("Text",
26             tableAuthor, "AuthorID");
27         txtAuthorName.DataBindings.Add("Text", tableAuthor, "Name");
28         dtpBirthDate.DataBindings.Add("Text",
29             tableAuthor, "BirthDate");
30         txtPhoto.DataBindings.Add("Text", tableAuthor, "PhotoFile");
31
```

```
32          // Creates data update
33          managerAuthor =
34              (CurrencyManager)this.BindingContext[tableAuthor];
35      }
36      catch (Exception ex)
37      {
38          MessageBox.Show(ex.Message,
39              "Error in reading Author table.",
40              MessageBoxButtons.OK, MessageBoxIcon.Error);
41          return;
42      }
43
44      this.Show();
45      DisplayPhoto();
46      SetState("View");
47  }
```

Step 4   When **Add New** button is clicked, you need to switch to **Add** state. Add the following
          code to **btnAddNew_Click** event method:

```
1   private void btnAddNew_Click(object sender, EventArgs e)
2   {
3       SetState("Add");
4   }
```

Step 5   When **Edit** button is clicked, the application will be switched to **Edit** state. Add the
          following code to **btnEdit_Click** event method:

```
1   private void btnEdit_Click(object sender, EventArgs e)
2   {
3       SetState("Edit");
4   }
```

Step 6   When **Cancel** or **Save** button is clicked (in **Add** or **Edit** state), application will return
          to the **View** state. Put this line of code in **btnCancel_Click** and **btnSave_Click** event
          methods:

```
1   private void btnCancel_Click(object sender, EventArgs e)
2   {
3       SetState("View");
4   }
5
6   private void btnSave_Click(object sender, EventArgs e)
7   {
8       SetState("View");
9   }
```

Step 7   Save and run the application. You will see the application in its initial state (**View**
          state):

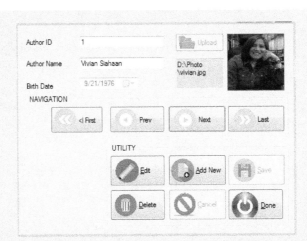

Figure 3.27 Author input form is in **View** state when it first runs

When user clicks the **Edit** or **Add New** button, she will see what is shown in Figure 3.28.

Figure 3.28 Author input form is in **Add** or **Edit** state

3.11 Tutorial Steps of Creating Form for Author Table: Error Trapping

Step 1   Modify **btnAddNew_Click**, **btnSave_Click**, and **btnDelete_Click** event methods to handle error trapping:

```
1  private void btnAddNew_Click(object sender, EventArgs e)
2  {
3      try
4      {
5          SetState("Add");
6      }
7      catch (Exception ex)
```

```
8     {
9         MessageBox.Show("Error adding new record.", "Error",
10            MessageBoxButtons.OK, MessageBoxIcon.Error);
11     }
12 }
```

```
1  private void btnSave_Click(object sender, EventArgs e)
2  {
3      try
4      {
5          MessageBox.Show("Records successfully saved", "Save",
6          MessageBoxButtons.OK, MessageBoxIcon.Information);
7          SetState("View");
8      }
9      catch (Exception ex)
10     {
11         MessageBox.Show("Error saving record.", "Error",
12             MessageBoxButtons.OK, MessageBoxIcon.Error);
13     }
14 }
```

```
1  private void btnDelete_Click(object sender, EventArgs e)
2  {
3      DialogResult response;
4      response = MessageBox.Show("Dou you really want to delete this record?",
5          "Delete", MessageBoxButtons.YesNo, MessageBoxIcon.Question,
6          MessageBoxDefaultButton.Button2);
7      if (response == DialogResult.No)
8      {
9          return;
10     }
11
12     try
13     {
14
15     }
16     catch (Exception ex)
17     {
18         MessageBox.Show("Error deleting record.", "Error",
19             MessageBoxButtons.OK, MessageBoxIcon.Error);
20     }
21 }
```

3.12 Tutorial Steps of Creating Form for Author Table: Editing Record

Step 1   You will now add editing capability and other related capabilities to save and/or cancel
edits. Before saving update into database, you need to validate data entered by user. In

this case, you need to validate author name and year range of birth date. Define a method named **ValidateData** to validate data entered by user:

```csharp
private bool ValidateData()
{
    string message = "";
    int yearInput, yearNow;
    bool allOK = true;

    // Checks name in txtAuthorName
    if (txtAuthorName.Text.Trim().Equals(""))
    {
        message = "You should enter author name." + "\r\n";
        txtAuthorName.Focus();
        allOK = false;
    }

    // Checks birth date range
    yearInput = dtpBirthDate.Value.Year;
    yearNow = DateTime.Now.Year;

    if (yearInput > yearNow || yearInput < yearNow - 150)
    {
        message += "Year should be between " +
            (yearNow - 150).ToString() +
            " and " + yearNow.ToString();
        dtpBirthDate.Focus();
        allOK = false;
    }

    if (!allOK)
    {
        MessageBox.Show(message, "Validation Error",
            MessageBoxButtons.OK, MessageBoxIcon.Information);
    }

    return (allOK);
}
```

Step 2   Add a **KeyPress** event for the **txtAuthorName** text box to accept only letters:

```csharp
private void txtAuthorName_KeyPress(object sender, KeyPressEventArgs e)
{
    if ((e.KeyChar >= 'a' && e.KeyChar <= 'z') ||
        (e.KeyChar >= 'A' && e.KeyChar <= 'Z') ||
        (int)e.KeyChar == 8 || (int)e.KeyChar == 32)
    {
        // Key can be accepted
        e.Handled = false;
    }
```

```
10      else
11      {
12          e.Handled = true;
13          Console.Beep();
14      }
15  }
```

Step 3   Modify **btnSave_Click** event method to save the change and reposition the pointer to the record just edited:

```
1   private void btnSave_Click(object sender, EventArgs e)
2   {
3       if (!ValidateData())
4       {
5           return;
6       }
7
8       string nameSaved = txtAuthorName.Text;
9       int rowSaved;
10
11      try
12      {
13          managerAuthor.EndCurrentEdit();
14          tableAuthor.DefaultView.Sort = "Name";
15          rowSaved = tableAuthor.DefaultView.Find(nameSaved);
16          managerAuthor.Position = rowSaved;
17
18          MessageBox.Show("Records successfully saved", "Save",
19              MessageBoxButtons.OK, MessageBoxIcon.Information);
20
21          SetState("View");
22      }
23      catch (Exception ex)
24      {
25          MessageBox.Show("Error saving record.", "Error",
26              MessageBoxButtons.OK, MessageBoxIcon.Error);
27      }
28  }
```

Step 4   Modify **btnCancel_Click** event method to restore controls if the edit is canceled:

```
1   private void btnCancel_Click(object sender, EventArgs e)
2   {
3       managerAuthor.CancelCurrentEdit();
4       SetState("View");
5   }
```

Figure 3.29 Editing operation is successfully performed

Step 5   Add the following code in line to the **FormAuthor_FormClosing** method to save any changes to the database file:

```
private void FormAuthor_FormClosing(object sender,
FormClosingEventArgs e)
{
    try
    {
        // Saves changes into database
        SqlCommandBuilder authorAdapterCommand =
            new SqlCommandBuilder(adapterAuthor);
        adapterAuthor.Update(tableAuthor);
    }
    catch (Exception ex)
    {
        MessageBox.Show("Error saving database into file: \r\n" +
            ex.Message, "Saving Error", MessageBoxButtons.OK,
            MessageBoxIcon.Error);
    }

    // Closes connection to database
    connBook.Close();

    // Deletes objects
    connBook.Dispose();
    commandAuthor.Dispose();
    adapterAuthor.Dispose();
}
```

Step 6   Save and run the application. Make sure Edit feature is working properly. Try changing the author name. Make sure the **Cancel** button is working properly. This is shown in Figure 3.29.

3.13 Tutorial Steps of Creating Form for Author Table: Adding New Record

Step 1   You now implement the capability on the form to add new records to the database. Add the following lines of code to the form-level declaration:

```csharp
string appState;
int myBookmark;
```

Step 2   Add this code in line 2 to **SetState** method:

```csharp
private void SetState(string stateStr) {
    appState = stateStr;

    switch (stateStr)
    {
        case "View":
            txtAuthorID.BackColor = Color.White;
            txtAuthorID.ForeColor = Color.Black;
            txtAuthorName.ReadOnly = true;
            dtpBirthDate.Enabled = false;
            btnPrev.Enabled = true;
            btnNext.Enabled = true;
            btnAddNew.Enabled = true;
            btnSave.Enabled = false;
            btnCancel.Enabled = false;
            btnEdit.Enabled = true;
            btnDelete.Enabled = true;
            btnFinish.Enabled = true;
            btnFirst.Enabled = true;
            btnLast.Enabled = true;
            txtAuthorName.Focus();
            break;

        default: // Add or Edit state
            txtAuthorID.BackColor = Color.Red;
            txtAuthorID.ForeColor = Color.White;
            txtAuthorName.ReadOnly = false;
            dtpBirthDate.Enabled = true;
            btnPrev.Enabled = false;
            btnNext.Enabled = false;
            btnAddNew.Enabled = false;
            btnSave.Enabled = true;
            btnCancel.Enabled = true;
            btnEdit.Enabled = false;
            btnDelete.Enabled = false;
            btnFinish.Enabled = false;
            btnFirst.Enabled = false;
            btnLast.Enabled = false;
            txtAuthorName.Focus();
            break;
    }
```

```
42  }
```

Step 3   Modify **btnAddNew_Click** event method to add a new record by adding code in line
          5 and 6:

```
1   private void btnAddNew_Click(object sender, EventArgs e)
2   {
3       try
4       {
5           myBookmark = managerAuthor.Position;
6           managerAuthor.AddNew();
7           SetState("Add");
8       }
9       catch (Exception ex)
10      {
11          MessageBox.Show("Error adding new record.", "Error",
12              MessageBoxButtons.OK, MessageBoxIcon.Error);
13      }
14  }
```

Figure 3.30 The new record has been successfully saved into the database

Step 4   Modify **btnCancel_Click** event method to differentiate between cancellation during
          Edit mode and **Add** mode by adding code in line 5-8:

```
1   private void btnCancel_Click(object sender, EventArgs e)
2   {
3       managerAuthor.CancelCurrentEdit();
4
5       if (appState.Equals("Add"))
6       {
7           managerAuthor.Position = myBookmark;
8       }
9
10      SetState("View");
```

Step 5   Save and run the application. Click **Add New** button. Note that all text boxes are blank (including **Author ID** text box. Type a specific name, then click **Save**. New record has been successfully saved as shown in Figure 3.30.

3.14 Tutorial Steps of Creating Form for Author Table: Deleting Record

Step 1   You will now add the capability to delete records from **Author** table. Modify the **btnDelete_Click** event method by adding code in line 14 to delete records if the user responds to **Yes** in the message box:

```
1   private void btnDelete_Click(object sender, EventArgs e)
2   {
3       DialogResult response;
4       response = MessageBox.Show("Dou you really want to delete this record?",
5           "Delete", MessageBoxButtons.YesNo, MessageBoxIcon.Question,
6           MessageBoxDefaultButton.Button2);
7       if (response == DialogResult.No)
8       {
9           return;
10      }
11
12      try
13      {
14          managerAuthor.RemoveAt(managerAuthor.Position);
15      }
16      catch (Exception ex)
17      {
18          MessageBox.Show("Error deleting record.", "Error",
19              MessageBoxButtons.OK, MessageBoxIcon.Error);
20      }
21  }
```

Step 2   Save the application and run it. Make sure the **Yes** and **No** responses in the message box give correct results. Delete only those records you added using **Add New** button. If you try to remove the original **Author** the table, you'll see a message box when you stop the application (from **FormClosing** event).

3.15 Tutorial Steps of Creating Form for Author Table: Stopping Application

Step 1   Add the following code in line 4-12 and line 34 to **FormAuthor_FormClosing** event method to ensure user doesn't close the application during **Edit** or **Add** mode:

```
1   private void FormAuthor_FormClosing(object sender,
2   FormClosingEventArgs e)
3   {
4       if (appState.Equals("Edit") || appState.Equals("Add"))
5       {
6           MessageBox.Show(
7               "You should finish editing before closing application.",
8               "", MessageBoxButtons.OK, MessageBoxIcon.Information);
9           e.Cancel = true;
10      }
11      else
12      {
13          try
14          {
15              // Saves changes into
16              SqlCommandBuilder authorAdapterCommand =
17                  new SqlCommandBuilder(adapterAuthor);
18              adapterAuthor.Update(tableAuthor);
19          }
20          catch (Exception ex)
21          {
22              MessageBox.Show("Error saving database into file: \r\n" +
23                  ex.Message, "Error Saving", MessageBoxButtons.OK,
24                  MessageBoxIcon.Error);
25          }
26
27          // Closes connection to database
28          connBook.Close();
29
30          // Deletes objects
31          connBook.Dispose();
32          commandAuthor.Dispose();
33          adapterAuthor.Dispose();
34      }
35  }
```

Step 2   Put this code in **btnDone_Click** event method:

```
1   private void btnDone_Click(object sender, EventArgs e)
2   {
3       this.Close();
4   }
```

Step 3   Save and run the application. Make sure the **Done** button is working properly. Make
sure the user cannot close the application in **Edit** or **Add** mode.

3.16 Tutorial Steps of Searching Capability

Step 1   Add a group box in the top-right corner of the form. Place a label, a text box, and a button on the group box. Set the properties as follows:

groupBox1 Control	
Name	grpSearchAuthor
Text	Find Author

label1 Control	
AutoSize	False
Text	Type the first few letters of the author
TextAlign	TopCenter

textBox1 Control	
Name	txtSearch
TabStop	False

button1 Control	
Name	btnSearch
Text	Search
TabStop	False

When finished, the modified form will look like in Figure 3.31.

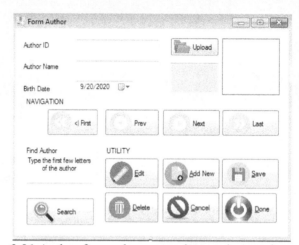

Figure 3.31 Author form when group box and controls are added

Step 2   In the **SetState** method, enable group box control in **View** mode and disable it in **Add** and **Edit** mode. Use its **Enabled** property.

Step 3   Add the following code to **btnSearch_Click** event method:

```
1  private void btnSearch_Click(object sender, EventArgs e)
2  {
3      if (txtSearch.Text.Equals(""))
4      {
```

```
 5          return;
 6      }
 7
 8      int rowSaved = managerAuthor.Position;
 9      DataRow[] rowFound;
10      tableAuthor.DefaultView.Sort = "Name";
11      rowFound = tableAuthor.Select("Name LIKE '" +
12          txtSearch.Text + "*'");
13
14      if (rowFound.Length == 0)
15      {
16          managerAuthor.Position = rowSaved;
17      }
18      else
19      {
20          managerAuthor.Position =
21              tableAuthor.DefaultView.Find(rowFound[0]["Name"]);
22          DisplayPhoto();
23      }
24  }
```

Step 4   Save and run the application. Try searching by providing the first letter or two of the author's name, as shown in Figure 3.32.

Figure 3.32 Author's name search feature added

3.17 Tutorial Steps of Adding Search Buttons

Step 1   Add a button control on the form. Set its **Name** property as **btnAll** and its **Text** poperty as **Show All Authors**. You add another **DataGridView** control and set its **Name** property as **grdAuthor**. You also need to add a label and set its **Text** property as **Number of Records:**. Then add a textbox on the form. Set its **Name** property as **txtNumberRecord**. The resulting form is shown in Figure 3.33.

Step 2   Add the following form-level declarations:

```
1   String SQLAll = "SELECT * FROM Author ";
2   Button[] buttonArr = new Button[26];
```

SQLAll is a variable that contains the default SQL statements, while **buttonArr** is an array containing the search buttons.

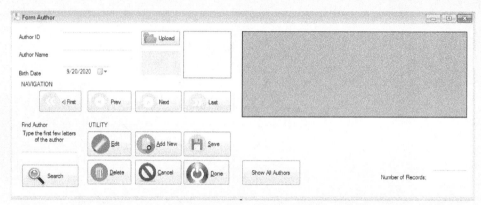

Figure 3.33 Author form after a number of controls added

Step 3   Define a new method named **createSearchButton()** as follows:

```
1    private void createSearchButton()
2    {
3        // Creates search buttons
4        int w, lStart, l, t;
5        int btnHeight = 35; // by trial and error
6
7        // Search buttons
8        // Button width - 13 buttons in a row
9        w = Convert.ToInt32(grdItem.Width / 13);
10
11       // Aligns buttons
12       lStart = Convert.ToInt32((grdItem.Width)) + 5;
13       l = lStart; t = grdItem.Top + grdItem.Height + 10;
14
15       // Creates and positions 26 buttons
16       for (int i = 0; i < 26; i++)
17       {
18           // Creates push button
19           buttonArr[i] = new Button();
20           buttonArr[i].TabStop = false;
21
22           // Sets Text property
23           buttonArr[i].Text = ((char)(65 + i)).ToString();
24           buttonArr[i].Font = new Font(buttonArr[i].Font.FontFamily,
25               9, FontStyle.Bold);
```

```
26
27        // Positions buttons
28        buttonArr[i].Width = w;
29        buttonArr[i].Height = btnHeight;
30        buttonArr[i].Left = l;
31        buttonArr[i].Top = t;
32
33        // Gives color
34        buttonArr[i].BackColor = Color.Red;
35        buttonArr[i].ForeColor = Color.White;
36
37        // Adds each button on form
38        this.Controls.Add(buttonArr[i]);
39
40        // Adds event handler
41        buttonArr[i].Click +=
42            new System.EventHandler(this.btnSQL_Click);
43        l += w+1;
44
45        if (i == 12)
46        {
47            // Next row
48            l = lStart; t += btnHeight;
49        }
50    }
51 }
```

This method creates search buttons A through Z using **buttonArrr** array. The code above then specifies the width of the button and places it on the form. Finally, the resulting records are displayed by programmatically clicking **btnSQL** button.

Step 4   Write the code for **btnSQL_Click** event method (handle **Click** event for all search buttons) as follows:

```
1  private void btnSQL_Click(object sender, EventArgs e)
2  {
3      SqlCommand commResult = null;
4      SqlDataAdapter adapterResult = new SqlDataAdapter();
5      DataTable tableResult = new DataTable();
6      String StatemenSQL;
7
8      // Determines which button is clicked and creates SQL statement
9      Button buttonClicked = (Button)sender;
10     switch (buttonClicked.Text)
11     {
12         case "Show All Authors":
13             StatemenSQL = SQLAll;
14             break;
15         case "Z":
```

```
16          // Z button is clicked
17          // Appends at SQLAll to limit records upto for item Z
18          StatemenSQL = SQLAll + " WHERE Name > 'Z' ";
19          break;
20      default:
21          // Letter keys except Z
22          // Appends at SQLAll to limit records
23          // for letter that is clicked
24          int idx = (int)(Convert.ToChar(buttonClicked.Text)) - 65;
25          StatemenSQL = SQLAll + " WHERE Name > '" +
26          buttonArr[idx].Text + " ' ";
27          StatemenSQL += " AND Name < '" +
28                  buttonArr[idx + 1].Text + " ' ";
29
30          // Binds to controls
31          int rowSaved = managerAuthor.Position;
32          DataRow[] rowFound;
33          tableAuthor.DefaultView.Sort = "Name";
34          rowFound = tableAuthor.Select("Name LIKE '" +
35              buttonArr[idx].Text + "*'");
36
37          if (rowFound.Length == 0)
38          {
39              managerAuthor.Position = rowSaved;
40          }
41          else
42          {
43              managerAuthor.Position =
44                  tableAuthor.DefaultView.Find(
45                      rowFound[0]["Name"]);
46              DisplayPhoto();
47          }
48          break;
49      }
50      StatemenSQL += " ORDER BY Name";
51
52      // Applies SQL statement
53      try
54      {
55          // Creates Command and DataAdapater objects
56          commResult = new SqlCommand(StatemenSQL, connBook);
57          adapterResult.SelectCommand = commResult;
58          adapterResult.Fill(tableResult);
59
60          // Binds DataGridView with data table
61          grdAuthor.DataSource = tableResult;
62          txtNumberRecord.Text = tableResult.Rows.Count.ToString();
63      }
64
65      catch (Exception ex)
66
```

```
67    {
68        MessageBox.Show(ex.Message, "Error Processing SQL",
69            MessageBoxButtons.OK, MessageBoxIcon.Error);
70    }
71    commResult.Dispose();
72    adapterResult.Dispose();
73    tableResult.Dispose();
74 }
```

This method determines which button is clicked and forms an SQL statement. If the button with the **Text** property of the button is **"Show All Authors"** is clicked, then all records will be displayed. When a key letter is clicked, the code determines which letter the user clicks on and attaches an additional test (using **AND**) to the **WHERE** field in the default SQL statement.

Step 5   Add the following code in line 48-53 to **FormAuthor_Load** event method. The code creates search buttons and perform **Click** event of **btnAll** programmatically:

```
1    private void FormAuthor_Load(object sender, EventArgs e)
2    {
3        try
4        {
5            // Connects to database
6            connBook = new SqlConnection("Data Source=.\\SQLEXPRESS;
7            AttachDbFilename=D:\\Database\\DBMS.mdf;
8            Integrated Security = True; Connect Timeout = 30;
9            User Instance = True");
10
11           connBook.Open();
12
13           // Creates Command object
14           commandAuthor = new
15               SqlCommand("SELECT * FROM Author ORDER BY Name",
16               connBook);
17
18           // Creates DataAdapter/DataTable objects
19           adapterAuthor = new SqlDataAdapter();
20           adapterAuthor.SelectCommand = commandAuthor;
21           tableAuthor = new DataTable();
22           adapterAuthor.Fill(tableAuthor);
23
24           // Binds controls to data table
25           txtAuthorID.DataBindings.Add("Text",
26               tableAuthor, "AuthorID");
27           txtAuthorName.DataBindings.Add("Text", tableAuthor, "Name");
28           dtpBirthDate.DataBindings.Add("Text",
29               tableAuthor, "BirthDate");
30           txtPhoto.DataBindings.Add("Text", tableAuthor, "PhotoFile");
31
```

```
32          // Creates data update
33          managerAuthor =
34              (CurrencyManager)this.BindingContext[tableAuthor];
35      }
36      catch (Exception ex)
37      {
38          MessageBox.Show(ex.Message,
39              "Error in reading Author table.",
40              MessageBoxButtons.OK, MessageBoxIcon.Error);
41          return;
42      }
43
44      this.Show();
45      DisplayPhoto();
46      SetState("View");
47
48      //Creates 26 search buttons
49      createSearchButton();
50
51      // Clicks all records when form starts
52      btnAll.Click += new System.EventHandler(this.btnSQL_Click);
53      btnAll.PerformClick();
54  }
```

Step 6   Define **Refresh_DGV** to refresh data grid view, **grdAuthor**, as follows:

```
1   private void Refresh_DGV()
2   {
3       // Connects to database
4       connBook = new SqlConnection("Data Source=.\\SQLEXPRESS;
5           AttachDbFilename=D:\\Database\\DBMS.mdf;
6           Integrated Security = True; Connect Timeout = 30;
7           User Instance = True");
8
9       connBook.Open();
10
11      // Save changes to database
12      SqlCommandBuilder authorDBAdapterCommand = new
13          SqlCommandBuilder(adapterAuthor);
14      adapterAuthor.Update(tableAuthor);
15
16      SqlCommand commandResult = null;
17      SqlDataAdapter adapterResult = new SqlDataAdapter();
18      DataTable tableResult = new DataTable();
19      string StatemenSQL = "SELECT * FROM Author ORDER BY Name";
20      try
21      {
22          // Creates Command and DataAdapter objects
23          commandResult = new SqlCommand(StatemenSQL, connBook);
24          adapterResult.SelectCommand = commandResult;
```

```
25          tableResult.Clear();
26          adapterResult.Fill(tableResult);
27
28          // Binds grid view to data table
29          grdAuthor.DataSource = tableResult;
30          txtNumberRecord.Text = tableResult.Rows.Count.ToString();
31      }
32      catch (Exception ex)
33      {
34          MessageBox.Show(ex.Message, "Error in processing SQL",
35              MessageBoxButtons.OK, MessageBoxIcon.Error);
36      }
37
38      commandResult.Dispose();
39      adapterResult.Dispose();
        tableResult.Dispose();
    }
```

Step 7   Call **Refresh_DGV** from **Click** event of **btnAll** as follows:

```
1   private void btnAll_Click(object sender, EventArgs e)
2   {
3       Refresh_DGV();
4   }
```

Step 8   Define **RowPostPaint** event of **grdAuthor** control to give it a row numbering:

```
1   private void grdAuthor_RowPostPaint(object sender,
2   DataGridViewRowPostPaintEventArgs e)
3   {
4       var grid = sender as DataGridView;
5       var rowIdx = (e.RowIndex + 1).ToString();
6
7       var centerFormat = new StringFormat()
8       {
9           // Aligns to middle
10          Alignment = StringAlignment.Center,
11          LineAlignment = StringAlignment.Center
12      };
13
14      var headerBounds = new Rectangle(e.RowBounds.Left,
15          e.RowBounds.Top, grid.RowHeadersWidth, e.RowBounds.Height);
16      e.Graphics.DrawString(rowIdx, this.Font,
17          SystemBrushes.ControlText, headerBounds, centerFormat);
18  }
```

Figure 3.34 The application when it first runs

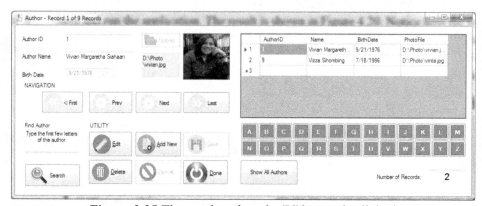

Figure 3.35 The results when the 'V' button is clicked

Step 8   Save and run the application. The result is shown in Figure 3.34. Notice how the search buttons are created. Also note that all records are displayed initially. Click on one of the search buttons. Only records with the item's initial matching the letter in the clicked button will be displayed. Figure 3.35 is the query result when the 'V' button is clicked.

3.18 Tutorial Steps of Reporting Author

Step 1   Now, you will add a feature to read all the data in the database. You need a database report. The report is quite simple. For each record, the data from each field will be displayed.

Add a button and a print preview dialog control to the project. Use the following properties:

button1 Control	
Name	btnPrint
Text	Print
TabStop	False

printPreviewDialog1 Control	
Name	dlgPreview

The form will look as shown in Figure 3.36.

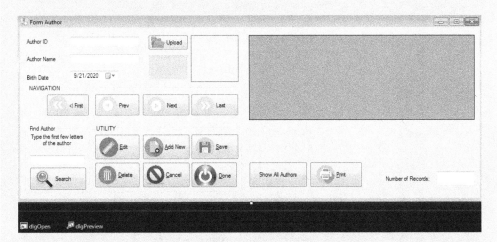

Figure 3.36 Another button, **Print**, and a **printPreviewDialog1** control added to the form

Step 2   Add this line of code at the top of the code window:

```
1   using System.Drawing.Printing;
```

Step 3   Add the page number variable to the form level declaration:

```
1   int pageNumber;
```

Step 4   Add code in line 25 and line 47 to the **SetState** method to set **Enabled** property of **btnPrint** to **true** in **View** mode and **false** in **Add/Edit** mode.

```
1   private void SetState(string appSate)
2   {
3       myState = appSate;
4       switch (myState)
5       {
6           case "View":
7               btnFirst.Enabled = true;
8               btnPrev.Enabled = true;
9               btnNext.Enabled = true;
10              btnLast.Enabled = true;
11              btnEdit.Enabled = true;
12              btnSave.Enabled = false;
13              btnCancel.Enabled = false;
14              txtItem.ReadOnly = true;
15              txtLocation.ReadOnly = true;
```

```
16        txtShop.ReadOnly = true;
17        dtpDatePurchased.Enabled = false;
18        txtCost.ReadOnly = true;
19        txtSerialNumber.ReadOnly = true;
20        chkFragile.Enabled = false;
21        btnLoadPhoto.Enabled = false;
22        btnAdd.Enabled = true;
23        btnDelete.Enabled = true;
24        grpSearchAuthor.Enabled = true;
25        btnPrint.Enabled = true;
26        break;
27
28    default: // "Edit", "Add"
29        btnFirst.Enabled = false;
30        btnPrev.Enabled = false;
31        btnNext.Enabled = false;
32        btnLast.Enabled = false;
33        btnEdit.Enabled = false;
34        btnSave.Enabled = true;
35        btnCancel.Enabled = true;
36        txtItem.ReadOnly = false;
37        txtLocation.ReadOnly = false;
38        txtShop.ReadOnly = false;
39        dtpDatePurchased.Enabled = true;
40        txtCost.ReadOnly = false;
41        txtSerialNumber.ReadOnly = false;
42        chkFragile.Enabled = true;
43        btnLoadPhoto.Enabled = true;
44        btnAdd.Enabled = false;
45        btnDelete.Enabled = false;
46        grpSearchAuthor.Enabled = false;
47        btnPrint.Enabled = false;
48        break;
49    }
50    txtItem.Focus();
51 }
```

Step 5   Add the following code to **btnPrint_Click** event method:

```
1  private void btnPrint_Click(object sender, EventArgs e)
2  {
3      // Declares document
4      PrintDocument docInventory;
5
6      // Creates document and gives it a name
7      docInventory = new PrintDocument();
8      docInventory.DocumentName = "Author Information";
9
10     // Adds code handler
11     docInventory.PrintPage += new
12         PrintPageEventHandler(this.PrintInventory);
```

```
13
14    // Prints document in preview control
15    pageNumber = 1;
16    int positionSaved = managerAuthor.Position;
17    dlgPreview.Document = docInventory;
18    dlgPreview.ShowDialog();
19
20    // Deletes document when finished printing
21    docInventory.Dispose();
22    managerAuthor.Position = positionSaved;
23
24    DisplayPhoto();
25 }
```

Step 6   Add the following code to **PrintInventory** method:

```
1    private void PrintInventory(object sender, PrintPageEventArgs e)
2    {
3        // Tracks every record, prints every record
4        managerAuthor.Position = pageNumber - 1;
5        DisplayPhoto();
6
7        // Prints header
8        Font myFont = new Font("Arial", 14, FontStyle.Bold);
9        int y = e.MarginBounds.Top + 50;
10
11       e.Graphics.DrawString("Author Information (" +
12           DateTime.Now.ToShortDateString() + ") - Page " +
13           pageNumber.ToString(), myFont, Brushes.Black,
14           e.MarginBounds.Left, y);
15       y += 2 * Convert.ToInt32(myFont.GetHeight(e.Graphics));
16
17       // Prints text information
18       myFont = new Font("Arial", 12, FontStyle.Regular);
19       e.Graphics.DrawString("Author ID:", myFont, Brushes.Black,
20           e.MarginBounds.X, y);
21       e.Graphics.DrawString(txtAuthorID.Text, myFont, Brushes.Black,
22           e.MarginBounds.X + 150, y);
23       y += Convert.ToInt32(myFont.GetHeight(e.Graphics));
24
25       e.Graphics.DrawString("Author Name:", myFont, Brushes.Black,
26           e.MarginBounds.X, y);
27       e.Graphics.DrawString(txtAuthorName.Text, myFont,
28           Brushes.Black, e.MarginBounds.X + 150, y);
29       y += Convert.ToInt32(myFont.GetHeight(e.Graphics));
30
31       e.Graphics.DrawString("Birth Date:", myFont, Brushes.Black,
32           e.MarginBounds.X, y);
33       e.Graphics.DrawString(dtpBirthDate.Text, myFont,
34           Brushes.Black, e.MarginBounds.X + 150, y);
```

```
35    y += 2* Convert.ToInt32(myFont.GetHeight(e.Graphics));
36
37    // Prints photo (width 4 inci, height depends on
38    // height/width ratio of photo)
39    int h = Convert.ToInt32(
40        400 * picAuthor.Image.Height / picAuthor.Image.Width);
41    e.Graphics.DrawImage(picAuthor.Image,
42        e.MarginBounds.X, y, 400, h);
43
44    pageNumber++;
45    if (pageNumber <= managerAuthor.Count)
46        e.HasMorePages = true;
47    else
48    {
49        e.HasMorePages = false;
50        pageNumber = 1;
51    }
52 }
```

On each page, a header is printed along with the data fields and author photo.

Step 7   Save and run the application. Click on the **Print** button. The print preview control will be displayed on all author pages, as shown in Figure 3.37.

Figure 3.37 Each record in the table can now be printed

3.19 Tutorial Steps of Creating Form for Publisher Table: Interface

Step 1　In this tutorial, you will build a framework for an interface so that the user can maintain the **Publisher** table in the book database (**DBMS**). The **Publisher** table interface is more or less the same as **Author** table interface. This **Publisher** table interface only requires more input fields. So you will use the interface for the **Author** table and modify it for the **Publisher** table. Adapting an existing application will save you a lot of time.

Copy the previous sample project folder (the latest version of **Author** input form). Give it another name. You now have a copy of **Author** table input form project which will be modified into **Publisher** table input form.

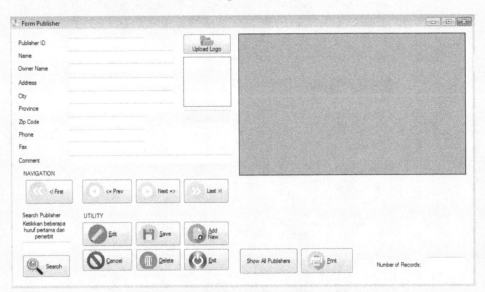

Figure 3.38 Form for **Publisher** table

Open the copy project in Visual C#. The **Publisher** table has eleven (11) input fields: **PublisherID**, **Name**, **OwnerName**, **Address**, **City**, **Province**, **ZipCode**, **Phone**, **Fax**, **Comment**, and **PhotoFile**.

Step 2　Change the properties of each control as follows:

Form1 Control	
Name	formPublisher
FormBorderStyle	FixedSingle
BackColor	DodgerBlue
StartPosition	CenterScreen
Text	Form Publisher

label1 Control	
Text	Publisher ID

txtPublisherID Control	

Name	txtPublisherID

label2 Control	
Text	Name

txtName Control	
Name	txtName

label3 Control	
Text	Owner Name

txtOwnerName Control	
Name	txtOwnerName

Step 3   Add seven additional labels and seven text boxes. Set the properties as follows:

label4 Control	
Text	Address
ForeColor	White

TextBox1 Control	
Name	txtAddress
BackColor	White
ReadOnly	True
TabIndex	3

label5 Control	
ForeColor	White
Text	Kota

TextBox2 Control	
Name	txtCity
BackColor	White
ReadOnly	True
TabIndex	4

label6 Control	
ForeColor	White
Text	Province

TextBox3 Control	
Name	txtProvince
BackColor	White
ReadOnly	True
TabIndex	5

label7 Control	
ForeColor	White
Text	Kode Pos

Kontrol TextBox4 Control	
Name	txtZipCode
BackColor	White
ReadOnly	True

TabIndex	6

label8 Control	
ForeColor	White
Text	Telepon

TextBox5 Control	
Name	txtPhone
BackColor	White
ReadOnly	True
TabIndex	7

label9 Control	
ForeColor	White
Text	Fax

TextBox6 Control	
Name	txtFax
BackColor	White
ReadOnly	True
TabIndex	8

label10 Control	
ForeColor	White
Text	Comment

TextBox6 Control	
Name	txtComment
BackColor	White
ReadOnly	True
TabIndex	9

At this point, the form will be displayed as in Figure 3.38. Don't forget to rename datagrid view control as **grdPublisher** and set Text property of **btnAll** as **Show All Publishers**.

Step 4   Rename the following form-level declarations for creating data objects:

```
1   SqlConnection connBook;
2   SqlCommand commandPublisher;
3   SqlDataAdapter adapterPublisher;
4   DataTable tablePublisher;
5   CurrencyManager managerPublisher;
```

Step 5   Make changes in line 13-42 to **FormPublisher_Load** event method:

```
1   private void FormPublisher_Load(object sender, EventArgs e)
2   {
3       try
4       {
5           // Connects to database
6           connBook = new SqlConnection("Data Source=.\\SQLEXPRESS;
```

```
7          AttachDbFilename=D:\\Database\\DBMS.mdf;
8          Integrated Security = True; Connect Timeout = 30;
9          User Instance = True");
10
11      connBook.Open();
12
13      // Creates Command object
14      commandPublisher = new
15          SqlCommand("SELECT * FROM Publisher ORDER BY Name",
16          connBook);
17
18      // Creates DataAdapter/DataTable objects
19      adapterPublisher = new SqlDataAdapter();
20      adapterPublisher.SelectCommand = commandPublisher;
21      tablePublisher = new DataTable();
22      adapterPublisher.Fill(tablePublisher);
23
24      // Binds controls to data table
25      txtPublisherID.DataBindings.Add("Text", tablePublisher,
26          "PublisherID");
27      txtPublisherName.DataBindings.Add("Text", tablePublisher,
28          "Name");
29      txtOwnerName.DataBindings.Add("Text", tablePublisher,
30          "OwnerName");
31      txtPhoto.DataBindings.Add("Text", tablePublisher, "PhotoFile");
32      txtAddress.DataBindings.Add("Text", tablePublisher, "Address");
33      txtCity.DataBindings.Add("Text", tablePublisher, "City");
34      txtProvince.DataBindings.Add("Text", tablePublisher, "Province");
35      txtZipCode.DataBindings.Add("Text", tablePublisher, "ZipCode");
36      txtPhone.DataBindings.Add("Text", tablePublisher, "Phone");
37      txtFax.DataBindings.Add("Text", tablePublisher, "Fax");
38      txtComment.DataBindings.Add("Text", tablePublisher, "Comment");
39
40      // Creates data update
41      managerPublisher =
42          (CurrencyManager)this.BindingContext[tablePublisher];
43  }
44  catch (Exception ex)
45  {
46      MessageBox.Show(ex.Message,
47          "Error in reading Publisher table.",
48          MessageBoxButtons.OK, MessageBoxIcon.Error);
49      return;
50  }
51
52  this.Show();
53  DisplayPhoto();
54 }
```

The code above reflects the naming of the new data object, the new SQL string and the appropriate data binding for the text box controls.

Step 6   Define **DisplayPhoto** to display publisher's logo in **picPublisher**:

```
1   private void DisplayPhoto()
2   {
3       // Displays photo
4       if (!txtPhoto.Text.Equals(""))
5       {
6           try
7           {
8               picPublisher.Image = Image.FromFile(txtPhoto.Text);
9           }
10          catch (Exception ex)
11          {
12              MessageBox.Show(ex.Message, "Error Loading Photo",
13                  MessageBoxButtons.OK, MessageBoxIcon.Error);
14          }
15      }
16      else
17      {
18          string dir =
19              Path.GetDirectoryName(Application.ExecutablePath);
20          string filename = Path.Combine(dir, @"logo.png");
21          picPublisher.Image = Image.FromFile(filename);
22      }
23  }
```

Step 7   Modify **FormPublisher_FormClosing** event method:

```
1   private void FormPublisher_FormClosing(object sender,
2   FormClosingEventArgs e)
3   {
4       // Closes connection to database
5       connBook.Close();
6
7       // Deletes objects
8       connPublisher.Dispose();
9       commandPublisher.Dispose();
10      adapterPublisher.Dispose();
11  }
```

Step 8   Make changes to four navigation event methods to reflect the new names for the update manager:

```
1   private void btnPrev_Click(object sender, EventArgs e)
2   {
3       if (managerPublisher.Position == 0)
```

```
4      {
5          Console.Beep();
6      }
7      managerPublisher.Position--;
8  }
9
10 private void btnNext_Click(object sender, EventArgs e)
11 {
12     if (managerPublisher.Position == managerPublishe.Count - 1)
13     {
14         Console.Beep();
15     }
16     managerPublisher.Position++;
17 }
18
19 private void btnFirst_Click(object sender, EventArgs e)
20 {
21     managerPublisher.Position = 0;
22 }
23
24 private void btnLast_Click(object sender, EventArgs e)
25 {
26     managerPublisher.Position = managerPublisher.Count - 1;
27 }
```

Step 9   Save and run the application to see the picture shown in Figure 3.39.

Figure 3.39 Publisher form when it first runs

3.20 Tutorial Steps of Creating Form for Publisher Table: Application State

Step 1   In this step, you will modify the code to reflect the proper state of the application. You'll be eliminating all old code, so when it's done, the app doesn't have any errors. The biggest change is in the **SetState** method. This modification will lock and unlock text boxes (using the **ReadOnly** property), depending on the circumstances:

```csharp
private void SetState(string stateStr)
{
    switch (stateStr)
    {
        case "View":
            txtPublisherID.BackColor = Color.White;
            txtPublisherID.ForeColor = Color.Black;
            txtName.ReadOnly = true;
            txtOwnerName.ReadOnly = true;
            txtAddress.ReadOnly = true;
            txtCity.ReadOnly = true;
            txtProvince.ReadOnly = true;
            txtZipCode.ReadOnly = true;
            txtPhone.ReadOnly = true;
            txtFax.ReadOnly = true;
            txtComment.ReadOnly = true;
            btnPrev.Enabled = true;
            btnNext.Enabled = true;
            btnAddNew.Enabled = true;
            btnSave.Enabled = false;
            btnCancel.Enabled = false;
            btnEdit.Enabled = true;
            btnDelete.Enabled = true;
            btnFinish.Enabled = true;
            btnFirst.Enabled = true;
            btnLast.Enabled = true;
            txtName.Focus();
            break;

        default: // Add or Edit
            txtPublisherID.BackColor = Color.Red;
            txtPublisherID.ForeColor = Color.White;
            txtName.ReadOnly = false;
            txtOwnerName.ReadOnly = false;
            txtAddress.ReadOnly = false;
            txtCity.ReadOnly = false;
            txtProvince.ReadOnly = false;
            txtZipCode.ReadOnly = false;
            txtPhone.ReadOnly = false;
            txtFax.ReadOnly = false;
            txtComment.ReadOnly = false;
            txtName.ReadOnly = false;
            btnPrev.Enabled = false;
```

```
44        btnNext.Enabled = false;
45        btnAddNew.Enabled = false;
46        btnSave.Enabled = true;
47        btnCancel.Enabled = true;
48        btnEdit.Enabled = false;
49        btnDelete.Enabled = false;
50        btnFinish.Enabled = false;
51        btnFirst.Enabled = false;
52        btnLast.Enabled = false;
53        txtName.Focus();
54        break;
55    }
56 }
```

Step 2   Delete **Author_KeyPressName** text event method. Add a **txtInput_KeyPress** event method (invoked by nine text box controls). This code implements programmatically to move from one text box to the next using the <Enter> key:

```
1  private void txtInput_KeyPress(object sender, KeyPressEventArgs e)
2  {
3      TextBox whichTextBox = (TextBox) sender;
4
5      if ((int) e.KeyChar == 13)
6      {
7          switch (whichTextBox.Name)
8          {
9              case "txtName":
10                 txtOwnerName.Focus();
11                 break;
12             case "txtOwnername":
13                 txtAddress.Focus();
14                 break;
15             case "txtAddress":
16                 txtCity.Focus();
17                 break;
18             case "txtCity":
19                 txtProvince.Focus();
20                 break;
21             case "txtProvince":
22                 txtZipCode.Focus();
23                 break;
24             case "txtZipCode":
25                 txtPhone.Focus();
26                 break;
27             case "txtPhone":
28                 txtFax.Focus();
29                 break;
30             case "txtFax":
31                 txtComment.Focus();
32                 break;
```

```
33          case "txtComment":
34              txtName.Focus();
35              break;
36      }
37  }
38 }
```

Step 3   Add this code at the end of **Load** event of form:

```
1  SetState("View");
```

Step 4   Save and run the application. You can now move from field to field using the **Enter**
          key, as shown in Figure 3.30.

Figure 3.30 User can move from one field to another by pressing the Enter key

3.21 Tutorial Steps of Creating Form for Publisher Table: Validating Input

Step 1   Again, you will ditch the old input validation and add new ones. Modify **ValidateData**
          method to be as follows:

```
1  private bool ValidateData() {
2      string message = "";
3      bool allOK = true;
4
5      // Checks txtName and txtOwnerName
6      if (txtName.Text.Trim().Equals("") ||
```

```
7          txtOwnerName.Text.Trim().Equals(""))
8      {
9          message =
10             "You should enter publisher name and its owner name." +
11             "\r\n";
12         txtName.Focus();
13         allOK = false;
14     }
15
16     if (!allOK) {
17         MessageBox.Show(message, "Validation error",
18         MessageBoxButtons.OK, MessageBoxIcon.Information);
19     }
20
21     return (allOK);
22 }
```

Step 2   You might ask, is it important to validate **PublisherID** field? Yes, but as primary key, it is treated differently. You will handle it later.

Step 3   Save and run the application. Click **Edit**. Clear Name or Owner Name fields and click Save. This message window will appear:

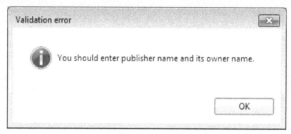

Figure 3.31 Message box to remind user to enter the publisher name and owner name

3.22 Tutorial Steps of Creating Form for Publisher Table: Error Trapping

Step 1   The code for handling and trapping errors in the previous application still applies to this new application, so nothing needs to be changed.

3.23 Tutorial Steps of Creating Form for Publisher Table: Editing Record

Step 1   You now will add editing capability and other related capabilities to save and/or cancel edits.

Modify **btnSave_Click** event method to save the edits and reposition the pointer to
the record just edited:

```csharp
private void btnSave_Click(object sender, EventArgs e)
{
    if (!ValidateData())
    {
        return;
    }

    string nameSaved = txtName.Text;
    int rowSaved;

    try
    {
        managerAuthor.EndCurrentEdit();
        tableAuthor.DefaultView.Sort = "Name";
        rowSaved = tableAuthor.DefaultView.Find(nameSaved);
        managerAuthor.Position = rowSaved;

        MessageBox.Show("Records successfully saved", "Save",
            MessageBoxButtons.OK, MessageBoxIcon.Information);

        SetState("View");
    }
    catch (Exception ex)
    {
        MessageBox.Show("Error saving record.", "Error",
            MessageBoxButtons.OK, MessageBoxIcon.Error);
    }
}
```

Step 2   Modify **btnCancel_Click** event method to restore controls if the edit is canceled:

```csharp
private void btnCancel_Click(object sender, EventArgs e)
{
    managerPublisher.CancelCurrentEdit();
    SetState("View");
}
```

Step 3   Add the following code in line to **FormPublisher_FormClosing** method to save any
changes to the database file:

```csharp
private void FormPublisher_FormClosing(object sender,
FormClosingEventArgs e)
{
    try
    {
        // Saves changes into
        SqlCommandBuilder publisherAdapterCommand =
```

```
8        new SqlCommandBuilder(adapterPublisher);
9        adapterPublisher.Update(tablePublisher);
10    }
11    catch (Exception ex)
12    {
13        MessageBox.Show("Error saving database into file: \r\n" +
14            ex.Message, "Error Saving", MessageBoxButtons.OK,
15            MessageBoxIcon.Error);
16    }
17
18    // Closes connection to database
19    connBook.Close();
20
21    // Deletes objects
22    connBook.Dispose();
23    commandPublisher.Dispose();
24    adapterPublisher.Dispose();
25 }
```

Step 4   Save and run the application. Make sure the **Edit** feature is working properly. Try changing the author name. Make sure the **Cancel** button is working properly. This is shown in Figure 3.32.

Figure 3.32 Record editing was successfully performed on **Publisher** table

3.24 Tutorial Steps of Creating Form for Publisher Table: Adding New Record

Step 1   You now implement the capability on the form to add new records to the database. Add the following lines of code to the form-level declaration:

```
1    string appState;
2    int myBookmark;
```

Step 2   Add this code in line 3 to **SetState** method:

```
1    private void SetState(string stateStr)
2    {
3        appState = stateStr;
4        switch (stateStr)
5        {
6            case "View":
7                txtPublisherID.BackColor = Color.White;
8                txtPublisherID.ForeColor = Color.Black;
9                txtName.ReadOnly = true;
10                txtOwnerName.ReadOnly = true;
11                txtAddress.ReadOnly = true;
12                txtCity.ReadOnly = true;
13                txtProvince.ReadOnly = true;
14                txtZipCode.ReadOnly = true;
15                txtPhone.ReadOnly = true;
16                txtFax.ReadOnly = true;
17                txtComment.ReadOnly = true;
18                btnPrev.Enabled = true;
19                btnNext.Enabled = true;
20                btnAddNew.Enabled = true;
21                btnSave.Enabled = false;
22                btnCancel.Enabled = false;
23                btnEdit.Enabled = true;
24                btnDelete.Enabled = true;
25                btnFinish.Enabled = true;
26                btnFirst.Enabled = true;
27                btnLast.Enabled = true;
28                txtName.Focus();
29                break;
30
31            default: // Add or Edit
32                txtPublisherID.BackColor = Color.Red;
33                txtPublisherID.ForeColor = Color.White;
34                txtName.ReadOnly = false;
35                txtOwnerName.ReadOnly = false;
36                txtAddress.ReadOnly = false;
37                txtCity.ReadOnly = false;
38                txtProvince.ReadOnly = false;
39                txtZipCode.ReadOnly = false;
40                txtPhone.ReadOnly = false;
41                txtFax.ReadOnly = false;
42                txtComment.ReadOnly = false;
```

```
43    txtName.ReadOnly = false;
44    btnPrev.Enabled = false;
45    btnNext.Enabled = false;
46    btnAddNew.Enabled = false;
47    btnSave.Enabled = true;
48    btnCancel.Enabled = true;
49    btnEdit.Enabled = false;
50    btnDelete.Enabled = false;
51    btnFinish.Enabled = false;
52    btnFirst.Enabled = false;
53    btnLast.Enabled = false;
54    txtName.Focus();
55    break;
56    }
57 }
```

Step 3   Modify **btnAddNew_Click** event method to add a new record by adding code in line 5 and 6:

```
1  private void btnAddNew_Click(object sender, EventArgs e)
2  {
3      try
4      {
5          myBookmark = managerPublisher.Position;
6          managerPublisher.AddNew();
7          SetState("Add");
8      }
9      catch (Exception ex)
10     {
11         MessageBox.Show("Error adding new record.", "Error",
12             MessageBoxButtons.OK, MessageBoxIcon.Error);
13     }
14 }
```

Step 4   Modify **btnCancel_Click** event method to differentiate between cancellation during **Edit** mode and **Add** mode by adding code in line 5-8:

```
1  private void btnCancel_Click(object sender, EventArgs e)
2  {
3      managerAuthor.CancelCurrentEdit();
4
5      if (appState.Equals("Add"))
6      {
7          managerPublisher.Position = myBookmark;
8      }
9
10     SetState("View");
11 }
```

Step 5　　Save and run the application. Click **Add New** button. Note that all text boxes are blank (including **Publisher ID** text box. Remember this field is the primary key that ADO.NET will provide when the database is resaved. Type a specific name, then click **Save**. New record has been successfully saved as shown in Figure 3.30.

Figure 3.33 The new record has been successfully saved into the database

3.25 Tutorial Steps of Creating Form for Publisher Table: Deleting Record

Step 1　　You will now add the capability to delete records from **Publisher** table. Modify the **btnDelete_Click** event method by adding code in line 14 to delete records if the user responds to **Yes** in the message box:

```
1   private void btnDelete_Click(object sender, EventArgs e)
2   {
3       DialogResult response;
4       response = MessageBox.Show("Dou you really want to delete this record?",
5           "Delete", MessageBoxButtons.YesNo, MessageBoxIcon.Question,
6           MessageBoxDefaultButton.Button2);
7       if (response == DialogResult.No)
8       {
9           return;
10      }
11
12      try
13      {
```

```
14    managerPublisher.RemoveAt(managerAuthor.Position);
15  }
16  catch (Exception ex)
17  {
18      MessageBox.Show("Error deleting record.", "Error",
19          MessageBoxButtons.OK, MessageBoxIcon.Error);
20  }
21 }
```

Step 2   Save the application and run it. Make sure the **Yes** and **No** responses in the message
box give correct results. Delete only those records you added using **Add New** button.
If you try to remove the original **Author** the table, you'll see a message box when you
stop the application (from **FormClosing** event).

3.26 Tutorial Steps of Creating Form for Publisher Table: Stopping Application

Step 1   Add the following code in line 4-10 and line 34 to **FormPublisher_FormClosing**
event method to ensure user doesn't close the application during **Edit** or **Add** mode:

```
1   private void FormPublisher_FormClosing(object sender,
2   FormClosingEventArgs e)
3   {
4       if (appState.Equals("Edit") || appState.Equals("Add"))
5       {
6           MessageBox.Show(
7               "You should finish editing before closing application.",
8               "", MessageBoxButtons.OK, MessageBoxIcon.Information);
9           e.Cancel = true;
10      }
11      else
12      {
13          try
14          {
15              // Saves changes into
16              SqlCommandBuilder publisherAdapterCommand =
17                  new SqlCommandBuilder(adapterPublisher);
18              adapterPublisher.Update(tablePublisher);
19          }
20          catch (Exception ex)
21          {
22              MessageBox.Show("Error saving database into file: \r\n" +
23                  ex.Message, "Error Saving", MessageBoxButtons.OK,
24                  MessageBoxIcon.Error);
25          }
26
27          // Closes connection to database
28          connBook.Close();
29
30          // Deletes objects
```

```
31        connBook.Dispose();
32        commandPublisher.Dispose();
33        adapterPublisher.Dispose();
34    }
35 }
```

Step 2   Put this code in **btnExit_Click** event method:

```
1 private void btnExit_Click(object sender, EventArgs e)
2 {
3     this.Close();
4 }
```

Step 3   Save and run the application. Make sure the **Finish** button is working properly. Make sure the user cannot close the application in **Edit** or **Add** mode.

3.27 Tutorial Steps of Searching Capability

Step 1   In the **SetState** method, enable **grpSearchPublisher** control in **View** mode and disable it in **Add** and **Edit** mode. Use its **Enabled** property.

Figure 3.34 Publisher's name search feature added

Step 2   Add the following code to **btnSearch_Click** event method:

```
1 private void btnSearch_Click(object sender, EventArgs e)
2 {
3     if (txtSearch.Text.Equals(""))
```

```
4      {
5          return;
6      }
7
8      int rowSaved = managerPublisher.Position;
9      DataRow[] rowFound;
10     tablePublisher.DefaultView.Sort = "Name";
11     rowFound = tablePublisher.Select("Name LIKE '" +
12         txtSearch.Text + "*'");
13
14     if (rowFound.Length == 0)
15     {
16         managerPublisher.Position = rowSaved;
17     }
18     else
19     {
20         managerPublisher.Position =
21             tablePublisher.DefaultView.Find(rowFound[0]["Name"]);
22         DisplayPhoto();
23     }
24 }
```

Step 3   Save and run the application. Try searching by providing the first letter or two of the author's name, as shown in Figure 3.31.

3.28 Tutorial Steps of Adding Search Buttons

Step 1   Add the following form-level declarations:

```
1  String SQLAll = "SELECT * FROM Publisher ";
2  Button[] buttonArr = new Button[26];
```

SQLAll is a variable that contains the default SQL statements, while **buttonArr** is an array containing the search buttons.

Step 2   Define a new method named **createSearchButton()** as follows:

```
1  private void createSearchButton()
2  {
3      // Creates search buttons
4      int w, lStart, l, t;
5      int btnHeight = 40; // by trial and error
6
7      // Search buttons
8      // Button width - 13 buttons in a row
9      w = Convert.ToInt32(grdPublisher.Width / 13);
10
11     // Aligns buttons
12     lStart = Convert.ToInt32((grdPublisher.Width)) -45;
```

```
13    l = lStart; t = grdPublisher.Top + grdPublisher.Height + 10;
14
15    // Creates and positions 26 buttons
16    for (int i = 0; i < 26; i++)
17    {
18        // Creates push button
19        buttonArr[i] = new Button();
20        buttonArr[i].TabStop = false;
21
22        // Sets Text property
23        buttonArr[i].Text = ((char)(65 + i)).ToString();
24        buttonArr[i].Font = new Font(buttonArr[i].Font.FontFamily,
25            9, FontStyle.Bold);
26
27        // Positions buttons
28        buttonArr[i].Width = w;
29        buttonArr[i].Height = btnHeight;
30        buttonArr[i].Left = l;
31        buttonArr[i].Top = t;
32
33        // Gives color
34        buttonArr[i].BackColor = Color.Red;
35        buttonArr[i].ForeColor = Color.White;
36
37        // Adds each button on form
38        this.Controls.Add(buttonArr[i]);
39
40        // Adds event handler
41        buttonArr[i].Click +=
42            new System.EventHandler(this.btnSQL_Click);
43        l += w;
44
45        if (i == 12)
46        {
47            // Next row
48            l = lStart; t += btnHeight;
49        }
50    }
}
```

This method creates search buttons A through Z using **buttonArrr** array. The code above then specifies the width of the button and places it on the form. Finally, the resulting records are displayed by programmatically clicking **btnSQL** button.

Step 4   Write the code for **btnSQL_Click** event method (handle **Click** event for all search buttons) as follows:

```
1    private void btnSQL_Click(object sender, EventArgs e)
2    {
3        SqlCommand commResult = null;
```

```
4    SqlDataAdapter adapterResult = new SqlDataAdapter();
5    DataTable tableResult = new DataTable();
6    String StatemenSQL;
7
8    // Determines which button is clicked and creates SQL statement
9    Button buttonClicked = (Button)sender;
10   switch (buttonClicked.Text)
11   {
12       case "Show All Authors":
13           StatemenSQL = SQLAll;
14           break;
15       case "Z":
16           // Z button is clicked
17           // Appends at SQLAll to limit records upto for item Z
18           StatemenSQL = SQLAll + " WHERE Name > 'Z' ";
19           break;
20       default:
21           // Letter keys except Z
22           // Appends at SQLAll to limit records
23           // for letter that is clicked
24           int idx = (int)(Convert.ToChar(buttonClicked.Text)) - 65;
25           StatemenSQL = SQLAll + " WHERE Name > '" +
26           buttonArr[idx].Text + " ' ";
27           StatemenSQL += " AND Name < '" +
28                   buttonArr[idx + 1].Text + " ' ";
29
30           // Binds to controls
31           int rowSaved = managerPublisher.Position;
32           DataRow[] rowFound;
33           tablePublisher.DefaultView.Sort = "Name";
34           rowFound = tablePublisher.Select("Name LIKE '" +
35               buttonArr[idx].Text + "*'");
36
37           if (rowFound.Length == 0)
38           {
39               managerPublisher.Position = rowSaved;
40           }
41           else
42           {
43               managerPublisher.Position =
44                   tablePublisher.DefaultView.Find(
45                       rowFound[0]["Name"]);
46               DisplayPhoto();
47           }
48           break;
49   }
50   StatemenSQL += " ORDER BY Name";
51
52   // Applies SQL statement
53   try
54   {
```

```
55      // Creates Command and DataAdapater objects
56      commResult = new SqlCommand(StatemenSQL, connBook);
57      adapterResult.SelectCommand = commResult;
58      adapterResult.Fill(tableResult);
59
60      // Binds DataGridView with data table
61      grdPublisher.DataSource = tableResult;
62      txtNumberRecord.Text = tableResult.Rows.Count.ToString();
63   }
64
65   catch (Exception ex)
66   {
67       MessageBox.Show(ex.Message, "Error Processing SQL",
68           MessageBoxButtons.OK, MessageBoxIcon.Error);
69   }
70   commResult.Dispose();
71   adapterResult.Dispose();
72   tableResult.Dispose();
73 }
```

This method determines which button is clicked and forms an SQL statement. If the
button with the **Text** property of the button is "**Show All Publishers**" is clicked, then
all records will be displayed. When a key letter is clicked, the code determines which
letter the user clicks on and attaches an additional test (using **AND**) to the **WHERE**
field in the default SQL statement.

Step 5   Add the following code in line 56-61 to **FormPublisher_Load** event method. The
code creates search buttons and perform **Click** event of **btnAll** programmatically:

```
1   private void FormPublisher_Load(object sender, EventArgs e)
2   {
3       try
4       {
5           // Connects to database
6           connBook = new SqlConnection("Data Source=.\\SQLEXPRESS;
7               AttachDbFilename=D:\\Database\\DBMS.mdf;
8               Integrated Security = True; Connect Timeout = 30;
9               User Instance = True");
10
11          connBook.Open();
12
13          // Creates Command object
14          commandPublisher = new
15              SqlCommand("SELECT * FROM Publisher ORDER BY Name",
16              connBook);
17
18          // Creates DataAdapter/DataTable objects
19          adapterPublisher = new SqlDataAdapter();
20          adapterPublisher.SelectCommand = commandPublisher;
```

```
21    tablePublisher = new DataTable();
22    adapterPublisher.Fill(tablePublisher);
23
24    // Binds controls to data table
25    txtPublisherID.DataBindings.Add("Text", tablePublisher,
26        "PublisherID");
27    txtPublisherName.DataBindings.Add("Text", tablePublisher,
28        "Name");
29    txtOwnerName.DataBindings.Add("Text", tablePublisher,
30        "OwnerName");
31    txtPhoto.DataBindings.Add("Text", tablePublisher, "PhotoFile");
32    txtAddress.DataBindings.Add("Text", tablePublisher, "Address");
33    txtCity.DataBindings.Add("Text", tablePublisher, "City");
34    txtProvince.DataBindings.Add("Text", tablePublisher, "Province");
35    txtZipCode.DataBindings.Add("Text", tablePublisher, "ZipCode");
36    txtPhone.DataBindings.Add("Text", tablePublisher, "Phone");
37    txtFax.DataBindings.Add("Text", tablePublisher, "Fax");
38    txtComment.DataBindings.Add("Text", tablePublisher, "Comment");
39
40    // Creates data update
41    managerPublisher =
42        (CurrencyManager)this.BindingContext[tablePublisher];
43    }
44    catch (Exception ex)
45    {
46        MessageBox.Show(ex.Message,
47            "Error in reading Publisher table.",
48            MessageBoxButtons.OK, MessageBoxIcon.Error);
49        return;
50    }
51
52    this.Show();
53    DisplayPhoto();
54    SetState("View");
55
56    //Creates 26 search buttons
57    createSearchButton();
58
59    // Clicks all records when form starts
60    btnAll.Click += new System.EventHandler(this.btnSQL_Click);
61    btnAll.PerformClick();
62  }
```

Step 6   Define **Refresh_DGV** to refresh data grid view, **grdPublisher**, as follows:

```
1    private void Refresh_DGV()
2    {
3        // Connects to database
4        connBook = new SqlConnection("Data Source=.\\SQLEXPRESS;
5            AttachDbFilename=D:\\Database\\DBMS.mdf;
```

```
 6        Integrated Security = True; Connect Timeout = 30;
 7        User Instance = True");
 8
 9    connBook.Open();
10
11    // Save changes to database
12    SqlCommandBuilder publisherDBAdapterCommand = new
13        SqlCommandBuilder(adapterPublisher);
14    adapterPublisher.Update(tablePublisher);
15
16    SqlCommand commandResult = null;
17    SqlDataAdapter adapterResult = new SqlDataAdapter();
18    DataTable tableResult = new DataTable();
19    string StatemenSQL = "SELECT * FROM Publisher ORDER BY Name";
20    try
21    {
22        // Creates Command and DataAdapter objects
23        commandResult = new SqlCommand(StatemenSQL, connBook);
24        adapterResult.SelectCommand = commandResult;
25        tableResult.Clear();
26        adapterResult.Fill(tableResult);
27
28        // Binds grid view to data table
29        grdPublisher.DataSource = tableResult;
30        txtNumberRecord.Text = tableResult.Rows.Count.ToString();
31    }
32    catch (Exception ex)
33    {
34        MessageBox.Show(ex.Message, "Error in processing SQL",
35            MessageBoxButtons.OK, MessageBoxIcon.Error);
36    }
37
38    commandResult.Dispose();
39    adapterResult.Dispose();
    tableResult.Dispose();
}
```

Step 7   Call **Refresh_DGV** from **Click** event of **btnAll** as follows:

```
1    private void btnAll_Click(object sender, EventArgs e)
2    {
3        Refresh_DGV();
4    }
```

Figure 3.35 The application when it first runs

Step 8   Define **RowPostPaint** event of **grdPublisher** control to give it a row numbering:

```
1   private void grdPublisher_RowPostPaint(object sender,
2   DataGridViewRowPostPaintEventArgs e)
3   {
4       var grid = sender as DataGridView;
5       var rowIdx = (e.RowIndex + 1).ToString();
6
7       var centerFormat = new StringFormat()
8       {
9           // Aligns to middle
10          Alignment = StringAlignment.Center,
11          LineAlignment = StringAlignment.Center
12      };
13
14      var headerBounds = new Rectangle(e.RowBounds.Left,
15          e.RowBounds.Top, grid.RowHeadersWidth, e.RowBounds.Height);
16      e.Graphics.DrawString(rowIdx, this.Font,
17          SystemBrushes.ControlText, headerBounds, centerFormat);
18  }
```

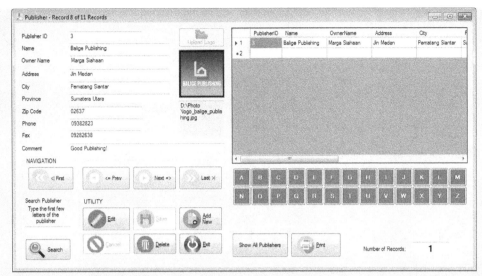

Figure 3.36 The results when the 'B' button is clicked

Step 8   Save and run the application. The result is shown in Figure 3.35. Notice how the search
buttons are created. Also note that all records are displayed initially. Click on one of
the search buttons. Only records with publisher's initial matching the letter in the
clicked button will be displayed. Figure 3.36 is the query result when the 'B' button is
clicked.

3.29 Tutorial Steps of Creating Form for Publisher Table: Stopping Application

Step 1   Add the following code in line 4-12 and line 34 to **FormPublisher_FormClosing**
event method to ensure user doesn't close the application during **Edit** or **Add** mode:

```
1    private void FormPublisher_FormClosing(object sender,
2    FormClosingEventArgs e)
3    {
4        if (appState.Equals("Edit") || appState.Equals("Add"))
5        {
6            MessageBox.Show(
7                "You should finish editing before closing application.",
8                "", MessageBoxButtons.OK, MessageBoxIcon.Information);
9            e.Cancel = true;
10       }
11       else
12       {
13           try
14           {
15               // Saves changes into
16               SqlCommandBuilder publisherAdapterCommand =
17                   new SqlCommandBuilder(adapterPublisher);
```

```
18        adapterPublisher.Update(tablePublisher);
19    }
20    catch (Exception ex)
21    {
22        MessageBox.Show("Error saving database into file: \r\n" +
23            ex.Message, "Error Saving", MessageBoxButtons.OK,
24            MessageBoxIcon.Error);
25    }
26
27    // Closes connection to database
28    connBook.Close();
29
30    // Deletes objects
31    connBook.Dispose();
32    commandPublisher.Dispose();
33    adapterPublisher.Dispose();
34    }
35 }
```

Step 2   Put this code in **btnExit_Click** event method:

```
1 private void btnExit_Click(object sender, EventArgs e)
2 {
3     this.Close();
4 }
```

Step 3   Save and run the application. Make sure the **Exit** button is working properly. Make sure the user cannot close the application in **Edit** or **Add** mode.

3.30 Tutorial Steps of Reporting Publisher

Step 1   Now, you will add a feature to read all the data in the database. You need a database report. The report is quite simple. For each record, the data from each field will be displayed.

Add a button and a print preview dialog control to the project. Use the following properties:

button1 Control	
Name	btnPrint
Text	Print
TabStop	False

printPreviewDialog1 Control	
Name	dlgPreview

Step 2   Add this line of code at the top of the code window:

```
1   using System.Drawing.Printing;
```

Step 3 Add the page number variable to the form level declaration:

```
1   int pageNumber;
```

Step 4 Add code in line 25 and line 47 to the **SetState** method to set **Enabled** property of **btnPrint** to **true** in **View** mode and **false** in **Add/Edit** mode.

```
1   private void SetState(string appSate)
2   {
3       myState = appSate;
4       switch (myState)
5       {
6           case "View":
7               btnFirst.Enabled = true;
8               btnPrev.Enabled = true;
9               btnNext.Enabled = true;
10              btnLast.Enabled = true;
11              btnEdit.Enabled = true;
12              btnSave.Enabled = false;
13              btnCancel.Enabled = false;
14              txtItem.ReadOnly = true;
15              txtLocation.ReadOnly = true;
16              txtShop.ReadOnly = true;
17              dtpDatePurchased.Enabled = false;
18              txtCost.ReadOnly = true;
19              txtSerialNumber.ReadOnly = true;
20              chkFragile.Enabled = false;
21              btnLoadPhoto.Enabled = false;
22              btnAdd.Enabled = true;
23              btnDelete.Enabled = true;
24              grpSearchPublisher.Enabled = true;
25              btnPrint.Enabled = true;
26              break;
27
28          default: // "Edit", "Add"
29              btnFirst.Enabled = false;
30              btnPrev.Enabled = false;
31              btnNext.Enabled = false;
32              btnLast.Enabled = false;
33              btnEdit.Enabled = false;
34              btnSave.Enabled = true;
35              btnCancel.Enabled = true;
36              txtItem.ReadOnly = false;
37              txtLocation.ReadOnly = false;
38              txtShop.ReadOnly = false;
39              dtpDatePurchased.Enabled = true;
40              txtCost.ReadOnly = false;
41              txtSerialNumber.ReadOnly = false;
```

```
42          chkFragile.Enabled = true;
43          btnLoadPhoto.Enabled = true;
44          btnAdd.Enabled = false;
45          btnDelete.Enabled = false;
46          grpSearchPublisher.Enabled = false;
47          btnPrint.Enabled = false;
48          break;
49      }
50      txtItem.Focus();
51  }
```

Step 5 Add the following code to **btnPrint_Click** event method:

```
1   private void btnPrint_Click(object sender, EventArgs e)
2   {
3       // Declares document
4       PrintDocument docInventory;
5
6       // Creates document and gives it a name
7       docInventory = new PrintDocument();
8       docInventory.DocumentName = "Publisher Information";
9
10      // Adds code handler
11      docInventory.PrintPage += new
12          PrintPageEventHandler(this.PrintInventory);
13
14      // Prints document in preview control
15      pageNumber = 1;
16      int positionSaved = managerPublisher.Position;
17      dlgPreview.Document = docInventory;
18      dlgPreview.ShowDialog();
19
20      // Deletes document when finished printing
21      docInventory.Dispose();
22      managerPublisher.Position = positionSaved;
23
24      DisplayPhoto();
25  }
```

Step 6 Add the following code to **PrintInventory** method:

```
1   private void PrintInventory(object sender, PrintPageEventArgs e)
2   {
3       // Tracks every record, prints every record
4       managerPublisher.Position = pageNumber - 1;
5       DisplayPhoto();
6
7       // Prints header
8       Font myFont = new Font("Arial", 14, FontStyle.Bold);
9       int y = e.MarginBounds.Top + 50;
10
```

```
11    e.Graphics.DrawString("Publisher Information (" +
12        DateTime.Now.ToShortDateString() + ") - Page " +
13        pageNumber.ToString(), myFont, Brushes.Black,
14        e.MarginBounds.Left, y);
15    y += 2 * Convert.ToInt32(myFont.GetHeight(e.Graphics));
16
17    // Prints text information
18    myFont = new Font("Arial", 12, FontStyle.Regular);
19        e.Graphics.DrawString("Publisher ID:", myFont,
20        Brushes.Black, e.MarginBounds.X, y);
21    e.Graphics.DrawString(txtPublisherID.Text, myFont,
22        Brushes.Black, e.MarginBounds.X + 150, y);
23    y += Convert.ToInt32(myFont.GetHeight(e.Graphics));
24
25    e.Graphics.DrawString("Owner Name:", myFont, Brushes.Black,
26        e.MarginBounds.X, y);
27    e.Graphics.DrawString(txtOwnerName.Text, myFont,
28        Brushes.Black, e.MarginBounds.X + 150, y);
29    y += Convert.ToInt32(myFont.GetHeight(e.Graphics));
30
31    e.Graphics.DrawString("Address:", myFont, Brushes.Black,
32        e.MarginBounds.X, y);
33    e.Graphics.DrawString(txtAddress.Text, myFont,
34        Brushes.Black, e.MarginBounds.X + 150, y);
35    y += 2 * Convert.ToInt32(myFont.GetHeight(e.Graphics));
36
37    e.Graphics.DrawString("City:", myFont, Brushes.Black,
38        e.MarginBounds.X, y);
39    e.Graphics.DrawString(txtCity.Text, myFont,
40        Brushes.Black, e.MarginBounds.X + 150, y);
41    y += 2 * Convert.ToInt32(myFont.GetHeight(e.Graphics));
42
43    e.Graphics.DrawString("Province:", myFont, Brushes.Black,
44        e.MarginBounds.X, y);
45    e.Graphics.DrawString(txtCity.Text, myFont,
46        Brushes.Black, e.MarginBounds.X + 150, y);
47    y += 2 * Convert.ToInt32(myFont.GetHeight(e.Graphics));
48
49    e.Graphics.DrawString("ZipCode:", myFont, Brushes.Black,
50        e.MarginBounds.X, y);
51    e.Graphics.DrawString(txtZipCode.Text, myFont,
52        Brushes.Black, e.MarginBounds.X + 150, y);
53    y += 2 * Convert.ToInt32(myFont.GetHeight(e.Graphics));
54
55    e.Graphics.DrawString("Phone:", myFont, Brushes.Black,
56        e.MarginBounds.X, y);
57    e.Graphics.DrawString(txtPhone.Text, myFont,
58        Brushes.Black, e.MarginBounds.X + 150, y);
59    y += 2 * Convert.ToInt32(myFont.GetHeight(e.Graphics));
60
61    e.Graphics.DrawString("Fax:", myFont, Brushes.Black,
```

```
62          e.MarginBounds.X, y);
63      e.Graphics.DrawString(txtFax.Text, myFont,
64          Brushes.Black, e.MarginBounds.X + 150, y);
65      y += 2 * Convert.ToInt32(myFont.GetHeight(e.Graphics));
66
67      e.Graphics.DrawString("Comment:", myFont, Brushes.Black,
68          e.MarginBounds.X, y);
69      e.Graphics.DrawString(txtComment.Text, myFont,
70          Brushes.Black, e.MarginBounds.X + 150, y);
71      y += 2 * Convert.ToInt32(myFont.GetHeight(e.Graphics));
72
73      // Prints photo (width 4 inci, height depends on
74      // height/width ratio of photo)
75      int h = Convert.ToInt32(
76          400 * picPublisher.Image.Height / picPublisher.Image.Width);
77      e.Graphics.DrawImage(picPublisher.Image,
78          e.MarginBounds.X, y, 400, h);
79
80      pageNumber++;
81      if (pageNumber <= managerPublisher.Count)
82          e.HasMorePages = true;
83      else
84      {
85          e.HasMorePages = false;
86          pageNumber = 1;
87      }
88  }
```

On each page, a header is printed along with the data fields and author photo.

Step 7   Save and run the application. Click on the **Print** button. The print preview control will be displayed on all publisher pages, as shown in Figure 3.37.

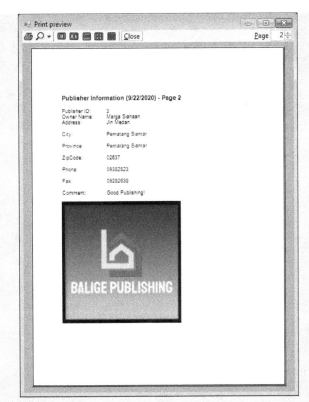

Figure 3.37 Each record in the table can now be printed

TUTORIAL 4
LIBRARY DATABASE PROJECT: PART 2

Description

In this tutorial, you will perform the steps necessary to design and implement title form, library member form, and book borrowal form.

4.1 Tutorial Steps of Creating Form for Title Table: Creating Form

Step 1   You start by designing and testing the basic entry form for book titles. The **Title** table has eight fields: **BookTitle**, **PublishYear**, **ISBN**, **PublishID**, **Description**, **Note**, **Subject**, and **Comment**.

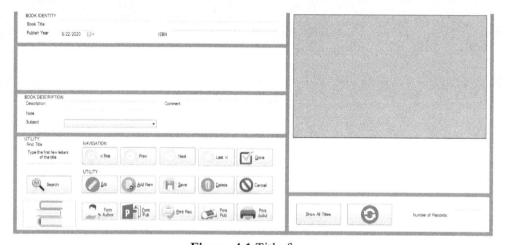

Figure 4.1 Title form

The SQL statement required for the **Command** object to read fields (sorted by the **BookTitle** field) are:

```
1    SELECT * FROM Title OREDER BY BookTitle
```

If this table field has an author name and a publisher name, then you don't need the other two tables. So how do you find authors and publishers? You need to use SQL to construct virtual data using all the tables in the book database. The **PublisherID** field, which corresponds to the **Publisher** table, will tell the publisher name. The **ISBN** field, which corresponds to the **Author_Title** table and the **Author** table, can provide author information. You will ignore it for the moment and only need to build the basic input form for the information in the **Title** table.

Remember how you built **Publisher** input form by modifying **Author** input form, not building them from scratch. You will take the same approach. You will copy the **Publisher** input form application and modify it to the **Title** input form.

Copy the **Publisher** input form folder. Give it another name. Open the project. Rename the form in the project to **FormTitle.cs**. You now have a copy of the **Publisher** input form with another name.

Step 2   Open the form. Remove the label controls and text boxes for **Phone**, **Fax**, and **Comment**. Also remov the text box for the **Name** field. Change the properties of each existing label and text box control on the form:

formPublisher (previous name)	
Name	formTitle
Text	Form Title

label1 (previous name)	
Text	Book Title

txtPublisherID (previous name)	
Name	txtBookTitle
TabIndex	0
TabStop	True

label2 (previous name)	
Text	Publish Year

dateTimePicker1 Conrol	
Name	dtpPublishYear
TabIndex	0
TabStop	True
Format	Short

label3 (previous name)	
Text	ISBN

txtOwnerName (previous name)	
Name	txtISBN
TabIndex	2
TabStop	True

label4 (previous name)	
Text	Description

txtAddress (previous name)	
Name	txtDescription
TabIndex	3

TabStop	True

label5 (previous name)	
Text	Note

txtCity (previous name)	
Name	txtNote
TabIndex	4
TabStop	True

Kontrol **label6** (previous name)	
Text	Subject

txtProvince (previous name)	
Name	cboSubject
TabIndex	5
TabStop	True

label7 (previous name)	
Text	Comment

txtZipCode (previous name)	
Name	txtComment
TabIndex	6
TabStop	True

When finished, the modified form will look as shown in Figure 4.1.

Step 3   Rename the data objects to reflect the **Title** table:

```
1   SqlConnection connTitle;
2   SqlCommand commandTitle;
3   SqlDataAdapter adapterTitle;
4   DataTable tableTitle;
5   CurrencyManager managerTitle;
```

Step 4   Modify the **FormTitle_Load** event method:

```
1   private void FormTitle_Load(object sender, EventArgs e)
2   {
3       try
4       {
5           // Connects to database
6           connTitle = new SqlConnection("Data Source=.\\SQLEXPRESS;
7           AttachDbFilename=D:\\Database\\DBMS.mdf;
8           Integrated Security = True; Connect Timeout = 30;
9           User Instance = True");
10
11          connTitle.Open();
12
13          // Creates Command object
14          commandTitle = new
15              SqlCommand("SELECT * FROM Title ORDER BY BookTitle",
16              connTitle);
```

```
17
18        // Creates DataAdapter/DataTable objects
19        adapterTitle = new SqlDataAdapter();
20        adapterTitle.SelectCommand = commandTitle;
21        tableTitle = new DataTable();
22        adapterTitle.Fill(tableTitle);
23
24        // Binds controls to data table
25        txtBookTitle.DataBindings.Add("Text", tableTitle, "BookTitle");
26        dtpPublishYear.DataBindings.Add("Text", tableTitle, "PublishYear");
27        txtISBN.DataBindings.Add("Text", tableTitle, "ISBN");
28        txtDescription.DataBindings.Add("Text", tableTitle, "Description");
29        txtNote.DataBindings.Add("Text", tableTitle, "Note");
30        txtSubject.DataBindings.Add("Text", tableTitle, "Subject");
31        txtComment.DataBindings.Add("Text", tableTitle, "Comment");
32
33        // Sets data update manager
34        managerTitle =
35            (CurrencyManager)this.BindingContext[tableTitle];
36    }
37    catch (Exception ex)
38    {
39        MessageBox.Show(ex.Message, "Error Creating Title table.",
40            MessageBoxButtons.OK, MessageBoxIcon.Error);
41        return;
42    }
43
44    this.Show();
45    SetState("View");
46 }
```

This reflects the name of the new data object, the new SQL string and the data binding
for the controls.

Step 5   Make the same changes to the **FormTitle_FormClosing** event method:

```
1  private void FormTitle_FormClosing(object sender,
2  FormClosingEventArgs e)
3  {
4      if (appState.Equals("Edit") || appState.Equals("Add"))
5      {
6          MessageBox.Show("You should finish editing before closing application.",
7              "", MessageBoxButtons.OK, MessageBoxIcon.Information);
8          e.Cancel = true;
9      }
10     else
11     {
12         try
13         {
14             // Saves changes into database
```

```
15        SqlCommandBuilder titleAdapterCommand = new
16            SqlCommandBuilder(adapterTitle);
17        adapterTitle.Update(tableTitle);
18    }
19    catch (Exception ex)
20    {
21        MessageBox.Show("Error saving into database: \r\n" +
22            ex.Message, "Saving Error", MessageBoxButtons.OK,
23            MessageBoxIcon.Error);
24    }
25
26    // Closes connection to database
27    connTitle.Close();
28
29    // Deletes objects
30    connTitle.Dispose();
31    commandTitle.Dispose();
32    adapterTitle.Dispose();
33    }
34 }
```

Step 6   Modify the four navigation methods:

```
1    private void btnPrev_Click(object sender, EventArgs e)
2    {
3        if (managerTitle.Position == 0)
4        {
5            Console.Beep();
6        }
7        managerTitle.Position--;
8    }
9
10   private void btnNext_Click(object sender, EventArgs e)
11   {
12       if (managerTitle.Position == managerTitle.Count - 1)
13       {
14           Console.Beep();
15       }
16       managerTitle.Position++;
17   }
18
19   private void btnFirst_Click(object sender, EventArgs e)
20   {
21       managerTitle.Position = 0;
22   }
23
24   private void btnLast_Click(object sender, EventArgs e)
25   {
26       managerTitle.Position = managerTitle.Count - 1;
27   }
```

Step 7   Delete the code for **txtInput_KeyPress** event method for the time being.

Step 8   Change **ValidateData** function so that it only has the following three lines of code (for
          the time being):

```
1  private bool ValidateData() {
2      string message = "";
3      bool allOK = true;
4      return (allOK);
5  }
```

Step 9   Modify the **SetState** method as follows:

```
1   private void SetState(string stateStr)
2   {
3       appState = stateStr;
4       switch (stateStr)
5       {
6           case "View":
7               txtBookTitle.BackColor = Color.White;
8               dtpPublishYear.Enabled = false;
9               txtISBN.ReadOnly = true;
10              txtISBN.BackColor = Color.White;
11              txtISBN.ForeColor = Color.Black;
12              txtDescription.ReadOnly = true;
13              txtNote.ReadOnly = true;
14              txtSubject.ReadOnly = true;
15              txtComment.ReadOnly = true;
16              btnPrev.Enabled = true;
17              btnNext.Enabled = true;
18              btnAddNew.Enabled = true;
19              btnSave.Enabled = false;
20              btnCancel.Enabled = false;
21              btnEdit.Enabled = true;
22              btnDelete.Enabled = true;
23              btnFinish.Enabled = true;
24              btnFirst.Enabled = true;
25              btnLast.Enabled = true;
26              txtBookTitle.Focus();
27              break;
28
29          default: // Add or Edit
30              txtBookTitle.ReadOnly = false;
31              dtpPublishYear.Enabled = true;
32              txtISBN.ReadOnly = false;
33
34              if (appState.Equals("Edit"))
35              {
36                  txtISBN.BackColor = Color.Red;
```

```
37          txtISBN.ForeColor = Color.White;
38          txtISBN.ReadOnly = true;
39          txtISBN.TabStop = false;
40      }
41      else
42      {
43          txtISBN.TabStop = true;
44      }
45
46      txtDescription.ReadOnly = false;
47      txtNote.ReadOnly = false;
48      txtSubject.ReadOnly = false;
49      txtComment.ReadOnly = false;
50      btnPrev.Enabled = false;
51      btnNext.Enabled = false;
52      btnAddNew.Enabled = false;
53      btnSave.Enabled = true;
54      btnCancel.Enabled = true;
55      btnEdit.Enabled = false;
56      btnDelete.Enabled = false;
57      btnFinish.Enabled = false;
58      btnFirst.Enabled = false;
59      btnLast.Enabled = false;
60      txtBookTitle.Focus();
61      break;
62  }
63 }
```

The code above reflects the new names in the text boxes and the **dateTimePicker**
controls. Additionally, you set the **ReadOnly** property to true for **txtISBN** control in
Edit mode and turn it red. This is the box where the **ISBN** (the primary key that
identifies a book) is entered. Note that you don't let the user edit the primary key. You
only allow the user to enter a new value here in **Add** mode.

Step 10   Modify **btnAddNew_Click**, **btnDelete_Click**, and **btnCancel_Click** event methods
to reflect the name of the data objects:

```
1   private void btnAddNew_Click(object sender, EventArgs e)
2   {
3       cboAuthor1.SelectedIndex = -1;
4       cboAuthor2.SelectedIndex = -1;
5       cboAuthor3.SelectedIndex = -1;
6       cboAuthor4.SelectedIndex = -1;
7       try
8       {
9           myBookmark = managerTitle.Position;
10          managerTitle.AddNew();
11          SetState("Add");
12          cboAuthor1.Enabled = false;
```

```
13              cboAuthor2.Enabled = false;
14              cboAuthor3.Enabled = false;
15                  cboAuthor4.Enabled = false;
16          }
17      catch (Exception ex)
18      {
19          MessageBox.Show("Adding new record error.", "Error",
20              MessageBoxButtons.OK, MessageBoxIcon.Error);
21      }
22  }
23
24  private void btnCancel_Click(object sender, EventArgs e)
25  {
26      managerTitle.CancelCurrentEdit();
27
28      if (appState.Equals("Add"))
29      {
30          managerTitle.Position = myBookmark;
31      }
32
33      SetState("View");
34  }
35
36  private void btnDelete_Click(object sender, EventArgs e)
37  {
38      DialogResult response;
39      response = MessageBox.Show("Do you really want to delete this record?",
40          "Delete", MessageBoxButtons.YesNo, MessageBoxIcon.Question,
41          MessageBoxDefaultButton.Button2);
42
43      if (response == DialogResult.No) {
44          return;
45      }
46      try
47      {
48          managerTitle.RemoveAt(managerTitle.Position);
49      }
50      catch (Exception ex)
51      {
52          MessageBox.Show("Record deletion error.", "Error",
53              MessageBoxButtons.OK, MessageBoxIcon.Error);
54      }
55  }
```

Step 11   Modify **btnSave_Click** event method to reflect the new data objects and look up the
Title table for new records:

```
1  private void btnSave_Click(object sender, EventArgs e)
2  {
3      if (!ValidateData())
```

```
4       {
5           return;
6       }
7
8       string nameSaved = txtBookTitle.Text;
9       int rowSaved;
10
11      try
12      {
13          managerTitle.EndCurrentEdit();
14          tableTitle.DefaultView.Sort = "BookTitle";
15          rowSaved = tableTitle.DefaultView.Find(nameSaved);
16          managerTitle.Position = rowSaved;
17
18          MessageBox.Show("Record is successfully saved", "Save",
19              MessageBoxButtons.OK, MessageBoxIcon.Information);
20
21          SetState("View");
22      }
23      catch (Exception ex)
24      {
25          MessageBox.Show("Error saving record.", "Error",
26              MessageBoxButtons.OK, MessageBoxIcon.Error);
27      }
28  }
```

Step 12   Modify **createSearchButton** method as follows:

```
1   private void createSearchButton()
2   {
3       // Creates search buttons
4       int w, lStart, l, t;
5       int btnHeight = 35; // by trial and error
6
7       // Search buttons
8       // Button width - 13 buttons in a row
9       w = Convert.ToInt32(grdTitle.ClientSize.Width / 13);
10
11      // Aligns buttons
12      lStart = Convert.ToInt32((grdTitle.Width)) + 250;
13      l = lStart; t = grdTitle.Top + grdTitle.Height + 10;
14
15      // Creates and positions 26 buttons
16      for (int i = 0; i < 26; i++)
17      {
18          // Creates push button
19          buttonArr[i] = new Button();
20          buttonArr[i].TabStop = false;
21
22          // Sets Text property
23          buttonArr[i].Text = ((char)(65 + i)).ToString();
```

```
24    buttonArr[i].Font = new Font(buttonArr[i].Font.FontFamily,
25        9, FontStyle.Bold);
26
27    // Positions buttons
28    buttonArr[i].Width = w;
29    buttonArr[i].Height = btnHeight;
30    buttonArr[i].Left = l;
31    buttonArr[i].Top = t;
32
33    // Gives color
34    buttonArr[i].BackColor = Color.Red;
35    buttonArr[i].ForeColor = Color.White;
36
37    // Adds each button on form
38    this.Controls.Add(buttonArr[i]);
39
40    // Adds event handler
41    buttonArr[i].Click +=
42        new System.EventHandler(this.btnSQL_Click);
43    l += w + 2;
44
45    if (i == 12)
46    {
47        // Next row
48        l = lStart; t += btnHeight;
49    }
50    }
51 }
```

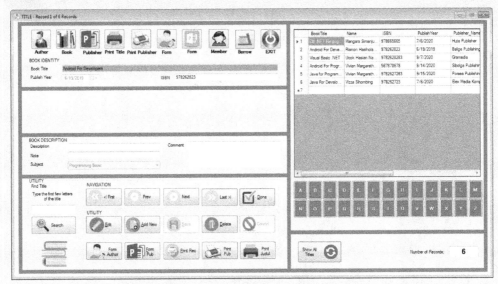

Figure 4.2 Application when it runs

Step 13   Define **createSQLStatement** method as follows:

```
1   private string createSQLStatement()
2   {
3       // Create SQL Statement
4       string SqlString = null;
5       SqlString += "SELECT Title.BookTitle, Author.Name, Title.ISBN,
6           Title.PublishYear, ";
7       SqlString += "Publisher.Name AS Publisher_Name, Publisher.City,
8           Publisher.Address, ";
9       SqlString += "Title.Description, Title.Subject ";
10      SqlString += "FROM Author, Title, Publisher, Title_Author ";
11      SqlString += "WHERE Title.ISBN = Title_Author.ISBN ";
12      SqlString += "AND Author.AuthorID = Title_Author.AuthorID ";
13      SqlString += "AND Title.PublisherID = Publisher.PublisherID ";
14
15      return SqlString;
16  }
```

Step 14   Modify **btnSQL_Click** method as follows:

```
1   private void btnSQL_Click(object sender, EventArgs e)
2   {
3       SqlCommand commResult = null;
4       SqlDataAdapter adapterResult = new SqlDataAdapter();
5       DataTable tableResult = new DataTable();
6       String StatemenSQL;
7
8       string SQLAll = createSQLStatement();
9
10      // Determines which button is clicked and creates SQL statement
11      Button buttonClicked = (Button)sender;
12      switch (buttonClicked.Text)
13      {
14          case "Show All Titles":
15              StatemenSQL = SQLAll;
16              break;
17          case "Z":
18              // Z button is clicked
19              // Appends at SQLAll to limit records upto for author Z
20              StatemenSQL = SQLAll + "AND Title.BookTitle > 'Z' ";
21              break;
22          default:
23              // Letter keys except Z
24              // Appends at SQLAll to limit records
25              // for letter that is clicked
26              int idx = (int)(Convert.ToChar(buttonClicked.Text)) - 65;
27              StatemenSQL = SQLAll + "AND Title.BookTitle > '" +
28              buttonArr[idx].Text + " ' ";
29              StatemenSQL += "AND Title.BookTitle < '" +
30                      buttonArr[idx + 1].Text + " ' ";
31              break;
32
```

```
33      }
34      StatemenSQL += "ORDER BY Author.Name";
35
36      // Applies SQL statement
37      try
38      {
39          // Creates Command and DataAdapater objects
40          commResult = new SqlCommand(StatemenSQL, connTitle);
41          adapterResult.SelectCommand = commResult;
42          adapterResult.Fill(tableResult);
43
44          // Binds DataGridView with data table
45          grdTitle.DataSource = tableResult;
46      }
47
48      catch (Exception ex)
49      {
50          MessageBox.Show(ex.Message, "Error Processing SQL",
51              MessageBoxButtons.OK, MessageBoxIcon.Error);
52      }
53      commResult.Dispose();
54      adapterResult.Dispose();
55      tableResult.Dispose();
    }
```

Step 15   Save and run the application. You will see a form as shown in Figure 4.2.

Try the navigation buttons if it can work properly. Try editing a recording to see if the **Save** and **Cancel** buttons work. Try adding a new record. Type a title and click **Save**. Then exit the application. You will get a database save error.

This is an error trapping code telling you that the new record cannot be saved to the database because you did not provide a valid **PublisherID**. You'll be fixing this in a moment.

4.2 Tutorial Steps of Creating Form for Title Table: Searching Record

Step 1   If you want to edit an entry beginning with the letter 'T', you will need to click the **Next** button tens or hundreds of times if the table contains thousands of entries. This is not practical. You need a way to find the recording location. You will add search capability for book titles that start with a specific letter.

Step 2   In **SetState** method, enable **grpSearchTitle** in **View** mode and disable it in **Add** and **Edit** mode. Use **Enabled** property of **grpSearchTitle**.

```
1   private void SetState(string stateStr)
```

```csharp
{
    appState = stateStr;
    switch (stateStr)
    {
        case "View":
            txtBookTitle.BackColor = Color.White;
            dtpPublishYear.Enabled = false;
            txtISBN.ReadOnly = true;
            txtISBN.BackColor = Color.White;
            txtISBN.ForeColor = Color.Black;
            txtDescription.ReadOnly = true;
            txtNote.ReadOnly = true;
            txtSubject.ReadOnly = true;
            txtComment.ReadOnly = true;
            grpSearchTitle.Enabled = true;
            btnPrev.Enabled = true;
            btnNext.Enabled = true;
            btnAddNew.Enabled = true;
            btnSave.Enabled = false;
            btnCancel.Enabled = false;
            btnEdit.Enabled = true;
            btnDelete.Enabled = true;
            btnFinish.Enabled = true;
            btnFirst.Enabled = true;
            btnLast.Enabled = true;
            txtBookTitle.Focus();
            break;

        default: // Add or Edit
            txtBookTitle.ReadOnly = false;
            dtpPublishYear.Enabled = true;
            txtISBN.ReadOnly = false;

            if (appState.Equals("Edit"))
            {
                txtISBN.BackColor = Color.Red;
                txtISBN.ForeColor = Color.White;
                txtISBN.ReadOnly = true;
                txtISBN.TabStop = false;
            }
            else
            {
                txtISBN.TabStop = true;
            }

            txtDescription.ReadOnly = false;
            txtNote.ReadOnly = false;
            txtSubject.ReadOnly = false;
            txtComment.ReadOnly = false;
            grpSearchTitle.Enabled = false;
```

```
53          btnPrev.Enabled = false;
54          btnNext.Enabled = false;
55          btnAddNew.Enabled = false;
56          btnSave.Enabled = true;
57          btnCancel.Enabled = true;
58          btnEdit.Enabled = false;
59          btnDelete.Enabled = false;
60          btnFinish.Enabled = false;
61          btnFirst.Enabled = false;
62          btnLast.Enabled = false;
63          txtBookTitle.Focus();
64          break;
65      }
}
```

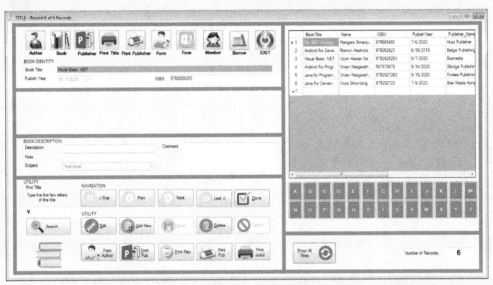

Figure 4.3 The resulting search is displayed in a number of controls

Step 3   Add the following code to **btnSearch_Click** event method:

```
1   private void btnSearch_Click(object sender, EventArgs e)
2   {
3       if (txtSearch.Text.Equals(""))
4       {
5           return;
6       }
7
8       int rowSaved = managerTitle.Position;
9       DataRow[] rowFound;
10      tableTitle.DefaultView.Sort = "BookTitle";
11      rowFound = tableTitle.Select("BookTitle LIKE '" +
12          txtSearch.Text + "*'");
13
14      if (rowFound.Length == 0)
```

```
15    {
16        managerTitle.Position = rowSaved;
17    }
18    else
19    {
20        managerTitle.Position =
21            tableTitle.DefaultView.Find(rowFound[0]["BookTitle"]);
22    }
23 }
```

This method first saves the positions of the update manager (**CurrencyManager**). The code then uses the **SELECT** method from the data table to find all rows with a **BookTitle** field starting with the first few letters using **LIKE**. If the search is unsuccessful, the saved position will be returned.

Step 4   Save and run the application. Type **V** in the text box. Click the **Search** button. You will get what is shown in Figure 4.3.

4.3 Tutorial Steps of Creating Form for Title Table: Navigational Information

Step 1   You now will add code for tracking and displaying viewed records and the number of records in the **Title** table. Add a method named **SetText** to your application. Use the following code:

```
1  private void SetText()
2  {
3      this.Text = "Title - Record " +
4          (managerTitle.Position + 1).ToString() + " of " +
5          managerTitle.Count.ToString() + " Records";
6  }
```

The code above sets the **Text** property of the form to reflect the current record (**Position**) and total number of records (**Count**).

Step 2   Add the following line of code at the bottom of **formTitle_Load** to initialize the display of the number of records:

```
1  SetText();
```

Step 3   When you move to a new record, the position of the update manager will change, so you need to update the information. Add this line of code at the end of the **btnSearch_Click** event method, **btnFirst_Click**, **btnPrev_Click**, **btnNext_Click**, and **btnLast_Click**:

```
1  private void btnFirst_Click(object sender, EventArgs e)
```

```
2   {
3       managerTitle.Position = 0;
4       SetText();
5   }
6
7   private void btnLast_Click(object sender, EventArgs e)
8   {
9       managerTitle.Position = managerTitle.Count - 1;
10      SetText();
11  }
12
13  private void btnPrev_Click(object sender, EventArgs e)
14  {
15      if (managerTitle.Position == 0)
16      {
17          Console.Beep();
18      }
19
20      managerTitle.Position--;
21      SetText();
22  }
23
24  private void btnNext_Click(object sender, EventArgs e)
25  {
26      if (managerTitle.Position == managerTitle.Count - 1)
27      {
28          Console.Beep();
29      }
30
31      managerTitle.Position++;
32      SetText();
33  }
```

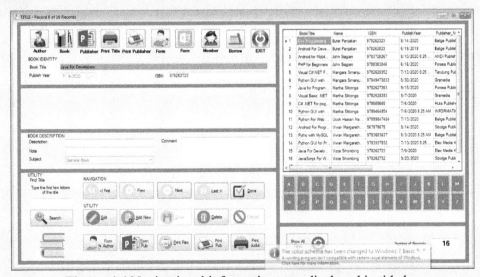

Figure 4.4 Navigational information now displayed in title bar

Step 4   When you add a new record, there will be a change in the number of records. Add this
line of code at the end of **btnAddNew_Click**, **btnSave_Click**, and **btnDelete_Click**
event methods to reflect these changes:

```csharp
private void btnAddNew_Click(object sender, EventArgs e)
{
    cboAuthor1.SelectedIndex = -1;
    cboAuthor2.SelectedIndex = -1;
    cboAuthor3.SelectedIndex = -1;
    cboAuthor4.SelectedIndex = -1;
    try
    {
        myBookmark = managerTitle.Position;
        managerTitle.AddNew();
        SetState("Add");
        cboAuthor1.Enabled = false;
        cboAuthor2.Enabled = false;
        cboAuthor3.Enabled = false;
                cboAuthor4.Enabled = false;
    }
    catch (Exception ex)
    {
        MessageBox.Show("Adding new record error.", "Error",
            MessageBoxButtons.OK, MessageBoxIcon.Error);
    }
    SetText();
}


private void btnDelete_Click(object sender, EventArgs e)
{
    DialogResult response;
    response = MessageBox.Show("Do you reallywant to delete this record?",
        "Delete", MessageBoxButtons.YesNo, MessageBoxIcon.Question,
        MessageBoxDefaultButton.Button2);

    if (response == DialogResult.No) {
        return;
    }
    try
    {
        managerTitle.RemoveAt(managerTitle.Position);
    }
    catch (Exception ex)
    {
        MessageBox.Show("Record deletion error.", "Error",
            MessageBoxButtons.OK, MessageBoxIcon.Error);
    }
    SetText();
}
```

```
47  private void btnSave_Click(object sender, EventArgs e)
48  {
49      if (!ValidateData())
50      {
51          return;
52      }
53
54      string nameSaved = txtBookTitle.Text;
55      int rowSaved;
56
57      try
58      {
59          managerTitle.EndCurrentEdit();
60          tableTitle.DefaultView.Sort = "BookTitle";
61          rowSaved = tableTitle.DefaultView.Find(nameSaved);
62          managerTitle.Position = rowSaved;
63
64          MessageBox.Show("Record is successfully saved", "Save",
65              MessageBoxButtons.OK, MessageBoxIcon.Information);
66
67          SetState("View");
68      }
69      catch (Exception ex)
70      {
71          MessageBox.Show("Error saving record.", "Error",
72              MessageBoxButtons.OK, MessageBoxIcon.Error);
73      }
74      this.Show();
75      SetState("View");
76
77      //Creates 26 search buttons
78      createSearchButton();
79
80      // Clicks all records when form starts
81      btnAll.Click += new System.EventHandler(this.btnSQL_Click);
82      btnAll.PerformClick();
83      SetText();
84  }
```

Step 5   Save and run the application. Notice that the navigational information is now displayed
in the form's title bar, as shown in Figure 4.4.

4.4 Tutorial Steps of Creating Form for Title Table: Adding Publisher's Name

Step 1   Previously, you tried to add and save records in the **Title** table, but received an error
message stating that no **PublisherID** field was supplied. You will correct it now. As
stated, every title in the book database requires **PublisherID**. This is a foreign key that

is related to the primary key in the **Publisher** table. This key tells who published the book.

For each existing record, the **PublisherID** value is recognized and can be changed, because it is a foreign key. For added records, the user must supply a value. But, how do users know **PublisherID** value? He may not know the name of the publisher. Instead of the user having to be asked to provide **PublisherID**, it would be better if the user could choose the publisher name and the database engine that determines the associated **PublisherID**. Likewise, when a user is navigating through existing records, the user should be able to see the publisher name, not the **PublisherID**.

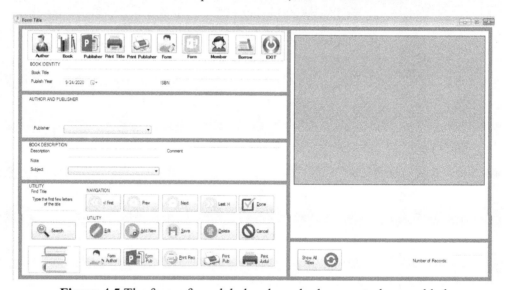

Figure 4.5 The form after a label and combo box controls are added

You will use a combo box control. The idea is that you use the **Name** field from the **Publisher** table to fill in the combo box. When the user has a publisher name, the combo box will pass the corresponding **PublisherID** to the **Title** table. Then, when the user navigates through the records, the corresponding **Publisher_ID** will be sent to the combo box to display the associated publisher name.

Add a label control and combo box to the **Title** input form. The form will look as shown in Figure 4.5.

Step 2   The two new controls have the following properties:

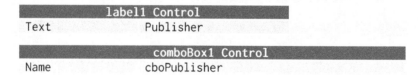

label1 Control	
Text	Publisher

comboBox1 Control	
Name	cboPublisher

BackColor	White (Changed so that user can see the values when **Enabled** is false)

Step 3 Add the following lines of code to the form-level declaration:

```
1  SqlCommand commandPublisher;
2  SqlDataAdapter adapterPublisher;
3  DataTable tablePublisher;
```

These objects will be used to populate combo box with publisher's names.

Step 4 Add the following code in line 37-48 to **FormTitle_Load** event method to set the binding to the combo box:

```
1   private void FormTitle_Load(object sender, EventArgs e)
2   {
3       try
4       {
5           // Connects to database
6           connTitle = new SqlConnection("Data Source=.\\SQLEXPRESS;
7           AttachDbFilename=D:\\Database\\DBMS.mdf;
8           Integrated Security = True; Connect Timeout = 30;
9           User Instance = True");
10
11          connTitle.Open();
12
13          // Creates Command object
14          commandTitle = new
15              SqlCommand("SELECT * FROM Title ORDER BY BookTitle",
16              connTitle);
17
18          // Creates DataAdapter/DataTable objects
19          adapterTitle = new SqlDataAdapter();
20          adapterTitle.SelectCommand = commandTitle;
21          tableTitle = new DataTable();
22          adapterTitle.Fill(tableTitle);
23
24          // Binds controls to data table
25          txtBookTitle.DataBindings.Add("Text", tableTitle, "BookTitle");
26          dtpPublishYear.DataBindings.Add("Text", tableTitle, "PublishYear");
27          txtISBN.DataBindings.Add("Text", tableTitle, "ISBN");
28          txtDescription.DataBindings.Add("Text", tableTitle, "Description");
29          txtNote.DataBindings.Add("Text", tableTitle, "Note");
30          txtSubject.DataBindings.Add("Text", tableTitle, "Subject");
31          txtComment.DataBindings.Add("Text", tableTitle, "Comment");
32
33          // Sets data update manager
34          managerTitle =
35              (CurrencyManager)this.BindingContext[tableTitle];
36
```

```
37      commandPublisher = new
38          SqlCommand("SELECT * FROM Publisher ORDER BY Name",
39          connTitle);
40      adapterPublisher = new SqlDataAdapter();
41      adapterPublisher.SelectCommand = commandPublisher;
42      tablePublisher = new DataTable();
43      adapterPublisher.Fill(tablePublisher);
44      cboPublisher.DataSource = tablePublisher;
45      cboPublisher.DisplayMember = "Name";
46      cboPublisher.ValueMember = "PublisherID";
47      cboPublisher.DataBindings.Add("SelectedValue",
48          tableTitle, "PublisherID");
49   }
50   catch (Exception ex)
51   {
52      MessageBox.Show(ex.Message, "Error Creating Title table.",
53          MessageBoxButtons.OK, MessageBoxIcon.Error);
54      return;
55   }
56
57   this.Show();
58   SetState("View");
59
60   // Creates 26 search buttons
61   createSearchButton();
62
63   // Creates SQLAll
64   SQLAll = createSQLStatement();
65
66   // Clicks all records when form starts
67   btnAll.Click += new System.EventHandler(this.btnSQL_Click);
68   btnAll.PerformClick();
     SetText();
   }
```

Step 5   Add the following code in line 32-34 to **FormTitle_FormClosing** to delete the newly
          created objects:

```
1    private void FormTitle_FormClosing(object sender,
2    FormClosingEventArgs e)
3    {
4        if (appState.Equals("Edit") || appState.Equals("Add"))
5        {
6            MessageBox.Show("You should finish editing before closing application.",
7                "", MessageBoxButtons.OK, MessageBoxIcon.Information);
8            e.Cancel = true;
9        }
10       else
11       {
12           try
```

```
13    {
14        // Saves changes to database
15        SqlCommandBuilder titleAdapterCommand = new
16            SqlCommandBuilder(adapterTitle);
17        adapterTitle.Update(tableTitle);
18    }
19    catch (Exception ex)
20    {
21        MessageBox.Show("Error saving into database: \r\n" +
22            ex.Message, "Saving Error", MessageBoxButtons.OK,
23            MessageBoxIcon.Error);
24    }
25    // Closes connection to database
26    connTitle.Close();
27
28    // Deletes objects
29    connTitle.Dispose();
30    commandTitle.Dispose();
31    adapterTitle.Dispose();
32    commandPublisher.Dispose();
33    adapterPublisher.Dispose();
34    tablePublisher.Dispose();
35    }
36 }
```

Step 6   Modify **SetState** method so that the combo box is disabled in **View** mode and enabled in **Add** and **Edit** mode.

Step 7   Save and run the application. You can now see publishers listed in the combo box. Navigate through the records and notice how the combo box displays the appropriate publisher name, as shown in Figure 4.6.

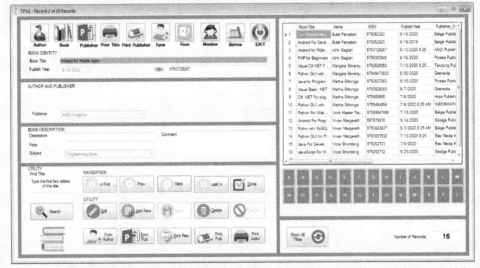

Figure 4.6 The combo box displays the appropriate publisher name for each title

Step 8   Try changing the publisher name or adding a new record.

4.5 Tutorial Steps of Creating Form for Title Table: Selecting Author

Step 1   You will add four authors to the **Title** input form. However, note that the **Title** table
in the book database does not have author information. So, if you enter the author in
the **Title** input form, what do you do with that information? You will need to link the
Title table (via th **ISBN** field) to the **Title_Author** table (which matches the **ISBN** to
AuthorID) and then to the **Author** table (which has author information, specifically
Name field).

The requirement for the user is to enter up to four author ids (**AuthorID** field) for each
title in **Title** table. These values will be matched against the corresponding **ISBN** field
in **Title_Author** table. As with the previously added **Publisher** information, you don't
want the user to know the author id, but you want the user to only know the author's
name.

Step 2   Reopen **Title** form. Add four label controls and four combo boxes to the form. Set the
properties as follows:

label1 Control	
Text	Author 1

label2 Control	
Text	Author 2

label3 Control	
Text	Author 3

label4 Control	
Text	Author 4

comboBox1 Control	
Name	cboAuthor1
BackColor	White
DropDownStyle	DropDownList

comboBox2 Control	
Name	cboAuthor2
BackColor	White
DropDownStyle	DropDownList

comboBox3 Control	
Name	cboAuthor3
BackColor	White
DropDownStyle	DropDownList

The form now looks as shown in Figure 4.7.

You will add four data table objects to provide the user with a number of author names to choose from in one of the four combo boxes.

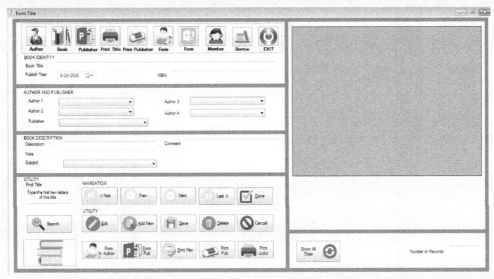

Figure 4.7 Form after new controls are added and their properties are set

Step 3   Add the following declarations at the form level:

```
1   ComboBox[] cboAuthorArr = new ComboBox[4];
2   SqlCommand commandAuthor;
3   SqlDataAdapter adapterAuthor;
4   DataTable[] tableAuthorArr = new DataTable[4];
```

Placing combo boxes into an array (**cboAuthorArr**) makes code simpler. An array containing data tables (**tableAuthorArr**) will be used to populate combo boxes with author names.

Step 4   Add the following code in line 50-69 to **FormTitle_Load** event method to create the data tables and bind the combo boxes:

```
1   private void FormTitle_Load(object sender, EventArgs e)
2   {
3       try
4       {
5           // Connects to database
6           connTitle = new SqlConnection("Data Source=.\\SQLEXPRESS;
7           AttachDbFilename=D:\\Database\\DBMS.mdf;
8           Integrated Security = True; Connect Timeout = 30;
9           User Instance = True");
10
11          connTitle.Open();
12
```

```
13    // Creates Command object
14    commandTitle = new
15        SqlCommand("SELECT * FROM Title ORDER BY BookTitle",
16        connTitle);
17
18    // Creates DataAdapter/DataTable objects
19    adapterTitle = new SqlDataAdapter();
20    adapterTitle.SelectCommand = commandTitle;
21    tableTitle = new DataTable();
22    adapterTitle.Fill(tableTitle);
23
24    // Binds controls to data table
25    txtBookTitle.DataBindings.Add("Text", tableTitle, "BookTitle");
26    dtpPublishYear.DataBindings.Add("Text", tableTitle, "PublishYear");
27    txtISBN.DataBindings.Add("Text", tableTitle, "ISBN");
28    txtDescription.DataBindings.Add("Text", tableTitle, "Description");
29    txtNote.DataBindings.Add("Text", tableTitle, "Note");
30    txtSubject.DataBindings.Add("Text", tableTitle, "Subject");
31    txtComment.DataBindings.Add("Text", tableTitle, "Comment");
32
33    // Sets data update manager
34    managerTitle =
35        (CurrencyManager)this.BindingContext[tableTitle];
36
37    commandPublisher = new
38        SqlCommand("SELECT * FROM Publisher ORDER BY Name",
39        connTitle);
40    adapterPublisher = new SqlDataAdapter();
41    adapterPublisher.SelectCommand = commandPublisher;
42    tablePublisher = new DataTable();
43    adapterPublisher.Fill(tablePublisher);
44    cboPublisher.DataSource = tablePublisher;
45    cboPublisher.DisplayMember = "Name";
46    cboPublisher.ValueMember = "PublisherID";
47    cboPublisher.DataBindings.Add("SelectedValue",
48        tableTitle, "PublisherID");
49
50    // Populates combo box cboPublisher
51    cboAuthorArr[0] = cboAuthor1;
52    cboAuthorArr[1] = cboAuthor2;
53    cboAuthorArr[2] = cboAuthor3;
54    cboAuthorArr[3] = cboAuthor4;
55    commandAuthor = new
56        SqlCommand("SELECT * FROM Author ORDER BY Name",
57        connTitle);
58    adapterAuthor = new SqlDataAdapter();
59    adapterAuthor.SelectCommand = commandAuthor;
60
61    for (int i = 0; i < 4; i++)
62    {
63        // Creates author table array
```

```
64          tableAuthorArr[i] = new DataTable();
65          adapterAuthor.Fill(tableAuthorArr[i]);
66          cboAuthorArr[i].DataSource = tableAuthorArr[i];
67          cboAuthorArr[i].DisplayMember = "Name";
68          cboAuthorArr[i].ValueMember = "AuthorID";
69          // deselects
70          cboAuthorArr[i].SelectedIndex = -1;
71       }
72    }
73    catch (Exception ex)
74    {
75        MessageBox.Show(ex.Message, "Error Creating Title table.",
76            MessageBoxButtons.OK, MessageBoxIcon.Error);
77        return;
78    }
79
80    this.Show();
81    SetState("View");
82
83    // Creates 26 search buttons
84    createSearchButton();
85
86    // Creates SQLAll
87    SQLAll = createSQLStatement();
88
89    // Clicks all records when form starts
90    btnAll.Click += new System.EventHandler(this.btnSQL_Click);
91    btnAll.PerformClick();
92    SetText();
93 }
```

Step 5   Add the following lines of code in line 36-41 to **FormTitle_FormClosing** method to delete new data objects:

```
1     private void FormTitle_FormClosing(object sender,
2     FormClosingEventArgs e)
3     {
4         if (appState.Equals("Edit") || appState.Equals("Add"))
5         {
6             MessageBox.Show("You should finish editing before closing application.",
7                 "", MessageBoxButtons.OK, MessageBoxIcon.Information);
8             e.Cancel = true;
9         }
10        else
11        {
12            try
13            {
14                // Saves changes to database
15                SqlCommandBuilder titleAdapterCommand = new
16                    SqlCommandBuilder(adapterTitle);
```

```
17        adapterTitle.Update(tableTitle);
18    }
19    catch (Exception ex)
20    {
21        MessageBox.Show("Error saving into database: \r\n" +
22            ex.Message, "Saving Error", MessageBoxButtons.OK,
23            MessageBoxIcon.Error);
24    }
25
26    // Closes connection to database
27    connTitle.Close();
28
29    // Deletes objects
30    connTitle.Dispose();
31    commandTitle.Dispose();
32    adapterTitle.Dispose();
33    commandPublisher.Dispose();
34    adapterPublisher.Dispose();
35    tablePublisher.Dispose();
36    commandAuthor.Dispose();
37    adapterAuthor.Dispose();
38    tableAuthorArr[0].Dispose();
39    tableAuthorArr[1].Dispose();
40    tableAuthorArr[2].Dispose();
41    tableAuthorArr[3].Dispose();
42    }
43 }
```

Step 6   Save and run the application. To restore the startup form again, open **Program.cs** file
and change **Main** method to the following:

```
1  static class Program
2  {
3      /// <summary>
4      /// The main entry point for the application.
5      /// </summary>
6      [STAThread]
7      static void Main()
8      {
9          Application.EnableVisualStyles();
10         Application.SetCompatibleTextRenderingDefault(false);
11         Application.Run(new formTitle());
12     }
13 }
```

After the title form is displayed, there are no authors listed in the author combo box.
Click **Edit**. Click a combo box to see a drop-down list of authors, as shown in Figure
4.8.

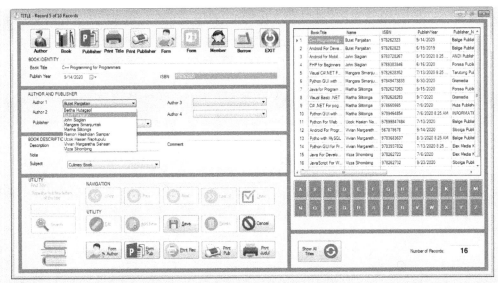

Figure 4.8 The four author combo boxes have been filled in by all authors from the
Author table

Step 7   Next to each combo box, put a small button control. Set their **Name** property as
btnAuthorX1, **btnAuthorX2**, **btnAuthorX3**, and **btnAuthorX4**. Set each **Text**
property as **X** (bold). Set **TabStop** property of each control to **False**.

Step 8   Add this code to **btnAuthorX_Click** event method (which handles the **Click** event for
the four buttons:

```
private void btnAuthorX_Click(object sender, EventArgs e)
{
    Button whichButton = (Button)sender;
    switch (whichButton.Name)
    {
        case "btnAuthorX1":
            cboAuthor1.SelectedIndex = -1;
            break;
        case "btnAuthorX2":
            cboAuthor2.SelectedIndex = -1;
            break;
        case "btnAuthorX3":
            cboAuthor3.SelectedIndex = -1;
            break;
        case "btnAuthorX4":
            cboAuthor4.SelectedIndex = -1;
            break;
    }
}
```

When a button is clicked, the combo box selection will be cleared.

Step 9   Save and run the application. Click **Edit**. Choose an author. Then, click the **X** button to delete it. Deletions will not be saved. You need a code to do this.

4.6 Tutorial Steps of Creating Form for Title Table: Viewing Author

Step 1   As a next step, you want the correct author names to appear when each title is displayed on the **Title** form. This is quite a complex coding. For specific title, you will create a small version of the **Title_ Author** window (using another data adapter) with the following format:

ISBN	AuthorID

The ISBN value will be the same for each row with up to four **AuthorID** values. To form such a table, you use SQL. If it is assumed that the displayed record has an ISBN with a **SearchString** value, the SQL statement for constructing such a table would be:

```
1   SELECT Title_Author.* FROM Title_Author
2   WHERE Title_Author.ISBN = 'SearchString'
```

After this SQL statement is processed, you determine how many records there are in the resulting data table. For each record, you set **ValueSelected** property of the associated combo box control to **AuthorID**. This will display the author's name. You will do it now.

Step 2   Return to the project Title input form. Add the following code to the form-level declaration to create the required objects:

```
1   SqlCommand commandISBNAuthor;
2   SqlDataAdapter adapterISBNAuthor;
3   DataTable tableISBNAuthor;
```

Step 3   Add **GetAuthor** method which reads author names for the current record:

```
1    private void GetAuthor()
2    {
3        string StatementSQL = "SELECT Title_Author.* FROM Title_Author
4            WHERE Title_Author.ISBN = '" + txtISBN.Text + "'";
5        for (int i = 0; i < 4; i++)
6        {
7            cboAuthorArr[i].SelectedIndex = -1;
8        }
9
10       // Creates combobox author array
```

```
11    commandISBNAuthor = new SqlCommand(StatementSQL, connTitle);
12    adapterISBNAuthor = new SqlDataAdapter();
13    adapterISBNAuthor.SelectCommand = commandISBNAuthor;
14    tableISBNAuthor = new DataTable();
15    adapterISBNAuthor.Fill(tableISBNAuthor);
16
17    if (tableISBNAuthor.Rows.Count == 0)
18    {
19        return;
20    }
21
22    for (int i = 0; i < tableISBNAuthor.Rows.Count; i++)
23    {
24        cboAuthorArr[i].SelectedValue =
25            tableISBNAuthor.Rows[i]["AuthorID"].ToString();
26    }
27 }
```

Step 4   Add the following lines of code in line 44-46 to **FormTitle_FormClosing** event
method to delete the newly created data objects:

```
1  private void FormTitle_FormClosing(object sender,
2  FormClosingEventArgs e)
3  {
4      if (appState.Equals("Edit") || appState.Equals("Add"))
5      {
6          MessageBox.Show("You should finish editing before closing
7  application.",
8              "", MessageBoxButtons.OK, MessageBoxIcon.Information);
9          e.Cancel = true;
10     }
11     else
12     {
13         try
14         {
15             // Saves changes to database
16             SqlCommandBuilder titleAdapterCommand = new
17                 SqlCommandBuilder(adapterTitle);
18             adapterTitle.Update(tableTitle);
19         }
20         catch (Exception ex)
21         {
22             MessageBox.Show("Error saving into database: \r\n" +
23                 ex.Message, "Saving Error", MessageBoxButtons.OK,
24                 MessageBoxIcon.Error);
25         }
26
27         // Closes connection to database
28         connTitle.Close();
29
```

```
30      // Deletes objects
31      connTitle.Dispose();
32      commandTitle.Dispose();
33      adapterTitle.Dispose();
34      commandPublisher.Dispose();
35      adapterPublisher.Dispose();
36      tablePublisher.Dispose();
37      commandAuthor.Dispose();
38      adapterAuthor.Dispose();
39      tableAuthorArr[0].Dispose();
40      tableAuthorArr[1].Dispose();
41      tableAuthorArr[2].Dispose();
42      tableAuthorArr[3].Dispose();
43
44      commandISBNAuthor.Dispose();
45      adapterISBNAuthor.Dispose();
46      tableISBNAuthor.Dispose();
47   }
48 }
```

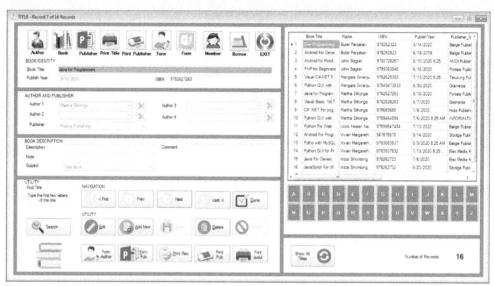

Figure 4.9 The combo box is now filled with the appropriate author name

Step 5   Add this one line as last code line to **formTitle_Load** event method to initialize the author view:

```
1   GetAuthor();
```

Step 6   When you move to a new record, the position (**Position** property) of the **CurrencyManager** object will change, so you need to update the author. Add the following line of code at the end of **btnSearch_Click**, **btnFirst_Click**, **btnPrev_Click**, **btnNext_Click**, and **btnLast_Click** button:

```
1    GetAuthor();
```

Step 7   When deleting a recording, the displayed information will change. Add the following
line of code at the end of **btnDelete_Click** event method:

```
1    GetAuthor();
```

Step 8   When canceling editing, combo boxes need to be returned to their pre-editing values.
Add this line of code at the end of **btnCancel_Click** event method:

```
1    GetAuthor();
```

Step 9   When adding a new title to the database (by clicking **Add New** button), you need to
clear the combo boxes. Add this line of code at the beginning of **btnAddNew_Click**
event method:

```
1    cboAuthor1.SelectedIndex = -1;
2    cboAuthor2.SelectedIndex = -1;
3    cboAuthor3.SelectedIndex = -1;
4    cboAuthor4.SelectedIndex = -1;
```

Step 10   Save and run the application. Navigate records. Note that for each title, the author can
be seen, as shown in Figure 4.9.

4.7 Tutorial Steps of Creating Form for Title Table: Saving Author

Step 1   You are now able to list authors and modify authors associated with a particular book,
but you still don't have the capability to save those changes. You can enter the code to
determine if the author's name has been changed, added or deleted. When **Save** button
is called, you create a new author data table filled with the names of the displayed
authors. The ADO .NET engine will then update these changes to the database.

Return to the **Title** input form. Add the following code in line 15-42 to **btnSave_Click**
event method:

```
1    private void btnSave_Click(object sender, EventArgs e)
2    {
3        if (!ValidateData())
4        {
5            return;
6        }
7
8        string nameSaved = txtBookTitle.Text;
9        int rowSaved;
10
```

```
11    try
12    {
13        managerTitle.EndCurrentEdit();
14
15        SqlCommandBuilder UpdateISBNCommand = new
16            SqlCommandBuilder(adapterISBNAuthor);
17
18        // Deletes all rows in table then reloads
19        if (tableISBNAuthor.Rows.Count != 0)
20        {
21            for (int i = 0; i < tableISBNAuthor.Rows.Count; i++)
22            {
23                tableISBNAuthor.Rows[i].Delete();
24            }
25
26            adapterISBNAuthor.Update(tableISBNAuthor);
27        }
28        for (int i = 0; i < 4; i++)
29        {
30            if (cboAuthorArr[i].SelectedIndex != -1)
31            {
32                tableISBNAuthor.Rows.Add();
33                tableISBNAuthor.Rows[
34                    tableISBNAuthor.Rows.Count - 1]["ISBN"] =
35                    txtISBN.Text;
36                tableISBNAuthor.Rows[
37                    tableISBNAuthor.Rows.Count - 1]["AuthorID"] =
38                    cboAuthorArr[i].SelectedValue;
39            }
40        }
41
42        adapterISBNAuthor.Update(tableISBNAuthor);
43
44        tableTitle.DefaultView.Sort = "BookTitle";
45        rowSaved = tableTitle.DefaultView.Find(nameSaved);
46        managerTitle.Position = rowSaved;
47
48        SqlCommandBuilder publisherAdapterCommand = new
49            SqlCommandBuilder(adapterTitle);
50        adapterTitle.Update(tableTitle);
51
52        MessageBox.Show("Record is successfully saved", "Save",
53            MessageBoxButtons.OK, MessageBoxIcon.Information);
54
55        SetState("View");
56    }
57    catch (Exception ex)
58    {
59        MessageBox.Show("Error saving record.", "Error",
60            MessageBoxButtons.OK, MessageBoxIcon.Error);
61    }
```

```
62    SetText();
63  }
```

The new code above deletes all records. Then, the code reads the author's names from the four combo boxes. If a combo box contains names, records will be added to the data table and field values (**ISBN**, **AuthorID**) will be created. The data adapter that contains the data table is then updated to save changes to the database.

Step 2   Save and run the project. You can now edit and add the title with the author name, as shown in Figure 4.10.

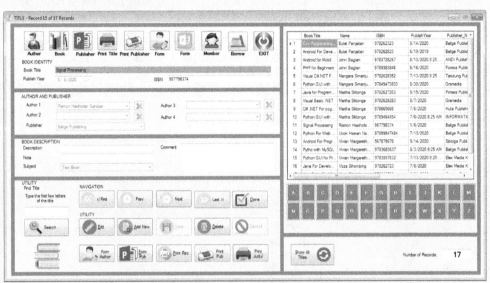

Figure 4.10 The new title was successfully added to the database with the author name selected from the combo box

4.8 Tutorial Steps of Reporting Every Title

Step 1   Now, you will add a feature to read all the data in the database. You need a database report. The report is quite simple. For each record, the data from each field will be displayed.

Add a button and a print preview dialog control to the project. Use the following properties:

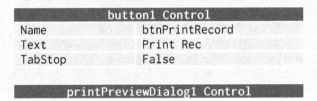

button1 Control	
Name	btnPrintRecord
Text	Print Rec
TabStop	False

printPreviewDialog1 Control	

Name	dlgPreview

Step 2 Add this line of code at the top of the code window:

```
1   using System.Drawing.Printing;
```

Step 3 Add the page number variable to the form level declaration:

```
1   int pageNumber;
```

Step 4 In **SetState** method to set **Enabled** property of **btnPrintRecord** to **true** in **View** mode and **false** in **Add/Edit** mode.

Step 5 Add the following code to **btnPrintRecord_Click** event method:

```
1   private void btnPrintRecord_Click(object sender, EventArgs e)
2   {
3       // Declares document
4       PrintDocument docRecord;
5
6       // Creates document and gives it a name
7       docRecord = new PrintDocument();
8       docRecord.DocumentName = "Title Record";
9
10      // Adds code handler
11      docRecord.PrintPage += new
12          PrintPageEventHandler(this.PrintRecordPage);
13
14      // Prints document in preview control
15      pageNumber = 1;
16      int positionSaved = managerTitle.Position;
17      dlgPreview.Document = docRecord;
18      dlgPreview.ShowDialog();
19
20
21      // Deletes document when finished printing
22      docRecord.Dispose();
23      managerTitle.Position = positionSaved;
24  }
```

Step 6 Add the following code to **PrintRecordPage** method:

```
1   private void PrintRecordPage(object sender, PrintPageEventArgs e) {
2       // Tracks every record, prints every record
3       Pen myPen = new Pen(Color.Black, 3);
4       e.Graphics.DrawRectangle(myPen, e.MarginBounds.Left,
5           e.MarginBounds.Top, e.MarginBounds.Width, 100);
6       e.Graphics.DrawImage(picBuku.Image, e.MarginBounds.Left + 10,
7           e.MarginBounds.Top + 10, 80, 80);
```

```
8
9        // Prints header
10       string s = "BOOK DATABASE MANAGEMENT SYSTEM";
11       Font myFont = new Font("Arial", 18, FontStyle.Bold);
12       SizeF sSize = e.Graphics.MeasureString(s, myFont);
13       e.Graphics.DrawString(s, myFont, Brushes.Black,
14           e.MarginBounds.Left + 100 + Convert.ToInt32(0.5 *
15           (e.MarginBounds.Width - 100 - sSize.Width)),
16           e.MarginBounds.Top + Convert.ToInt32(0.5 * (100 -
17           sSize.Height)));
18       myFont = new Font("Arial", 12, FontStyle.Regular);
19       int y = 275;
20       int dy = Convert.ToInt32(e.Graphics.MeasureString("S",
21           myFont).Height);
22
23       // Prints title
24       e.Graphics.DrawString("Title: " + txtBookTitle.Text, myFont,
25           Brushes.Black, e.MarginBounds.Left, y);
26
27       // Prints author
28       y += 2 * dy; e.Graphics.DrawString("Author: ", myFont,
29           Brushes.Black, e.MarginBounds.Left, y);
30       int x = e.MarginBounds.Left +
31           Convert.ToInt32(e.Graphics.MeasureString("Author: ",
32           myFont).Width);
33
34       if (tableISBNAuthor.Rows.Count != 0) {
35           for (int i = 0; i < tableISBNAuthor.Rows.Count; i++) {
36               e.Graphics.DrawString(cboAuthorArr[i].Text, myFont,
37                   Brushes.Black, x, y);
38               y += dy;
39           }
40       }
41       else {
42           e.Graphics.DrawString("None", myFont, Brushes.Black, x, y);
43           y += dy;
44       }
45
46       x = e.MarginBounds.Left; y += dy;
47
48       // Prints other fields
49       e.Graphics.DrawString("ISBN: " + txtISBN.Text, myFont,
50           Brushes.Black, x, y);
51       y += 2 * dy;
52       e.Graphics.DrawString("Year Published: " + dtpPublishYear.Value,
53           myFont, Brushes.Black, x, y);
54       y += 2 * dy;
55       e.Graphics.DrawString("Publisher: " + cboPublisher.Text, myFont,
56           Brushes.Black, x, y);
57       y += 2 * dy;
58       e.Graphics.DrawString("Description: " + txtDescription.Text,
```

```
59      myFont, Brushes.Black, x, y);
60    y += 2 * dy;
61    e.Graphics.DrawString("Note: " + txtNote.Text, myFont,
62      Brushes.Black, x, y);
63    y += 2 * dy;
64    e.Graphics.DrawString("Subject: " + cboSubject.Text, myFont,
65      Brushes.Black, x, y);
66    y += 2 * dy;
67    e.Graphics.DrawString("Comment: " + txtComment.Text, myFont,
68      Brushes.Black, x, y);
69    e.HasMorePages = false;
70  }
```

On each page, a header is printed along with the data fields and author photo.

Step 7   Save and run the application. Click on the **Print Rec** button. The print preview control will be displayed on every title page, as shown in Figure 4.11.

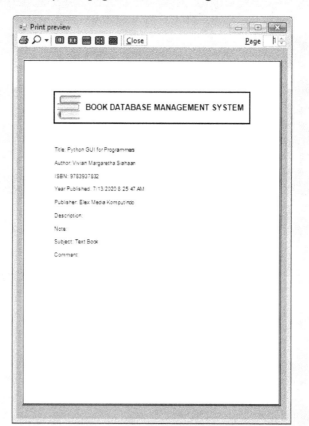

Figure 4.11 Each record in the table can now be printed

4.9 Tutorial Steps of Reporting All Titles

Step 1   Add a button and a print preview dialog control to the project. Use the following properties:

button1 Control	
Name	btnPrintTitle
Text	Print Title
TabStop	False

Step 2   Add the page number variable to the form level declaration:

```
1  const int titlePerPage = 45;
```

Step 3   In **SetState** method to set **Enabled** property of **btnPrintTitle** to **true** in **View** mode and **false** in **Add/Edit** mode.

Step 5   Add the following code to **btnPrintTitle_Click** event method:

```
1   private void btnPrintTitle_Click(object sender, EventArgs e)
2   {
3       // Starts processing printing on first record
4       pageNumber = 1;
5       btnFirst.PerformClick();
6       PrintDocument docTitle;
7
8       // Creates document and gives it a name
9       docTitle = new PrintDocument();
10      docTitle.DocumentName = "Book Title List";
11
12      // Adds code handler
13      docTitle.PrintPage += new
14          PrintPageEventHandler(this.PrintPageTitle);
15
16      // Prints document
17      dlgPreview.Document = docTitle;
18      dlgPreview.ShowDialog();
19
20      // Deletes document
21      docTitle.Dispose();
22  }
```

Step 6   Add the following code to **PrintPageTitle** method:

```
1   private void PrintPageTitle(object sender, PrintPageEventArgs e) {
2       // For every page
3       // Prints header
4       Font myFont = new Font("Courier New", 14, FontStyle.Bold);
5       e.Graphics.DrawString("Title - Page " + pageNumber.ToString(),
6           myFont, Brushes.Black, e.MarginBounds.Left,
7           e.MarginBounds.Top);
```

```
8     myFont = new Font("Courier New", 12, FontStyle.Underline);
9     int y = Convert.ToInt32(e.MarginBounds.Top + 50);
10    e.Graphics.DrawString("Title", myFont, Brushes.Black,
11        e.MarginBounds.Left, y);
12    e.Graphics.DrawString("Author", myFont, Brushes.Black,
13        e.MarginBounds.Left +
14        Convert.ToInt32(0.6 * (e.MarginBounds.Width)), y);
15    y += Convert.ToInt32(2 * myFont.GetHeight());
16    myFont = new Font("Courier New", 12, FontStyle.Regular);
17    int iLast = titlePerPage * pageNumber;
18
19    if (iLast > tableTitle.Rows.Count) {
20        iLast = tableTitle.Rows.Count;
21        e.HasMorePages = false;
22    }
23    else {
24        e.HasMorePages = true;
25    }
26
27    for (int i = 1 + titlePerPage * (pageNumber - 1); i <= iLast;
28    i++) {
29        // Moves to all records
30        if (txtBookTitle.Text.Length < 35) {
31            e.Graphics.DrawString(txtBookTitle.Text, myFont,
32            Brushes.Black, e.MarginBounds.Left, y);
33        }
34
35        else {
36            e.Graphics.DrawString(
37                txtBookTitle.Text.Substring(0, 35),
38                myFont, Brushes.Black, e.MarginBounds.Left, y);
39        }
40
41        if (cboAuthor1.Text.Length < 20) {
42            e.Graphics.DrawString(
43                cboAuthor1.Text, myFont, Brushes.Black,
44                e.MarginBounds.Left +
45                Convert.ToInt32(0.6 * (e.MarginBounds.Width)), y);
46        }
47
48        else {
49            e.Graphics.DrawString(
50                cboAuthor1.Text.Substring(0, 20), myFont,
51                Brushes.Black, e.MarginBounds.Left +
52                Convert.ToInt32(0.6 * (e.MarginBounds.Width)), y);
53        }
54
55        btnNext.PerformClick();
56        y += Convert.ToInt32(myFont.GetHeight());
57    }
58
```

```
59    if (e.HasMorePages)
60        pageNumber++;
61    else
62        pageNumber = 1;
63  }
```

On each page, a header is printed along with the data fields and author photo.

Step 7   Save and run the application. Click on the **Print Title** button. The print preview control will be displayed on every title list page, as shown in Figure 4.12.

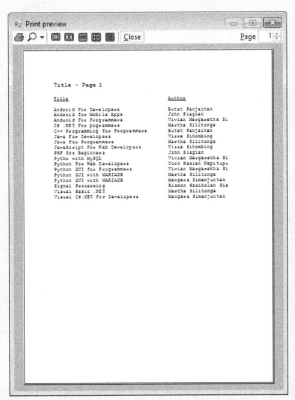

Figure 4.12 Each record in the table can now be printed

4.10 Tutorial Steps of Modifying Main Form and Global Variable LoginState

Step 1   Back in the main form, define the click event of **btnLibrary** in line 81-85 as follows:

```
FormMain.cs
1  using System;
2  using System.Collections.Generic;
3  using System.ComponentModel;
4  using System.Data;
5  using System.Drawing;
```

```csharp
6   using System.Linq;
7   using System.Text;
8   using System.Threading.Tasks;
9   using System.Windows.Forms;
10  using System.Threading;
11
12  namespace Balige_HighSchool_DMBS
13  {
14      public partial class FormMain : Form
15      {
16
17          public FormMain()
18          {
19              InitializeComponent();
20          }
21
22          public Button showButtonLibrary
23          {
24              get { return btnLibrary; }
25              set { btnLibrary = value; }
26          }
27
28          public Button showButtonInventory
29          {
30              get { return btnInventory; }
31              set { btnInventory = value; }
32          }
33
34          public Button showButtonAcademy
35          {
36              get { return btnAcademy; }
37              set { btnAcademy = value; }
38          }
39
40          public Button showButtonLogin
41          {
42              get { return btnLogin; }
43              set { btnLogin = value; }
44          }
45
46          public Button showButtonTuition
47          {
48              get { return btnTuition; }
49              set { btnTuition = value; }
50          }
51
52          public Button showButtonSetting
53          {
54              get { return btnSetting; }
55              set { btnSetting = value; }
56          }
```

```
57
58    private void FormMain_Load(object sender, EventArgs e)
59    {
60        btnLibrary.Enabled = false;
61        btnInventory.Enabled = false;
62        btnAcademy.Enabled = false;
63        btnTuition.Enabled = false;
64        btnSetting.Enabled = false;
65        btnExit.Enabled = true;
66    }
67
68    private void btnLogin_Click(object sender, EventArgs e)
69    {
70        FormLogin formlogin = new FormLogin();
71        formlogin.Show();
72        this.Hide();
73    }
74
75    private void btnExit_Click(object sender, EventArgs e)
76    {
77        //this.Close();
78        Application.Exit();
79    }
80
81    private void btnLibrary_Click(object sender, EventArgs e)
82    {
83        FormTitle frm = new FormTitle();
84        frm.Show();
85    }
86    }
87 }
```

Step 2   In **FormTitle.cs**, define **LoginState** method to disable a number of buttons if user, admin, or boss logins:

```
1    private void LoginState()
2    {
3        // If user logins
4        if (Balige_HighSchool_DMBS.Global_Var.LoginState == 1)
5        {
6            SetState("View");
7            btnEdit.Enabled = false;
8            btnAddNew.Enabled = false;
9            btnAuthor.Enabled = false;
10           btnPublisher.Enabled = false;
11           btnDelete.Enabled = false;
12       }
13
14       // If admin logins
15       else if (Balige_HighSchool_DMBS.Global_Var.LoginState == 2)
```

```
16      {
17          SetState("View");
18          btnAddNew.Enabled = false;
19          btnDelete.Enabled = false;
20      }
21
22      // If boss logins
23      else if (Balige_HighSchool_DMBS.Global_Var.LoginState == 3)
24      {
25          SetState("View");
26      }
27  }
```

Step 3   Call **LoginState** method in **Load** event of **FormTitle** in line 99 as follows:

```
1   private void FormTitle_Load(object sender, EventArgs e)
2   {
3       try
4       {
5           // Connects to database
6           connTitle = new SqlConnection("Data Source=.\\SQLEXPRESS;
7               AttachDbFilename=D:\\Database\\DBMS.mdf;
8               Integrated Security = True; Connect Timeout = 30;
9               User Instance = True");
10
11          connTitle.Open();
12
13          // Creates Command object
14          commandTitle = new
15              SqlCommand("SELECT * FROM Title ORDER BY BookTitle",
16              connTitle);
17
18          // Creates DataAdapter/DataTable objects
19          adapterTitle = new SqlDataAdapter();
20          adapterTitle.SelectCommand = commandTitle;
21          tableTitle = new DataTable();
22          adapterTitle.Fill(tableTitle);
23
24          // Binds controls to data table
25          txtBookTitle.DataBindings.Add("Text", tableTitle,
26              "BookTitle");
27          dtpPublishYear.DataBindings.Add("Text", tableTitle,
28              "PublishYear");
29          txtISBN.DataBindings.Add("Text", tableTitle, "ISBN");
30          txtDescription.DataBindings.Add("Text", tableTitle,
31              "Description");
32          txtNote.DataBindings.Add("Text", tableTitle, "Note");
33          txtSubject.DataBindings.Add("Text", tableTitle, "Subject");
34          txtComment.DataBindings.Add("Text", tableTitle, "Comment");
35
```

```
36          // Sets data update manager
37          managerTitle =
38              (CurrencyManager)this.BindingContext[tableTitle];
39
40          commandPublisher = new
41              SqlCommand("SELECT * FROM Publisher ORDER BY Name",
42              connTitle);
43          adapterPublisher = new SqlDataAdapter();
44          adapterPublisher.SelectCommand = commandPublisher;
45          tablePublisher = new DataTable();
46          adapterPublisher.Fill(tablePublisher);
47          cboPublisher.DataSource = tablePublisher;
48          cboPublisher.DisplayMember = "Name";
49          cboPublisher.ValueMember = "PublisherID";
50          cboPublisher.DataBindings.Add("SelectedValue",
51              tableTitle, "PublisherID");
52
53          // Populates combo box cboPublisher
54          cboAuthorArr[0] = cboAuthor1;
55          cboAuthorArr[1] = cboAuthor2;
56          cboAuthorArr[2] = cboAuthor3;
57          cboAuthorArr[3] = cboAuthor4;
58          commandAuthor = new
596             SqlCommand("SELECT * FROM Author ORDER BY Name",
0               connTitle);
61          adapterAuthor = new SqlDataAdapter();
62          adapterAuthor.SelectCommand = commandAuthor;
63
64          for (int i = 0; i < 4; i++)
65          {
66              // Creates author table array
67              tableAuthorArr[i] = new DataTable();
68              adapterAuthor.Fill(tableAuthorArr[i]);
69              cboAuthorArr[i].DataSource = tableAuthorArr[i];
70              cboAuthorArr[i].DisplayMember = "Name";
71              cboAuthorArr[i].ValueMember = "AuthorID";
72              // deselects
73              cboAuthorArr[i].SelectedIndex = -1;
74          }
75      }
76      catch (Exception ex)
77      {
78          MessageBox.Show(ex.Message, "Error Creating Title table.",
79              MessageBoxButtons.OK, MessageBoxIcon.Error);
80          return;
81      }
82
83      this.Show();
84      SetState("View");
85
86      // Creates 26 search buttons
```

```
87    createSearchButton();
88
89    // Creates SQLAll
90    SQLAll = createSQLStatement();
91
92    // Clicks all records when form starts
93    btnAll.Click += new System.EventHandler(this.btnSQL_Click);
94    btnAll.PerformClick();
95    SetText();
96    GetAuthor();
97
98    // Determines who logins
99    LoginState();
100 }
```

Step 5   Run application. Try to login as user. Then click on **Library DBMS** and you will see
a number of button controls are disabled as shown in Figure 4.13.

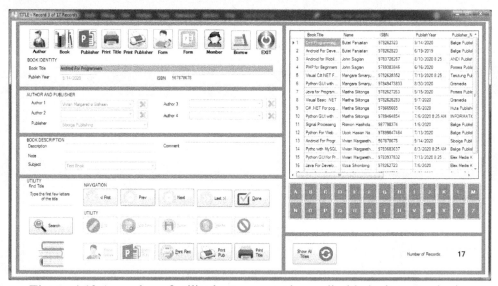

Figure 4.13 A number of utility button controls are disabled when user logins

Quit application. Run again the application. Try to login as admin. Then click on
Library DBMS and you will see that only **Edit** button control is enabled as shown in
Figure 4.14.

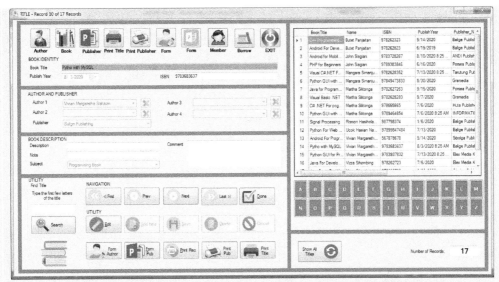

Figure 4.14 Only Edit button is enabled when admin logins

Quit application. Run again the application. Try to login as boss. Then click on
Library DBMS and you will see that all utility button controls (edit, add new, and
delete) are enabled as shown in Figure 4.15.

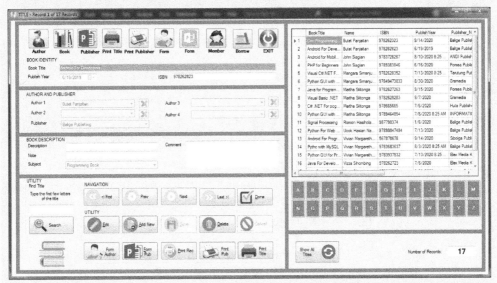

Figure 4.15 All utility button controls (edit, add new, and delete) are enabled

4.11 Tutorial Steps of Creating Form for Member Table: Interface

Step 1   In this tutorial, you will build such a form for **Member** table. This table has twelve fields: **MemberID**, **FirstName**, **LastName**, **BirthDate**, **Status**, **Ethnicity**, **Nationality**, **Mobile**, **Phone**, **Religion**, **Gender**, and **PhotoFile**).

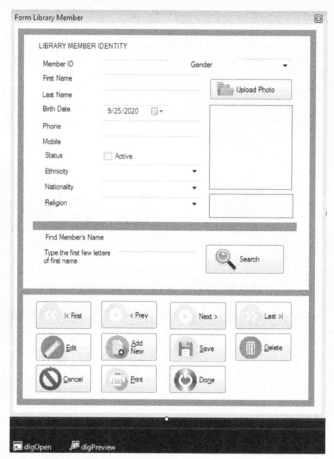

Figure 4.16 Design of member's library form

You need an input form so that user can edit existing records, delete records, or add new records. The form will also have the capability of navigating from one record to another. The steps that need to be done are as follows.

Start a new Visual C# application. You need thirteen label controls, one picture box, six text boxes, four comboxes, one check box, one date time picker, one openfiledialog, and one printpreviewdialog. You also need four buttons for navigation, six buttons for controlling editing features, one button for searching member's name, and one button to upload member's photo. Place these controls on the form. The complete form looks as shown in Figure 4.16.

Step 2   Set the properties of each control as follows:

Form1 Control

Name	FormMember
BackColor	Control
FormBorderStyle	FixedSingle
StartPosition	CenterScreen
Text	Form Library Member

label1 Control

Text	Member ID

textBox1 Control

Name	txtMemberID
ReadOnly	True

label2 Control

Text	Gender

checkbox1 Control

Text	Gender
BackColor	White
Items	{Male, Female}

label3 Control

Text	First Name

textBox2 Control

Name	txtFirstName

label4 Control

Text	Last Name

textBox3 Control

Name	txtLastName

label5 Control

Text	Birth Date

dateTimePicker1 Control

Name	dtpBirthDate
Format	short

label6 Control

Text	Phone

textBox4 Control

Name	txtPhone

label7 Control

Text	Mobile

textBox5 Control

Name	txtMobile

label8 Control	
Text	Status

checkbox1 Control	
Name	chkStatus
Text	Active

label9 Control	
Text	Ethnicity

checkbox2 Control	
Name	cboEthnicity
Items	{Jawa, Sasak, Sunda, Batak, Betawi, Minang, Papua Bima, Melayu}

label10 Control	
Text	Nationality

checkbox3 Control	
Name	cboNationality
Items	{ Indonesia, Inggris Jepang, Amerika Korea Selatan, Malaysia, Singapur Vietnam}

label11 Control	
Text	Religion

checkbox4 Control	
Name	cboReligion
Items	{ Islam, Kristen Protestan, Kristen Katolik, Buddha, Hindu, Konguchu, Kepercayaan}

label12 Control	
Name	lblPhotoFile

pictureBox1 Control	
Name	picMember
SizeMode	StretchImage

label13 Control	

Text	Type the first few letters of first name

textBox6 Control	
Name	txtFind

button1 Control	
Name	btnFirst
Text	|< First

button2 Control	
Name	btnPrev
Text	< Prev

button3 Control	
Name	btnNext
Text	Next >

button4 Control	
Name	btnLast
Text	Last >|

button5 Control	
Name	btnSearch
Text	Search

button6 Control	
Name	btnEdit
Text	&Edit

button7 Control	
Name	btnSave
Text	&Save

button8 Control	
Name	btnCancel
Text	&Cancel

button9 Control	
Name	btnAddNew
Text	&Add New

button10 Control	
Name	btnDelete
Text	&Delete

button11 Control	
Name	btnDone
Text	Do&ne

button12 Control	
Name	btnUpload
Text	&Upload Photo

button13 Control	
Name	btnPrint
Text	&Print

openFileDialog1 Control	
Name	dlgOpen

printPreviewDialog1 Control	
Name	dlgPreview

Step 3   You will add features to this member form gradually. At this point, you will add code to construct the data table and to navigate the records in the **Member** table. Add these lines of code at the top of the window:

```
1  using System.Data.SqlClient;
2  using System.IO;
3  using System.Drawing.Printing;
```

Step 4   Write the following form-level declarations for creating data objects:

```
1  SqlConnection connBook;
2  SqlCommand commandMember;
3  SqlDataAdapter adapterMember;
4  DataTable tableMember;
5  CurrencyManager managerMember;
```

Step 5   Add the following code to the **FormMember_Load** event method:

```
1   private void FormMember_Load(object sender, EventArgs e)
2   {
3       try
4       {
5           // Connects to database
6           connBook = new SqlConnection("Data Source=.\\SQLEXPRESS;
7               AttachDbFilename=D:\\Database\\DBMS.mdf;
8               Integrated Security = True; Connect Timeout = 30;
9               User Instance = True");
10
11          // Opens connection
12          connBook.Open();
13
14          // Creates Command object
15          commandMember = new SqlCommand(
16              "SELECT * FROM Member ORDER BY FirstName", connBook);
17
18          // Creates DataAdapter/DataTable objects
19          adapterMember = new SqlDataAdapter();
20          adapterMember.SelectCommand = commandMember;
21          tableMember = new DataTable();
```

```
22      adapterMember.Fill(tableMember);
23
24      // Binds controls to data table
25      txtMemberID.DataBindings.Add("Text",
26          tableMember, "MemberID");
27      txtFirstName.DataBindings.Add("Text",
28          tableMember, "FirstName");
29      txtLastName.DataBindings.Add("Text",
30          tableMember, "LastName");
31      dtpBirthDate.DataBindings.Add("Text",
32          tableMember, "BirthDate");
33      lblPhotoFile.DataBindings.Add("Text",
34          tableMember, "PhotoFile");
35      txtPhone.DataBindings.Add("Text", tableMember, "Phone");
36      txtMobile.DataBindings.Add("Text", tableMember, "Mobile");
37      chkStatus.DataBindings.Add("Checked",
38          tableMember, "Status");
39      cboEthnicity.DataBindings.Add("Text",
40          tableMember, "Ethnicity");
41      cboNationality.DataBindings.Add("Text",
42          tableMember, "Nationality");
43      cboReligion.DataBindings.Add("Text",
44          tableMember, "Religion");
45      cboGender.DataBindings.Add("Text", tableMember, "Gender");
46
47      // Creates data update
48      managerMember =
49          (CurrencyManager)BindingContext[tableMember];
50
51      DisplayPhoto();
52      this.Show();
53    }
54    catch (Exception ex)
55    {
56      MessageBox.Show(ex.Message,
57        "Error in reading Member table.",
58        MessageBoxButtons.OK, MessageBoxIcon.Error);
59      return;
60    }
}
```

The code above creates the data objects needed to open the database and construct the
Member table (includes all fields). The code above then binds the controls with the
update manager object (**CurrencyManager**).

Step 6   Define **DisplayPhoto** to display member's photo in **picMember**:

```
1   private void DisplayPhoto()
2   {
3       // Displays photo
```

```
4    if (!lblPhotoFile.Text.Equals(""))
5    {
6        try
7        {
8            picMember.Image = Image.FromFile(lblPhotoFile.Text);
9        }
10       catch (Exception ex)
11       {
12           MessageBox.Show(ex.Message, "Error Loading Photo File",
13               MessageBoxButtons.OK, MessageBoxIcon.Error);
14       }
15   }
16   else
17   {
18       string dir =
19           Path.GetDirectoryName(Application.ExecutablePath);
20       string filename = Path.Combine(dir, @"member.png");
21       picMember.Image = Image.FromFile(filename);
22   }
23 }
```

Step 7   Add the following code to **FormMember_FormClosing** event method to close the
database connection:

```
1  private void FormMember_FormClosing(object sender,
2  FormClosingEventArgs e)
3  {
4      // Closes connection to database
5      connBook.Close();
6
7      // Deletes objects
8      connBook.Dispose();
9      commandMember.Dispose();
10     adapterMember.Dispose();
11 }
```

Step 8   Write the following code for the **Click** event of the four navigation buttons:

```
1  private void btnPrev_Click(object sender, EventArgs e)
2  {
3      if (managerMember.Position == 0)
4      {
5          Console.Beep();
6      }
7      managerMember.Position--;
8      DisplayPhoto();
9  }
10
11 private void btnNext_Click(object sender, EventArgs e)
12 {
```

```
13      if (managerMember.Position == managerMember.Count - 1)
14      {
15          Console.Beep();
16      }
17      managerMember.Position++;
18      DisplayPhoto();
19  }
20
21  private void btnFirst_Click(object sender, EventArgs e)
22  {
23      managerMember.Position = 0;
24      DisplayPhoto();
25  }
26
27  private void btnLast_Click(object sender, EventArgs e)
28  {
29      managerMember.Position = managerMember.Count - 1;
30      DisplayPhoto();
31  }
```

Step 9   Insert some data into **Member** table using **Visual C#** as shown in Figure 4.17.

Figure 4.17 Inserting some data into **Member** table

Step 10 Save and run the application. What is displayed first is the first record in **Member** table. Click on four navigation buttons to prove the result.

Figure 4.18 Member form when it first runs

Figure 4.19 The result when user clicks **Last >|** button

4.12 Tutorial Steps of Creating Form for Member Table: Message Box

Step 1   There are two places where you can use the message box in **Member** table input form. One message box is provided after saving updates to let the user know that the save was successful and another message box is related to record deletion.

Use the following code in **btnSave_Click** event method:

```
1  private void btnSave_Click(object sender, EventArgs e)
2  {
3      MessageBox.Show("Records successfully saved", "Save",
4          MessageBoxButtons.OK, MessageBoxIcon.Information);
5  }
```

There will be more code in this event. The code implements only message box.

Step 2   Use this code on **btnDelete_Click** event method:

```
1  private void btnDelete_Click(object sender, EventArgs e)
2  {
3      DialogResult response;
4      response = MessageBox.Show("Dou you really want to delete this record?",
5          "Delete", MessageBoxButtons.YesNo, MessageBoxIcon.Question,
6          MessageBoxDefaultButton.Button2);
7  }
```

Step 3   Save the application and run it. Click on **Delete** button to see as shown in Figure 4.20.

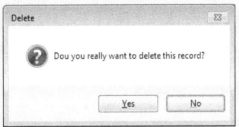

Figure 4.20 Message box is displayed when user clicks **Delete** button

4.13 Tutorial Steps of Creating Form for Member Table: Application State

Step 1   The **Member** form operates in one of three states: **View** state, **Add** state, or **Edit** state. In the **View** state, user can navigate one record to another, user can switch to **Edit** state, user can add and/or delete records, or user can exit the application.

In **Add** and **Edit** state, no navigation is made possible, data can be updated, and user can have access to **Save** and **Cancel** operations. Each of these steps can be implemented using the **Enabled** property of the button and the **ReadOnly** property of the text box. You use **TabIndex** (and **TabOrder**) to shift focus on the text box controls. You will use a method of moving from one state to another.

Clear all tab ordering for the ten buttons by setting the **TabStop** property to **False**. Additionally, set the **TabStop** property to **False** for the **Member ID** text box.

Step 2   Add a method named **SetState** as follows:

```
1   private void SetState(string stateStr) {
2       switch (stateStr)
3       {
4           case "View":
5               txtMemberID.BackColor = Color.Red;
6               txtMemberID.ForeColor = Color.Black;
7               txtFirstName.ReadOnly = true;
8               txtLastName.ReadOnly = true;
9               dtpBirthDate.Enabled = false;
10              txtPhone.ReadOnly = true;
11              txtMobile.ReadOnly = true;
12              chkStatus.Enabled = false;
13              cboEthnicity.Enabled = false;
14              cboNationality.Enabled = false;
15              cboReligion.Enabled = false;
16              cboGender.Enabled = false;
17              btnUpload.Enabled = false;
18              btnFirst.Enabled = true;
19              btnPrev.Enabled = true;
20              btnNext.Enabled = true;
21              btnLast.Enabled = true;
22              btnAddNew.Enabled = true;
23              btnSave.Enabled = false;
24              btnDelete.Enabled = true;
25              btnCancel.Enabled = false;
26              btnEdit.Enabled = true;
27              btnDone.Enabled = true;
28              txtFirstName.Focus();
29              break;
30
31          default: // Edit or Add
32              txtMemberID.ReadOnly = false;
33              txtMemberID.BackColor = Color.Red;
34              txtMemberID.ForeColor = Color.Black;
35              txtFirstName.ReadOnly = false;
36              txtLastName.ReadOnly = false;
37              dtpBirthDate.Enabled = true;
38              dtpBirthDate.Value = DateTime.Now;
39              txtPhone.ReadOnly = false;
40              txtMobile.ReadOnly = false;
41              chkStatus.Enabled = true;
42              cboEthnicity.Enabled = true;
```

```
43        cboNationality.Enabled = true;
44        cboNationality.SelectedIndex = -1;
45        cboReligion.Enabled = true;
46        cboReligion.SelectedIndex = -1;
47        cboGender.Enabled = true;
48        cboReligion.SelectedIndex = -1;
49        btnUpload.Enabled = true;
50        btnFirst.Enabled = false;
51        btnPrev.Enabled = false;
52        btnNext.Enabled = false;
53        btnLast.Enabled = false;
54        btnAddNew.Enabled = false;
55        btnSave.Enabled = true;
56        btnDelete.Enabled = false;
57        btnCancel.Enabled = true;
58        btnEdit.Enabled = false;
59        btnDone.Enabled = false;
60        btnPrint.Enabled = false;
61        txtFirstName.Focus();
62        break;
63    }
64 }
```

The code above specifies **View**, **Add**, or **Edit** state for the application. Pay attention to which buttons are available and which are not. Note that **Member ID** text box is given red back color if it is in **Add** or **Edit** state to indicate that it cannot be changed.

Step 3   Set the **View** state when the application first runs. Add the following code in line 53 to **FormMember_Load** event method:

```
1  private void FormMember_Load(object sender, EventArgs e)
2  {
3      try
4      {
5          // Connects to database
6          connBook = new SqlConnection("Data Source=.\\SQLEXPRESS;
7              AttachDbFilename=D:\\Database\\DBMS.mdf;
8              Integrated Security = True; Connect Timeout = 30;
9              User Instance = True");
10
11         // Opens connection
12         connBook.Open();
13
14         // Creates Command object
15         commandMember = new SqlCommand(
16             "SELECT * FROM Member ORDER BY FirstName", connBook);
17
18         // Creates DataAdapter/DataTable objects
19         adapterMember = new SqlDataAdapter();
20         adapterMember.SelectCommand = commandMember;
```

```
21    tableMember = new DataTable();
22    adapterMember.Fill(tableMember);
23
24    // Binds controls to data table
25    txtMemberID.DataBindings.Add("Text",
26        tableMember, "MemberID");
27    txtFirstName.DataBindings.Add("Text",
28        tableMember, "FirstName");
29    txtLastName.DataBindings.Add("Text",
30        tableMember, "LastName");
31    dtpBirthDate.DataBindings.Add("Text",
32        tableMember, "BirthDate");
33    lblPhotoFile.DataBindings.Add("Text",
34        tableMember, "PhotoFile");
35    txtPhone.DataBindings.Add("Text", tableMember, "Phone");
36    txtMobile.DataBindings.Add("Text", tableMember, "Mobile");
37    chkStatus.DataBindings.Add("Checked",
38        tableMember, "Status");
39    cboEthnicity.DataBindings.Add("Text",
40        tableMember, "Ethnicity");
41    cboNationality.DataBindings.Add("Text",
42        tableMember, "Nationality");
43    cboReligion.DataBindings.Add("Text",
44        tableMember, "Religion");
45    cboGender.DataBindings.Add("Text", tableMember, "Gender");
46
47    // Creates data update
48    managerMember =
49        (CurrencyManager)BindingContext[tableMember];
50
51    DisplayPhoto();
52    this.Show();
53    SetState("View");
54    }
55  catch (Exception ex)
56  {
57    MessageBox.Show(ex.Message,
58      "Error in reading Member table.",
59      MessageBoxButtons.OK, MessageBoxIcon.Error);
60    return;
61  }
62 }
```

Step 4   When **Add New** button is clicked, you need to switch to **Add** state. Add the following code to **btnAddNew_Click** event method:

```
1  private void btnAddNew_Click(object sender, EventArgs e)
2  {
3      SetState("Add");
4  }
```

Step 5   When **Edit** button is clicked, the application will be switched to **Edit** state. Add the
          following code to **btnEdit_Click** event method:

```
1  private void btnEdit_Click(object sender, EventArgs e)
2  {
3      SetState("Edit");
4  }
```

Figure 4.21 Member form is in **Add** or **Edit** state

Step 6   When **Cancel** or **Save** button is clicked (in **Add** or **Edit** state), application will return
          to the **View** state. Put this line of code in **btnCancel_Click** and **btnSave_Click** event
          methods:

```
1  private void btnCancel_Click(object sender, EventArgs e)
2  {
3      SetState("View");
4  }
5
6  private void btnSave_Click(object sender, EventArgs e)
7  {
8      SetState("View");
9  }
```

Step 7   Save and run the application. When user clicks the **Edit** or **Add New** button, you will
          see what is shown in Figure 4.21.

4.14 Tutorial Steps of Creating Form for Member Table: Error Trapping

Step 1   Modify **btnAddNew_Click**, **btnSave_Click**, and **btnDelete_Click** event methods to handle error trapping:

```csharp
private void btnAddNew_Click(object sender, EventArgs e)
{
    try
    {
        SetState("Add");
    }
    catch (Exception ex)
    {
        MessageBox.Show("Error adding new record.", "Error",
            MessageBoxButtons.OK, MessageBoxIcon.Error);
    }
}
```

```csharp
private void btnSave_Click(object sender, EventArgs e)
{
    try
    {
        MessageBox.Show("Record successfully saved", "Save",
        MessageBoxButtons.OK, MessageBoxIcon.Information);
        SetState("View");
    }
    catch (Exception ex)
    {
        MessageBox.Show("Error saving record.", "Error",
            MessageBoxButtons.OK, MessageBoxIcon.Error);
    }
}
```

```csharp
private void btnDelete_Click(object sender, EventArgs e)
{
    DialogResult response;
    response = MessageBox.Show("Dou you really want to delete this record?",
        "Delete", MessageBoxButtons.YesNo, MessageBoxIcon.Question,
        MessageBoxDefaultButton.Button2);
    if (response == DialogResult.No)
    {
        return;
    }

    try
    {

    }
    catch (Exception ex)
    {
        MessageBox.Show("Error deleting record.", "Error",
```

```
19              MessageBoxButtons.OK, MessageBoxIcon.Error);
20          }
21  }
```

4.15 Tutorial Steps of Creating Form for Member Table: Editing Record

Step 1   You will now add editing capability and other related capabilities to save and/or cancel edits. Before saving update into database, you need to validate data entered by user. In this case, you need to validate member name and year range of birth date. Define a method named **ValidateData** to validate data entered by user:

```
1   private bool ValidateData()
2   {
3       string message = "";
4       int yearInput, yearNow;
5       bool allOK = true;
6
7       // Checks name in txtFirstName and txtLastName
8       if (txtFirstName.Text.Trim().Equals("") &&
9           txtLastName.Text.Trim().Equals(""))
10      {
11          message = "You should enter first and last name." + "\r\n";
12          txtFirstName.Focus();
13          allOK = false;
14
15      }
16      // Checks birth date range
17      yearInput = dtpBirthDate.Value.Year;
18      yearNow = DateTime.Now.Year;
19
20      if (yearInput > yearNow || yearInput < yearNow - 150)
21      {
22          message += "Year should be between " +
23              (yearNow - 150).ToString() +
24              " and " + yearNow.ToString();
25          dtpBirthDate.Focus();
26          allOK = false;
27      }
28
29      if (!allOK)
30      {
31          MessageBox.Show(message, "Validation Error",
32              MessageBoxButtons.OK, MessageBoxIcon.Information);
33      }
34
35      return (allOK);
36  }
```

Step 2   Add a **KeyPress** event for the **txtFirstName** and **txtLastName** text boxes to accept
only letters:

```csharp
private void txtFirstName_KeyPress(object sender, KeyPressEventArgs e)
{
    if ((e.KeyChar >= 'a' && e.KeyChar <= 'z') ||
        (e.KeyChar >= 'A' && e.KeyChar <= 'Z') ||
        (int)e.KeyChar == 8 || (int)e.KeyChar == 32)
    {
        // Key can be accepted
        e.Handled = false;
    }
    else
    {
        e.Handled = true;
        Console.Beep();
    }

    if ((int)e.KeyChar == 13)
        txtLastName.Focus();
}
```

```csharp
private void txtLastName_KeyPress(object sender, KeyPressEventArgs e)
{
    if ((e.KeyChar >= 'a' && e.KeyChar <= 'z') ||
        (e.KeyChar >= 'A' && e.KeyChar <= 'Z') ||
        (int)e.KeyChar == 8 || (int)e.KeyChar == 32)
    {
        // Key can be accepted
        e.Handled = false;
    }
    else
    {
        e.Handled = true;
        Console.Beep();
    }

    if ((int)e.KeyChar == 13)
        txtLastName.Focus();
}
```

Step 3   Add a **KeyPress** event for the **txtMobile** and **txtPhone** text boxes to accept only digits:

```csharp
private void txtMobile_KeyPress(object sender, KeyPressEventArgs e)
{
    e.Handled = !char.IsDigit(e.KeyChar) &&
        !char.IsControl(e.KeyChar);

    if ((int)e.KeyChar == 13)
        chkStatus.Focus();
```

```
8              }
9
10   private void txtPhone_KeyPress(object sender, KeyPressEventArgs e)
11   {
12       e.Handled = !char.IsDigit(e.KeyChar) &&
13           !char.IsControl(e.KeyChar);
14
15       if ((int)e.KeyChar == 13)
16           txtMobile.Focus();
17   }
```

Step 4   Add a **KeyPress** event for other controls to move to the next control:

```
1    private void chkStatus_KeyPress(object sender, KeyPressEventArgs e)
2    {
3        if ((int)e.KeyChar == 13)
4            cboEthnicity.Focus();
5    }
6
7    private void cboEthnicity_KeyPress(object sender, KeyPressEventArgs e)
8    {
9        if ((int)e.KeyChar == 13)
10           cboNationality.Focus();
11   }
12
13   private void cboNationality_KeyPress(object sender, KeyPressEventArgs e)
14   {
15       if ((int)e.KeyChar == 13)
16           cboReligion.Focus();
17   }
18
19   private void cboReligion_KeyPress(object sender, KeyPressEventArgs e)
20   {
21       if ((int)e.KeyChar == 13)
22           txtFirstName.Focus();
23   }
```

Step 5   Add the following line of code to the form-level declaration:

```
1    string appState;
```

step 6   Add this code in line 2 to **SetState** method:

```
1    private void SetState(string stateStr) {
2        appState = stateStr;
3
4        switch (stateStr)
5        {
6            case "View":
7                txtMemberID.BackColor = Color.Red;
```

```
8          txtMemberID.ForeColor = Color.Black;
9          txtFirstName.ReadOnly = true;
10         txtLastName.ReadOnly = true;
11         dtpBirthDate.Enabled = false;
12         txtPhone.ReadOnly = true;
13         txtMobile.ReadOnly = true;
14         chkStatus.Enabled = false;
15         cboEthnicity.Enabled = false;
16         cboNationality.Enabled = false;
17         cboReligion.Enabled = false;
18         cboGender.Enabled = false;
19         btnUpload.Enabled = false;
20         btnFirst.Enabled = true;
21         btnPrev.Enabled = true;
22         btnNext.Enabled = true;
23         btnLast.Enabled = true;
24         btnAddNew.Enabled = true;
25         btnSave.Enabled = false;
26         btnDelete.Enabled = true;
27         btnCancel.Enabled = false;
28         btnEdit.Enabled = true;
29         btnDone.Enabled = true;
30         txtFirstName.Focus();
31         break;
32
33     default: // Edit or Add
34         txtMemberID.ReadOnly = false;
35         txtMemberID.BackColor = Color.Red;
36         txtMemberID.ForeColor = Color.Black;
37         txtFirstName.ReadOnly = false;
38         txtLastName.ReadOnly = false;
39         dtpBirthDate.Enabled = true;
40         dtpBirthDate.Value = DateTime.Now;
41         txtPhone.ReadOnly = false;
42         txtMobile.ReadOnly = false;
43         chkStatus.Enabled = true;
44         cboEthnicity.Enabled = true;
45         cboNationality.Enabled = true;
46         cboNationality.SelectedIndex = -1;
47         cboReligion.Enabled = true;
48         cboReligion.SelectedIndex = -1;
49         cboGender.Enabled = true;
50         cboReligion.SelectedIndex = -1;
51         btnUpload.Enabled = true;
52         btnFirst.Enabled = false;
53         btnPrev.Enabled = false;
54         btnNext.Enabled = false;
55         btnLast.Enabled = false;
56         btnAddNew.Enabled = false;
57         btnSave.Enabled = true;
58         btnDelete.Enabled = false;
```

```
59          btnCancel.Enabled = true;
60          btnEdit.Enabled = false;
61          btnDone.Enabled = false;
62          txtFirstName.Focus();
63          break;
64      }
65  }
```

Step 7   Modify **btnSave_Click** event method to save the change and reposition the pointer to the record just edited:

```
1   private void btnSave_Click(object sender, EventArgs e)
2   {
3       if (!ValidateData())
4       {
5           return;
6       }
7
8       string nameSaved = txtFirstName.Text;
9       int rowSaved;
10
11      try
12      {
13          managerMember.EndCurrentEdit();
14
15          if (appState.Equals("Add"))
16          {
17              tableMember.Rows[managerMember.Count - 1]["Status"] =
18                  chkStatus.Checked;
19              chkStatus.DataBindings.Add("Checked",
20                  tableMember, "Status");
21          }
22
23          tableMember.DefaultView.Sort = "FirstName";
24          rowSaved = tableMember.DefaultView.Find(nameSaved);
25          managerMember.Position = rowSaved;
26
27          MessageBox.Show("Records successfully saved", "Save",
28              MessageBoxButtons.OK, MessageBoxIcon.Information);
29
30          SetState("View");
31      }
32      catch (Exception ex)
33      {
34          MessageBox.Show("Error saving record.", "Error",
35              MessageBoxButtons.OK, MessageBoxIcon.Error);
36      }
37  }
```

Step 8   Modify **btnCancel_Click** event method to restore controls if the edit is canceled:

```
1  private void btnCancel_Click(object sender, EventArgs e)
2  {
3      managerMember.CancelCurrentEdit();
4
5      SetState("View");
6      DisplayPhoto();
7  }
```

Figure 4.22 Editing operation is successfully performed

Step 9   Add the following code in line to the **FormMember_FormClosing** method to save
any changes to the database file:

```
1   private void FormMember_FormClosing(object sender,
2   FormClosingEventArgs e)
3   {
4       try
5       {
6           // Saves changes into database
7           SqlCommandBuilder memberAdapterCommand =
8               new SqlCommandBuilder(adapterMember);
9           adapterMember.Update(tableMember);
10      }
11      catch (Exception ex)
12      {
13          MessageBox.Show("Error saving database into file: \r\n" +
14              ex.Message, "Saving Error", MessageBoxButtons.OK,
```

```
15              MessageBoxIcon.Error);
16          }
17
18          // Closes connection to database
19          connBook.Close();
20
21          // Deletes objects
22          connBook.Dispose();
23          commandMember.Dispose();
24          adapterMember.Dispose();
25      }
```

Step 10   Define Click event of **btnUpload** as follows:

```
1    private void btnUpload_Click(object sender, EventArgs e)
2    {
3        try
4        {
5            if (dlgOpen.ShowDialog() == DialogResult.OK)
6            {
7                lblPhotoFile.Text = dlgOpen.FileName;
8                DisplayPhoto();
9            }
10       }
11       catch (Exception ex)
12       {
13           MessageBox.Show(ex.Message, "Error in loading photo",
14               MessageBoxButtons.OK, MessageBoxIcon.Error);
15       }
16   }
```

Step 11   Save and run the application. Make sure Edit feature is working properly. Try changing
           member name or filling other fields. Make sure the **Cancel** button is working properly.
           This is shown in Figure 4.22.

4.16 Tutorial Steps of Creating Form for Member Table: Adding New Record

Step 1   You now implement the capability on the form to add new records to the database.
           Add the following line of code to the form-level declaration:

```
1    int myBookmark;
```

Figure 4.23 The new record has been successfully saved into the database

Step 2   Modify **btnAddNew_Click** event method to add a new record by adding code in line 5-9:

```
1   private void btnAddNew_Click(object sender, EventArgs e)
2   {
3       try
4       {
5           // Deletes binding from checkbox chkStatus
6           chkStatus.DataBindings.Clear();
7           chkStatus.Checked = false;
8
9           lblPhotoFile.Text = "";
10          DisplayPhoto();
11
12          myBookmark = managerMember.Position;
13          managerMember.AddNew();
14          SetState("Add");
15      }
16      catch (Exception ex)
17      {
18          MessageBox.Show("Error adding new record.", "Error",
19              MessageBoxButtons.OK, MessageBoxIcon.Error);
20      }
21  }
```

Step 3   Modify **btnCancel_Click** event method to differentiate between cancellation during
Edit mode and **Add** mode by adding code in line 5-10:

```
1   private void btnCancel_Click(object sender, EventArgs e)
2   {
3       managerMember.CancelCurrentEdit();
4
5       if (appState.Equals("Add"))
6       {
7           managerMember.Position = myBookmark;
8           chkStatus.DataBindings.Add("Checked",
9               tableMember, "Status");
10      }
11      SetState("View");
12      DisplayPhoto();
13  }
```

Step 4   Save and run the application. Click **Add New** button. Note that all text boxes are blank
(including **Member ID** text box. Fill first name, last name, and other fields, then click
Save. New record has been successfully saved as shown in Figure 4.23.

4.17 Tutorial Steps of Creating Form for Member Table: Deleting Record

Step 1   You will now add the capability to delete records from **Member** table. Modify the
btnDelete_Click event method by adding code in line 14 to delete records if the user
responds to **Yes** in the message box:

```
1   private void btnDelete_Click(object sender, EventArgs e)
2   {
3       DialogResult response;
4       response = MessageBox.Show("Dou you really want to delete this record?",
5           "Delete", MessageBoxButtons.YesNo, MessageBoxIcon.Question,
6           MessageBoxDefaultButton.Button2);
7       if (response == DialogResult.No)
8       {
9           return;
10      }
11
12      try
13      {
14          managerMember.RemoveAt(managerMember.Position);
15      }
16      catch (Exception ex)
17      {
18          MessageBox.Show("Error deleting record.", "Error",
19              MessageBoxButtons.OK, MessageBoxIcon.Error);
20      }
```

```
21  }
```

Step 2   Save the application and run it. Make sure the **Yes** and **No** responses in the message box give correct results. Delete only those records you added using **Add New** button.

4.18 Tutorial Steps of Creating Form for Member Table: Stopping Application

Step 1   Add the following code in line 4-12 and line 34 to **FormMember_FormClosing** event method to ensure user doesn't close the application during **Edit** or **Add** mode:

```
1   private void FormMember_FormClosing(object sender,
2   FormClosingEventArgs e)
3   {
4       if (appState.Equals("Edit") || appState.Equals("Add"))
5       {
6           MessageBox.Show(
7               "You should finish editing before closing application.",
8               "", MessageBoxButtons.OK, MessageBoxIcon.Information);
9           e.Cancel = true;
10      }
11      else
12      {
13          try
14          {
15              // Saves changes into
16              SqlCommandBuilder memberAdapterCommand =
17                  new SqlCommandBuilder(adapterMember);
18              adapterMember.Update(tableMember);
19          }
20          catch (Exception ex)
21          {
22              MessageBox.Show("Error saving database into file: \r\n" +
23                  ex.Message, "Error Saving", MessageBoxButtons.OK,
24                  MessageBoxIcon.Error);
25          }
26
27          // Closes connection to database
28          connBook.Close();
29
30          // Deletes objects
31          connBook.Dispose();
32          commandMember.Dispose();
33          adapterMember.Dispose();
34      }
35  }
```

Step 2   Put this code in **btnDone_Click** event method:

```
1   private void btnDone_Click(object sender, EventArgs e)
2   {
3       this.Close();
4   }
```

Step 3   Save and run the application. Make sure the **Done** button is working properly. Make sure the user cannot close the application in **Edit** or **Add** mode.

4.19 Tutorial Steps of Searching Capability

Step 1   In the **SetState** method, enable group box control in **View** mode and disable it in **Add** and **Edit** mode. Use its **Enabled** property.

Figure 4.24 Member's name search feature added

Step 3   Add the following code to **btnSearch_Click** event method:

```
1   private void btnSearch_Click(object sender, EventArgs e)
2   {
3       if (txtFind.Text.Equals(""))
4       {
5           return;
6       }
```

```
7
8       int rowSaved = managerMember.Position;
9       DataRow[] rowFound;
10      tableMember.DefaultView.Sort = "FirstName";
11      rowFound = tableMember.Select("FirstName LIKE '" +
12          txtFind.Text + "*'");
13
14      if (rowFound.Length == 0)
15      {
16          managerMember.Position = rowSaved;
17      }
18      else
19      {
20          managerMember.Position =
21              tableMember.DefaultView.Find(rowFound[0][" FirstName "]);
22          DisplayPhoto();
23      }
24  }
```

Step 4   Save and run the application. Try searching by providing the first or two letters of the member's name, as shown in Figure 4.24.

4.20 Tutorial Steps of Adding Search Buttons

Step 1   Add a button control on the form. Set its **Name** property as **btnAll** and its **Text** property as **Show All Members**. You add another **DataGridView** control and set its **Name** property as **grdMember**. You also need to add a label and set its **Text** property as **Number of Records:**. Then add a textbox on the form. Set its **Name** property as **txtNumberRecord**. The resulting form is shown in Figure 4.25.

Step 2   Add the following form-level declarations:

```
1   String SQLAll = "SELECT * FROM Member ";
2   Button[] buttonArr = new Button[26];
```

SQLAll is a variable that contains the default SQL statements, while **buttonArr** is an array containing the search buttons.

Step 3   Define a new method named **createSearchButton()** as follows:

```
1   private void createSearchButton()
2   {
3       // Creates search buttons
4       int w, lStart, l, t;
5       int btnHeight = 35; // by trial and error
6
7       // Search buttons
```

```
8      // Button width - 13 buttons in a row
9      w = Convert.ToInt32(grdMember.Width / 13);
10
11     // Aligns buttons
12     lStart = Convert.ToInt32((grdMember.Width));
13     l = lStart; t = grdMember.Top + grdMember.Height + 10;
14
15     // Creates and positions 26 buttons
16     for (int i = 0; i < 26; i++)
17     {
18         // Creates push button
19         buttonArr[i] = new Button();
20         buttonArr[i].TabStop = false;
21
22         // Sets Text property
23         buttonArr[i].Text = ((char)(65 + i)).ToString();
24         buttonArr[i].Font = new Font(buttonArr[i].Font.FontFamily,
25             9, FontStyle.Bold);
26
27         // Positions buttons
28         buttonArr[i].Width = w;
29         buttonArr[i].Height = btnHeight;
30         buttonArr[i].Left = l;
31         buttonArr[i].Top = t;
32
33         // Gives color
34         buttonArr[i].BackColor = Color.Red;
35         buttonArr[i].ForeColor = Color.White;
36
37         // Adds each button on form
38         this.Controls.Add(buttonArr[i]);
39
40         // Adds event handler
41         buttonArr[i].Click +=
42             new System.EventHandler(this.btnSQL_Click);
43         l += w+1;
44
45         if (i == 12)
46         {
47             // Next row
48             l = lStart; t += btnHeight;
49         }
50     }
51 }
```

This method creates search buttons A through Z using **buttonArrr** array. The code above then specifies the width of the button and places it on the form. Finally, the resulting records are displayed by programmatically clicking **btnSQL** button.

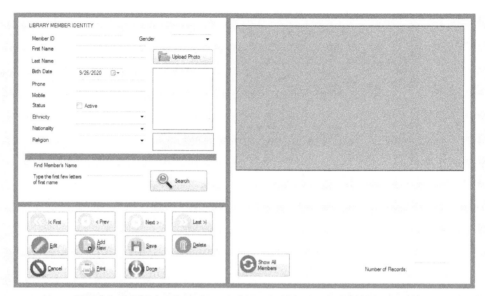

Figure 4.25 Member form after a number of controls added

Step 4   Write the code for **btnSQL_Click** event method (handle **Click** event for all search buttons) as follows:

```
1    private void btnSQL_Click(object sender, EventArgs e)
2    {
3        SqlCommand commResult = null;
4        SqlDataAdapter adapterResult = new SqlDataAdapter();
5        DataTable tableResult = new DataTable();
6        String StatemenSQL;
7
8        // Determines which button is clicked and creates SQL statement
9        Button buttonClicked = (Button)sender;
10       switch (buttonClicked.Text)
11       {
12           case "Show All Members":
13               StatemenSQL = SQLAll;
14               break;
15           case "Z":
16               // Z button is clicked
17               // Appends at SQLAll to limit records upto for item Z
18               StatemenSQL = SQLAll + " WHERE FirstName > 'Z' ";
19               break;
20           default:
21               // Letter keys except Z
22               // Appends at SQLAll to limit records
23               // for letter that is clicked
24               int idx = (int)(Convert.ToChar(buttonClicked.Text)) - 65;
25               StatemenSQL = SQLAll + " WHERE FirstName > '" +
26               buttonArr[idx].Text + " ' ";
```

```
27          StatemenSQL += " AND FirstName < '" +
28              buttonArr[idx + 1].Text + " ' ";
29
30          // Binds to controls
31          int rowSaved = managerMember.Position;
32          DataRow[] rowFound;
33          tableMember.DefaultView.Sort = "FirstName";
34          rowFound = tableMember.Select("FirstName LIKE '" +
35              buttonArr[idx].Text + "*'");
36
37          if (rowFound.Length == 0)
38          {
39              managerMember.Position = rowSaved;
40          }
41          else
42          {
43              managerMember.Position =
44                  tableMember.DefaultView.Find(
45                      rowFound[0]["FirstName"]);
46              DisplayPhoto();
47          }
48          break;
49      }
50  StatemenSQL += " ORDER BY FirstName";
51
52  // Applies SQL statement
53  try
54  {
55      // Creates Command and DataAdapater objects
56      commResult = new SqlCommand(StatemenSQL, connBook);
57      adapterResult.SelectCommand = commResult;
58      adapterResult.Fill(tableResult);
59
60      // Binds DataGridView with data table
61      grdMember.DataSource = tableResult;
62      txtNumberRecord.Text = tableResult.Rows.Count.ToString();
63  }
64
65  catch (Exception ex)
66  {
67      MessageBox.Show(ex.Message, "Error Processing SQL",
68          MessageBoxButtons.OK, MessageBoxIcon.Error);
69  }
70  commResult.Dispose();
71  adapterResult.Dispose();
72  tableResult.Dispose();
73 }
```

This method determines which button is clicked and forms an SQL statement. If the button with the **Text** property of the button is **"Show All Members"** is clicked, then all records will be displayed. When a key letter is clicked, the code determines which letter the user clicks on and attaches an additional test (using **AND**) to the **WHERE** field in the default SQL statement.

Step 5 Add the following code in line 55-60 to **FormMember_Load** event method. The code creates search buttons and perform **Click** event of **btnAll** programmatically:

```csharp
1   private void FormMember_Load(object sender, EventArgs e)
2   {
3       try
4       {
5           // Connects to database
6           connBook = new SqlConnection("Data Source=.\\SQLEXPRESS;
7               AttachDbFilename=D:\\Database\\DBMS.mdf;
8               Integrated Security = True; Connect Timeout = 30;
9               User Instance = True");
10
11          // Opens connection
12          connBook.Open();
13
14          // Creates Command object
15          commandMember = new SqlCommand(
16              "SELECT * FROM Member ORDER BY FirstName", connBook);
17
18          // Creates DataAdapter/DataTable objects
19          adapterMember = new SqlDataAdapter();
20          adapterMember.SelectCommand = commandMember;
21          tableMember = new DataTable();
22          adapterMember.Fill(tableMember);
23
24          // Binds controls to data table
25          txtMemberID.DataBindings.Add("Text",
26              tableMember, "MemberID");
27          txtFirstName.DataBindings.Add("Text",
28              tableMember, "FirstName");
29          txtLastName.DataBindings.Add("Text",
30              tableMember, "LastName");
31          dtpBirthDate.DataBindings.Add("Text",
32              tableMember, "BirthDate");
33          lblPhotoFile.DataBindings.Add("Text",
34              tableMember, "PhotoFile");
35          txtPhone.DataBindings.Add("Text", tableMember, "Phone");
36          txtMobile.DataBindings.Add("Text", tableMember, "Mobile");
37          chkStatus.DataBindings.Add("Checked",
38              tableMember, "Status");
39          cboEthnicity.DataBindings.Add("Text",
40              tableMember, "Ethnicity");
41          cboNationality.DataBindings.Add("Text",
42              tableMember, "Nationality");
```

```
43    cboReligion.DataBindings.Add("Text",
44        tableMember, "Religion");
45    cboGender.DataBindings.Add("Text", tableMember, "Gender");
46
47    // Creates data update
48    managerMember =
49        (CurrencyManager)BindingContext[tableMember];
50
51    DisplayPhoto();
52    this.Show();
53    SetState("View");
54
55    //Creates 26 search buttons
56    createSearchButton();
57
58    // Clicks all records when form starts
59    btnAll.Click += new System.EventHandler(this.btnSQL_Click);
60    btnAll.PerformClick();
61    }
62    catch (Exception ex)
63    {
64        MessageBox.Show(ex.Message,
65          "Error in reading Member table.",
66          MessageBoxButtons.OK, MessageBoxIcon.Error);
67        return;
68    }
69 }
```

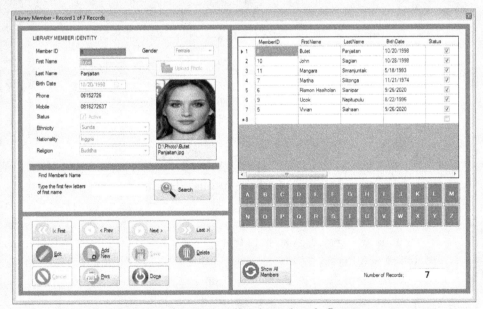

Figure 4.26 The application when it first runs

Step 6   Define **RowPostPaint** event of **grdMember** control to give it a row numbering:

```
1   private void grdMember_RowPostPaint(object sender,
2   DataGridViewRowPostPaintEventArgs e)
3   {
4       var grid = sender as DataGridView;
5       var rowIdx = (e.RowIndex + 1).ToString();
6
7       var centerFormat = new StringFormat()
8       {
9           // Aligns to middle
10          Alignment = StringAlignment.Center,
11          LineAlignment = StringAlignment.Center
12      };
13
14      var headerBounds = new Rectangle(e.RowBounds.Left,
15          e.RowBounds.Top, grid.RowHeadersWidth, e.RowBounds.Height);
16      e.Graphics.DrawString(rowIdx, this.Font,
17          SystemBrushes.ControlText, headerBounds, centerFormat);
18  }
```

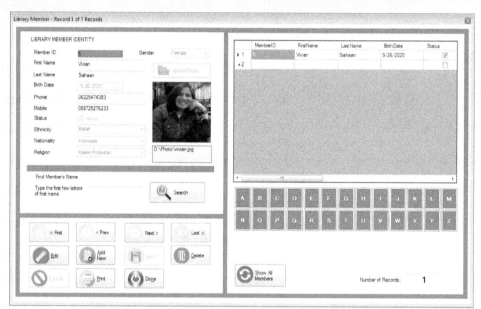

Figure 4.27 The results when the 'V' button is clicked

Step 7   Save and run the application. The result is shown in Figure 4.26. Notice how the search
buttons are created. Also note that all records are displayed initially. Click on one of
the search buttons. Only records with the member's initial matching the letter in the
clicked button will be displayed. Figure 4.27 is the query result when the 'V' button is
clicked.

4.21 Tutorial Steps of Reporting Members

Step 1 Now, you will add a feature to read all the data in the database. You need a database report. The report is quite simple. For each record, the data from each field will be displayed.

Add this line of code at the top of the code window:

```
1    using System.Drawing.Printing;
```

Step 2 Add the page number variable to the form level declaration:

```
1    int pageNumber;
```

Step 3 Add code in line 30 and line 63 to the **SetState** method to set **Enabled** property of **btnPrint** to **true** in **View** mode and **false** in **Add/Edit** mode.

```
1    private void SetState(string stateStr) {
2        appState = stateStr;
3
4        switch (stateStr)
5        {
6            case "View":
7                txtMemberID.BackColor = Color.Red;
8                txtMemberID.ForeColor = Color.Black;
9                txtFirstName.ReadOnly = true;
10                txtLastName.ReadOnly = true;
11                dtpBirthDate.Enabled = false;
12                txtPhone.ReadOnly = true;
13                txtMobile.ReadOnly = true;
14                chkStatus.Enabled = false;
15                cboEthnicity.Enabled = false;
16                cboNationality.Enabled = false;
17                cboReligion.Enabled = false;
18                cboGender.Enabled = false;
19                btnUpload.Enabled = false;
20                btnFirst.Enabled = true;
21                btnPrev.Enabled = true;
22                btnNext.Enabled = true;
23                btnLast.Enabled = true;
24                btnAddNew.Enabled = true;
25                btnSave.Enabled = false;
26                btnDelete.Enabled = true;
27                btnCancel.Enabled = false;
28                btnEdit.Enabled = true;
29                btnDone.Enabled = true;
30                btnPrint.Enabled = true;
31                txtFirstName.Focus();
32                break;
33
```

```
34    default: // Edit or Add
35        txtMemberID.ReadOnly = false;
36        txtMemberID.BackColor = Color.Red;
37        txtMemberID.ForeColor = Color.Black;
38        txtFirstName.ReadOnly = false;
39        txtLastName.ReadOnly = false;
40        dtpBirthDate.Enabled = true;
41        dtpBirthDate.Value = DateTime.Now;
42        txtPhone.ReadOnly = false;
43        txtMobile.ReadOnly = false;
44        chkStatus.Enabled = true;
45        cboEthnicity.Enabled = true;
46        cboNationality.Enabled = true;
47        cboNationality.SelectedIndex = -1;
48        cboReligion.Enabled = true;
49        cboReligion.SelectedIndex = -1;
50        cboGender.Enabled = true;
51        cboReligion.SelectedIndex = -1;
52        btnUpload.Enabled = true;
53        btnFirst.Enabled = false;
54        btnPrev.Enabled = false;
55        btnNext.Enabled = false;
56        btnLast.Enabled = false;
57        btnAddNew.Enabled = false;
58        btnSave.Enabled = true;
59        btnDelete.Enabled = false;
60        btnCancel.Enabled = true;
61        btnEdit.Enabled = false;
62        btnDone.Enabled = false;
63        btnPrint.Enabled = false;
64        txtFirstName.Focus();
65        break;
66    }
67 }
```

Step 4   Add the following code to **btnPrint_Click** event method:

```
1  private void btnPrint_Click(object sender, EventArgs e)
2  {
3      // Declares document
4      PrintDocument docMember;
5
6      // Creates document and gives it a name
7      docMember = new PrintDocument();
8      docMember.DocumentName = "Member Data";
9
10     // Adds code handler
11     docMember.PrintPage += new
12         PrintPageEventHandler(this.PrintMember);
13
14     // Prints document in preview control
```

```
15    pageNumber = 1;
16    int positionSaved = managerMember.Position;
17    dlgPreview.Document = docMember;
18    dlgPreview.ShowDialog();
19
20    // Deletes document when finished printing
21    docMember.Dispose();
22    managerMember.Position = positionSaved;
23
24    DisplayPhoto();
25  }
```

Step 5   Add the following code to **PrintMember** method:

```
1   private void PrintMember(object sender, PrintPageEventArgs e)
2   {
3       // Tracks every record, prints every record
4       managerMember.Position = pageNumber - 1;
5       DisplayPhoto();
6
7       Font myFont = new Font("Arial", 14, FontStyle.Bold);
8       int y = e.MarginBounds.Top + 50;
9
10      // Prints Header
11      e.Graphics.DrawString("Member's Data (" +
12          DateTime.Now.ToShortDateString() + ") - Page " +
13          pageNumber.ToString(), myFont, Brushes.Black,
14          e.MarginBounds.Left, y);
15      y += 2 * Convert.ToInt32(myFont.GetHeight(e.Graphics));
16
17      e.Graphics.DrawString("*****************************
18          ***************************", myFont, Brushes.Black,
19          e.MarginBounds.X, y);
20      y += Convert.ToInt32(myFont.GetHeight(e.Graphics));
21
22      // Prints photo (width 4 inci, height depends on
23      // height/width ratio of photo)
24      int h = Convert.ToInt32(
25          150 * picMember.Image.Height / picMember.Image.Width);
26      e.Graphics.DrawImage(picMember.Image,
27          e.MarginBounds.X, y, 150, h);
28
29      int slideRight = 175;
30
31      // Prints text information
32      myFont = new Font("Arial", 12, FontStyle.Regular);
33      e.Graphics.DrawString("Member ID:", myFont, Brushes.Black,
34          e.MarginBounds.X + slideRight, y);
35      e.Graphics.DrawString(txtMemberID.Text, myFont, Brushes.Black,
36          e.MarginBounds.X + slideRight + slideRight, y);
```

```
37      y += Convert.ToInt32(myFont.GetHeight(e.Graphics));
38
39      e.Graphics.DrawString("Full Name:", myFont, Brushes.Black,
40          e.MarginBounds.X + slideRight, y);
41      e.Graphics.DrawString(txtFirstName.Text + txtLastName.Text,
42          myFont, Brushes.Black, e.MarginBounds.X + 2*slideRight, y);
43      y += Convert.ToInt32(myFont.GetHeight(e.Graphics));
44
45      e.Graphics.DrawString("Gender:", myFont, Brushes.Black,
46          e.MarginBounds.X + slideRight, y);
47      e.Graphics.DrawString(cboGender.Text, myFont, Brushes.Black,
48          e.MarginBounds.X + 2 * slideRight, y);
49      y += Convert.ToInt32(myFont.GetHeight(e.Graphics));
50
51      e.Graphics.DrawString("Birth Date:", myFont, Brushes.Black,
52          e.MarginBounds.X + slideRight, y);
53      e.Graphics.DrawString(dtpBirthDate.Text, myFont, Brushes.Black,
54          e.MarginBounds.X + 2 * slideRight, y);
55      y += Convert.ToInt32(myFont.GetHeight(e.Graphics));
56
57      e.Graphics.DrawString("Phone:", myFont, Brushes.Black,
58          e.MarginBounds.X + slideRight, y);
59      e.Graphics.DrawString(txtPhone.Text, myFont, Brushes.Black,
60          e.MarginBounds.X + 2* slideRight, y);
61      y += Convert.ToInt32(myFont.GetHeight(e.Graphics));
62
63      e.Graphics.DrawString("Mobile:", myFont, Brushes.Black,
64          e.MarginBounds.X + slideRight, y);
65      e.Graphics.DrawString(txtMobile.Text, myFont,
66          Brushes.Black, e.MarginBounds.X + 2 * slideRight, y);
67      y += Convert.ToInt32(myFont.GetHeight(e.Graphics));
68
69      e.Graphics.DrawString("Status:", myFont, Brushes.Black,
70          e.MarginBounds.X + slideRight, y);
71      e.Graphics.DrawString(chkStatus.Text, myFont, Brushes.Black,
72          e.MarginBounds.X + 2 * slideRight, y);
73      y += Convert.ToInt32(myFont.GetHeight(e.Graphics));
74
75      e.Graphics.DrawString("Ethnicity:", myFont, Brushes.Black,
76          e.MarginBounds.X + slideRight, y);
77      e.Graphics.DrawString(cboEthnicity.Text, myFont, Brushes.Black,
78          e.MarginBounds.X + 2 * slideRight, y);
79      y += Convert.ToInt32(myFont.GetHeight(e.Graphics));
80
81      e.Graphics.DrawString("Nationality:", myFont, Brushes.Black,
82          e.MarginBounds.X + slideRight, y);
83      e.Graphics.DrawString(cboNationality.Text, myFont,
84          Brushes.Black, e.MarginBounds.X + 2 * slideRight, y);
85      y += Convert.ToInt32(myFont.GetHeight(e.Graphics));
86
87      e.Graphics.DrawString("Religion:", myFont, Brushes.Black,
```

```
88          e.MarginBounds.X + slideRight, y);
89      e.Graphics.DrawString(cboReligion.Text, myFont, Brushes.Black,
90          e.MarginBounds.X + 2 * slideRight, y);
91      y += Convert.ToInt32(myFont.GetHeight(e.Graphics));
92
93      Font myFont2 = new Font("Arial", 14, FontStyle.Bold);
94      e.Graphics.DrawString("***************************
95      ****************************", myFont2, Brushes.Black,
96          e.MarginBounds.X, y);
97
98      pageNumber++;
99      if (pageNumber <= managerMember.Count)
100         e.HasMorePages = true;
101     else
102     {
103         e.HasMorePages = false;
104         pageNumber = 1;
105     }
106 }
```

On each page, a header is printed along with the data fields and member's photo.

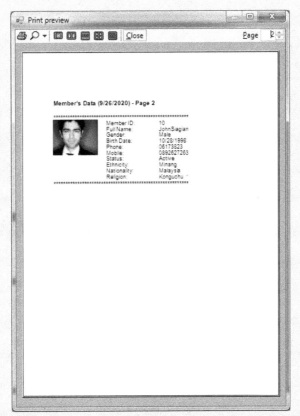

Figure 4.28 Each record in the table can now be printed

Step 6   Save and run the application. Click on the **Print** button. The print preview control will be displayed on all member pages, as shown in Figure 4.28.

4.22 Tutorial Steps of Creating Form for Borrow Table: Interface

Step 1   In this tutorial, you will build such a form for **Borrow** table. This table has seven fields: **BorrowID**, **MemberID**, **BorrowCode**, **ISBN**, **BorrowDate**, **ReturnDate**, and **Penalty**).

Figure 4.29 Design of book borrowal form

You need an input form so that user can edit existing records, delete records, or add new records. The form will also have the capability of navigating from one record to another. The steps that need to be done are as follows.

Start a new Visual C# application. You need twelve label controls, six text boxes, two comboxes, two date time pickers, one openfiledialog, and one printpreviewdialog. You also need four buttons for navigation, seven buttons for other utilities, one button for searching borrowal code, one button to generate borrowal code, one buton to open member form, one button to open title form, and one button to return book. Place these controls on the form. The complete form looks as shown in Figure 4.29.

Step 2   Set the properties of each control as follows:

Form1 Control	
Name	FormBorrow
BackColor	Control
FormBorderStyle	FixedSingle
StartPosition	CenterScreen
Text	Form Borrow

label1 Control	
Text	Borrow ID

textBox1 Control	
Name	txtBorrowID
ReadOnly	True

label2 Control	
Text	Borrowal Code

textBox2 Control	
Name	txtBorrowCode
ReadOnly	True

label3 Control	
Text	Borrower's Name

comboBox1 Control	
Name	cboMember

label4 Control	
Text	Borrow Date

dateTimePicker1 Control	
Name	dtpBorrow
Format	Short

label5 Control	
Text	Return Date

dateTimePicker2 Control	
Name	dtpReturn
Format	short

label6 Control	
Text	Book Borrowed

comboBox2 Control	
Name	cboBookBorrowed

label7 Control	
Text	ISBN

textBox3 Control	
Name	txtISBN
ReadOnly	True

label8 Control	
Text	Type a few first letters of borrowal code

textBox4 Control	
Name	txtSearch

label19 Control	
Text	Total Penalty

textBox5 Control	
Name	txtPenalty
BackColor	Gold
ReadOnly	True

label10 Control	
Text	Penalty/Day

textBox6 Control	
Name	txtPenaltyPerDay
Text	1000
BackColor	LightCyan

label11 Control	
Text	Assume that fine of Rp. 1000 per day if borrowing is more than one week

label12 Control	
Text	MAKE SURE the return date

pictureBox1 Control	
Name	picMember
SizeMode	StretchImage

label13 Control	
Text	Type the first few letters of first name

button1 Control	
Name	btnMember
Text	View/Edit/Add Member

button2 Control	
Name	btnBorrowalCode
Text	Borrowal Code

button3 Control	
Name	btnViewEditBook
Text	View/Edit Book

button4 Control	
Name	btnSearch
Text	Search

button5 Control	
Name	btnReturn
Text	Return Book

button6 Control	
Name	btnFirst
Text	|< First

button7 Control	
Name	btnPrev
Text	< Prev

button8 Control	
Name	btnNext
Text	Next >

button9 Control	
Name	btnLast
Text	Last >|

button10 Control	
Name	btnEdit
Text	&Edit

button11 Control	
Name	btnSave
Text	&Save

button12 Control	
Name	btnCancel
Text	&Cancel

button13 Control	
Name	btnAddNew
Text	&Add New

button14 Control	
Name	btnDelete
Text	&Delete

button15 Control	
Name	btnDone
Text	Do&ne

button16 Control	
Name	btnPrint
Text	&Print

openFileDialog1 Control	
Name	dlgOpen

printPreviewDialog1 Control	
Name	dlgPreview

Step 3   You will add features to this author form gradually. At this point, you will add code to
construct the data table and to navigate the records in the **Member** table. Add these
lines of code at the top of the window:

```
1    using System.Data.SqlClient;
2    using System.IO;
3    using System.Drawing.Printing;
```

Step 4   Write the following form-level declarations for creating data objects:

```
1    SqlConnection connBook;
2    SqlCommand commandBorrow;
3    SqlDataAdapter adapterBorrow;
4    DataTable tableBorrow;
5    CurrencyManager managerBorrow;
6
7    SqlCommand commandMember;
8    SqlDataAdapter adapterMember;
9    DataTable tableMember;
10
11   SqlCommand commandTitle;
12   SqlDataAdapter adapterTitle;
13   DataTable tableTitle;
```

Step 5   Add the following code to the **FormBorrow_Load** event method:

```
1    private void FormBorrow_Load(object sender, EventArgs e)
2    {
3        try
4        {
5            // Connects to database
6            connBook = new SqlConnection("Data Source=.\\SQLEXPRESS;
7                AttachDbFilename=D:\\Database\\DBMS.mdf;
8                Integrated Security = True; Connect Timeout = 30;
9                User Instance = True");
10
11           // Opens connection
12           connBook.Open();
13
14           // Creates Command object
15           commandBorrow = new SqlCommand(
16               "SELECT * FROM Borrow ORDER BY MemberID", connBook);
17
18           // Creates DataAdapter/DataTable objects
19           adapterBorrow = new SqlDataAdapter();
20           adapterBorrow.SelectCommand = commandBorrow;
21           tableBorrow = new DataTable();
22           adapterBorrow.Fill(tableBorrow);
23
24           // Binds controls to data table
```

```
25        txtBorrowID.DataBindings.Add("Text", tableBorrow, "BorrowID");
26        cboMember.DataBindings.Add("Text", tableBorrow, "MemberID");
27        dtpBorrow.DataBindings.Add("Text", tableBorrow, "BorrowDate");
28        dtpReturn.DataBindings.Add("Text", tableBorrow, "ReturnDate");
29        txtPenalty.DataBindings.Add("Text", tableBorrow, "Penalty");
30        txtBorrowCode.DataBindings.Add("Text", tableBorrow, "BorrowCode");
31
32        // Populates cboMember
33        commandMember = new SqlCommand(
34            "SELECT * FROM Member ORDER BY FirstName", connBook);
35        adapterMember = new SqlDataAdapter();
36        adapterMember.SelectCommand = commandMember;
37        tableMember = new DataTable();
38        adapterMember.Fill(tableMember);
39        cboMember.DataSource = tableMember;
40        cboMember.DisplayMember = "FirstName";
41        cboMember.ValueMember = "MemberID";
42        cboMember.DataBindings.Add("SelectedValue",
43            tableBorrow, "MemberID");
44
45        // Populates cboBookBorrowed and txtISBN
46        commandTitle = new SqlCommand(
47            "SELECT * FROM Title ORDER BY BookTitle", connBook);
48        adapterTitle = new SqlDataAdapter();
49        adapterTitle.SelectCommand = commandTitle;
50        tableTitle = new DataTable();
51        adapterTitle.Fill(tableTitle);
52        cboBookBorrowed.DataSource = tableTitle;
53        cboBookBorrowed.DisplayMember = "BookTitle";
54        cboBookBorrowed.ValueMember = "ISBN";
55        cboBookBorrowed.DataBindings.Add("SelectedValue",
56            tableBorrow, "ISBN");
57        txtISBN.DataBindings.Add("Text", tableBorrow, "ISBN");
58
59        // Creates data update
60        managerBorrow =
61            (CurrencyManager)BindingContext[tableBorrow];
62
63        this.Show();
64    }
65    catch (Exception ex)
66    {
67        MessageBox.Show(ex.Message, "Error in reading table.",
68            MessageBoxButtons.OK, MessageBoxIcon.Error);
69        return;
70    }
71 }
```

The code above creates the data objects needed to open the database and construct the **Borrow** table (includes all fields). The code above then binds the controls with the update manager object (**CurrencyManager**).

Step 6   Add the following code to **FormBorrow_FormClosing** event method to close the database connection:

```
private void FormBorrow_FormClosing(object sender,
FormClosingEventArgs e)
{
    // Closes connection to database
    connBook.Close();

    // Deletes objects
    connBook.Dispose();
    commandBorrow.Dispose();
    adapterBorrow.Dispose();
    commandMember.Dispose();
    adapterMember.Dispose();
    tableMember.Dispose();
    commandTitle.Dispose();
    adapterTitle.Dispose();
    tableTitle.Dispose();
}
```

Step 7   Write the following code for the **Click** event of the four navigation buttons:

```
private void btnPrev_Click(object sender, EventArgs e)
{
    if (managerBorrow.Position == 0)
    {
        Console.Beep();
    }
    managerBorrow.Position--;
}

private void btnNext_Click(object sender, EventArgs e)
{
    if (managerBorrow.Position == managerBorrow.Count - 1)
    {
        Console.Beep();
    }
    managerBorrow.Position++;
}

private void btnFirst_Click(object sender, EventArgs e)
{
    managerBorrow.Position = 0;
}
```

```
24  private void btnLast_Click(object sender, EventArgs e)
25  {
26      managerBorrow.Position = managerBorrow.Count - 1;
27  }
```

Step 8   Save and run the application. You will see the borrow form when it first runs as shown in Figure 4.30.

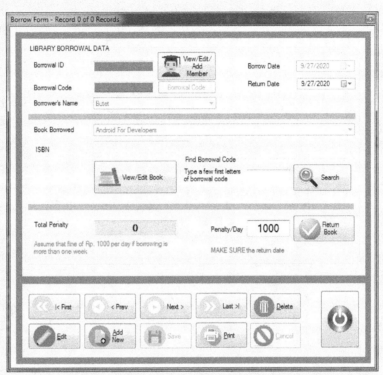

Figure 4.30 Borrow form when it first runs

4.23 Tutorial Steps of Creating Form for Borrow Table: Open Member and Title Forms

Step 1   Define **Click** event of **btnMember** to open Member form:

```
1  private void btnMember_Click(object sender, EventArgs e)
2  {
3      FormMember frmMember = new FormMember();
4      frmMember.Show();
5  }
```

Step 2   Define **Click** event of **btnViewEditBook** to open Title form:

```
1  private void btnViewEditBook_Click(object sender, EventArgs e)
2  {
```

```
3    FormTitle frmTitle = new FormTitle();
4    frmTitle.Show();
5    }
```

Step 3   Run application. Click on both buttons to see whether they work properly.

4.24 Tutorial Steps of Creating Form for Borrow Table: Generate Borrowal Code

Step 1   Define **Click** event of **btnBorrowalCode** to generate borrowal code:

```
1    private void btnBorrowalCode_Click(object sender, EventArgs e)
2    {
3        string borr_code = GenerateCode(8);
4        txtBorrowCode.Text = borr_code;
5    }
```

Figure 4.31 Generating borrowal code

Step 2   Define **GenerateCode** method as follows:

```
1    public static string GenerateCode(int length)
2    {
3        Random myRandom = new Random();
4        string chars =
5          "0123456789ABCDEFGHIJKLMNOPQRSTUVWXYZabcdefghijklmnopqrstuvwxyz";
6        StringBuilder result = new StringBuilder(length);
```

```
7
8        for (int i = 0; i < length; i++)
9        {
10           result.Append(chars[myRandom.Next(chars.Length)]);
11       }
12
13       return result.ToString();
14   }
```

Step 3   Run application. Click on **btnBorrowalCode** button to see the generated code as shown in Figure 4.31.

4.25 Tutorial Steps of Creating Form for Borrow Table: Message Box

Step 1   There are two places where you can use the message box in **Borrow** table input form. One message box is provided after saving updates to let the user know that the save was successful and another message box is related to record deletion.

Use the following code in **btnSave_Click** event method:

```
1   private void btnSave_Click(object sender, EventArgs e)
2   {
3       MessageBox.Show("Records successfully saved", "Save",
4           MessageBoxButtons.OK, MessageBoxIcon.Information);
5   }
```

There will be more code in this event. The code implements only message box.

Step 2   Use this code on **btnDelete_Click** event method:

```
1   private void btnDelete_Click(object sender, EventArgs e)
2   {
3       DialogResult response;
4       response = MessageBox.Show("Dou you really want to delete this record?",
5           "Delete", MessageBoxButtons.YesNo, MessageBoxIcon.Question,
6           MessageBoxDefaultButton.Button2);
7   }
```

Step 3   Save the application and run it. Click on **Delete** button to see as shown in Figure 4.32.

Figure 4.32 Message box is displayed when user clicks **Delete** button

4.26 Tutorial Steps of Creating Form for Borrow Table: Application State

Step 1   The **Borrow** form operates in one of three states: **View** state, **Add** state, or **Edit** state. In the **View** state, user can navigate one record to another, user can switch to **Edit** state, user can add and/or delete records, or user can exit the application.

In **Add** and **Edit** state, no navigation is made possible, data can be updated, and user can have access to **Save** and **Cancel** operations. Each of these steps can be implemented using the **Enabled** property of the button and the **ReadOnly** property of the text box. You use **TabIndex** (and **TabOrder**) to shift focus on the text box controls. You will use a method of moving from one state to another.

Clear all tab ordering for the ten buttons by setting the **TabStop** property to **False**. Additionally, set the **TabStop** property to **False** for the **Borrow ID** text box.

Step 2   Add a method named **SetState** as follows:

```csharp
private void SetState(string stateStr) {
    switch (stateStr)
    {
        case "View":
            txtBorrowID.BackColor = Color.Red;
            txtBorrowID.ForeColor = Color.Black;
            cboMember.Enabled = false;
            cboBookBorrowed.Enabled = false;
            dtpBorrow.Enabled = false;
            dtpReturn.Enabled = true;
            txtPenalty.ReadOnly = true;
            btnFirst.Enabled = true;
            btnPrev.Enabled = true;
            btnNext.Enabled = true;
            btnLast.Enabled = true;
            btnAddNew.Enabled = true;
            btnSave.Enabled = false;
            btnDelete.Enabled = true;
            btnCancel.Enabled = false;
            btnEdit.Enabled = true;
            btnDone.Enabled = true;
            btnReturn.Enabled = true;
            btnPrint.Enabled = true;
            btnBorrowalCode.Enabled = false;
            break;

        default: // Edit or Add
            txtBorrowID.ReadOnly = true;
            txtBorrowID.BackColor = Color.Red;
            txtBorrowID.ForeColor = Color.Black;
            cboMember.Enabled = true;
            cboBookBorrowed.Enabled = true;
```

```
29        dtpBorrow.Enabled = true;
30        dtpReturn.Enabled = true;
31        txtPenalty.ReadOnly = true;
32        btnFirst.Enabled = false;
33        btnPrev.Enabled = false;
34        btnNext.Enabled = false;
35        btnLast.Enabled = false;
36        btnAddNew.Enabled = false;
37        btnSave.Enabled = true;
38        btnDelete.Enabled = false;
39        btnCancel.Enabled = true;
40        btnEdit.Enabled = false;
41        btnDone.Enabled = false;
42        btnPrint.Enabled = false;
43        btnReturn.Enabled = false;
44        btnBorrowalCode.Enabled = true;
45        break;
      }
}
```

The code above specifies **View**, **Add**, or **Edit** state for the application. Pay attention
to which buttons are available and which are not. Note that **BorrowID** text box is given
red back color if it is in **Add** or **Edit** state to indicate that it cannot be changed.

Step 3   Set the **View** state when the application first runs. Add the following code in line 64
to **FormBorrow_Load** event method:

```
1   private void FormBorrow_Load(object sender, EventArgs e)
2   {
3       try
4       {
5           // Connects to database
6           connBook = new SqlConnection("Data Source=.\\SQLEXPRESS;
7               AttachDbFilename=D:\\Database\\DBMS.mdf;
8               Integrated Security = True; Connect Timeout = 30;
9               User Instance = True");
10
11          // Opens connection
12          connBook.Open();
13
14          // Creates Command object
15          commandBorrow = new SqlCommand(
16              "SELECT * FROM Borrow ORDER BY MemberID", connBook);
17
18          // Creates DataAdapter/DataTable objects
19          adapterBorrow = new SqlDataAdapter();
20          adapterBorrow.SelectCommand = commandBorrow;
21          tableBorrow = new DataTable();
22          adapterBorrow.Fill(tableBorrow);
23
24          // Binds controls to data table
25          txtBorrowID.DataBindings.Add("Text", tableBorrow, "BorrowID");
```

```
26      cboMember.DataBindings.Add("Text", tableBorrow, "MemberID");
27      dtpBorrow.DataBindings.Add("Text", tableBorrow, "BorrowDate");
28      dtpReturn.DataBindings.Add("Text", tableBorrow, "ReturnDate");
29      txtPenalty.DataBindings.Add("Text", tableBorrow, "Penalty");
30      txtBorrowCode.DataBindings.Add("Text", tableBorrow, "BorrowCode");
31
32      // Populates cboMember
33      commandMember = new SqlCommand(
34          "SELECT * FROM Member ORDER BY FirstName", connBook);
35      adapterMember = new SqlDataAdapter();
36      adapterMember.SelectCommand = commandMember;
37      tableMember = new DataTable();
38      adapterMember.Fill(tableMember);
39      cboMember.DataSource = tableMember;
40      cboMember.DisplayMember = "FirstName";
41      cboMember.ValueMember = "MemberID";
42      cboMember.DataBindings.Add("SelectedValue",
43          tableBorrow, "MemberID");
44
45      // Populates cboBookBorrowed and txtISBN
46      commandTitle = new SqlCommand(
47          "SELECT * FROM Title ORDER BY BookTitle", connBook);
48      adapterTitle = new SqlDataAdapter();
49      adapterTitle.SelectCommand = commandTitle;
50      tableTitle = new DataTable();
51      adapterTitle.Fill(tableTitle);
52      cboBookBorrowed.DataSource = tableTitle;
53      cboBookBorrowed.DisplayMember = "BookTitle";
54      cboBookBorrowed.ValueMember = "ISBN";
55      cboBookBorrowed.DataBindings.Add("SelectedValue",
56          tableBorrow, "ISBN");
57      txtISBN.DataBindings.Add("Text", tableBorrow, "ISBN");
58
59      // Creates data update
60      managerBorrow =
61          (CurrencyManager)BindingContext[tableBorrow];
62
63      this.Show();
64      SetState("View");
65  }
66  catch (Exception ex)
67  {
68      MessageBox.Show(ex.Message, "Error in reading table.",
69          MessageBoxButtons.OK, MessageBoxIcon.Error);
70      return;
71  }
72 }
```

Step 4   When **Add New** button is clicked, you need to switch to **Add** state. Add the following code to **btnAddNew_Click** event method:

```
1   private void btnAddNew_Click(object sender, EventArgs e)
2   {
3       SetState("Add");
4   }
```

Figure 4.33 Member form is in **View** state when it first runs

Step 5   When **Edit** button is clicked, the application will be switched to **Edit** state. Add the following code to **btnEdit_Click** event method:

```
1   private void btnEdit_Click(object sender, EventArgs e)
2   {
3       SetState("Edit");
4   }
```

Step 6   When **Cancel** or **Save** button is clicked (in **Add** or **Edit** state), application will return to the **View** state. Put this line of code in **btnCancel_Click** and **btnSave_Click** event methods:

```
1   private void btnCancel_Click(object sender, EventArgs e)
2   {
3       SetState("View");
4   }
5
6   private void btnSave_Click(object sender, EventArgs e)
7   {
```

```
8       SetState("View");
9   }
```

Step 7   Save and run the application. You will see the application in its initial state (**View** state) as shown in Figure 4.33.

When user clicks the **Edit** or **Add New** button, you will see what is shown in Figure 4.34.

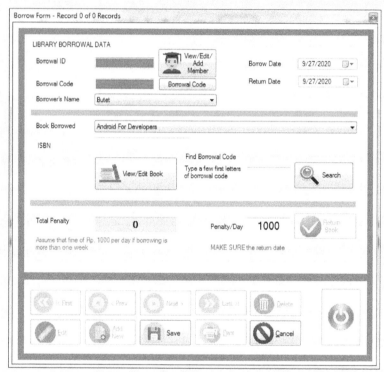

Figure 4.34 Member form is in **Add** or **Edit** state

4.27 Tutorial Steps of Creating Form for Borrow Table: Error Trapping

Step 1   Modify **btnAddNew_Click**, **btnSave_Click**, and **btnDelete_Click** event methods to handle error trapping:

```
1   private void btnAddNew_Click(object sender, EventArgs e)
2   {
3       try
4       {
5           SetState("Add");
6       }
7       catch (Exception ex)
8       {
9           MessageBox.Show("Error adding new record.", "Error",
```

```
10          MessageBoxButtons.OK, MessageBoxIcon.Error);
11      }
12  }
```

```
1   private void btnSave_Click(object sender, EventArgs e)
2   {
3       try
4       {
5           MessageBox.Show("Record successfully saved", "Save",
6           MessageBoxButtons.OK, MessageBoxIcon.Information);
7           SetState("View");
8       }
9       catch (Exception ex)
10      {
11          MessageBox.Show("Error saving record.", "Error",
12              MessageBoxButtons.OK, MessageBoxIcon.Error);
13      }
14  }
```

```
1   private void btnDelete_Click(object sender, EventArgs e)
2   {
3       DialogResult response;
4       response = MessageBox.Show("Dou you really want to delete this record?",
5           "Delete", MessageBoxButtons.YesNo, MessageBoxIcon.Question,
6           MessageBoxDefaultButton.Button2);
7       if (response == DialogResult.No)
8       {
9           return;
10      }
11
12      try
13      {
14
15      }
16      catch (Exception ex)
17      {
18          MessageBox.Show("Error deleting record.", "Error",
19              MessageBoxButtons.OK, MessageBoxIcon.Error);
20      }
21  }
```

4.28 Tutorial Step of Creating Form for Borrow Table: Calculate Penalty

Step 1   Define **Click** event of **btnReturn** to calculate penalty and delete corresponding record:

```
1   private void btnReturn_Click(object sender, EventArgs e)
2   {
3       dtpReturn.Enabled = true;
4
```

```
5    DateTime start = dtpBorrow.Value.Date;
6    DateTime last = dtpReturn.Value.Date;
7
8    double penalty_cost;
9    double penaltyPerDay = Convert.ToDouble(txtPenaltyPerDay.Text);
10
11   if ((last.Subtract(start).Days) > 7)
12   {
13       penalty_cost =
14           penaltyPerDay * Convert.ToInt32(last.Subtract(start).Days);
15       txtPenalty.Text = penalty_cost.ToString();
16   }
17   else
18   {
19       txtPenalty.Text = 0.ToString();
20   }
21
22   // Delays
23   Thread.Sleep(1000);
24
25   if (MessageBox.Show("Do you really want to delete this record?",
26       "Delete", MessageBoxButtons.OKCancel,
27       MessageBoxIcon.Question) == DialogResult.OK)
28   {
29       btnDelete.PerformClick();
30   }
31   else
32   {
33       this.Show();
34   }
35 }
```

4.29 Tutorial Steps of Creating Form for Borrow Table: Editing Record

Step 1   You will now add editing capability and other related capabilities to save and/or cancel
edits. Before saving update into database, you need to validate data entered by user. In
this case, you need to validate borrowal code, borrow date, borrowed book, borrower's
name, and year range. Define a method named **ValidateData** to validate data entered
by user:

```
1    private bool ValidateData()
2    {
3        string message = "";
4        int yearInput, yearNow;
5        bool allOK = true;
6
7        // Checks borrowal code, borrow date, borrowed book,
```

```
8      // and borrowers name
9      if ((dtpBorrow.Text.Length == 0) || (cboMember.SelectedIndex == -1)
10         || (cboBookBorrowed.SelectedIndex == -1) ||
11         (txtBorrowCode.Text.Length == 0))
12     {
13         message = "You should enter borrowal code, borrow date,
14             borrowed book, and borrowers name." + "\r\n";
15         dtpBorrow.Focus();
16         allOK = false;
17     }
18
19     // Checks year range
20     yearInput = dtpBorrow.Value.Year;
21     yearNow = DateTime.Now.Year;
22
23     if (yearInput > yearNow || yearInput < yearNow - 150)
24     {
25         message += "Year should be between " +
26             (yearNow - 150).ToString() +
27             " and " + yearNow.ToString();
28         dtpBorrow.Focus();
29         allOK = false;
30     }
31
32     if (!allOK)
33     {
34         MessageBox.Show(message, "Validation Error",
35             MessageBoxButtons.OK, MessageBoxIcon.Information);
36     }
37
38     return (allOK);
39 }
```

Step 2   Modify **btnSave_Click** event method to save the change and reposition the pointer to the record just edited:

```
1      private void btnSave_Click(object sender, EventArgs e)
2      {
3          if (!ValidateData())
4          {
5              return;
6          }
7
8          int nameSaved = cboMember.SelectedIndex;
9          int rowSaved;
10
11         try
12         {
13             managerBorrow.EndCurrentEdit();
14             tableBorrow.DefaultView.Sort = "MemberID";
```

```
15      rowSaved = tableBorrow.DefaultView.Find(nameSaved);
16      managerBorrow.Position = rowSaved;
17
18      MessageBox.Show("Records successfully saved", "Save",
19          MessageBoxButtons.OK, MessageBoxIcon.Information);
20      SetState("View");
21      connBook.Close();
22  }
23  catch (Exception ex)
24  {
25      MessageBox.Show("Error in saving record.", "Error",
26          MessageBoxButtons.OK, MessageBoxIcon.Error);
27  }
28  }
```

Step 3   Modify **btnCancel_Click** event method to restore controls if the edit is canceled:

```
1  private void btnCancel_Click(object sender, EventArgs e)
2  {
3      managerBorrow.CancelCurrentEdit();
4
5      SetState("View");
6  }
```

Figure 4.35 Editing operation is successfully performed

Step 4   Add the following code in line to the **FormBorrow_FormClosing** method to save any changes to the database file:

```
private void FormBorrow_FormClosing(object sender,
FormClosingEventArgs e)
{
    try
    {
        // Saves changes into database
        SqlCommandBuilder borrowAdapterCommand =
            new SqlCommandBuilder(adapterBorrow);
        adapterBorrow.Update(tableBorrow);
    }
    catch (Exception ex)
    {
        MessageBox.Show("Error saving database into file: \r\n" +
            ex.Message, "Saving Error", MessageBoxButtons.OK,
            MessageBoxIcon.Error);
    }

    // Closes connection to database
    connBook.Close();

    // Deletes objects
    connBook.Dispose();
    commandBorrow.Dispose();
    adapterBorrow.Dispose();
    commandMember.Dispose();
    adapterMember.Dispose();
    tableMember.Dispose();
    commandTitle.Dispose();
    adapterTitle.Dispose();
    tableTitle.Dispose();
}
```

Step 5   Save and run the application. Make sure Edit feature is working properly. Try changing the author name. Make sure the **Cancel** button is working properly. This is shown in Figure 4.35.

4.30 Tutorial Steps of Creating Form for Borrow Table: Adding New Record

Step 1   You now implement the capability on the form to add new records to the database. Add the following lines of code to the form-level declaration:

```
string appState;
int myBookmark;
```

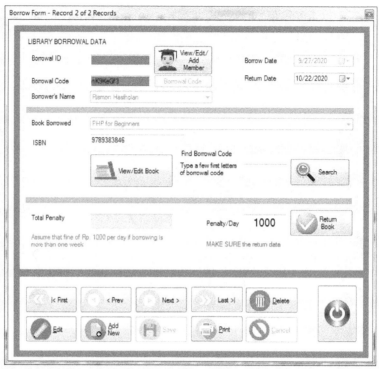

Figure 4.36 The new record has been successfully saved into the database

Step 2   Modify **SetState** method in line 2 as follows:

```
private void SetState(string stateStr) {
    appState = stateStr;

    switch (stateStr)
    {
        case "View":
            txtBorrowID.BackColor = Color.Red;
            txtBorrowID.ForeColor = Color.Black;
            cboMember.Enabled = false;
            cboBookBorrowed.Enabled = false;
            dtpBorrow.Enabled = false;
            dtpReturn.Enabled = true;
            txtPenalty.ReadOnly = true;
            btnFirst.Enabled = true;
            btnPrev.Enabled = true;
            btnNext.Enabled = true;
            btnLast.Enabled = true;
            btnAddNew.Enabled = true;
            btnSave.Enabled = false;
            btnDelete.Enabled = true;
            btnCancel.Enabled = false;
            btnEdit.Enabled = true;
            btnDone.Enabled = true;
```

```
24          btnReturn.Enabled = true;
25          btnPrint.Enabled = true;
26          btnBorrowalCode.Enabled = false;
27          break;
28
29      default: // Edit or Add
30          txtBorrowID.ReadOnly = true;
31          txtBorrowID.BackColor = Color.Red;
32          txtBorrowID.ForeColor = Color.Black;
33          cboMember.Enabled = true;
34          cboBookBorrowed.Enabled = true;
35          dtpBorrow.Enabled = true;
36          dtpReturn.Enabled = true;
37          txtPenalty.ReadOnly = true;
38          btnFirst.Enabled = false;
39          btnPrev.Enabled = false;
40          btnNext.Enabled = false;
41          btnLast.Enabled = false;
42          btnAddNew.Enabled = false;
43          btnSave.Enabled = true;
44          btnDelete.Enabled = false;
45          btnCancel.Enabled = true;
46          btnEdit.Enabled = false;
47          btnDone.Enabled = false;
48          btnPrint.Enabled = false;
49          btnReturn.Enabled = false;
50          btnBorrowalCode.Enabled = true;
51          break;
52      }
53  }
```

Step 3   Modify **btnAddNew_Click** event method to add a new record by adding code as
follows:

```
1   private void btnAddNew_Click(object sender, EventArgs e)
2   {
3       try
4       {
5           btnBorrowalCode.PerformClick();
6           SetState("Add");
7           myBookmark = managerBorrow.Position;
8           managerBorrow.AddNew();
9       }
10      catch (Exception ex)
11      {
12          MessageBox.Show("Error in adding new record.", "Error",
13              MessageBoxButtons.OK, MessageBoxIcon.Error);
14      }
15  }
```

Step 4   Modify **btnCancel_Click** event method to differentiate between cancellation during
          Edit mode and **Add** mode by adding code in line 5-9:

```
1   private void btnCancel_Click(object sender, EventArgs e)
2   {
3       managerBorrow.CancelCurrentEdit();
4
5       if (appState.Equals("Add"))
6       {
7           managerBorrow.Position = myBookmark;
8       }
9       SetState("View");
10  }
```

Step 5   Save and run the application. Click **Add New** button. Click **Borrowal Code** button,
          choose borrow date and return date, choose borrower's name, and choose book to
          borrow, then click **Save**. New record has been successfully saved as shown in Figure
          4.36.

4.31 Tutorial Steps of Creating Form for Borrow Table: Deleting Record

Step 1   You will now add the capability to delete records from **Borrow** table. Modify the
          btnDelete_Click event method by adding code in line 14 to delete records if the user
          responds to **Yes** in the message box:

```
1   private void btnDelete_Click(object sender, EventArgs e)
2   {
3       DialogResult response;
4       response = MessageBox.Show("Dou you really want to delete this record?",
5           "Delete", MessageBoxButtons.YesNo, MessageBoxIcon.Question,
6           MessageBoxDefaultButton.Button2);
7       if (response == DialogResult.No)
8       {
9           return;
10      }
11
12      try
13      {
14          managerBorrow.RemoveAt(managerBorrow.Position);
15      }
16      catch (Exception ex)
17      {
18          MessageBox.Show("Error deleting record.", "Error",
19              MessageBoxButtons.OK, MessageBoxIcon.Error);
20      }
21  }
```

Step 2   Save the application and run it. Make sure the **Yes** and **No** responses in the message box give correct results. Delete only those records you added using **Add New** button.

4.32 Tutorial Steps of Creating Form for Borrow Table: Stopping Application

Step 1   Add the following code in line 4-12 to **FormBorrow_FormClosing** event method to ensure user doesn't close the application during **Edit** or **Add** mode:

```csharp
private void FormBorrow_FormClosing(object sender,
FormClosingEventArgs e)
{
    if (appState.Equals("Edit") || appState.Equals("Add"))
    {
        MessageBox.Show(
            "You should finish editing before closing application.",
            "", MessageBoxButtons.OK, MessageBoxIcon.Information);
        e.Cancel = true;
    }
    else
    {
        try
        {
            // Saves changes into
            SqlCommandBuilder borrowAdapterCommand =
                new SqlCommandBuilder(adapterBorrow);
            adapterBorrow.Update(tableBorrow);
        }
        catch (Exception ex)
        {
            MessageBox.Show("Error saving database into file: \r\n" +
                ex.Message, "Error Saving", MessageBoxButtons.OK,
                MessageBoxIcon.Error);
        }

        // Closes connection to database
        connBook.Close();

        // Deletes objects
        connBook.Dispose();
        commandBorrow.Dispose();
        adapterBorrow.Dispose();
        commandMember.Dispose();
        adapterMember.Dispose();
        tableMember.Dispose();
        commandTitle.Dispose();
        adapterTitle.Dispose();
        tableTitle.Dispose();
    }
```

```
41  }
```

Step 2   Put this code in **btnDone_Click** event method:

```
1   private void btnDone_Click(object sender, EventArgs e)
2   {
3       this.Close();
4   }
```

Step 3   Save and run the application. Make sure the **Done** button is working properly. Make sure the user cannot close the application in **Edit** or **Add** mode.

4.33 Tutorial Steps of Searching Capability

Step 1   In the **SetState** method, enable group box control in **View** mode and disable it in **Add** and **Edit** mode. Use its **Enabled** property.

Step 3   Add the following code to **btnSearch_Click** event method:

```
1   private void btnSearch_Click(object sender, EventArgs e)
2   {
3       if (txtSearch.Text.Equals(""))
4       {
5           return;
6       }
7
8       int rowSaved = managerBorrow.Position;
9       DataRow[] rowFound;
10      tableBorrow.DefaultView.Sort = "BorrowCode";
11
12      rowFound = tableBorrow.Select("BorrowCode LIKE '" +
13          txtSearch.Text + "*'");
14
15      if (rowFound.Length == 0)
16      {
17          managerBorrow.Position = rowSaved;
18      }
19      else
20      {
21          managerBorrow.Position =
22              tableBorrow.DefaultView.Find(rowFound[0]["BorrowCode"]);
23      }
24  }
```

Step 4   Save and run the application. Try searching by providing the first or two letters of the borrowal code, as shown in Figure 4.37.

Figure 4.37 Searching capability in borrow form

4.34 Tutorial Steps of Adding Search Buttons

Step 1   Add a button control on the form. Set its **Name** property as **btnAll** and its **Text** property as **Show All Borrowers**. You add another **DataGridView** control and set its **Name** property as **grdBorrow**. You also need to add a label and set its **Text** property as **Number of Records:**. Then add a textbox on the form. Set its **Name** property as **txtNumberRecord**.

Step 2   Add the following form-level declaration:

```
1   Button[] buttonArr = new Button[26];
```

buttonArr is an array containing the search buttons.

Step 3   Define a new method named **createSearchButton()** as follows:

```
1   private void createSearchButton()
2   {
3       // Creates search buttons
4       int w, lStart, l, t;
5       int btnHeight = 50; // by trial and error
6
```

```
7     // Search buttons
8     // Button width - 13 buttons in a row
9     w = Convert.ToInt32(grdBorrow.Width / 13);
10
11    // Aligns buttons
12    lStart = Convert.ToInt32((grdBorrow.Width)) + 150;
13    l = lStart; t = grdBorrow.Top + grdBorrow.Height + 10;
14
15    // Creates and positions 26 buttons
16    for (int i = 0; i < 26; i++)
17    {
18        // Creates push button
19        buttonArr[i] = new Button();
20        buttonArr[i].TabStop = false;
21
22        // Sets Text property
23        buttonArr[i].Text = ((char)(65 + i)).ToString();
24        buttonArr[i].Font = new Font(buttonArr[i].Font.FontFamily,
25            9, FontStyle.Bold);
26
27        // Positions buttons
28        buttonArr[i].Width = w;
29        buttonArr[i].Height = btnHeight;
30        buttonArr[i].Left = l;
31        buttonArr[i].Top = t;
32
33        // Gives color
34        buttonArr[i].BackColor = Color.Red;
35        buttonArr[i].ForeColor = Color.White;
36
37        // Adds each button on form
38        this.Controls.Add(buttonArr[i]);
39
40        // Adds event handler
41        buttonArr[i].Click +=
42            new System.EventHandler(this.btnSQL_Click);
43        l += w+1;
44
45        if (i == 12)
46        {
47            // Next row
48            l = lStart; t += btnHeight;
49        }
50    }
51 }
```

This method creates search buttons A through Z using **buttonArrr** array. The code above then specifies the width of the button and places it on the form. Finally, the resulting records are displayed by programmatically clicking **btnSQL** button.

Step 4   Define **createSQLStatement** method as follows:

```
1   private string createSQLStatement()
2   {
3       // Create SQL Statement
4       string SqlString = null;
5       SqlString += "SELECT Borrow.BorrowID, Borrow.BorrowCode, Member.FirstName, ";
6       SqlString += "Title.BookTitle, Title.ISBN, Title.PublishYear, ";
7       SqlString += "Publisher.Name AS Publisher_Name, Publisher.City, Publisher.Address, ";
8       SqlString += "Title.Description, Title.Subject ";
9       SqlString += "FROM Title, Publisher, Member, Borrow ";
10      SqlString += "WHERE Borrow.ISBN = Title.ISBN ";
11      SqlString += "AND Member.MemberID = Borrow.MemberID ";
12      SqlString += "AND Title.PublisherID = Publisher.PublisherID ";
13
14      return SqlString;
15  }
```

Step 5   Write the code for **btnSQL_Click** event method (handle **Click** event for all search buttons) as follows:

```
1   private void btnSQL_Click(object sender, EventArgs e)
2   {
3       SqlCommand commResult = null;
4       SqlDataAdapter adapterResult = new SqlDataAdapter();
5       DataTable tableResult = new DataTable();
6       String StatementSQL;
7
8       string SQLAll = createSQLStatement();
9
10      // Determines which button is clicked and creates SQL statement
11      Button buttonClicked = (Button)sender;
12      switch (buttonClicked.Text)
13      {
14          case "Show All Borrowers":
15              StatementSQL = SQLAll;
16              break;
17          case "Z":
18              // Z button is clicked
19              // Appends at SQLAll to limit records upto for item Z
20              StatementSQL = SQLAll + " AND Member.FirstName > 'Z' ";
21              break;
22          default:
23              // Letter keys except Z
24              // Appends at SQLAll to limit records
25              // for letter that is clicked
26              int idx = (int)(Convert.ToChar(buttonClicked.Text)) - 65;
27              StatementSQL = SQLAll + " AND Member.FirstName > '" +
28                  buttonArr[idx].Text + " ' ";
29                  StatementSQL += " AND Member.FirstName < '" +
```

```
30              buttonArr[idx + 1].Text + " ' ";
31          break;
32      }
33      StatementSQL += " ORDER BY Member.FirstName";
34
35      // Applies SQL statement
36      try
37      {
38          // Creates Command and DataAdapater objects
39          commResult = new SqlCommand(StatementSQL, connBook);
40          adapterResult.SelectCommand = commResult;
41          adapterResult.Fill(tableResult);
42
43          // Binds DataGridView with data table
44          grdBorrow.DataSource = tableResult;
45          txtNumberRecord.Text = tableResult.Rows.Count.ToString();
46      }
47
48      catch (Exception ex)
49      {
50          MessageBox.Show(ex.Message, "Error Processing SQL",
51              MessageBoxButtons.OK, MessageBoxIcon.Error);
52      }
53
54      commResult.Dispose();
55      adapterResult.Dispose();
56      tableResult.Dispose();
57  }
```

This method determines which button is clicked and forms an SQL statement. If the button with the **Text** property of the button is **"Show All Borrowers"** is clicked, then all records will be displayed. When a key letter is clicked, the code determines which letter the user clicks on and attaches an additional test (using **AND**) to the **WHERE** field in the default SQL statement.

Step 6   Add the following code in line 66-71 to **FormBorrower_Load** event method. The code creates search buttons and perform **Click** event of **btnAll** programmatically:

```
1   private void FormBorrow_Load(object sender, EventArgs e)
2   {
3       try
4       {
5           // Connects to database
6           connBook = new SqlConnection("Data Source=.\\SQLEXPRESS;
7               AttachDbFilename=D:\\Database\\DBMS.mdf;
8               Integrated Security = True; Connect Timeout = 30;
9               User Instance = True");
10
11          // Opens connection
```

```csharp
12        connBook.Open();
13
14        // Creates Command object
15        commandBorrow = new SqlCommand(
16            "SELECT * FROM Borrow ORDER BY MemberID", connBook);
17
18        // Creates DataAdapter/DataTable objects
19        adapterBorrow = new SqlDataAdapter();
20        adapterBorrow.SelectCommand = commandBorrow;
21        tableBorrow = new DataTable();
22        adapterBorrow.Fill(tableBorrow);
23
24        // Binds controls to data table
25        txtBorrowID.DataBindings.Add("Text", tableBorrow, "BorrowID");
26        cboMember.DataBindings.Add("Text", tableBorrow, "MemberID");
27        dtpBorrow.DataBindings.Add("Text", tableBorrow, "BorrowDate");
28        dtpReturn.DataBindings.Add("Text", tableBorrow, "ReturnDate");
29        txtPenalty.DataBindings.Add("Text", tableBorrow, "Penalty");
30        txtBorrowCode.DataBindings.Add("Text", tableBorrow, "BorrowCode");
31
32        // Populates cboMember
33        commandMember = new SqlCommand(
34            "SELECT * FROM Member ORDER BY FirstName", connBook);
35        adapterMember = new SqlDataAdapter();
36        adapterMember.SelectCommand = commandMember;
37        tableMember = new DataTable();
38        adapterMember.Fill(tableMember);
39        cboMember.DataSource = tableMember;
40        cboMember.DisplayMember = "FirstName";
41        cboMember.ValueMember = "MemberID";
42        cboMember.DataBindings.Add("SelectedValue",
43            tableBorrow, "MemberID");
44
45        // Populates cboBookBorrowed and txtISBN
46        commandTitle = new SqlCommand(
47            "SELECT * FROM Title ORDER BY BookTitle", connBook);
48        adapterTitle = new SqlDataAdapter();
49        adapterTitle.SelectCommand = commandTitle;
50        tableTitle = new DataTable();
51        adapterTitle.Fill(tableTitle);
52        cboBookBorrowed.DataSource = tableTitle;
53        cboBookBorrowed.DisplayMember = "BookTitle";
54        cboBookBorrowed.ValueMember = "ISBN";
55        cboBookBorrowed.DataBindings.Add("SelectedValue",
56            tableBorrow, "ISBN");
57        txtISBN.DataBindings.Add("Text", tableBorrow, "ISBN");
58
59        // Creates data update
60        managerBorrow =
61            (CurrencyManager)BindingContext[tableBorrow];
62
```

```
63      this.Show();
64      SetState("View");
65
66      //Creates 26 search buttons
67      createSearchButton();
68
69      // Clicks all records when form starts
70      btnAll.Click += new System.EventHandler(this.btnSQL_Click);
71      btnAll.PerformClick();
72    }
73    catch (Exception ex)
74    {
75      MessageBox.Show(ex.Message, "Error in reading table.",
76          MessageBoxButtons.OK, MessageBoxIcon.Error);
77      return;
78    }
79  }
```

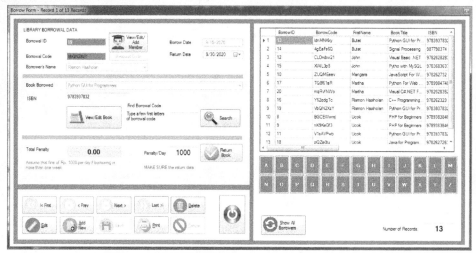

Figure 4.38 The application when it first runs

Step 7   Define **RowPostPaint** event of **grdBorrow** control to give it a row numbering:

```
1   private void grdBorrow_RowPostPaint(object sender,
2   DataGridViewRowPostPaintEventArgs e)
3   {
4       var grid = sender as DataGridView;
5       var rowIdx = (e.RowIndex + 1).ToString();
6
7       var centerFormat = new StringFormat()
8       {
9           // Aligns to middle
10          Alignment = StringAlignment.Center,
11          LineAlignment = StringAlignment.Center
12      };
13
```

```
14      var headerBounds = new Rectangle(e.RowBounds.Left,
15          e.RowBounds.Top, grid.RowHeadersWidth, e.RowBounds.Height);
16      e.Graphics.DrawString(rowIdx, this.Font,
17          SystemBrushes.ControlText, headerBounds, centerFormat);
18  }
```

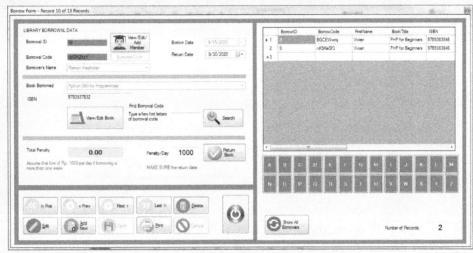

Figure 4.39 The results when the 'V' button is clicked

Step 8   Define **Refresh_DGV** to refresh data grid view, **grdBorrow**, as follows:

```
1   private void Refresh_DGV()
2   {
3       // Connects to database
4       connBook = new SqlConnection("Data Source=.\\SQLEXPRESS;
5           AttachDbFilename=D:\\Database\\DBMS.mdf;
6           Integrated Security = True; Connect Timeout = 30;
7           User Instance = True");
8
9       connBook.Open();
10
11      // Save changes to database
12      SqlCommandBuilder publisherDBAdapterCommand = new
13          SqlCommandBuilder(adapterBorrow);
14      adapterBorrow.Update(tableBorrow);
15
16      SqlCommand commandResult = null;
17      SqlDataAdapter adapterResult = new SqlDataAdapter();
18      DataTable tableResult = new DataTable();
19      string SQLAll = createSQLStatement();
20
21      try
22      {
23          // Creates Command and DataAdapter objects
24          commandResult = new SqlCommand(SQLAll, connBook);
```

```
25        adapterResult.SelectCommand = commandResult;
26        tableResult.Clear();
27        adapterResult.Fill(tableResult);
28
29        // Binds grid view to data table
30        grdBorrow.DataSource = tableResult;
31        txtNumberRecord.Text = tableResult.Rows.Count.ToString();
32    }
33
34    catch (Exception ex)
35    {
36        MessageBox.Show(ex.Message, "Error in processing SQL",
37            MessageBoxButtons.OK, MessageBoxIcon.Error);
38    }
39
40    commandResult.Dispose();
41    adapterResult.Dispose();
      tableResult.Dispose();
  }
```

Step 9   Call **Refresh_DGV** from **Click** event of **btnAll** as follows:

```
1    private void btnAll_Click(object sender, EventArgs e)
2    {
3        Refresh_DGV();
4    }
```

Step 10   Save and run the application. The result is shown in Figure 4.38. Notice how the search
buttons are created. Also note that all records are displayed initially. Click on one of
the search buttons. Only records with the member's initial matching the letter in the
clicked button will be displayed. Figure 4.39 is the query result when the 'V' button is
clicked.

4.35 Tutorial Steps of Reporting Borrowers

Step 1   Now, you will add a feature to read all the data in the database. You need a database
report. The report is quite simple. For each record, the data from each field will be
displayed.

Add this line of code at the top of the code window:

```
1    using System.Drawing.Printing;
```

Step 2   Add the page number variable to the form level declaration:

```
1    int pageNumber;
```

Step 3 In the **SetState** method, set **Enabled** property of **btnPrint** to **true** in **View** mode and **false** in **Add/Edit** mode.

Step 4 Add the following code to **btnPrint_Click** event method:

```
private void btnPrint_Click(object sender, EventArgs e)
{
    // Declares document
    PrintDocument docBorrow;

    // Creates document and gives it a name
    docBorrow = new PrintDocument();
    docBorrow.DocumentName = "Borrower Data";

    // Adds code handler
    docBorrow.PrintPage += new
        PrintPageEventHandler(this.PrintBorrower);

    // Prints document in preview control
    pageNumber = 1;
    int positionSaved = managerBorrow.Position;
    dlgPreview.Document = docBorrow;
    dlgPreview.ShowDialog();

    // Deletes document when finished printing
    docBorrow.Dispose();
    managerBorrow.Position = positionSaved;
}
```

Step 5 Add the following code to **PrintBorrow** method:

```
private void PrintBorrower(object sender, PrintPageEventArgs e)
{
    // Tracks every record, prints every record
    managerBorrow.Position = pageNumber - 1;

    Font myFont = new Font("Arial", 14, FontStyle.Bold);
    int y = e.MarginBounds.Top + 50;

    // Prints header
    e.Graphics.DrawString("Borrower's Data (" +
        DateTime.Now.ToShortDateString() + ") - Page " +
        pageNumber.ToString(), myFont, Brushes.Black,
        e.MarginBounds.Left, y);
    y += 2 * Convert.ToInt32(myFont.GetHeight(e.Graphics));

    e.Graphics.DrawString("*****************************
    ***************************", myFont, Brushes.Black,
        e.MarginBounds.X, y);
    y += Convert.ToInt32(myFont.GetHeight(e.Graphics));
```

```
20
21      int shift = 5;
22
23      // Prints Header
24      myFont = new Font("Arial", 12, FontStyle.Regular);
25      e.Graphics.DrawString("Borrow ID:", myFont, Brushes.Black,
26          e.MarginBounds.X + shift, y);
27      e.Graphics.DrawString(txtBorrowID.Text, myFont, Brushes.Black,
28          e.MarginBounds.X + shift + 200, y);
29      y += Convert.ToInt32(myFont.GetHeight(e.Graphics));
30
31      e.Graphics.DrawString("Borrowal Code:", myFont, Brushes.Black,
32          e.MarginBounds.X + shift, y);
33      e.Graphics.DrawString(txtBorrowCode.Text, myFont,
34          Brushes.Black, e.MarginBounds.X + shift + 200, y);
35      y += Convert.ToInt32(myFont.GetHeight(e.Graphics));
36
37      e.Graphics.DrawString("Borrower's Name:", myFont,
38          Brushes.Black, e.MarginBounds.X + shift, y);
39      e.Graphics.DrawString(cboMember.Text, myFont, Brushes.Black,
40          e.MarginBounds.X + shift + 200, y);
41      y += Convert.ToInt32(myFont.GetHeight(e.Graphics));
42
43      e.Graphics.DrawString("Book Borrowed:", myFont, Brushes.Black,
44          e.MarginBounds.X + shift, y);
45      e.Graphics.DrawString(cboBookBorrowed.Text, myFont,
46          Brushes.Black, e.MarginBounds.X + shift + 200, y);
47      y += Convert.ToInt32(myFont.GetHeight(e.Graphics));
48
49      e.Graphics.DrawString("Borrow Date:", myFont, Brushes.Black,
50          e.MarginBounds.X + shift, y);
51      e.Graphics.DrawString(dtpBorrow.Text, myFont, Brushes.Black,
52          e.MarginBounds.X + 200, y);
53      y += Convert.ToInt32(myFont.GetHeight(e.Graphics));
54
55      e.Graphics.DrawString("Return Date:", myFont, Brushes.Black,
56          e.MarginBounds.X + shift, y);
57      e.Graphics.DrawString(dtpReturn.Text, myFont, Brushes.Black,
58          e.MarginBounds.X + 200, y);
59      y += Convert.ToInt32(myFont.GetHeight(e.Graphics));
60
61      e.Graphics.DrawString("Penalty:", myFont, Brushes.Black,
62          e.MarginBounds.X + shift, y);
63      e.Graphics.DrawString(txtPenalty.Text, myFont, Brushes.Black,
64          e.MarginBounds.X + 200, y);
65      y += Convert.ToInt32(myFont.GetHeight(e.Graphics));
66
67      Font myFont2 = new Font("Arial", 14, FontStyle.Bold);
68      e.Graphics.DrawString("**********************
69          *********************************", myFont2,
70          Brushes.Black, e.MarginBounds.X, y);
```

```
71
72        pageNumber++;
73        if (pageNumber <= managerBorrow.Count)
74            e.HasMorePages = true;
75        else
76        {
77            e.HasMorePages = false;
78            pageNumber = 1;
79        }
80    }
```

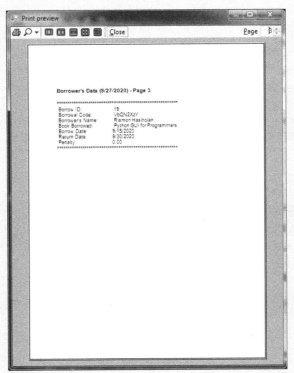

Figure 4.40 Each record in the table can now be printed

Step 6   Save and run the application. Click on the **Print** button. The print preview control will
be displayed on all borrower pages, as shown in Figure 4.40.

TUTORIAL 5
BALIGE ACADEMY
DATABASE PROJECT: PART 1

Description

In this tutorial, you will perform the steps necessary to add 6 tables using Visual C# into **DBMS** database. You will build each table and add the associated fields as needed.

5.1 Tutorial Steps of Creating Six More Tables

Step 1   Add the first table and name it as **Parent** and add twelve fields to the table. Set the fields using the following options:

Name	Data Type
ParentID	bigint
FirstName	varchar(50)
LastName	varchar(50)
BirthDate	datetime
Status	bit
Ethnicity	varchar(100)
Nationality	varchar(100)
Mobile	varchar(20)
Phone	varchar(20)
Religion	varchar(50)
Gender	varchar(10)
PhotoFile	varchar(200)

Set **Allow Nulls** to **Yes** for all fields except **ParentID**, **FirstName**, and **LastName**. Also set **ParentID** as the primary key. For **ParentID**, set its **Is Identity** property as **True**. Make **FirstName** and **LastName** fields as indexes.

Below is the SQL Server query to create this table:

```
1   CREATE TABLE [dbo].[Parent]
2   (
3       [ParentID] BIGINT NOT NULL PRIMARY KEY IDENTITY,
4       [FirstName] VARCHAR(50) NOT NULL,
5       [LastName] VARCHAR(50) NOT NULL,
```

```
6      [BirthDate] DATETIME NULL,
7      [Status] BIT NULL,
8      [Ethnicity] VARCHAR(100) NULL,
9      [Nationality] VARCHAR(100) NULL,
10     [Mobile] VARCHAR(20) NULL,
11     [Phone] VARCHAR(20) NULL,
12     [Religion] VARCHAR(50) NULL,
13     [Gender] VARCHAR(20) NULL,
14     [PhotoFile] VARCHAR(200) NULL
15  );
16  GO
17  CREATE INDEX [IX_Parent_Column] ON [dbo].[Parent] ([FirstName])
18
19  GO
20  CREATE INDEX [IX_Parent_Column_1] ON [dbo].[Parent] ([LastName])
```

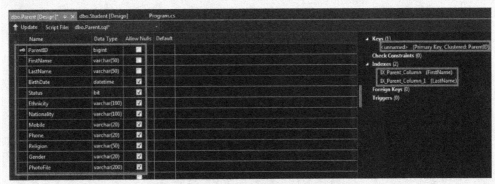

Figure 5.1 Panel for **Parent** table

In the top-left corner of the **Table Designer**, select the **Update** button. In the **Preview Database Updates** dialog box, select the **Update Database** button to create the table.

Step 2   Create a second table named **Student**. It has 14 fields. Add the following fields:

Name	Data Type
StudentID	bigint
ParentID	bigint
FirstName	varchar(50)
LastName	varchar(50)
BirthDate	datetime
YearEntry	datetime
Status	bit
Ethnicity	varchar(100)
Nationality	varchar(100)
Mobile	varchar(20)
Phone	varchar(20)
Religion	varchar(50)
Gender	varchar(10)

```
PhotoFile            varchar(200)
```

Set **Allow Null** to **Yes** for all fields except **StudentID**, **ParentID**, **FirstName**, and **LastName**. Also set **StudentID** as the primary key. For **StudentID**, set its **Is Identity** property as **True**. Make **FirstName** and **LastName** fields as indexes.

```
1    CREATE TABLE [dbo].[Student] (
2        [StudentID]   BIGINT         PRIMARY KEY IDENTITY,
3        [ParentID]    BIGINT         NOT NULL,
4        [FirstName]   VARCHAR (50)   NOT NULL,
5        [LastName]    VARCHAR (50)   NOT NULL,
6        [BirthDate]   DATETIME       NULL,
7        [YearEntry]   DATETIME       NULL,
8        [Status]      BIT            NULL,
9        [Ethnicity]   VARCHAR (100)  NULL,
10       [Nationality] VARCHAR (100)  NULL,
11       [Mobile]      VARCHAR (20)   NULL,
12       [Phone]       VARCHAR (20)   NULL,
13       [Religion]    VARCHAR (50)   NULL,
14       [Gender]      VARCHAR (20)   NULL,
15       [PhotoFile]   VARCHAR (200)  NULL,
16   );
17
18   GO
19   CREATE INDEX [IX_Student_Column] ON [dbo].[Student] ([FirstName])
20
21   GO
22   CREATE INDEX [IX_Student_Column_1] ON [dbo].[Student] ([LastName])
```

Then, you need to associate the **ParentID** (foreign key) field in **Student** table with **ParentID** (primary key) in the **Parent** table. Modify SQL Server query of creating **Student** table as follows:

```
1    CREATE TABLE [dbo].[Student] (
2        [StudentID]   BIGINT         PRIMARY KEY IDENTITY,
3        [ParentID]    BIGINT         NOT NULL,
4        [FirstName]   VARCHAR (50)   NOT NULL,
5        [LastName]    VARCHAR (50)   NOT NULL,
6        [BirthDate]   DATETIME       NULL,
7        [YearEntry]   DATETIME       NULL,
8        [Status]      BIT            NULL,
9        [Ethnicity]   VARCHAR (100)  NULL,
10       [Nationality] VARCHAR (100)  NULL,
11       [Mobile]      VARCHAR (20)   NULL,
12       [Phone]       VARCHAR (20)   NULL,
13       [Religion]    VARCHAR (50)   NULL,
14       [Gender]      VARCHAR (20)   NULL,
15       [PhotoFile]   VARCHAR (200)  NULL,
16       CONSTRAINT [FK_Student_Parent] FOREIGN KEY ([ParentID])
17       REFERENCES [Parent]([ParentID]),
```

```
18  );
19
20  GO
21  CREATE INDEX [IX_Student_Column] ON [dbo].[Student] ([FirstName])
22
23  GO
24  CREATE INDEX [IX_Student_Column_1] ON [dbo].[Student] ([LastName])
```

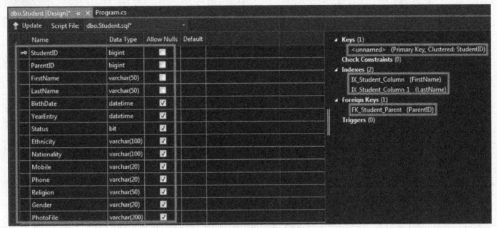

Figure 5.2 Panel for **Student** table

In the top-left corner of the **Table Designer**, select the **Update** button. In the **Preview Database Updates** dialog box, select the **Update Database** button to create the table.

Step 3   Create a third table named **Teacher**. It has 14 fields. Add the following fields:

Name	Data Type
TeacherID	bigint
RegNumber	varchar(50)
FirstName	varchar(50)
LastName	varchar(50)
BirthDate	datetime
Rank	varchar(20)
Status	bit
Ethnicity	varchar(100)
Nationality	varchar(100)
Mobile	varchar(20)
Phone	varchar(20)
Religion	varchar(50)
Gender	varchar(10)
PhotoFile	varchar(200)

Set **Allow Null** to **Yes** for all fields except **TeacherID**, **RegNumber**, **FirstName**, and **LastName**. Also set **TeacherID** as the primary key. For **TeacherID**, set its **Is Identity** property as **True**. Make **FirstName** and **LastName** fields as indexes.

Below is the SQL Server query to create this table:

```sql
CREATE TABLE [dbo].[Teacher]
(
    [TeacherID] BIGINT NOT NULL PRIMARY KEY IDENTITY,
    [RegNumber] VARCHAR(20) NOT NULL,
    [FirstName] VARCHAR(50) NOT NULL,
    [LastName] VARCHAR(50) NOT NULL,
    [BirthDate] DATETIME NULL,
        [Rank] VARCHAR(20) NULL,
    [Status] BIT NULL,
    [Ethnicity] VARCHAR(100) NULL,
    [Nationality] VARCHAR(100) NULL,
    [Mobile] VARCHAR(20) NULL,
    [Phone] VARCHAR(20) NULL,
    [Religion] VARCHAR(50) NULL,
    [Gender] VARCHAR(20) NULL,
    [PhotoFile] VARCHAR(200) NULL
)

GO
CREATE INDEX [IX_Teacher_Column] ON [dbo].[Teacher] ([FirstName])

GO
CREATE INDEX [IX_Teacher_Column_1] ON [dbo].[Teacher] ([LastName])
```

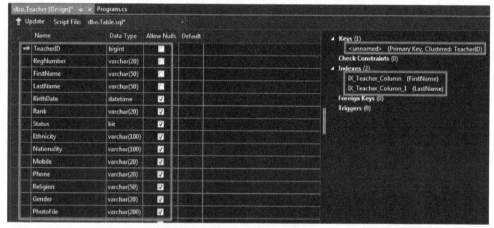

Figure 5.3 Panel for **Teacher** table

In the top-left corner of the **Table Designer**, select the **Update** button. In the **Preview Database Updates** dialog box, select the **Update Database** button to create the table.

Step 4   Create a fourth table named **Subject**. It has only 3 fields. Add the following fields:

Name	Data Type
SubjectID	bigint
Name	varchar(100)

```
Description          varchar(200)
```

Set **Allow Null** to **Yes** only for **Description**. Also set **SubjectID** as the primary key. For **SubjectID**, set its **Is Identity** property as **True**. Make **Name** field as index.

Below is the SQL Server query to create this table:

```
1  CREATE TABLE [dbo].[Subject]
2  (
3      [SubjectID] BIGINT NOT NULL PRIMARY KEY IDENTITY,
4      [Name] VARCHAR(100) NOT NULL,
5      [Description] VARCHAR(200) NULL
6  )
7
8  GO
9  CREATE INDEX [IX_Subject_Column] ON [dbo].[Subject] ([Name])
```

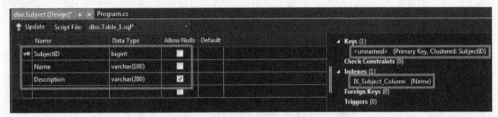

Figure 5.4 Panel for **Subject** table

In the top-left corner of the **Table Designer**, select the **Update** button. In the **Preview Database Updates** dialog box, select the **Update Database** button to create the table.

Step 5   Create a fifth table named **Grade**. It has 7 fields. Add the following fields:

Name	Data Type
GradeID	bigint
Name	varchar(50)
SubjectID	bigint
TeacherID	bigint
SchoolYear	varchar(50)
TimeStart	time
TimeFinish	time

```
1  CREATE TABLE [dbo].[Grade]
2  (
3      [GradeID] BIGINT NOT NULL PRIMARY KEY IDENTITY,
4      [Name] VARCHAR(50) NOT NULL,
5      [SubjectID] BIGINT NOT NULL,
6      [TeacherID] BIGINT NOT NULL,
7      [SchoolYear] VARCHAR(50) NULL,
8      [TimeStart] TIME NULL,
9      [TimeFinish] TIME NULL
```

```
10  )
11
12  GO
13  CREATE INDEX [IX_Grade_Column] ON [dbo].[Grade] ([Name])
```

Set **Allow Null** to **Yes** for all fields except **GradeID**, **Name**, **SubjectID**, and **TeacherID**. Also set **GradeID** as the primary key. For **GradeID**, set its **Is Identity** property as **True**. Make **Name** fields as index.

Then, you need to associate the **SubjectID** (foreign key) field in **Grade** table with **SubjectID** (primary key) in the **Subject** table. And you also need to associate the **TeacherID** (foreign key) field in **Grade** table with **TeacherID** (primary key) in the **Teacher** table.

Modify SQL query of creating **Grade** table as follows:

```
1   CREATE TABLE [dbo].[Grade]
2   (
3       [GradeID] BIGINT NOT NULL PRIMARY KEY IDENTITY,
4       [Name] VARCHAR(50) NOT NULL,
5       [SubjectID] BIGINT NOT NULL,
6       [TeacherID] BIGINT NOT NULL,
7       [SchoolYear] VARCHAR(50) NULL,
8       [TimeStart] TIME NULL,
9       [TimeFinish] TIME NULL,
10      CONSTRAINT FK_Grade_Subject FOREIGN KEY (SubjectID)
11      REFERENCES Subject(SubjectID),
12      CONSTRAINT FK_Grade_Teacher  FOREIGN KEY (TeacherID)
13      REFERENCES Teacher(TeacherID)
14  )
15
16  GO
17  CREATE INDEX [IX_Grade_Column] ON [dbo].[Grade] ([Name])
```

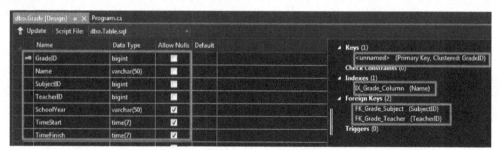

Figure 5.5 Panel for **Grade** table

In the top-left corner of the **Table Designer**, select the **Update** button. In the **Preview Database Updates** dialog box, select the **Update Database** button to create the table.

Step 6 Create a sixth table named **Grade_Student**. It has only 3 fields. Add the following fields:

Name	Data Type
Grade_StudentID	bigint
GradeID	bigint
StudentID	bigint

```
1   CREATE TABLE [dbo].[Grade_Student]
2   (
3       [Grade_StudentID] BIGINT NOT NULL PRIMARY KEY IDENTITY,
4       [GradeID] BIGINT NOT NULL,
5       [StudentID] BIGINT NOT NULL
6   )
```

Set **NOT NULL** for all fields. Also set **Grade_StudentID** as the primary key. For **Grade_StudentID**, set its **Is Identity** property as **True**.

Then, you need to associate the **GradeID** (foreign key) field in **Grade_Student** table with **GradeID** (primary key) in the **Grade** table. And you also need to associate the **StudentID** (foreign key) field in **Grade_Student** table with **StudentID** (primary key) in the **Student** table.

Modify SQL query of creating **Grade_Student** table as follows:

```
1   CREATE TABLE [dbo].[Grade_Student]
2   (
3       [Grade_StudentID] BIGINT NOT NULL PRIMARY KEY,
4       [GradeID] BIGINT NOT NULL,
5       [StudentID] BIGINT NOT NULL,
6       CONSTRAINT FK_Grade_Student_Grade FOREIGN KEY (GradeID)
7       REFERENCES Grade(GradeID),
8       CONSTRAINT FK_Grade_Student_Student FOREIGN KEY (StudentID)
9       REFERENCES Student(StudentID)
10  )
```

Figure 5.6 Panel for **Grade_Student** table

In the top-left corner of the **Table Designer**, select the **Update** button. In the **Preview Database Updates** dialog box, select the **Update Database** button to create the table.

Step 7   In **Server Explorer** window, you can see now that you have 14 tables as shown in Figure 5.7.

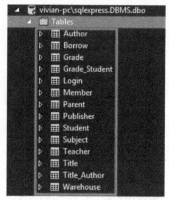

Figure 5.7 All tables in **DBMS** database

5.2 Tutorial Steps of Creating Form for Parent Table: Interface

Step 1   In this tutorial, you will build such a form for **Parent** table. This table has twelve fields: **ParentID**, **FirstName**, **LastName**, **BirthDate**, **Status**, **Ethnicity**, **Nationality**, **Mobile**, **Phone**, **Religion**, **Gender**, and **PhotoFile**).

You need an input form so that user can edit existing records, delete records, or add new records. The form will also have the capability of navigating from one record to another. The steps that need to be done are as follows.

Start a new Visual C# application. You need thirteen label controls, one picture box, six text boxes, four comboxes, one check box, one date time picker, one openfiledialog, and one printpreviewdialog. You also need four buttons for navigation, six buttons for controlling editing features, one button for searching member's name, and one button to upload member's photo. Place these controls on the form. The complete form looks as shown in Figure 5.10.

Step 2   Set the properties of each control as follows:

Form1 Control	
Name	FormParent
BackColor	Control
FormBorderStyle	FixedSingle
StartPosition	CenterScreen
Text	Form Parent

label1 Control	
Text	Parent ID

textBox1 Control

Name	txtParentID
ReadOnly	True

label2 Control

Text	Gender

combobox1 Control

Text	Gender
BackColor	White
Items	{Male, Female}

label3 Control

Text	First Name

textBox2 Control

Name	txtFirstName

label4 Control

Text	Last Name

textBox3 Control

Name	txtLastName

label5 Control

Text	Birth Date

dateTimePicker1 Control

Name	dtpBirthDate
Format	short

label6 Control

Text	Phone

textBox4 Control

Name	txtPhone

label7 Control

Text	Mobile

textBox5 Control

Name	txtMobile

label8 Control

Text	Status

checkbox1 Control

Name	chkStatus
Text	Single Parent

label9 Control

Text	Ethnicity

combobox2 Control

Name	cboEthnicity
Items	{Jawa, Sasak, Sunda, Batak, Betawi, Minang, Papua Bima, Melayu}

label10 Control
Text	Nationality

combobox3 Control
Name	cboNationality
Items	{Indonesia, Inggris Jepang, Amerika Korea Selatan, Malaysia, Singapur Vietnam}

label11 Control
Text	Religion

combobox4 Control
Name	cboReligion
Items	{ Islam, Kristen Protestan, Kristen Katolik, Buddha, Hindu, Konguchu, Kepercayaan}

label12 Control
Name	lblPhotoFile

pictureBox1 Control
Name	picParent
SizeMode	StretchImage

label13 Control
Text	Type the first few letters of first name

textBox6 Control
Name	txtFind

button1 Control
Name	btnFirst
Text	|< First

button2 Control
Name	btnPrev
Text	< Prev

button3 Control	
Name	btnNext
Text	Next >

button4 Control	
Name	btnLast
Text	Last >|

button5 Control	
Name	btnSearch
Text	Search

button6 Control	
Name	btnEdit
Text	&Edit

button7 Control	
Name	btnSave
Text	&Save

button8 Control	
Name	btnCancel
Text	&Cancel

button9 Control	
Name	btnAddNew
Text	&Add New

button10 Control	
Name	btnDelete
Text	&Delete

button11 Control	
Name	btnDone
Text	Do&ne

button12 Control	
Name	btnUpload
Text	&Upload Photo

button13 Control	
Name	btnPrint
Text	&Print

openFileDialog1 Control	
Name	dlgOpen

printPreviewDialog1 Control	
Name	dlgPreview

Step 3   You will add features to this parent form gradually. At this point, you will add code to construct the data table and to navigate the records in the **Parent** table. Add these lines of code at the top of the window:

```
1  using System.Data.SqlClient;
2  using System.IO;
3  using System.Drawing.Printing;
```

Figure 5.8 Design of parent form

Step 4   Write the following form-level declarations for creating data objects:

```
1  SqlConnection connBook;
2  SqlCommand commandParent;
3  SqlDataAdapter adapterParent;
4  DataTable tableParent;
5  CurrencyManager managerParent;
```

Step 5   Add the following code to the **FormParent_Load** event method:

```
1  private void FormParent_Load(object sender, EventArgs e)
2  {
3      try
4      {
5          // Connects to database
6          connBook = new SqlConnection("Data Source=.\\SQLEXPRESS;
7              AttachDbFilename=D:\\Database\\DBMS.mdf;
8              Integrated Security = True; Connect Timeout = 30;
9              User Instance = True");
10
11         // Opens connection
```

```
12          connBook.Open();
13
14              // Creates Command object
15              commandParent = new SqlCommand(
16                  "SELECT * FROM Parent ORDER BY FirstName", connBook);
17
18              // Creates DataAdapter/DataTable objects
19              adapterParent = new SqlDataAdapter();
20              adapterParent.SelectCommand = commandParent;
21              tableParent = new DataTable();
22              adapterParent.Fill(tableParent);
23
24              // Binds controls to data table
25              txtParentID.DataBindings.Add("Text",
26                  tableParent, "ParentID");
27              txtFirstName.DataBindings.Add("Text",
28                  tableParent, "FirstName");
29              txtLastName.DataBindings.Add("Text",
30                  tableParent, "LastName");
31              dtpBirthDate.DataBindings.Add("Text",
32                  tableParent, "BirthDate");
33              lblPhotoFile.DataBindings.Add("Text",
34                  tableParent, "PhotoFile");
35              txtPhone.DataBindings.Add("Text", tableParent, "Phone");
36              txtMobile.DataBindings.Add("Text", tableParent, "Mobile");
37              chkStatus.DataBindings.Add("Checked",
38                  tableParent, "Status");
39              cboEthnicity.DataBindings.Add("Text",
40                  tableParent, "Ethnicity");
41              cboNationality.DataBindings.Add("Text",
42                  tableParent, "Nationality");
43              cboReligion.DataBindings.Add("Text",
44                  tableParent, "Religion");
45              cboGender.DataBindings.Add("Text", tableParent, "Gender");
46
47              // Creates data update
48              managerParent =
49                  (CurrencyManager)BindingContext[tableParent];
50
51          DisplayPhoto();
52          this.Show();
53      }
54  catch (Exception ex)
55  {
56      MessageBox.Show(ex.Message,
57        "Error in reading Parent table.",
58        MessageBoxButtons.OK, MessageBoxIcon.Error);
59      return;
60  }
61 }
```

The code above creates the data objects needed to open the database and construct the **Parent** table (includes all fields). The code above then binds the controls with the update manager object (**CurrencyManager**).

Step 6   Define **DisplayPhoto** to display parent photo in **picParent**:

```
private void DisplayPhoto()
{
    // Displays photo
    if (!lblPhotoFile.Text.Equals(""))
    {
        try
        {
            picParent.Image = Image.FromFile(lblPhotoFile.Text);
        }
        catch (Exception ex)
        {
            MessageBox.Show(ex.Message, "Error Loading Photo File",
                MessageBoxButtons.OK, MessageBoxIcon.Error);
        }
    }
    else
    {
        string dir =
            Path.GetDirectoryName(Application.ExecutablePath);
        string filename = Path.Combine(dir, @"parent.png");
        picParent.Image = Image.FromFile(filename);
    }
}
```

Step 7   Add the following code to **FormParent_FormClosing** event method to close the database connection:

```
private void FormParent_FormClosing(object sender,
FormClosingEventArgs e)
{
    // Closes connection to database
    connBook.Close();

    // Deletes objects
    connBook.Dispose();
    commandParent.Dispose();
    adapterParent.Dispose();
}
```

Step 8   Write the following code for the **Click** event of the four navigation buttons:

```
private void btnPrev_Click(object sender, EventArgs e)
{
```

```
3        if (managerParent.Position == 0)
4        {
5            Console.Beep();
6        }
7        managerParent.Position--;
8        DisplayPhoto();
9    }
10
11   private void btnNext_Click(object sender, EventArgs e)
12   {
13        if (managerParent.Position == managerParent.Count - 1)
14        {
15            Console.Beep();
16        }
17        managerParent.Position++;
18        DisplayPhoto();
19   }
20
21   private void btnFirst_Click(object sender, EventArgs e)
22   {
23        managerParent.Position = 0;
24        DisplayPhoto();
25   }
26
27   private void btnLast_Click(object sender, EventArgs e)
28   {
29        managerParent.Position = managerParent.Count - 1;
30        DisplayPhoto();
31   }
```

Figure 5.9 Inserting some data into **Parent** table

Step 9   Save and run the application. What is displayed first is the first record in **Parent** table. Click on four navigation buttons to prove the result.

Figure 5.10 Parent form when it first runs

Figure 5.11 The result when user clicks **Last >|** button

5.3 Tutorial Steps of Creating Form for Parent Table: Message Box

Step 1   There are two places where you can use the message box in **Parent** table input form.
One message box is provided after saving updates to let the user know that the save
was successful and another message box is related to record deletion.

Use the following code in **btnSave_Click** event method:

```
1  private void btnSave_Click(object sender, EventArgs e)
2  {
3      MessageBox.Show("Records successfully saved", "Save",
4          MessageBoxButtons.OK, MessageBoxIcon.Information);
5  }
```

There will be more code in this event. The code implements only message box.

Step 2   Use this code on **btnDelete_Click** event method:

```
1  private void btnDelete_Click(object sender, EventArgs e)
2  {
3      DialogResult response;
4      response = MessageBox.Show("Dou you really want to delete this record?",
5          "Delete", MessageBoxButtons.YesNo, MessageBoxIcon.Question,
6          MessageBoxDefaultButton.Button2);
7  }
```

Step 3   Save the application and run it. Click on **Delete** button to see as shown in Figure 5.12.

Figure 5.12 Message box is displayed when user clicks **Delete** button

5.4 Tutorial Steps of Creating Form for Parent Table: Application State

Step 1   The **Parent** form operates in one of three states: **View** state, **Add** state, or **Edit** state.
In the **View** state, user can navigate one record to another, user can switch to **Edit**
state, user can add and/or delete records, or user can exit the application.

In **Add** and **Edit** state, no navigation is made possible, data can be updated, and user
can have access to **Save** and **Cancel** operations. Each of these steps can be
implemented using the **Enabled** property of the button and the **ReadOnly** property of

the text box. You use **TabIndex** (and **TabOrder**) to shift focus on the text box controls. You will use a method of moving from one state to another.

Clear all tab ordering for the ten buttons by setting the **TabStop** property to **False**. Additionally, set the **TabStop** property to **False** for the **Parent ID** text box.

Step 2   Add a method named **SetState** as follows:

```
private void SetState(string stateStr) {
    switch (stateStr)
    {
        case "View":
            txtParentID.BackColor = Color.Red;
            txtParentID.ForeColor = Color.Black;
            txtFirstName.ReadOnly = true;
            txtLastName.ReadOnly = true;
            dtpBirthDate.Enabled = false;
            txtPhone.ReadOnly = true;
            txtMobile.ReadOnly = true;
            chkStatus.Enabled = false;
            cboEthnicity.Enabled = false;
            cboNationality.Enabled = false;
            cboReligion.Enabled = false;
            cboGender.Enabled = false;
            btnUpload.Enabled = false;
            btnFirst.Enabled = true;
            btnPrev.Enabled = true;
            btnNext.Enabled = true;
            btnLast.Enabled = true;
            btnAddNew.Enabled = true;
            btnSave.Enabled = false;
            btnDelete.Enabled = true;
            btnCancel.Enabled = false;
            btnEdit.Enabled = true;
            btnDone.Enabled = true;
            txtFirstName.Focus();
            break;

        default: // Edit or Add
            txtParentID.ReadOnly = false;
            txtParentID.BackColor = Color.Red;
            txtParentID.ForeColor = Color.Black;
            txtFirstName.ReadOnly = false;
            txtLastName.ReadOnly = false;
            dtpBirthDate.Enabled = true;
            dtpBirthDate.Value = DateTime.Now;
            txtPhone.ReadOnly = false;
            txtMobile.ReadOnly = false;
            chkStatus.Enabled = true;
            cboEthnicity.Enabled = true;
```

```
43        cboNationality.Enabled = true;
44        cboNationality.SelectedIndex = -1;
45        cboReligion.Enabled = true;
46        cboReligion.SelectedIndex = -1;
47        cboGender.Enabled = true;
48        cboReligion.SelectedIndex = -1;
49        btnUpload.Enabled = true;
50        btnFirst.Enabled = false;
51        btnPrev.Enabled = false;
52        btnNext.Enabled = false;
53        btnLast.Enabled = false;
54        btnAddNew.Enabled = false;
55        btnSave.Enabled = true;
56        btnDelete.Enabled = false;
57        btnCancel.Enabled = true;
58        btnEdit.Enabled = false;
59        btnDone.Enabled = false;
60        txtFirstName.Focus();
61        break;
62    }
63 }
```

The code above specifies **View**, **Add**, or **Edit** state for the application. Pay attention
to which buttons are available and which are not. Note that **Parent ID** text box is given
red back color if it is in **Add** or **Edit** state to indicate that it cannot be changed.

Step 3   Set the **View** state when the application first runs. Add the following code in line 53
to **FormParent_Load** event method:

```
1  private void FormParent_Load(object sender, EventArgs e)
2  {
3      try
4      {
5          // Connects to database
6          connBook = new SqlConnection("Data Source=.\\SQLEXPRESS;
7          AttachDbFilename=D:\\Database\\DBMS.mdf;
8          Integrated Security = True; Connect Timeout = 30;
9          User Instance = True");
10
11         // Opens connection
12         connBook.Open();
13
14         // Creates Command object
15         commandParent = new SqlCommand(
16             "SELECT * FROM Parent ORDER BY FirstName", connBook);
17
18         // Creates DataAdapter/DataTable objects
19         adapterParent = new SqlDataAdapter();
20         adapterParent.SelectCommand = commandParent;
21         tableParent = new DataTable();
```

```
22      adapterParent.Fill(tableParent);
23
24      // Binds controls to data table
25      txtParentID.DataBindings.Add("Text",
26          tableParent, "ParentID");
27      txtFirstName.DataBindings.Add("Text",
28          tableParent, "FirstName");
29      txtLastName.DataBindings.Add("Text",
30          tableParent, "LastName");
31      dtpBirthDate.DataBindings.Add("Text",
32          tableParent, "BirthDate");
33      lblPhotoFile.DataBindings.Add("Text",
34          tableParent, "PhotoFile");
35      txtPhone.DataBindings.Add("Text", tableParent, "Phone");
36      txtMobile.DataBindings.Add("Text", tableParent, "Mobile");
37      chkStatus.DataBindings.Add("Checked",
38          tableParent, "Status");
39      cboEthnicity.DataBindings.Add("Text",
40          tableParent, "Ethnicity");
41      cboNationality.DataBindings.Add("Text",
42          tableParent, "Nationality");
43      cboReligion.DataBindings.Add("Text",
44          tableParent, "Religion");
45      cboGender.DataBindings.Add("Text", tableParent, "Gender");
46
47      // Creates data update
48      managerParent =
49          (CurrencyManager)BindingContext[tableParent];
50
51      DisplayPhoto();
52      this.Show();
53      SetState("View");
54  }
55  catch (Exception ex)
56  {
57      MessageBox.Show(ex.Message,
58        "Error in reading Parent table.",
59        MessageBoxButtons.OK, MessageBoxIcon.Error);
60      return;
61  }
}
```

Step 4 When **Add New** button is clicked, you need to switch to **Add** state. Add the following code to **btnAddNew_Click** event method:

```
1  private void btnAddNew_Click(object sender, EventArgs e)
2  {
3      SetState("Add");
4  }
```

Step 5   When **Edit** button is clicked, the application will be switched to **Edit** state. Add the
following code to **btnEdit_Click** event method:

```
1  private void btnEdit_Click(object sender, EventArgs e)
2  {
3      SetState("Edit");
4  }
```

Step 6   When **Cancel** or **Save** button is clicked (in **Add** or **Edit** state), application will return
to the **View** state. Put this line of code in **btnCancel_Click** and **btnSave_Click** event
methods:

```
1  private void btnCancel_Click(object sender, EventArgs e)
2  {
3      SetState("View");
4  }
5
6  private void btnSave_Click(object sender, EventArgs e)
7  {
8      SetState("View");
9  }
```

Step 7   Save and run the application. You will see the application in its initial state (**View**
state) as shown in Figure 5.13.

Figure 5.13 Parent form is in **View** state when it first runs

When user clicks the **Edit** or **Add New** button, you will see what is shown in Figure 5.14.

Figure 5.14 Parent form is in **Add** or **Edit** state

5.5 Tutorial Steps of Creating Form for Parent Table: Error Trapping

Step 1   Modify **btnAddNew_Click**, **btnSave_Click**, and **btnDelete_Click** event methods to handle error trapping:

```
private void btnAddNew_Click(object sender, EventArgs e)
{
    try
    {
        SetState("Add");
    }
    catch (Exception ex)
    {
        MessageBox.Show("Error adding new record.", "Error",
            MessageBoxButtons.OK, MessageBoxIcon.Error);
    }
}
```

```
private void btnSave_Click(object sender, EventArgs e)
```

```
 2   {
 3       try
 4       {
 5           MessageBox.Show("Record successfully saved", "Save",
 6           MessageBoxButtons.OK, MessageBoxIcon.Information);
 7           SetState("View");
 8       }
 9       catch (Exception ex)
10       {
11           MessageBox.Show("Error saving record.", "Error",
12               MessageBoxButtons.OK, MessageBoxIcon.Error);
13       }
14   }
```

```
 1   private void btnDelete_Click(object sender, EventArgs e)
 2   {
 3       DialogResult response;
 4       response = MessageBox.Show("Dou you really want to delete this record?",
 5           "Delete", MessageBoxButtons.YesNo, MessageBoxIcon.Question,
 6           MessageBoxDefaultButton.Button2);
 7       if (response == DialogResult.No)
 8       {
 9           return;
10       }
11
12       try
13       {
14
15       }
16       catch (Exception ex)
17       {
18           MessageBox.Show("Error deleting record.", "Error",
19               MessageBoxButtons.OK, MessageBoxIcon.Error);
20       }
21   }
```

5.6 Tutorial Steps of Creating Form for Parent Table: Editing Record

Step 1   You will now add editing capability and other related capabilities to save and/or cancel edits. Before saving update into database, you need to validate data entered by user. In this case, you need to validate parent name and year range of birth date. Define a method named **ValidateData** to validate data entered by user:

```
 1   private bool ValidateData()
 2   {
 3       string message = "";
 4       int yearInput, yearNow;
 5       bool allOK = true;
 6
```

```
7      // Checks name in txtFirstName and txtLastName
8      if (txtFirstName.Text.Trim().Equals("") &&
9          txtLastName.Text.Trim().Equals(""))
10     {
11         message = "You should enter first and last name." + "\r\n";
12         txtFirstName.Focus();
13         allOK = false;
14
15     }
16     // Checks birth date range
17     yearInput = dtpBirthDate.Value.Year;
18     yearNow = DateTime.Now.Year;
19
20     if (yearInput > yearNow || yearInput < yearNow - 150)
21     {
22         message += "Year should be between " +
23             (yearNow - 150).ToString() +
24             " and " + yearNow.ToString();
25         dtpBirthDate.Focus();
26         allOK = false;
27     }
28
29     if (!allOK)
30     {
31         MessageBox.Show(message, "Validation Error",
32             MessageBoxButtons.OK, MessageBoxIcon.Information);
33     }
34
35     return (allOK);
36 }
```

Step 2   Add a **KeyPress** event for the **txtFirstName** and **txtLastName** text boxes to accept
only letters:

```
1      private void txtFirstName_KeyPress(object sender, KeyPressEventArgs e)
2      {
3          if ((e.KeyChar >= 'a' && e.KeyChar <= 'z') ||
4              (e.KeyChar >= 'A' && e.KeyChar <= 'Z') ||
5              (int)e.KeyChar == 8 || (int)e.KeyChar == 32)
6          {
7              // Key can be accepted
8              e.Handled = false;
9          }
10         else
11         {
12             e.Handled = true;
13             Console.Beep();
14         }
15
16         if ((int)e.KeyChar == 13)
```

```
17      txtLastName.Focus();
18  }
```

```
1   private void txtLastName_KeyPress(object sender, KeyPressEventArgs e)
2   {
3       if ((e.KeyChar >= 'a' && e.KeyChar <= 'z') ||
4           (e.KeyChar >= 'A' && e.KeyChar <= 'Z') ||
5           (int)e.KeyChar == 8 || (int)e.KeyChar == 32)
6       {
7           // Key can be accepted
8           e.Handled = false;
9       }
10      else
11      {
12          e.Handled = true;
13          Console.Beep();
14      }
15
16      if ((int)e.KeyChar == 13)
17          dtpBirthDate.Focus();
18  }
```

Step 3   Add a **KeyPress** event for the **txtMobile** and **txtPhone** text boxes to accept only digits:

```
1   private void txtMobile_KeyPress(object sender, KeyPressEventArgs e)
2   {
3       e.Handled = !char.IsDigit(e.KeyChar) &&
4           !char.IsControl(e.KeyChar);
5
6       if ((int)e.KeyChar == 13)
7           chkStatus.Focus();
8   }
9
10  private void txtPhone_KeyPress(object sender, KeyPressEventArgs e)
11  {
12      e.Handled = !char.IsDigit(e.KeyChar) &&
13          !char.IsControl(e.KeyChar);
14
15      if ((int)e.KeyChar == 13)
16          txtMobile.Focus();
17  }
```

Step 4   Add a **KeyPress** event for other controls to move to the next control:

```
1   private void dtpBirthDate_KeyPress(object sender, KeyPressEventArgs e)
2   {
3       if ((int)e.KeyChar == 13)
4           txtPhone.Focus();
5   }
6
7   private void chkStatus_KeyPress(object sender, KeyPressEventArgs e)
```

```
8    {
9        if ((int)e.KeyChar == 13)
10           cboEthnicity.Focus();
11   }
12
13   private void cboEthnicity_KeyPress(object sender, KeyPressEventArgs e)
14   {
15       if ((int)e.KeyChar == 13)
16           cboNationality.Focus();
17   }
18
19   private void cboNationality_KeyPress(object sender, KeyPressEventArgs e)
20   {
21       if ((int)e.KeyChar == 13)
22           cboReligion.Focus();
23   }
24
25   private void cboReligion_KeyPress(object sender, KeyPressEventArgs e)
26   {
27       if ((int)e.KeyChar == 13)
28           txtFirstName.Focus();
29   }
```

Step 5   Add the following line of code to the form-level declaration:

```
1    string appState;
```

step 6   Add this code in line 2 to **SetState** method:

```
1    private void SetState(string stateStr) {
2        appState = stateStr;
3
4        switch (stateStr)
5        {
6            case "View":
7                txtParentID.BackColor = Color.Red;
8                txtParentID.ForeColor = Color.Black;
9                txtFirstName.ReadOnly = true;
10               txtLastName.ReadOnly = true;
11               dtpBirthDate.Enabled = false;
12               txtPhone.ReadOnly = true;
13               txtMobile.ReadOnly = true;
14               chkStatus.Enabled = false;
15               cboEthnicity.Enabled = false;
16               cboNationality.Enabled = false;
17               cboReligion.Enabled = false;
18               cboGender.Enabled = false;
19               btnUpload.Enabled = false;
20               btnFirst.Enabled = true;
21               btnPrev.Enabled = true;
```

```
22        btnNext.Enabled = true;
23        btnLast.Enabled = true;
24        btnAddNew.Enabled = true;
25        btnSave.Enabled = false;
26        btnDelete.Enabled = true;
27        btnCancel.Enabled = false;
28        btnEdit.Enabled = true;
29        btnDone.Enabled = true;
30        txtFirstName.Focus();
31        break;
32
33    default: // Edit or Add
34        txtParentID.ReadOnly = false;
35        txtParentID.BackColor = Color.Red;
36        txtParentID.ForeColor = Color.Black;
37        txtFirstName.ReadOnly = false;
38        txtLastName.ReadOnly = false;
39        dtpBirthDate.Enabled = true;
40        dtpBirthDate.Value = DateTime.Now;
41        txtPhone.ReadOnly = false;
42        txtMobile.ReadOnly = false;
43        chkStatus.Enabled = true;
44        cboEthnicity.Enabled = true;
45        cboNationality.Enabled = true;
46        cboNationality.SelectedIndex = -1;
47        cboReligion.Enabled = true;
48        cboReligion.SelectedIndex = -1;
49        cboGender.Enabled = true;
50        cboReligion.SelectedIndex = -1;
51        btnUpload.Enabled = true;
52        btnFirst.Enabled = false;
53        btnPrev.Enabled = false;
54        btnNext.Enabled = false;
55        btnLast.Enabled = false;
56        btnAddNew.Enabled = false;
57        btnSave.Enabled = true;
58        btnDelete.Enabled = false;
59        btnCancel.Enabled = true;
60        btnEdit.Enabled = false;
61        btnDone.Enabled = false;
62        txtFirstName.Focus();
63        break;
64    }
65 }
```

Step 7   Modify **btnSave_Click** event method to save the change and reposition the pointer to the record just edited:

```
1  private void btnSave_Click(object sender, EventArgs e)
2  {
```

```
3    if (!ValidateData())
4    {
5        return;
6    }
7
8    string nameSaved = txtFirstName.Text;
9    int rowSaved;
10
11   try
12   {
13       managerParent.EndCurrentEdit();
14
15       if (appState.Equals("Add"))
16       {
17           tableParent.Rows[managerParent.Count - 1]["Status"] =
18               chkStatus.Checked;
19           chkStatus.DataBindings.Add("Checked",
20               tableParent, "Status");
21       }
22
23       tableParent.DefaultView.Sort = "FirstName";
24       rowSaved = tableParent.DefaultView.Find(nameSaved);
25       managerParent.Position = rowSaved;
26
27       MessageBox.Show("Records successfully saved", "Save",
28           MessageBoxButtons.OK, MessageBoxIcon.Information);
29
30       SetState("View");
31   }
32   catch (Exception ex)
33   {
34       MessageBox.Show("Error saving record.", "Error",
35           MessageBoxButtons.OK, MessageBoxIcon.Error);
36   }
37 }
```

Step 8   Modify **btnCancel_Click** event method to restore controls if the edit is canceled:

```
1    private void btnCancel_Click(object sender, EventArgs e)
2    {
3        managerParent.CancelCurrentEdit();
4
5        SetState("View");
6        DisplayPhoto();
7    }
```

Step 9   Add the following code in line to the **FormParent_FormClosing** method to save any
          changes to the database file:

```
1   private void FormParent_FormClosing(object sender,
2   FormClosingEventArgs e)
3   {
4       try
5       {
6           // Saves changes into database
7           SqlCommandBuilder parentAdapterCommand =
8               new SqlCommandBuilder(adapterParent);
9           adapterParent.Update(tableParent);
10      }
11      catch (Exception ex)
12      {
13          MessageBox.Show("Error saving database into file: \r\n" +
14              ex.Message, "Saving Error", MessageBoxButtons.OK,
15              MessageBoxIcon.Error);
16      }
17
18      // Closes connection to database
19      connBook.Close();
20
21      // Deletes objects
22      connBook.Dispose();
23      commandParent.Dispose();
24      adapterParent.Dispose();
25  }
```

Figure 5.15 Editing operation is successfully performed

Step 10   Define Click event of **btnUpload** as follows:

```
1   private void btnUpload_Click(object sender, EventArgs e)
2   {
3       try
4       {
5           if (dlgOpen.ShowDialog() == DialogResult.OK)
6           {
7               lblPhotoFile.Text = dlgOpen.FileName;
8               DisplayPhoto();
9           }
10      }
11      catch (Exception ex)
12      {
13          MessageBox.Show(ex.Message, "Error in loading photo",
14              MessageBoxButtons.OK, MessageBoxIcon.Error);
15      }
16  }
```

Step 11   Save and run the application. Make sure Edit feature is working properly. Try filling other fields. Make sure the **Cancel** button is working properly. This is shown in Figure 5.15.

5.7 Tutorial Steps of Creating Form for Parent Table: Adding New Record

Step 1   You now implement the capability on the form to add new records to the database. Add the following line of code to the form-level declaration:

```
1   int myBookmark;
```

Step 2   Modify **btnAddNew_Click** event method to add a new record by adding code in line 6-13:

```
1   private void btnAddNew_Click(object sender, EventArgs e)
2   {
3       try
4       {
5           // Deletes binding from checkbox chkStatus
6           chkStatus.DataBindings.Clear();
7           chkStatus.Checked = false;
8
9           lblPhotoFile.Text = "";
10          DisplayPhoto();
11
12          myBookmark = managerParent.Position;
13          managerParent.AddNew();
14          SetState("Add");
```

```
15        }
16    catch (Exception ex)
17    {
18        MessageBox.Show("Error adding new record.", "Error",
19            MessageBoxButtons.OK, MessageBoxIcon.Error);
20    }
21 }
```

Figure 5.16 The new record has been successfully saved into the database

Step 3   Modify **btnCancel_Click** event method to differentiate between cancellation during
Edit mode and **Add** mode by adding code in line 5-10:

```
1  private void btnCancel_Click(object sender, EventArgs e)
2  {
3      managerParent.CancelCurrentEdit();
4
5      if (appState.Equals("Add"))
6      {
7          managerParent.Position = myBookmark;
8          chkStatus.DataBindings.Add("Checked",
9              tableParent, "Status");
10     }
11     SetState("View");
12     DisplayPhoto();
13 }
```

Step 4   Save and run the application. Click **Add New** button. Note that all text boxes are blank (including **Parent ID** text box. Fill first name, last name, and other fields, then click **Save**. New record has been successfully saved as shown in Figure 5.16.

5.8 Tutorial Steps of Creating Form for Parent Table: Deleting Record

Step 1   You will now add the capability to delete records from **Parent** table. Modify the **btnDelete_Click** event method by adding code in line 14 to delete records if the user responds to **Yes** in the message box:

```
1   private void btnDelete_Click(object sender, EventArgs e)
2   {
3       DialogResult response;
4       response = MessageBox.Show("Dou you really want to delete this record?",
5           "Delete", MessageBoxButtons.YesNo, MessageBoxIcon.Question,
6           MessageBoxDefaultButton.Button2);
7       if (response == DialogResult.No)
8       {
9           return;
10      }
11
12      try
13      {
14          managerParent.RemoveAt(managerParent.Position);
15      }
16      catch (Exception ex)
17      {
18          MessageBox.Show("Error deleting record.", "Error",
19              MessageBoxButtons.OK, MessageBoxIcon.Error);
20      }
21  }
```

Step 2   Save the application and run it. Make sure the **Yes** and **No** responses in the message box give correct results. Delete only those records you added using **Add New** button.

5.9 Tutorial Steps of Creating Form for Parent Table: Stopping Application

Step 1   Add the following code in line 4-12 and line 34 to **FormParent_FormClosing** event method to ensure user doesn't close the application during **Edit** or **Add** mode:

```
1   private void FormParent_FormClosing(object sender,
2   FormClosingEventArgs e)
3   {
4       if (appState.Equals("Edit") || appState.Equals("Add"))
5       {
```

```
6          MessageBox.Show(
7              "You should finish editing before closing application.",
8              "", MessageBoxButtons.OK, MessageBoxIcon.Information);
9          e.Cancel = true;
10     }
11     else
12     {
13         try
14         {
15             // Saves changes into
16             SqlCommandBuilder parentAdapterCommand =
17                 new SqlCommandBuilder(adapterParent);
18             adapterParent.Update(tableParent);
19         }
20         catch (Exception ex)
21         {
22             MessageBox.Show("Error saving database into file: \r\n" +
23                 ex.Message, "Error Saving", MessageBoxButtons.OK,
24                 MessageBoxIcon.Error);
25         }
26
27         // Closes connection to database
28         connBook.Close();
29
30         // Deletes objects
31         connBook.Dispose();
32         commandParent.Dispose();
33         adapterParent.Dispose();
34     }
35 }
```

Step 2   Put this code in **btnDone_Click** event method:

```
1  private void btnDone_Click(object sender, EventArgs e)
2  {
3      this.Close();
4  }
```

Step 3   Save and run the application. Make sure the **Done** button is working properly. Make sure the user cannot close the application in **Edit** or **Add** mode.

5.10 Tutorial Steps of Searching Capability

Step 1   In the **SetState** method, enable group box control in **View** mode and disable it in **Add** and **Edit** mode. Use its **Enabled** property.

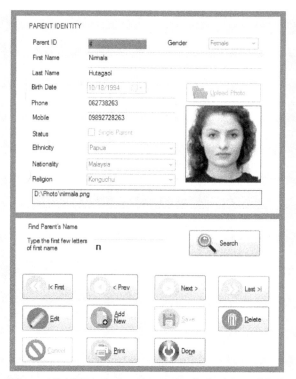

Figure 5.17 Parent's name search feature added

Step 3   Add the following code to **btnSearch_Click** event method:

```
1   private void btnSearch_Click(object sender, EventArgs e)
2   {
3       if (txtFind.Text.Equals(""))
4       {
5           return;
6       }
7
8       int rowSaved = managerParent.Position;
9       DataRow[] rowFound;
10      tableParent.DefaultView.Sort = "FirstName";
11      rowFound = tableParent.Select("FirstName LIKE '" +
12          txtFind.Text + "*'");
13
14      if (rowFound.Length == 0)
15      {
16          managerParent.Position = rowSaved;
17      }
18      else
19      {
20          managerParent.Position =
21              tableParent.DefaultView.Find(rowFound[0]["FirstName"]);
22          DisplayPhoto();
```

```
23      }
24  }
```

Step 4   Save and run the application. Try searching by providing the first or two letters of the parent's name, as shown in Figure 5.17.

5.11 Tutorial Steps of Adding Search Buttons

Step 1   Add a button control on the form. Set its **Name** property as **btnAll** and its **Text** property as **Show All Parents**. You add another **DataGridView** control and set its **Name** property as **grdParent**. You also need to add a label and set its **Text** property as **Number of Records:**. Then add a textbox on the form. Set its **Name** property as **txtNumberRecord**. The resulting form is shown in Figure 5.18.

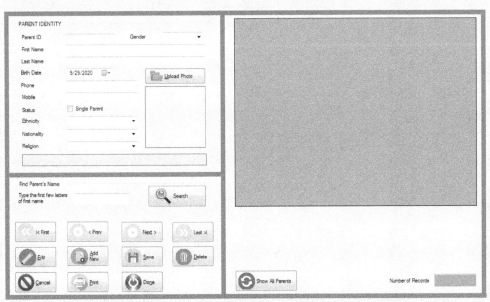

Figure 5.18 Parent form after a number of controls added

Step 2   Add the following form-level declarations:

```
1  String SQLAll = "SELECT * FROM Parent ";
2  Button[] buttonArr = new Button[26];
```

SQLAll is a variable that contains the default SQL statements, while **buttonArr** is an array containing the search buttons.

Step 3   Define a new method named **createSearchButton()** as follows:

```
1  private void createSearchButton()
2  {
```

```
3    // Creates search buttons
4    int w, lStart, l, t;
5    int btnHeight = 35; // by trial and error
6
7    // Search buttons
8    // Button width - 13 buttons in a row
9    w = Convert.ToInt32(grdParent.Width / 13);
10
11   // Aligns buttons
12   lStart = Convert.ToInt32((grdParent.Width))-20;
13   l = lStart; t = grdParent.Top + grdParent.Height + 10;
14
15   // Creates and positions 26 buttons
16   for (int i = 0; i < 26; i++)
17   {
18       // Creates push button
19       buttonArr[i] = new Button();
20       buttonArr[i].TabStop = false;
21
22       // Sets Text property
23       buttonArr[i].Text = ((char)(65 + i)).ToString();
24       buttonArr[i].Font = new Font(buttonArr[i].Font.FontFamily,
25           9, FontStyle.Bold);
26
27       // Positions buttons
28       buttonArr[i].Width = w;
29       buttonArr[i].Height = btnHeight;
30       buttonArr[i].Left = l;
31       buttonArr[i].Top = t;
32
33       // Gives color
34       buttonArr[i].BackColor = Color.Red;
35       buttonArr[i].ForeColor = Color.White;
36
37       // Adds each button on form
38       this.Controls.Add(buttonArr[i]);
39
40       // Adds event handler
41       buttonArr[i].Click +=
42           new System.EventHandler(this.btnSQL_Click);
43       l += w+1;
44
45       if (i == 12)
46       {
47           // Next row
48           l = lStart; t += btnHeight;
49       }
50   }
51 }
```

This method creates search buttons A through Z using **buttonArrr** array. The code above then specifies the width of the button and places it on the form. Finally, the resulting records are displayed by programmatically clicking **btnSQL** button.

Step 4   Write the code for **btnSQL_Click** event method (handle **Click** event for all search buttons) as follows:

```
private void btnSQL_Click(object sender, EventArgs e)
{
    SqlCommand commResult = null;
    SqlDataAdapter adapterResult = new SqlDataAdapter();
    DataTable tableResult = new DataTable();
    String StatementSQL;

    // Determines which button is clicked and creates SQL statement
    Button buttonClicked = (Button)sender;
    switch (buttonClicked.Text)
    {
        case "Show All Members":
            StatementSQL = SQLAll;
            break;
        case "Z":
            // Z button is clicked
            // Appends at SQLAll to limit records upto for item Z
            StatementSQL = SQLAll + " WHERE FirstName > 'Z' ";
            break;
        default:
            // Letter keys except Z
            // Appends at SQLAll to limit records
            // for letter that is clicked
            int idx = (int)(Convert.ToChar(buttonClicked.Text)) - 65;
            StatementSQL = SQLAll + " WHERE FirstName > '" +
            buttonArr[idx].Text + " ' ";
            StatementSQL += " AND FirstName < '" +
                    buttonArr[idx + 1].Text + " ' ";

            // Binds to controls
            int rowSaved = managerParent.Position;
            DataRow[] rowFound;
            tableParent.DefaultView.Sort = "FirstName";
            rowFound = tableParent.Select("FirstName LIKE '" +
                buttonArr[idx].Text + "*'");

            if (rowFound.Length == 0)
            {
                managerParent.Position = rowSaved;
            }
            else
            {
```

```
43          managerParent.Position =
44              tableParent.DefaultView.Find(
45                  rowFound[0]["FirstName"]);
46          DisplayPhoto();
47      }
48      break;
49  }
50  StatementSQL += " ORDER BY FirstName";
51
52  // Applies SQL statement
53  try
54  {
55      // Creates Command and DataAdapater objects
56      commResult = new SqlCommand(StatementSQL, connBook);
57      adapterResult.SelectCommand = commResult;
58      adapterResult.Fill(tableResult);
59
60      // Binds DataGridView with data table
61      grdParent.DataSource = tableResult;
62      txtNumberRecord.Text = tableResult.Rows.Count.ToString();
63  }
64
65  catch (Exception ex)
66  {
67      MessageBox.Show(ex.Message, "Error Processing SQL",
68          MessageBoxButtons.OK, MessageBoxIcon.Error);
69  }
70  commResult.Dispose();
71  adapterResult.Dispose();
72  tableResult.Dispose();
73  }
```

This method determines which button is clicked and forms an SQL statement. If the
button with the **Text** property of the button is "**Show All Parents**" is clicked, then all
records will be displayed. When a key letter is clicked, the code determines which
letter the user clicks on and attaches an additional test (using **AND**) to the **WHERE**
field in the default SQL statement.

Step 5   Add the following code in line 59-61 to **FormParent_Load** event method. The code
creates search buttons and perform **Click** event of **btnAll** programmatically:

```
1  private void FormParent_Load(object sender, EventArgs e)
2  {
3      try
4      {
5          // Connects to database
6          connBook = new SqlConnection("Data Source=.\\SQLEXPRESS;
7              AttachDbFilename=D:\\Database\\DBMS.mdf;
8              Integrated Security = True; Connect Timeout = 30;
9              User Instance = True");
```

```
10
11        // Opens connection
12        connBook.Open();
13
14        // Creates Command object
15        commandParent = new SqlCommand(
16            "SELECT * FROM Parent ORDER BY FirstName", connBook);
17
18        // Creates DataAdapter/DataTable objects
19        adapterParent = new SqlDataAdapter();
20        adapterParent.SelectCommand = commandParent;
21        tableParent = new DataTable();
22        adapterParent.Fill(tableParent);
23
24        // Binds controls to data table
25        txtParentID.DataBindings.Add("Text",
26            tableParent, "ParentID");
27        txtFirstName.DataBindings.Add("Text",
28            tableParent, "FirstName");
29        txtLastName.DataBindings.Add("Text",
30            tableParent, "LastName");
31        dtpBirthDate.DataBindings.Add("Text",
32            tableParent, "BirthDate");
33        lblPhotoFile.DataBindings.Add("Text",
34            tableParent, "PhotoFile");
35        txtPhone.DataBindings.Add("Text", tableParent, "Phone");
36        txtMobile.DataBindings.Add("Text", tableParent, "Mobile");
37        chkStatus.DataBindings.Add("Checked",
38            tableParent, "Status");
39        cboEthnicity.DataBindings.Add("Text",
40            tableParent, "Ethnicity");
41        cboNationality.DataBindings.Add("Text",
42            tableParent, "Nationality");
43        cboReligion.DataBindings.Add("Text",
44            tableParent, "Religion");
45        cboGender.DataBindings.Add("Text", tableParent, "Gender");
46
47        // Creates data update
48        managerParent =
49            (CurrencyManager)BindingContext[tableParent];
50
51        DisplayPhoto();
52        this.Show();
53        SetState("View");
54
55        //Creates 26 search buttons
56        createSearchButton();
57
58        // Clicks all records when form starts
59        btnAll.Click += new System.EventHandler(this.btnSQL_Click);
60
```

```
61          btnAll.PerformClick();
62      }
63      catch (Exception ex)
64      {
65          MessageBox.Show(ex.Message,
66            "Error in reading Parent table.",
67            MessageBoxButtons.OK, MessageBoxIcon.Error);
68          return;
69      }
70  }
```

Figure 5.19 The application when it first runs

Step 6   Define **RowPostPaint** event of **grdParent** control to give it a row numbering:

```
1   private void grdParent_RowPostPaint(object sender,
2   DataGridViewRowPostPaintEventArgs e)
3   {
4       var grid = sender as DataGridView;
5       var rowIdx = (e.RowIndex + 1).ToString();
6
7       var centerFormat = new StringFormat()
8       {
9           // Aligns to middle
10          Alignment = StringAlignment.Center,
11          LineAlignment = StringAlignment.Center
12      };
13
14      var headerBounds = new Rectangle(e.RowBounds.Left,
15          e.RowBounds.Top, grid.RowHeadersWidth, e.RowBounds.Height);
16      e.Graphics.DrawString(rowIdx, this.Font,
17          SystemBrushes.ControlText, headerBounds, centerFormat);
```

```
18    }
```

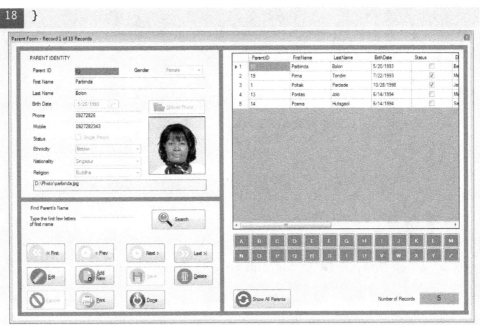

Figure 5.20 The results when the 'P' button is clicked

Step 7   Define **Refresh_DGV** to refresh data grid view, **grdParent**, as follows:

```
1    private void Refresh_DGV()
2    {
3        // Connects to database
4            connBook = new SqlConnection("Data Source=.\\SQLEXPRESS;
5            AttachDbFilename=D:\\Database\\DBMS.mdf;
6            Integrated Security = True; Connect Timeout = 30;
7            User Instance = True");
8        connBook.Open();
9
10       // Save changes to database
11       SqlCommandBuilder parentDBAdapterCommand = new
12           SqlCommandBuilder(adapterParent);
13       adapterParent.Update(tableParent);
14
15       SqlCommand commandResult = null;
16       SqlDataAdapter adapterResult = new SqlDataAdapter();
17       DataTable tableResult = new DataTable();
18
19       try
20       {
21           // Creates Command and DataAdapter objects
22           commandResult = new SqlCommand(SQLAll, connBook);
23           adapterResult.SelectCommand = commandResult;
24           tableResult.Clear();
25           adapterResult.Fill(tableResult);
26
```

```
27        // Binds grid view to data table
28        grdParent.DataSource = tableResult;
29        txtNumberRecord.Text = tableResult.Rows.Count.ToString();
30    }
31
32    catch (Exception ex)
33    {
34        MessageBox.Show(ex.Message, "Error in processing SQL",
35            MessageBoxButtons.OK, MessageBoxIcon.Error);
36    }
37
38    commandResult.Dispose();
39    adapterResult.Dispose();
40    tableResult.Dispose();
41 }
```

Step 8   Call **Refresh_DGV** from **Click** event of **btnAll** as follows:

```
1    private void btnAll_Click(object sender, EventArgs e)
2    {
3        Refresh_DGV();
4    }
```

Step 9   Save and run the application. The result is shown in Figure 5.19. Notice how the search
buttons are created. Also note that all records are displayed initially. Click on one of
the search buttons. Only records with the parent's initial matching the letter in the
clicked button will be displayed. Figure 5.20 is the query result when the 'P' button is
clicked.

5.12 Tutorial Steps of Reporting Parents

Step 1   Now, you will add a feature to read all the data in the database. You need a database
report. The report is quite simple. For each record, the data from each field will be
displayed.

Add this line of code at the top of the code window:

```
1    using System.Drawing.Printing;
```

Step 2   Add the page number variable to the form level declaration:

```
1    int pageNumber;
```

Step 3   Add code in line 30 and line 63 to the **SetState** method to set **Enabled** property of
btnPrint to **true** in **View** mode and **false** in **Add/Edit** mode.

```
1   private void SetState(string stateStr) {
2       appState = stateStr;
3
4       switch (stateStr)
5       {
6           case "View":
7               txtParentID.BackColor = Color.Red;
8               txtParentID.ForeColor = Color.Black;
9               txtFirstName.ReadOnly = true;
10              txtLastName.ReadOnly = true;
11              dtpBirthDate.Enabled = false;
12              txtPhone.ReadOnly = true;
13              txtMobile.ReadOnly = true;
14              chkStatus.Enabled = false;
15              cboEthnicity.Enabled = false;
16              cboNationality.Enabled = false;
17              cboReligion.Enabled = false;
18              cboGender.Enabled = false;
19              btnUpload.Enabled = false;
20              btnFirst.Enabled = true;
21              btnPrev.Enabled = true;
22              btnNext.Enabled = true;
23              btnLast.Enabled = true;
24              btnAddNew.Enabled = true;
25              btnSave.Enabled = false;
26              btnDelete.Enabled = true;
27              btnCancel.Enabled = false;
28              btnEdit.Enabled = true;
29              btnDone.Enabled = true;
30              btnPrint.Enabled = true;
31              txtFirstName.Focus();
32              break;
33
34          default: // Edit or Add
35              txtParentID.ReadOnly = false;
36              txtParentID.BackColor = Color.Red;
37              txtParentID.ForeColor = Color.Black;
38              txtFirstName.ReadOnly = false;
39              txtLastName.ReadOnly = false;
40              dtpBirthDate.Enabled = true;
41              dtpBirthDate.Value = DateTime.Now;
42              txtPhone.ReadOnly = false;
43              txtMobile.ReadOnly = false;
44              chkStatus.Enabled = true;
45              cboEthnicity.Enabled = true;
46              cboNationality.Enabled = true;
47              cboNationality.SelectedIndex = -1;
48              cboReligion.Enabled = true;
49              cboReligion.SelectedIndex = -1;
50              cboGender.Enabled = true;
51              cboReligion.SelectedIndex = -1;
```

```
52        btnUpload.Enabled = true;
53        btnFirst.Enabled = false;
54        btnPrev.Enabled = false;
55        btnNext.Enabled = false;
56        btnLast.Enabled = false;
57        btnAddNew.Enabled = false;
58        btnSave.Enabled = true;
59        btnDelete.Enabled = false;
60        btnCancel.Enabled = true;
61        btnEdit.Enabled = false;
62        btnDone.Enabled = false;
63        btnPrint.Enabled = false;
64        txtFirstName.Focus();
65        break;
66    }
67 }
```

Step 4   Add the following code to **btnPrint_Click** event method:

```
1  private void btnPrint_Click(object sender, EventArgs e)
2  {
3      // Declares document
4      PrintDocument docParent;
5
6      // Creates document and gives it a name
7      docParent = new PrintDocument();
8      docParent.DocumentName = "Parent Data";
9
10     // Adds code handler
11     docParent.PrintPage += new
12         PrintPageEventHandler(this.PrintParent);
13
14     // Prints document in preview control
15     pageNumber = 1;
16     int positionSaved = managerParent.Position;
17     dlgPreview.Document = docParent;
18     dlgPreview.ShowDialog();
19
20     // Deletes document when finished printing
21     docParent.Dispose();
22     managerParent.Position = positionSaved;
23
24     DisplayPhoto();
25 }
```

Step 5   Add the following code to **PrintParent** method:

```
1  private void PrintParent(object sender, PrintPageEventArgs e)
2  {
3      // Tracks every record, prints every record
4      managerParent.Position = pageNumber - 1;
```

```
 5      DisplayPhoto();
 6
 7      Font myFont = new Font("Arial", 14, FontStyle.Bold);
 8      int y = e.MarginBounds.Top + 50;
 9
10      // Prints Header
11      e.Graphics.DrawString("Member's Data (" +
12          DateTime.Now.ToShortDateString() + ") - Page " +
13          pageNumber.ToString(), myFont, Brushes.Black,
14          e.MarginBounds.Left, y);
15      y += 2 * Convert.ToInt32(myFont.GetHeight(e.Graphics));
16
17      e.Graphics.DrawString("****************************
18          ***************************", myFont, Brushes.Black,
19          e.MarginBounds.X, y);
20      y += Convert.ToInt32(myFont.GetHeight(e.Graphics));
21
22      // Prints photo (width 4 inci, height depends on
23      // height/width ratio of photo)
24      int h = Convert.ToInt32(
25          150 * picParent.Image.Height / picParent.Image.Width);
26      e.Graphics.DrawImage(picParent.Image,
27          e.MarginBounds.X, y, 150, h);
28
29      int slideRight = 175;
30
31      // Prints text information
32      myFont = new Font("Arial", 12, FontStyle.Regular);
33      e.Graphics.DrawString("Parent ID:", myFont, Brushes.Black,
34          e.MarginBounds.X + slideRight, y);
35      e.Graphics.DrawString(txtParentID.Text, myFont, Brushes.Black,
36          e.MarginBounds.X + slideRight + slideRight, y);
37      y += Convert.ToInt32(myFont.GetHeight(e.Graphics));
38
39      e.Graphics.DrawString("Full Name:", myFont, Brushes.Black,
40          e.MarginBounds.X + slideRight, y);
41      e.Graphics.DrawString(txtFirstName.Text + txtLastName.Text,
42          myFont, Brushes.Black, e.MarginBounds.X + 2*slideRight, y);
43      y += Convert.ToInt32(myFont.GetHeight(e.Graphics));
44
45      e.Graphics.DrawString("Gender:", myFont, Brushes.Black,
46          e.MarginBounds.X + slideRight, y);
47      e.Graphics.DrawString(cboGender.Text, myFont, Brushes.Black,
48          e.MarginBounds.X + 2 * slideRight, y);
49      y += Convert.ToInt32(myFont.GetHeight(e.Graphics));
50
51      e.Graphics.DrawString("Birth Date:", myFont, Brushes.Black,
52          e.MarginBounds.X + slideRight, y);
53      e.Graphics.DrawString(dtpBirthDate.Text, myFont, Brushes.Black,
54          e.MarginBounds.X + 2 * slideRight, y);
55      y += Convert.ToInt32(myFont.GetHeight(e.Graphics));
```

```csharp
56
57      e.Graphics.DrawString("Phone:", myFont, Brushes.Black,
58          e.MarginBounds.X + slideRight, y);
59      e.Graphics.DrawString(txtPhone.Text, myFont, Brushes.Black,
60          e.MarginBounds.X + 2* slideRight, y);
61      y += Convert.ToInt32(myFont.GetHeight(e.Graphics));
62
63      e.Graphics.DrawString("Mobile:", myFont, Brushes.Black,
64          e.MarginBounds.X + slideRight, y);
65      e.Graphics.DrawString(txtMobile.Text, myFont,
66          Brushes.Black, e.MarginBounds.X + 2 * slideRight, y);
67      y += Convert.ToInt32(myFont.GetHeight(e.Graphics));
68
69      e.Graphics.DrawString("Status:", myFont, Brushes.Black,
70          e.MarginBounds.X + slideRight, y);
71      e.Graphics.DrawString(chkStatus.Text, myFont, Brushes.Black,
72          e.MarginBounds.X + 2 * slideRight, y);
73      y += Convert.ToInt32(myFont.GetHeight(e.Graphics));
74
75      e.Graphics.DrawString("Ethnicity:", myFont, Brushes.Black,
76          e.MarginBounds.X + slideRight, y);
77      e.Graphics.DrawString(cboEthnicity.Text, myFont, Brushes.Black,
78          e.MarginBounds.X + 2 * slideRight, y);
79      y += Convert.ToInt32(myFont.GetHeight(e.Graphics));
80
81      e.Graphics.DrawString("Nationality:", myFont, Brushes.Black,
82          e.MarginBounds.X + slideRight, y);
83      e.Graphics.DrawString(cboNationality.Text, myFont,
84          Brushes.Black, e.MarginBounds.X + 2 * slideRight, y);
85      y += Convert.ToInt32(myFont.GetHeight(e.Graphics));
86
87      e.Graphics.DrawString("Religion:", myFont, Brushes.Black,
88          e.MarginBounds.X + slideRight, y);
89      e.Graphics.DrawString(cboReligion.Text, myFont, Brushes.Black,
90          e.MarginBounds.X + 2 * slideRight, y);
91      y += Convert.ToInt32(myFont.GetHeight(e.Graphics));
92
93      Font myFont2 = new Font("Arial", 14, FontStyle.Bold);
94      e.Graphics.DrawString("***************************
95          ***************************", myFont2, Brushes.Black,
96          e.MarginBounds.X, y);
97
98      pageNumber++;
99      if (pageNumber <= managerParent.Count)
100         e.HasMorePages = true;
101     else
102     {
103         e.HasMorePages = false;
104         pageNumber = 1;
105     }
106 }
```

On each page, a header is printed along with the data fields and parent's photo.

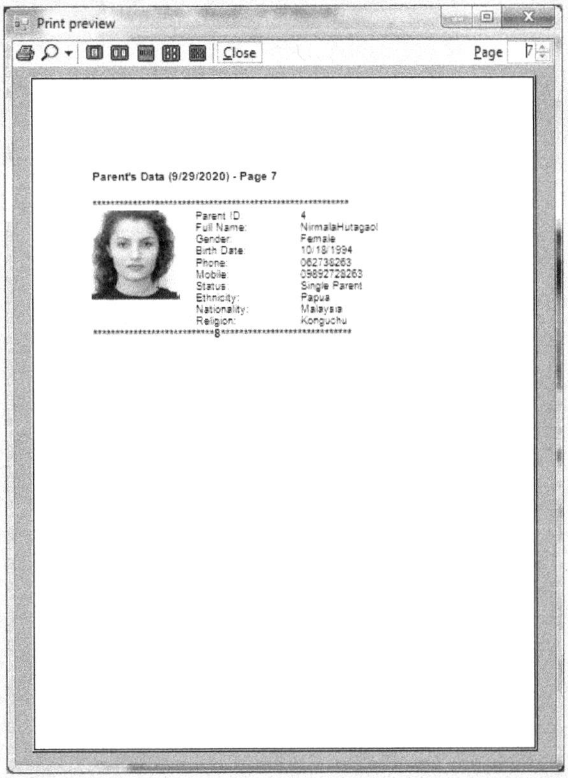

Figure 5.21 Each record in the table can now be printed

Step 6   Save and run the application. Click on the **Print** button. The print preview control will
be displayed on all parent pages, as shown in Figure 5.21.

5.13 Tutorial Steps of Creating Form for Student Table: Interface

Step 1   In this tutorial, you will build such a form for **Student** table. This table has fourteen
fields: **StudentID**, **ParentID**, **FirstName**, **LastName**, **BirthDate**, **YearEntry**,
Status, **Ethnicity**, **Nationality**, **Mobile**, **Phone**, **Religion**, **Gender**, and **PhotoFile**).

You need an input form so that user can edit existing records, delete records, or add
new records. The form will also have the capability of navigating from one record to
another. The steps that need to be done are as follows.

Start a new Visual C# application. You need fourteen label controls, one picture box,
six text boxes, five comboxes, one check box, two date time pickers, one
openfiledialog, and one printpreviewdialog. You also need four buttons for navigation,
seven buttons for controlling editing features, one button for searching parent's name,

one button to open parent form, and one button to upload member's photo. Place these controls on the form. The complete form looks as shown in Figure 5.22.

Step 2   Set the properties of each control as follows:

Form1 Control	
Name	FormParent
BackColor	Control
FormBorderStyle	FixedSingle
StartPosition	CenterScreen
Text	Form Parent

label1 Control	
Text	Parent ID

textBox1 Control	
Name	txtParentID
ReadOnly	True

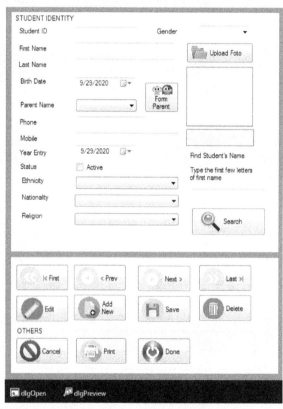

Figure 5.22 Design of parent form

label2 Control	
Text	Gender

combobox1 Control

Name	cboGender
BackColor	White
Items	{Male, Female}

label3 Control

Text	First Name

textBox2 Control

Name	txtFirstName

label4 Control

Text	Last Name

textBox3 Control

Name	txtLastName

label5 Control

Text	Birth Date

dateTimePicker1 Control

Name	dtpBirthDate
Format	short

label6 Control

Text	Phone

textBox4 Control

Name	txtPhone

label7 Control

Text	Mobile

textBox5 Control

Name	txtMobile

label18 Control

Text	Status

checkbox1 Control

Name	chkStatus
Text	Active

label19 Control

Text	Ethnicity

combobox2 Control

Name	cboEthnicity
Items	{Jawa, Sasak, Sunda, Batak, Betawi, Minang, Papua Bima, Melayu}

label10 Control	
Text	Nationality

combobox3 Control	
Name	cboNationality
Items	{Indonesia, Inggris
	Jepang, Amerika
	Korea Selatan,
	Malaysia, Singapur
	Vietnam}

label11 Control	
Text	Religion

combobox4 Control	
Name	cboReligion
Items	{ Islam,
	Kristen Protestan,
	Kristen Katolik,
	Buddha,
	Hindu,
	Konguchu,
	Kepercayaan}

label12 Control	
Name	lblPhotoFile

pictureBox1 Control	
Name	picStudent
SizeMode	StretchImage

label13 Control	
Text	Type the first few letters of first name

textBox6 Control	
Name	txtFind

label14 Control	
Text	Parent Name

comboBox5 Control	
Name	cboParent

label15 Control	
Text	Year Entry

dateTimePicker2 Control	
Name	dtpYearEntry

button1 Control	
Name	btnFirst

Text	|< First

button2 Control	
Name	btnPrev
Text	< Prev

button3 Control	
Name	btnNext
Text	Next >

button4 Control	
Name	btnLast
Text	Last >|

button5 Control	
Name	btnSearch
Text	Search

button6 Control	
Name	btnEdit
Text	&Edit

button7 Control	
Name	btnSave
Text	&Save

button8 Control	
Name	btnCancel
Text	&Cancel

button9 Control	
Name	btnAddNew
Text	&Add New

button10 Control	
Name	btnDelete
Text	&Delete

button11 Control	
Name	btnDone
Text	Do&ne

button12 Control	
Name	btnUpload
Text	&Upload Photo

button13 Control	
Name	btnPrint
Text	&Print

button14 Control	
Name	btnFormParent
Text	&Form Parent

openFileDialog1 Control	

Name	dlgOpen

printPreviewDialog1 Control

Name	dlgPreview

Step 3   You will add features to this parent form gradually. At this point, you will add code to construct the data table and to navigate the records in the **Student** table. Add these lines of code at the top of the window:

```
1  using System.Data.SqlClient;
2  using System.IO;
3  using System.Drawing.Printing;
```

Step 4   Write the following form-level declarations for creating data objects:

```
1  SqlConnection connBook;
2  SqlCommand commandStudent;
3  SqlDataAdapter adapterStudent;
4  DataTable tableStudent;
5  CurrencyManager managerStudent;
6
7  SqlCommand commandParent;
8  SqlDataAdapter adapterParent;
   DataTable tableParent;
```

Step 5   Add the following code to the **FormStudent_Load** event method:

```
1  private void FormStudent_Load(object sender, EventArgs e)
2  {
3      try
4      {
5          // Connects to database
6          connBook = new SqlConnection("Data Source=.\\SQLEXPRESS;
7              AttachDbFilename=D:\\Database\\DBMS.mdf;
8              Integrated Security = True; Connect Timeout = 30;
9              User Instance = True");
10
11         // Opens connection
12         connBook.Open();
13
14         // Creates Command object
15         commandStudent = new SqlCommand(
16             "SELECT * FROM Student ORDER BY FirstName", connBook);
17
18         // Creates DataAdapter/DataTable objects
19         adapterStudent = new SqlDataAdapter();
20         adapterStudent.SelectCommand = commandStudent;
21         tableStudent = new DataTable();
22         adapterStudent.Fill(tableStudent);
23
24         // Binds controls to data table
25         txtStudentID.DataBindings.Add("Text",
```

```
26              tableStudent, "StudentID");
27          txtFirstName.DataBindings.Add("Text",
28              tableStudent, "FirstName");
29          txtLastName.DataBindings.Add("Text",
30              tableStudent, "LastName");
31          dtpBirthDate.DataBindings.Add("Text",
32              tableStudent, "BirthDate");
33          lblPhotoFile.DataBindings.Add("Text",
34              tableStudent, "PhotoFile");
35          txtPhone.DataBindings.Add("Text", tableStudent, "Phone");
36          txtMobile.DataBindings.Add("Text", tableStudent, "Mobile");
37          dtpYearEntry.DataBindings.Add("Text",
38              tableStudent, "YearEntry");
39          chkStatus.DataBindings.Add("Checked",
40              tableStudent, "Status");
41          cboEthnicity.DataBindings.Add("Text",
42              tableStudent, "Ethnicity");
43          cboNationality.DataBindings.Add("Text",
44              tableStudent, "Nationality");
45          cboReligion.DataBindings.Add("Text",
46              tableStudent, "Religion");
47          cboGender.DataBindings.Add("Text", tableStudent, "Gender");
48
49          // Creates data update manager
50          managerStudent =
51              (CurrencyManager)BindingContext[tableStudent];
52
53          // Populates combobox cboParent
54          commandParent = new SqlCommand("SELECT ParentID,
55              CONCAT(FirstName, ' ', LastName) AS Name FROM Parent",
56              connBook);
57          adapterParent = new SqlDataAdapter();
58          adapterParent.SelectCommand = commandParent;
59          tableParent = new DataTable();
60          adapterParent.Fill(tableParent);
61          cboParent.DataSource = tableParent;
62
63          cboParent.DisplayMember = "Name";
64          cboParent.ValueMember = "ParentID";
65          cboParent.DataBindings.Add("SelectedValue",
66              tableStudent, "ParentID");
67
68          DisplayPhoto();
69          this.Show();
70      }
71      catch (Exception ex)
72      {
73          MessageBox.Show(ex.Message,
74            "Error in reading Parent table.",
75            MessageBoxButtons.OK, MessageBoxIcon.Error);
76          return;
```

```
77        }
78    }
79
```

The code above creates the data objects needed to open the database and construct the **Student** table (includes all fields). The code above then binds the controls with the update manager object (**CurrencyManager**). It also populates **cboParent**.

Step 6   Define **DisplayPhoto** to display author photo in **picStudent**:

```
1    private void DisplayPhoto()
2    {
3        // Displays photo
4        if (!lblPhotoFile.Text.Equals(""))
5        {
6            try
7            {
8                picStudent.Image = Image.FromFile(lblPhotoFile.Text);
9            }
10           catch (Exception ex)
11           {
12               MessageBox.Show(ex.Message, "Error Loading Photo File",
13                   MessageBoxButtons.OK, MessageBoxIcon.Error);
14           }
15       }
16       else
17       {
18           string dir =
19               Path.GetDirectoryName(Application.ExecutablePath);
20           string filename = Path.Combine(dir, @"student.png");
21           picStudent.Image = Image.FromFile(filename);
22       }
23   }
```

Step 7   Add the following code to **FormStudent_FormClosing** event method to close the database connection:

```
1    private void FormStudent_FormClosing(object sender,
2    FormClosingEventArgs e)
3    {
4        // Closes connection to database
5        connBook.Close();
6
7        // Deletes objects
8        connBook.Dispose();
9        commandStudent.Dispose();
10       adapterStudent.Dispose();
11       commandParent.Dispose();
12       adapterParent.Dispose();
13       tableParent.Dispose();
```

```
14 }
```

Step 8   Write the following code for the **Click** event of the four navigation buttons:

```
1   private void btnPrev_Click(object sender, EventArgs e)
2   {
3       if (managerStudent.Position == 0)
4       {
5           Console.Beep();
6       }
7       managerStudent.Position--;
8       DisplayPhoto();
9   }
10
11  private void btnNext_Click(object sender, EventArgs e)
12  {
13      if (managerStudent.Position == managerStudent.Count - 1)
14      {
15          Console.Beep();
16      }
17      managerStudent.Position++;
18      DisplayPhoto();
19  }
20
21  private void btnFirst_Click(object sender, EventArgs e)
22  {
23      managerStudent.Position = 0;
24      DisplayPhoto();
25  }
26
27  private void btnLast_Click(object sender, EventArgs e)
28  {
29      managerStudent.Position = managerStudent.Count - 1;
30      DisplayPhoto();
31  }
```

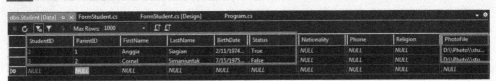

Figure 5.23 Inserting some data into **Student** table

Figure 5.24 Student form when it first runs

Figure 5.25 The result when user clicks **Last >|** button

Step 9   Insert some data into **Student** table as shown in Figure 5.23.

Step 10   Save and run the application. What is displayed first is the first record in **Student** table. Click on four navigation buttons to prove the result.

5.14 Tutorial Steps of Creating Form for Student Table: Message Box

Step 1   There are two places where you can use the message box in **Student** table input form. One message box is provided after saving updates to let the user know that the save was successful and another message box is related to record deletion.

Use the following code in **btnSave_Click** event method:

```
1  private void btnSave_Click(object sender, EventArgs e)
2  {
3      MessageBox.Show("Records successfully saved", "Save",
4          MessageBoxButtons.OK, MessageBoxIcon.Information);
5  }
```

There will be more code in this event. The code implements only message box.

Step 2   Use this code on **btnDelete_Click** event method:

```
1  private void btnDelete_Click(object sender, EventArgs e)
2  {
3      DialogResult response;
4      response = MessageBox.Show("Dou you really want to delete this record?",
5          "Delete", MessageBoxButtons.YesNo, MessageBoxIcon.Question,
6          MessageBoxDefaultButton.Button2);
7  }
```

Step 3   Save the application and run it. Click on **Delete** button to see as shown in Figure 5.26.

Figure 5.26 Message box is displayed when user clicks **Delete** button

5.15 Tutorial Steps of Creating Form for Student Table: Application State

Step 1   The **Student** form operates in one of three states: **View** state, **Add** state, or **Edit** state. In the **View** state, user can navigate one record to another, user can switch to **Edit** state, user can add and/or delete records, or user can exit the application.

In **Add** and **Edit** state, no navigation is made possible, data can be updated, and user can have access to **Save** and **Cancel** operations. Each of these steps can be implemented using the **Enabled** property of the button and the **ReadOnly** property of the text box. You use **TabIndex** (and **TabOrder**) to shift focus on the text box controls. You will use a method of moving from one state to another.

Clear all tab ordering for the ten buttons by setting the **TabStop** property to **False**. Additionally, set the **TabStop** property to **False** for the **Student ID** text box.

Step 2   Add a method named **SetState** as follows:

```
1   private void SetState(string stateStr) {
2       switch (stateStr)
3       {
4           case "View":
5               txtStudentID.BackColor = Color.Red;
6               txtStudentID.ForeColor = Color.Black;
7               txtFirstName.ReadOnly = true;
8               txtLastName.ReadOnly = true;
9               dtpBirthDate.Enabled = false;
10              txtPhone.ReadOnly = true;
11              txtMobile.ReadOnly = true;
12              cboParent.Enabled = false;
13              dtpYearEntry.Enabled = false;
14              chkStatus.Enabled = false;
15              cboEthnicity.Enabled = false;
16              cboNationality.Enabled = false;
17              cboReligion.Enabled = false;
18              cboGender.Enabled = false;
19              btnUpload.Enabled = false;
20              btnFirst.Enabled = true;
21              btnPrev.Enabled = true;
22              btnNext.Enabled = true;
23              btnLast.Enabled = true;
24              btnAddNew.Enabled = true;
25              btnSave.Enabled = false;
26              btnDelete.Enabled = true;
27              btnCancel.Enabled = false;
28              btnEdit.Enabled = true;
29              btnDone.Enabled = true;
30              txtFirstName.Focus();
31              break;
32
```

```
33          case "Add":
34              txtStudentID.ReadOnly = false;
35              txtStudentID.BackColor = Color.Red;
36              txtStudentID.ForeColor = Color.Black;
37              txtFirstName.ReadOnly = false;
38              txtLastName.ReadOnly = false;
39              dtpBirthDate.Enabled = true;
40              dtpBirthDate.Value = DateTime.Now;
41              txtPhone.ReadOnly = false;
42              txtMobile.ReadOnly = false;
43              cboParent.Enabled = false;
44              dtpYearEntry.Enabled = false;
45              chkStatus.Enabled = true;
46              cboEthnicity.Enabled = true;
47              cboEthnicity.DataBindings.Clear();
48              cboEthnicity.SelectedIndex = -1;
49              cboNationality.Enabled = true;
50              cboNationality.DataBindings.Clear();
51              cboNationality.SelectedIndex = -1;
52              cboReligion.Enabled = true;
53              cboReligion.DataBindings.Clear();
54              cboReligion.SelectedIndex = -1;
55              cboGender.Enabled = true;
56              cboReligion.SelectedIndex = -1;
57              btnUpload.Enabled = true;
58              btnFirst.Enabled = false;
59              btnPrev.Enabled = false;
60              btnNext.Enabled = false;
61              btnLast.Enabled = false;
62              btnAddNew.Enabled = false;
63              btnSave.Enabled = true;
64              btnDelete.Enabled = false;
65              btnCancel.Enabled = true;
66              btnEdit.Enabled = false;
67              btnDone.Enabled = false;
68              lblPhotoFile.Text = "";
69              chkStatus.DataBindings.Clear();
70              chkStatus.Checked = false;
71              txtFirstName.Focus();
72              break;
73
74          case "Edit":
75              txtStudentID.ReadOnly = false;
76              txtStudentID.BackColor = Color.Red;
77              txtStudentID.ForeColor = Color.Black;
78              txtFirstName.ReadOnly = false;
79              txtLastName.ReadOnly = false;
80              dtpBirthDate.Enabled = true;
81              txtPhone.ReadOnly = false;
82              txtMobile.ReadOnly = false;
83              cboParent.Enabled = false;
```

```
84        dtpYearEntry.Enabled = true;
85        chkStatus.Enabled = true;
86        cboEthnicity.Enabled = true;
87        cboNationality.Enabled = true;
88        cboReligion.Enabled = true;
89        cboGender.Enabled = true;
90        btnUpload.Enabled = true;
91        btnFirst.Enabled = false;
92        btnPrev.Enabled = false;
93        btnNext.Enabled = false;
94        btnLast.Enabled = false;
95        btnAddNew.Enabled = false;
96        btnSave.Enabled = true;
97        btnDelete.Enabled = false;
98        btnCancel.Enabled = true;
99        btnEdit.Enabled = false;
100       btnDone.Enabled = false;
101       txtFirstName.Focus();
102       break;
103    }
104 }
```

The code above specifies **View**, **Add**, or **Edit** state for the application. Pay attention
to which buttons are available and which are not. Note that **Student ID** text box is
given red back color if it is in **Add** or **Edit** state to indicate that it cannot be changed.

Step 3   Set the **View** state when the application first runs. Add the following code in line 70
to **FormStudent_Load** event method:

```
1  private void FormStudent_Load(object sender, EventArgs e)
2  {
3      try
4      {
5          // Connects to database
6          connBook = new SqlConnection("Data Source=.\\SQLEXPRESS;
7              AttachDbFilename=D:\\Database\\DBMS.mdf;
8              Integrated Security = True; Connect Timeout = 30;
9              User Instance = True");
10
11         // Opens connection
12         connBook.Open();
13
14         // Creates Command object
15         commandStudent = new SqlCommand(
16             "SELECT * FROM Student ORDER BY FirstName", connBook);
17
18         // Creates DataAdapter/DataTable objects
19         adapterStudent = new SqlDataAdapter();
20         adapterStudent.SelectCommand = commandStudent;
21         tableStudent = new DataTable();
```

```
22    adapterStudent.Fill(tableStudent);
23
24    // Binds controls to data table
25    txtStudentID.DataBindings.Add("Text",
26        tableStudent, "StudentID");
27    txtFirstName.DataBindings.Add("Text",
28        tableStudent, "FirstName");
29    txtLastName.DataBindings.Add("Text",
30        tableStudent, "LastName");
31    dtpBirthDate.DataBindings.Add("Text",
32        tableStudent, "BirthDate");
33    lblPhotoFile.DataBindings.Add("Text",
34        tableStudent, "PhotoFile");
35    txtPhone.DataBindings.Add("Text", tableStudent, "Phone");
36    txtMobile.DataBindings.Add("Text", tableStudent, "Mobile");
37    dtpYearEntry.DataBindings.Add("Text",
38        tableStudent, "YearEntry");
39    chkStatus.DataBindings.Add("Checked",
40        tableStudent, "Status");
41    cboEthnicity.DataBindings.Add("Text",
42        tableStudent, "Ethnicity");
43    cboNationality.DataBindings.Add("Text",
44        tableStudent, "Nationality");
45    cboReligion.DataBindings.Add("Text",
46        tableStudent, "Religion");
47    cboGender.DataBindings.Add("Text", tableStudent, "Gender");
48
49    // Creates data update manager
50    managerStudent =
51        (CurrencyManager)BindingContext[tableStudent];
52
53    // Populates combobox cboParent
54    commandParent = new SqlCommand("SELECT ParentID,
55        CONCAT(FirstName, ' ', LastName) AS Name FROM Parent",
56        connBook);
57    adapterParent = new SqlDataAdapter();
58    adapterParent.SelectCommand = commandParent;
59    tableParent = new DataTable();
60    adapterParent.Fill(tableParent);
61    cboParent.DataSource = tableParent;
62
63    cboParent.DisplayMember = "Name";
64    cboParent.ValueMember = "ParentID";
65    cboParent.DataBindings.Add("SelectedValue",
66        tableStudent, "ParentID");
67
68    DisplayPhoto();
69    this.Show();
70    SetState("View");
71  }
72
```

```
73    catch (Exception ex)
74    {
75        MessageBox.Show(ex.Message,
76          "Error in reading Parent table.",
77          MessageBoxButtons.OK, MessageBoxIcon.Error);
78        return;
79    }
    }
```

Step 4 When **Add New** button is clicked, you need to switch to **Add** state. Add the following code to **btnAddNew_Click** event method:

```
1    private void btnAddNew_Click(object sender, EventArgs e)
2    {
3        SetState("Add");
4    }
```

Step 5 When **Edit** button is clicked, the application will be switched to **Edit** state. Add the following code to **btnEdit_Click** event method:

```
1    private void btnEdit_Click(object sender, EventArgs e)
2    {
3        SetState("Edit");
4    }
```

Step 6 When **Cancel** or **Save** button is clicked (in **Add** or **Edit** state), application will return to the **View** state. Put this line of code in **btnCancel_Click** and **btnSave_Click** event methods:

```
1    private void btnCancel_Click(object sender, EventArgs e)
2    {
3        SetState("View");
4    }
5
6    private void btnSave_Click(object sender, EventArgs e)
7    {
8        SetState("View");
9    }
```

Step 7 Save and run the application. You will see the application in its initial state (**View** state) as shown in Figure 5.27.

Figure 5.27 Student form is in **View** state when it first runs

Figure 5.28 Student form is in **Edit** state

Figure 5.29 Student form is in **Add** state

When user clicks the **Edit** or **Add New** button, you will see what is shown in Figure
5.28 and 5.29.

5.20 Tutorial Steps of Creating Form for Student Table: Error Trapping

Step 1   Modify **btnAddNew_Click**, **btnSave_Click**, and **btnDelete_Click** event methods to
handle error trapping:

```
private void btnAddNew_Click(object sender, EventArgs e)
{
    try
    {
        SetState("Add");
        DisplayPhoto();
    }
    catch (Exception ex)
    {
        MessageBox.Show("Error adding new record.", "Error",
            MessageBoxButtons.OK, MessageBoxIcon.Error);
    }
}
```

```
private void btnSave_Click(object sender, EventArgs e)
{
```

```
3    try
4    {
5        MessageBox.Show("Record successfully saved", "Save",
6        MessageBoxButtons.OK, MessageBoxIcon.Information);
7        SetState("View");
8    }
9    catch (Exception ex)
10   {
11       MessageBox.Show("Error saving record.", "Error",
12           MessageBoxButtons.OK, MessageBoxIcon.Error);
13   }
14 }
```

```
1  private void btnDelete_Click(object sender, EventArgs e)
2  {
3      DialogResult response;
4      response = MessageBox.Show("Dou you really want to delete this record?",
5          "Delete", MessageBoxButtons.YesNo, MessageBoxIcon.Question,
6          MessageBoxDefaultButton.Button2);
7      if (response == DialogResult.No)
8      {
9          return;
10     }
11
12     try
13     {
14
15     }
16     catch (Exception ex)
17     {
18         MessageBox.Show("Error deleting record.", "Error",
19             MessageBoxButtons.OK, MessageBoxIcon.Error);
20     }
21 }
```

5.21 Tutorial Steps of Creating Form for Student Table: Editing Record

Step 1   You will now add editing capability and other related capabilities to save and/or cancel
edits. Before saving update into database, you need to validate data entered by user. In
this case, you need to validate student and parent name and year range of birth date.
Define a method named **ValidateData** to validate data entered by user:

```
1  private bool ValidateData()
2  {
3      string message = "";
4      int yearInput, yearNow;
5      bool allOK = true;
6
```

```
7       // Checks name in txtFirstName, txtLastName, and cboParent
8       if (txtFirstName.Text.Trim().Equals("") ||
9           txtLastName.Text.Trim().Equals("") ||
10          cboParent.SelectedIndex == -1)      {
11          message = "You should enter first and last name and choose
12              parent's name." + "\r\n";
13          txtFirstName.Focus();
14          allOK = false;
15      }
16
17      // Checks birth date range
18      yearInput = dtpBirthDate.Value.Year;
19      yearNow = DateTime.Now.Year;
20
21      if (yearInput > yearNow || yearInput < yearNow - 150)
22      {
23          message += "Year should be between " +
24              (yearNow - 150).ToString() +
25              " and " + yearNow.ToString();
26          dtpBirthDate.Focus();
27          allOK = false;
28      }
29
30      if (!allOK)
31      {
32          MessageBox.Show(message, "Validation Error",
33              MessageBoxButtons.OK, MessageBoxIcon.Information);
34      }
35
36      return (allOK);
37  }
```

Step 2   Add a **KeyPress** event for the **txtFirstName** and **txtLastName** text boxes to accept only letters:

```
1   private void txtFirstName_KeyPress(object sender, KeyPressEventArgs e)
2   {
3       if ((e.KeyChar >= 'a' && e.KeyChar <= 'z') ||
4           (e.KeyChar >= 'A' && e.KeyChar <= 'Z') ||
5           (int)e.KeyChar == 8 || (int)e.KeyChar == 32)
6       {
7           // Key can be accepted
8           e.Handled = false;
9       }
10      else
11      {
12          e.Handled = true;
13          Console.Beep();
14      }
15
```

```
16      if ((int)e.KeyChar == 13)
17          txtLastName.Focus();
18  }
```

```
1   private void txtLastName_KeyPress(object sender, KeyPressEventArgs e)
2   {
3       if ((e.KeyChar >= 'a' && e.KeyChar <= 'z') ||
4           (e.KeyChar >= 'A' && e.KeyChar <= 'Z') ||
5           (int)e.KeyChar == 8 || (int)e.KeyChar == 32)
6       {
7           // Key can be accepted
8           e.Handled = false;
9       }
10      else
11      {
12          e.Handled = true;
13          Console.Beep();
14      }
15
16      if ((int)e.KeyChar == 13)
17          dtpBirthDate.Focus();
18  }
```

Step 3   Add a **KeyPress** event for other fields:

```
1   private void dtpBirthDate_KeyPress(object sender, KeyPressEventArgs e)
2   {
3       if ((int)e.KeyChar == 13)
4           cboParent.Focus();
5   }
6
7   private void cboParent_KeyPress(object sender, KeyPressEventArgs e)
8   {
9       if ((int)e.KeyChar == 13)
10          txtMobile.Focus();
11  }
12
13  private void txtPhone_KeyPress(object sender, KeyPressEventArgs e)
14  {
15      e.Handled = !char.IsDigit(e.KeyChar) &&
16          !char.IsControl(e.KeyChar);
17
18      if ((int)e.KeyChar == 13)
19          txtMobile.Focus();
20  }
21
22  private void txtMobile_KeyPress(object sender, KeyPressEventArgs e)
23  {
24      e.Handled = !char.IsDigit(e.KeyChar) &&
25          !char.IsControl(e.KeyChar);
26
```

```
27        if ((int)e.KeyChar == 13)
28            dtpYearEntry.Focus();
29    }
30
31    private void dtpYearEntry_KeyPress(object sender, KeyPressEventArgs e)
32    {
33        if ((int)e.KeyChar == 13)
34            chkStatus.Focus();
35    }
36
37    private void chkStatus_KeyPress(object sender, KeyPressEventArgs e)
38    {
39        if ((int)e.KeyChar == 13)
40            cboEthnicity.Focus();
41    }
42
43    private void cboEthnicity_KeyPress(object sender, KeyPressEventArgs e)
44    {
45        if ((int)e.KeyChar == 13)
46            cboNationality.Focus();
47    }
48
49    private void cboNationality_KeyPress(object sender, KeyPressEventArgs e)
50    {
51        if ((int)e.KeyChar == 13)
52            cboReligion.Focus();
53    }
54
55    private void cboReligion_KeyPress(object sender, KeyPressEventArgs e)
56    {
57        if ((int)e.KeyChar == 13)
58            cboGender.Focus();
59    }
60
61    private void cboGender_KeyPress(object sender, KeyPressEventArgs e)
62    {
63        if ((int)e.KeyChar == 13)
64            txtFirstName.Focus();
65    }
66
```

Step 4   Add the following line of code to the form-level declaration:

```
1    string appState;
```

step 5   Add this code in line 2 to **SetState** method:

```
1    private void SetState(string stateStr) {
2        appState = stateStr;
3        switch (stateStr)
```

```
4      {
5          case "View":
6              txtStudentID.BackColor = Color.Red;
7              txtStudentID.ForeColor = Color.Black;
8              txtFirstName.ReadOnly = true;
9              txtLastName.ReadOnly = true;
10             dtpBirthDate.Enabled = false;
11             txtPhone.ReadOnly = true;
12             txtMobile.ReadOnly = true;
13             cboParent.Enabled = false;
14             dtpYearEntry.Enabled = false;
15             chkStatus.Enabled = false;
16             cboEthnicity.Enabled = false;
17             cboNationality.Enabled = false;
18             cboReligion.Enabled = false;
19             cboGender.Enabled = false;
20             btnUpload.Enabled = false;
21             btnFirst.Enabled = true;
22             btnPrev.Enabled = true;
23             btnNext.Enabled = true;
24             btnLast.Enabled = true;
25             btnAddNew.Enabled = true;
26             btnSave.Enabled = false;
27             btnDelete.Enabled = true;
28             btnCancel.Enabled = false;
29             btnEdit.Enabled = true;
30             btnDone.Enabled = true;
31             txtFirstName.Focus();
32             break;
33
34         case "Add":
35             txtStudentID.ReadOnly = false;
36             txtStudentID.BackColor = Color.Red;
37             txtStudentID.ForeColor = Color.Black;
38             txtFirstName.ReadOnly = false;
39             txtLastName.ReadOnly = false;
40             dtpBirthDate.Enabled = true;
41             dtpBirthDate.Value = DateTime.Now;
42             txtPhone.ReadOnly = false;
43             txtMobile.ReadOnly = false;
44             cboParent.Enabled = false;
45             dtpYearEntry.Enabled = false;
46             chkStatus.Enabled = true;
47             cboEthnicity.Enabled = true;
48             cboEthnicity.DataBindings.Clear();
49             cboEthnicity.SelectedIndex = -1;
50             cboNationality.Enabled = true;
51             cboNationality.DataBindings.Clear();
52             cboNationality.SelectedIndex = -1;
53             cboReligion.Enabled = true;
54             cboReligion.DataBindings.Clear();
```

```
55          cboReligion.SelectedIndex = -1;
56          cboGender.Enabled = true;
57          cboReligion.SelectedIndex = -1;
58          btnUpload.Enabled = true;
59          btnFirst.Enabled = false;
60          btnPrev.Enabled = false;
61          btnNext.Enabled = false;
62          btnLast.Enabled = false;
63          btnAddNew.Enabled = false;
64          btnSave.Enabled = true;
65          btnDelete.Enabled = false;
66          btnCancel.Enabled = true;
67          btnEdit.Enabled = false;
68          btnDone.Enabled = false;
69          lblPhotoFile.Text = "";
70          chkStatus.DataBindings.Clear();
71          chkStatus.Checked = false;
72          txtFirstName.Focus();
73          break;
74
75      case "Edit":
76          txtStudentID.ReadOnly = false;
77          txtStudentID.BackColor = Color.Red;
78          txtStudentID.ForeColor = Color.Black;
79          txtFirstName.ReadOnly = false;
80          txtLastName.ReadOnly = false;
81          dtpBirthDate.Enabled = true;
82          txtPhone.ReadOnly = false;
83          txtMobile.ReadOnly = false;
84          cboParent.Enabled = false;
85          dtpYearEntry.Enabled = true;
86          chkStatus.Enabled = true;
87          cboEthnicity.Enabled = true;
88          cboNationality.Enabled = true;
89          cboReligion.Enabled = true;
90          cboGender.Enabled = true;
91          btnUpload.Enabled = true;
92          btnFirst.Enabled = false;
93          btnPrev.Enabled = false;
94          btnNext.Enabled = false;
95          btnLast.Enabled = false;
96          btnAddNew.Enabled = false;
97          btnSave.Enabled = true;
98          btnDelete.Enabled = false;
99          btnCancel.Enabled = true;
100         btnEdit.Enabled = false;
101         btnDone.Enabled = false;
102         txtFirstName.Focus();
103         break;
104     }
105 }
```

Step 6 Modify **btnSave_Click** event method to save the change and reposition the pointer to the record just edited:

```
private void btnSave_Click(object sender, EventArgs e)
{
    if (!ValidateData())
    {
        return;
    }

    string nameSaved = txtFirstName.Text;
    int rowSaved;

    try
    {
        managerStudent.EndCurrentEdit();

        if (appState.Equals("Add"))
        {
            tableStudent.Rows[managerStudent.Count - 1]["Status"] =
                chkStatus.Checked;
            chkStatus.DataBindings.Add("Checked", tableStudent,
                "Status");
        }

        tableStudent.DefaultView.Sort = "FirstName";
        rowSaved = tableStudent.DefaultView.Find(nameSaved);
        managerStudent.Position = rowSaved;

        // Saves changes into database
        SqlCommandBuilder studentAdapterCommand = new
            SqlCommandBuilder(adapterStudent);
        adapterStudent.Update(tableStudent);

        MessageBox.Show("Records successfully saved", "Save",
            MessageBoxButtons.OK, MessageBoxIcon.Information);

        SetState("View");
    }
    catch (Exception ex)
    {
        MessageBox.Show("Error saving record.", "Error",
            MessageBoxButtons.OK, MessageBoxIcon.Error);
    }
}
```

Step 7 Modify **btnCancel_Click** event method to restore controls if the edit is canceled:

```
private void btnCancel_Click(object sender, EventArgs e)
{
```

```
3        managerStudent.CancelCurrentEdit();
4
5        SetState("View");
6        DisplayPhoto();
7    }
```

Step 8   Add the following code in line to the **FormStudent_FormClosing** method to save any
changes to the database file:

```
1    private void FormStudent_FormClosing(object sender,
2    FormClosingEventArgs e)
3    {
4        try
5        {
6            // Saves changes into database
7            SqlCommandBuilder studentAdapterCommand =
8                new SqlCommandBuilder(adapterStudent);
9            adapterStudent.Update(tableStudent);
10       }
11       catch (Exception ex)
12       {
13           MessageBox.Show("Error saving database into file: \r\n" +
14               ex.Message, "Saving Error", MessageBoxButtons.OK,
15               MessageBoxIcon.Error);
16       }
17
18       // Closes connection to database
19       connBook.Close();
20
21       // Deletes objects
22       connBook.Dispose();
23       commandStudent.Dispose();
24       adapterStudent.Dispose();
25       commandParent.Dispose();
26       adapterParent.Dispose();
27       tableParent.Dispose();
28   }
```

Figure 5.30 Editing operation is successfully performed

Step 9   Define Click event of **btnUpload** as follows:

```
1   private void btnUpload_Click(object sender, EventArgs e)
2   {
3       try
4       {
5           if (dlgOpen.ShowDialog() == DialogResult.OK)
6           {
7               lblPhotoFile.Text = dlgOpen.FileName;
8               DisplayPhoto();
9           }
10      }
11      catch (Exception ex)
12      {
13          MessageBox.Show(ex.Message, "Error in loading photo",
14              MessageBoxButtons.OK, MessageBoxIcon.Error);
15      }
16  }
```

Step 10   Save and run the application. Make sure Edit feature is working properly. Try filling other fields. Make sure the **Cancel** button is working properly. This is shown in Figure 5.30.

5.22 Tutorial Steps of Creating Form for Student Table: Adding New Record

Step 1   You now implement the capability on the form to add new records to the database. Add the following line of code to the form-level declaration:

```
1    int myBookmark;
```

Figure 5.31 The new record has been successfully saved into the database

Step 2   Modify **btnAddNew_Click** event method to add a new record by adding code in line 6-13:

```
1    private void btnAddNew_Click(object sender, EventArgs e)
2    {
3        try
4        {
5            // Deletes binding from checkbox chkStatus
6            chkStatus.DataBindings.Clear();
7            chkStatus.Checked = false;
8
9            lblPhotoFile.Text = "";
10           DisplayPhoto();
11
12           myBookmark = managerStudent.Position;
13           managerStudent.AddNew();
14           SetState("Add");
```

```
15      }
16      catch (Exception ex)
17      {
18          MessageBox.Show("Error adding new record.", "Error",
19              MessageBoxButtons.OK, MessageBoxIcon.Error);
20      }
21  }
```

Step 3   Modify **btnCancel_Click** event method to differentiate between cancellation during **Edit** mode and **Add** mode by adding code in line 5-10:

```
1   private void btnCancel_Click(object sender, EventArgs e)
2   {
3       managerStudent.CancelCurrentEdit();
4
5       if (appState.Equals("Add"))
6       {
7           managerStudent.Position = myBookmark;
8           chkStatus.DataBindings.Add("Checked",
9               tableStudent, "Status");
10      }
11      SetState("View");
12      DisplayPhoto();
13  }
```

Step 4   Save and run the application. Click **Add New** button. Note that all text boxes are blank (including **Student ID** text box. Fill first name, last name, and other fields, then click **Save**. New record has been successfully saved as shown in Figure 5.31.

5.23 Tutorial Steps of Creating Form for Student Table: Deleting Record

Step 1   You will now add the capability to delete records from **Student** table. Modify the **btnDelete_Click** event method by adding code in line 14 to delete records if the user responds to **Yes** in the message box:

```
1   private void btnDelete_Click(object sender, EventArgs e)
2   {
3       DialogResult response;
4       response = MessageBox.Show("Dou you really want to delete this record?",
5           "Delete", MessageBoxButtons.YesNo, MessageBoxIcon.Question,
6           MessageBoxDefaultButton.Button2);
7       if (response == DialogResult.No)
8       {
9           return;
10      }
11
12      try
```

```
13    {
14        managerStudent.RemoveAt(managerStudent.Position);
15    }
16    catch (Exception ex)
17    {
18        MessageBox.Show("Error deleting record.", "Error",
19            MessageBoxButtons.OK, MessageBoxIcon.Error);
20    }
21 }
```

Step 2   Save the application and run it. Make sure the **Yes** and **No** responses in the message box give correct results. Delete only those records you added using **Add New** button.

5.24 Tutorial Steps of Creating Form for Student Table: Stopping Application

Step 1   Add the following code in line 4-12 and line 34 to **FormStudent_FormClosing** event method to ensure user doesn't close the application during **Edit** or **Add** mode:

```
1    private void FormStudent_FormClosing(object sender,
2    FormClosingEventArgs e)
3    {
4        if (appState.Equals("Edit") || appState.Equals("Add"))
5        {
6            MessageBox.Show(
7                "You should finish editing before closing application.",
8                "", MessageBoxButtons.OK, MessageBoxIcon.Information);
9            e.Cancel = true;
10        }
11        else
12        {
13            try
14            {
15                // Saves changes into database
16                SqlCommandBuilder studentAdapterCommand =
17                    new SqlCommandBuilder(adapterStudent);
18                adapterStudent.Update(tableStudent);
19            }
20            catch (Exception ex)
21            {
22                MessageBox.Show("Error saving database into file: \r\n" +
23                    ex.Message, "Error Saving", MessageBoxButtons.OK,
24                    MessageBoxIcon.Error);
25            }
26
27            // Closes connection to database
28            connBook.Close();
29
30            // Deletes objects
```

```
31        connBook.Dispose();
32        commandStudent.Dispose();
33        adapterStudent.Dispose();
34        commandParent.Dispose();
35        adapterParent.Dispose();
36        tableParent.Dispose();
37    }
38 }
```

Step 2   Put this code in **btnDone_Click** event method:

```
1 private void btnDone_Click(object sender, EventArgs e)
2 {
3     this.Close();
4 }
```

Step 3   Save and run the application. Make sure the **Done** button is working properly. Make sure the user cannot close the application in **Edit** or **Add** mode.

5.25 Tutorial Steps of Searching Capability

Step 1   In the **SetState** method, enable group box control in **View** mode and disable it in **Add** and **Edit** mode. Use its **Enabled** property.

Step 3   Add the following code to **btnSearch_Click** event method:

```
1 private void btnSearch_Click(object sender, EventArgs e)
2 {
3     if (txtFind.Text.Equals(""))
4     {
5         return;
6     }
7
8     int rowSaved = managerStudent.Position;
9     DataRow[] rowFound;
10    tableStudent.DefaultView.Sort = "FirstName";
11    rowFound = tableStudent.Select("FirstName LIKE '" +
12        txtFind.Text + "*'");
13
14    if (rowFound.Length == 0)
15    {
16        managerStudent.Position = rowSaved;
17    }
18    else
19    {
20        managerStudent.Position =
21            tableStudent.DefaultView.Find(rowFound[0]["FirstName"]);
22        DisplayPhoto();
```

```
23        }
24    }
```

Step 4   Save and run the application. Try searching by providing the first or two letters of the parent's name, as shown in Figure 5.32.

Figure 5.32 Student's name search feature added

5.26 Tutorial Steps of Adding Search Buttons

Step 1   Add a button control on the form. Set its **Name** property as **btnAll** and its **Text** poperty as **Show All Students**. You add another **DataGridView** control and set its **Name** property as **grdStudent**. You also need to add a label and set its **Text** property as **Number of Records:**. Then add a textbox on the form. Set its **Name** property as **txtNumberRecord**. The resulting form is shown in Figure 5.33.

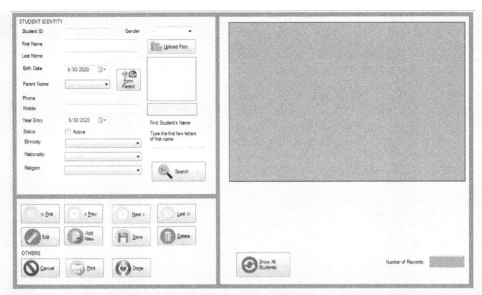

Figure 5.33 Student form after a number of controls added

Step 2   Add the following form-level declarations:

```
1  Button[] buttonArr = new Button[26];
```

Variable **buttonArr** is an array containing the search buttons.

Step 3   Define a new method named **createSearchButton()** as follows:

```
1   private void createSearchButton()
2   {
3       // Creates search buttons
4       int w, lStart, l, t;
5       int btnHeight = 50; // by trial and error
6
7       // Search buttons
8       // Button width - 13 buttons in a row
9       w = Convert.ToInt32(grdStudent.Width / 13);
10
11      // Aligns buttons
12      lStart = Convert.ToInt32((grdStudent.Width))-50;
13      l = lStart; t = grdStudent.Top + grdStudent.Height + 10;
14
15      // Creates and positions 26 buttons
16      for (int i = 0; i < 26; i++)
17      {
18          // Creates push button
19          buttonArr[i] = new Button();
20          buttonArr[i].TabStop = false;
21
22          // Sets Text property
```

```
23    buttonArr[i].Text = ((char)(65 + i)).ToString();
24    buttonArr[i].Font = new Font(buttonArr[i].Font.FontFamily,
25        9, FontStyle.Bold);
26
27    // Positions buttons
28    buttonArr[i].Width = w;
29    buttonArr[i].Height = btnHeight;
30    buttonArr[i].Left = l;
31    buttonArr[i].Top = t;
32
33    // Gives color
34    buttonArr[i].BackColor = Color.Red;
35    buttonArr[i].ForeColor = Color.White;
36
37    // Adds each button on form
38    this.Controls.Add(buttonArr[i]);
39
40    // Adds event handler
41    buttonArr[i].Click +=
42        new System.EventHandler(this.btnSQL_Click);
43    l += w+1;
44
45    if (i == 12)
46    {
47        // Next row
48        l = lStart; t += btnHeight;
49    }
50    }
51 }
```

This method creates search buttons A through Z using **buttonArrr** array. The code above then specifies the width of the button and places it on the form. Finally, the resulting records are displayed by programmatically clicking **btnSQL** button.

Step 4   Define **createSQLStatement** method as follows:

```
1    private string createSQLStatement()
2    {
3        // Create SQL Statement
4        string SqlString = null;
5        SqlString += "SELECT Student.StudentID, ";
6        SqlString += "CONCAT(Student.FirstName, ' ', Student.LastName)
7            AS Student_Name, ";
8        SqlString += "CONCAT(Parent.FirstName, ' ', Parent.LastName) AS
9            Parent_Name, ";
10       SqlString += "Student.BirthDate, Student.YearEntry, ";
11       SqlString += "Student.Status, Student.nationality ";
12       SqlString += "FROM Student, Parent ";
13       SqlString += "WHERE Student.ParentID = Parent.ParentID ";
14
```

```
15    return SqlString;
16  }
```

Step 5   Write the code for **btnSQL_Click** event method (handle **Click** event for all search buttons) as follows:

```
1   private void btnSQL_Click(object sender, EventArgs e)
2   {
3       SqlCommand commResult = null;
4       SqlDataAdapter adapterResult = new SqlDataAdapter();
5       DataTable tableResult = new DataTable();
6       String StatementSQL;
7       string SQLAll = createSQLStatement();
8       // Determines which button is clicked and creates SQL statement
9       Button buttonClicked = (Button)sender;
10      switch (buttonClicked.Text)
11      {
12          case "Show All Students":
13              StatementSQL = SQLAll;
14              break;
15          case "Z":
16              // Z button is clicked
17              // Appends at SQLAll to limit records upto for item Z
18              StatementSQL = SQLAll + " WHERE Student.FirstName > 'Z' ";
19              break;
20          default:
21              // Letter keys except Z
22              // Appends at SQLAll to limit records
23              // for letter that is clicked
24              int idx = (int)(Convert.ToChar(buttonClicked.Text)) - 65;
25              StatementSQL = SQLAll + " WHERE Student.FirstName > '" +
26              buttonArr[idx].Text + " ' ";
27              StatementSQL += " AND Student.FirstName < '" +
28                      buttonArr[idx + 1].Text + " ' ";
29              break;
30      }
31      StatementSQL += " ORDER BY FirstName";
32
33      // Applies SQL statement
34      try
35      {
36          // Creates Command and DataAdapater objects
37          commResult = new SqlCommand(StatementSQL, connBook);
38          adapterResult.SelectCommand = commResult;
39          adapterResult.Fill(tableResult);
40
41          // Binds DataGridView with data table
42          grdStudent.DataSource = tableResult;
43          txtNumberRecord.Text = tableResult.Rows.Count.ToString();
44
```

```
45        // Colors DGV
46        setRowColor(grdStudent);
47    }
48
49    catch (Exception ex)
50    {
51        MessageBox.Show(ex.Message, "Error Processing SQL",
52            MessageBoxButtons.OK, MessageBoxIcon.Error);
53    }
54    commResult.Dispose();
55    adapterResult.Dispose();
56    tableResult.Dispose();
57 }
```

This method determines which button is clicked and forms an SQL statement. If the button with the **Text** property of the button is **"Show All Students"** is clicked, then all records will be displayed. When a key letter is clicked, the code determines which letter the user clicks on and attaches an additional test (using **AND**) to the **WHERE** field in the default SQL statement.

Step 6   Add the following code in line 73-77 to **FormStudent_Load** event method. The code creates search buttons and perform **Click** event of **btnAll** programmatically:

```
1    private void FormStudent_Load(object sender, EventArgs e)
2    {
3        try
4        {
5            // Connects to database
6            connBook = new SqlConnection("Data Source=.\\SQLEXPRESS;
7                AttachDbFilename=D:\\Database\\DBMS.mdf;
8                Integrated Security = True; Connect Timeout = 30;
9                User Instance = True");
10
11           // Opens connection
12           connBook.Open();
13
14           // Creates Command object
15           commandStudent = new SqlCommand(
16               "SELECT * FROM Student ORDER BY FirstName", connBook);
17
18           // Creates DataAdapter/DataTable objects
19           adapterStudent = new SqlDataAdapter();
20           adapterStudent.SelectCommand = commandStudent;
21           tableStudent = new DataTable();
22           adapterStudent.Fill(tableStudent);
23
24           // Binds controls to data table
25           txtStudentID.DataBindings.Add("Text",
26               tableStudent, "StudentID");
```

```
27    txtFirstName.DataBindings.Add("Text",
28        tableStudent, "FirstName");
29    txtLastName.DataBindings.Add("Text",
30        tableStudent, "LastName");
31    dtpBirthDate.DataBindings.Add("Text",
32        tableStudent, "BirthDate");
33    lblPhotoFile.DataBindings.Add("Text",
34        tableStudent, "PhotoFile");
35    txtPhone.DataBindings.Add("Text", tableStudent, "Phone");
36    txtMobile.DataBindings.Add("Text", tableStudent, "Mobile");
37    dtpYearEntry.DataBindings.Add("Text",
38        tableStudent, "YearEntry");
39    chkStatus.DataBindings.Add("Checked",
40        tableStudent, "Status");
41    cboEthnicity.DataBindings.Add("Text",
42        tableStudent, "Ethnicity");
43    cboNationality.DataBindings.Add("Text",
44        tableStudent, "Nationality");
45    cboReligion.DataBindings.Add("Text",
46        tableStudent, "Religion");
47    cboGender.DataBindings.Add("Text", tableStudent, "Gender");
48
49    // Creates data update manager
50    managerStudent =
51        (CurrencyManager)BindingContext[tableStudent];
52
53    // Populates combobox cboParent
54    commandParent = new SqlCommand("SELECT ParentID,
55        CONCAT(FirstName, ' ', LastName) AS Name FROM Parent",
56        connBook);
57    adapterParent = new SqlDataAdapter();
58    adapterParent.SelectCommand = commandParent;
59    tableParent = new DataTable();
60    adapterParent.Fill(tableParent);
61    cboParent.DataSource = tableParent;
62
63    cboParent.DisplayMember = "Name";
64    cboParent.ValueMember = "ParentID";
65    cboParent.DataBindings.Add("SelectedValue",
66        tableStudent, "ParentID");
67
68    DisplayPhoto();
69    this.Show();
70    SetState("View");
71
72    createSearchButton();
73
74    // Clicks all records when form starts
75    btnAll.Click += new System.EventHandler(this.btnSQL_Click);
76    btnAll.PerformClick();
77 }
```

```
78      catch (Exception ex)
79      {
80          MessageBox.Show(ex.Message,
81            "Error in reading Parent table.",
82            MessageBoxButtons.OK, MessageBoxIcon.Error);
83          return;
84      }
85  }
86
```

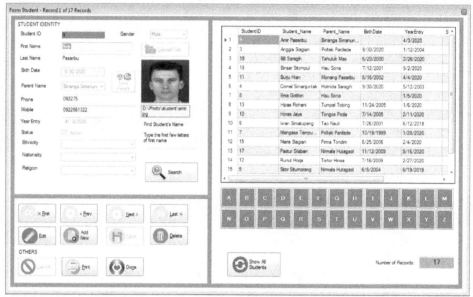

Figure 5.34 The application when it first runs

Step 7   Define **RowPostPaint** event of **grdStudent** control to give it a row numbering:

```
1   private void grdStudent_RowPostPaint(object sender,
2   DataGridViewRowPostPaintEventArgs e)
3   {
4       var grid = sender as DataGridView;
5       var rowIdx = (e.RowIndex + 1).ToString();
6
7       var centerFormat = new StringFormat()
8       {
9           // Aligns to middle
10          Alignment = StringAlignment.Center,
11          LineAlignment = StringAlignment.Center
12      };
13
14      var headerBounds = new Rectangle(e.RowBounds.Left,
15          e.RowBounds.Top, grid.RowHeadersWidth, e.RowBounds.Height);
16      e.Graphics.DrawString(rowIdx, this.Font,
17          SystemBrushes.ControlText, headerBounds, centerFormat);
18  }
```

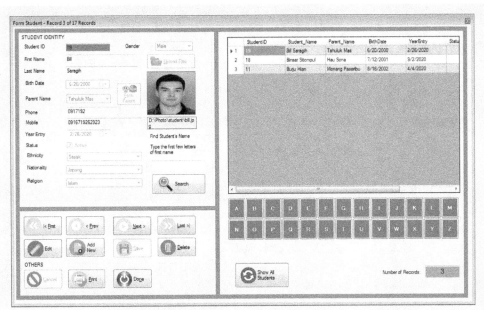

Figure 5.35 The results when the 'B' button is clicked

Step 8   Define **setRowColor** method to alternately give color to rows of **grdStudent**. This method is called from **btnSQL_Click**:

```
1   // Altenately colors row
2   private void setRowColor(DataGridView dgv)
3   {
4       for (int i = 0; i < dgv.Rows.Count; i++)
5       {
6           if (i % 2 == 0)
7           {
8               for (int j = 0; j < dgv.Columns.Count; j++ )
9                   dgv.Rows[i].Cells[j].Style.BackColor =
10                      System.Drawing.Color.LightGreen;
11          }
12          else
13          {
14              for (int j = 0; j < dgv.Columns.Count; j++)
15                  dgv.Rows[i].Cells[j].Style.BackColor =
16                      System.Drawing.Color.LightYellow;
17          }
18      }
19  }
```

Step 9   Define **Refresh_DGV** to refresh data grid view, **grdParent**, as follows:

```
1   private void Refresh_DGV()
2   {
3       // Connects to database
```

```
 4   connBook = new SqlConnection("Data Source=.\\SQLEXPRESS;
 5       AttachDbFilename=D:\\Database\\DBMS.mdf;
 6       Integrated Security = True; Connect Timeout = 30;
 7       User Instance = True");
 8   connBook.Open();
 9
10   // Save changes to database
11   SqlCommandBuilder studentAdapterCommand = new
12       SqlCommandBuilder(adapterStudent);
13   adapterStudent.Update(tableStudent);
14
15   SqlCommand commandResult = null;
16   SqlDataAdapter adapterResult = new SqlDataAdapter();
17   DataTable tableResult = new DataTable();
18   string SQLAll = createSQLStatement();
19
20   try
21   {
22       // Creates Command and DataAdapter objects
23       commandResult = new SqlCommand(SQLAll, connBook);
24       adapterResult.SelectCommand = commandResult;
25       tableResult.Clear();
26       adapterResult.Fill(tableResult);
27
28       // Binds grid view to data table
29       grdStudent.DataSource = tableResult;
30       txtNumberRecord.Text = tableResult.Rows.Count.ToString();
31   }
32
33   catch (Exception ex)
34   {
35       MessageBox.Show(ex.Message, "Error in processing SQL",
36           MessageBoxButtons.OK, MessageBoxIcon.Error);
37   }
38
39   commandResult.Dispose();
40   adapterResult.Dispose();
41   tableResult.Dispose();
42 }
```

Step 10   Call **Refresh_DGV** from **Click** event of **btnAll** as follows:

```
1   private void btnAll_Click(object sender, EventArgs e)
2   {
3       Refresh_DGV();
4   }
```

Step 11   Save and run the application. The result is shown in Figure 5.34. Notice how the search
buttons are created. Also note that all records are displayed initially. Click on one of

the search buttons. Only records with the student's initial matching the letter in the
clicked button will be displayed. Figure 5.35 is the query result when the 'B' button is
clicked.

5.27 Tutorial Steps of Selecting Gender

Step 1   You can add a feature to select student's gender. Add a label and a combo box on form.
Set **Text** property of the label **"Choose Gender"** and set **Name** property of combo
box as **cboSelectGender**. Define SelectedIndexChanged event of combo box as
follows:

```
1   private void cboSelectGender_SelectedIndexChanged(object sender,
2   EventArgs e)
3   {
4       // Connects to database
5       connBook = new SqlConnection("Data Source=.\\SQLEXPRESS;
6           AttachDbFilename=D:\\Database\\DBMS.mdf;
7           Integrated Security = True; Connect Timeout = 30;
8           User Instance = True");
9       connBook.Open();
10
11      // Creates data objects
12      SqlDataAdapter adapterResult = new SqlDataAdapter();
13      DataTable tableResult = new DataTable();
14      SqlCommand commandResult;
15
16      try
17      {
18          if (cboSelectGender.SelectedItem != null)
19          {
20              // Creates command and data adapter objects
21              string SQLAll = createSQLStatement();
22
23              SQLAll += "AND Student.Gender = '" +
24                  cboSelectGender.SelectedItem.ToString() +
25                  "' ORDER BY Student.FirstName";
26
27              commandResult = new SqlCommand(SQLAll, connBook);
28              adapterResult.SelectCommand = commandResult;
29              adapterResult.Fill(tableResult);
30
31              // binds DataGridView to data table
32              grdStudent.DataSource = tableResult;
33              txtNumberRecord.Text =
34                  tableResult.Rows.Count.ToString();
35
36              setRowColor(grdStudent);
```

```
37              }
38
39          }
40      catch (Exception ex)
41      {
42          MessageBox.Show(ex.Message, "Error in processing SQL",
43              MessageBoxButtons.OK, MessageBoxIcon.Error);
44      }
45  }
```

Step 2   Run the application. Choose gender as shown in Figure 5.36 and Figure 5.37.

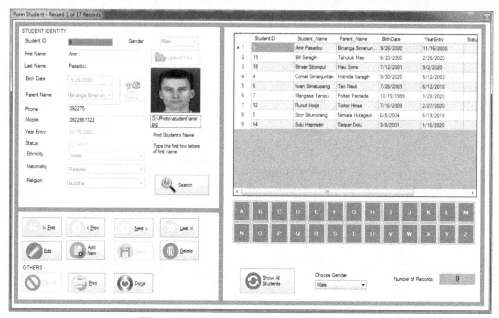

Figure 5.36 User chooses male gender

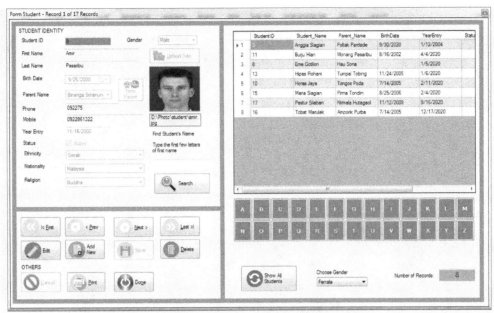

Figure 5.37 User chooses female gender

5.28 Tutorial Steps of Reporting Students

Step 1   Now, you will add a feature to read all the data in the database. You need a database
report. The report is quite simple. For each record, the data from each field will be
displayed.

Add this line of code at the top of the code window:

```
1  using System.Drawing.Printing;
```

Step 2   Add the page number variable to the form level declaration:

```
1  int pageNumber;
```

Step 3   In **SetState** method, set **Enabled** property of **btnPrint** to **true** in **View** mode and **false**
in **Add/Edit** mode.

Step 4   Add the following code to **btnPrint_Click** event method:

```
1  private void btnPrint_Click(object sender, EventArgs e)
2  {
3      // Declares document
4      PrintDocument docParent;
5
6      // Creates document and gives it a name
7      docParent = new PrintDocument();
```

```
8     docParent.DocumentName = "Student Data";
9
10    // Adds code handler
11    docParent.PrintPage += new
12        PrintPageEventHandler(this.PrintStudent);
13
14    // Prints document in preview control
15    pageNumber = 1;
16    int positionSaved = managerStudent.Position;
17    dlgPreview.Document = docParent;
18    dlgPreview.ShowDialog();
19
20    // Deletes document when finished printing
21    docParent.Dispose();
22    managerStudent.Position = positionSaved;
23
24    DisplayPhoto();
25 }
```

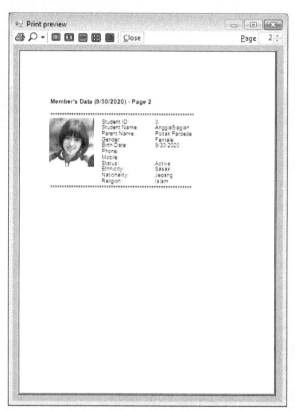

Figure 5.38 Each record in the table can now be printed

Step 5   Add the following code to **PrintStudent** method:

```
1    private void PrintStudent(object sender, PrintPageEventArgs e)
2    {
```

```
3    // Tracks every record, prints every record
4    managerStudent.Position = pageNumber - 1;
5    DisplayPhoto();
6
7    Font myFont = new Font("Arial", 14, FontStyle.Bold);
8    int y = e.MarginBounds.Top + 50;
9
10   // Prints Header
11   e.Graphics.DrawString("Member's Data (" +
12       DateTime.Now.ToShortDateString() + ") - Page " +
13       pageNumber.ToString(), myFont, Brushes.Black,
14       e.MarginBounds.Left, y);
15   y += 2 * Convert.ToInt32(myFont.GetHeight(e.Graphics));
16
17   e.Graphics.DrawString("*****************************
18       ***************************", myFont, Brushes.Black,
19       e.MarginBounds.X, y);
20   y += Convert.ToInt32(myFont.GetHeight(e.Graphics));
21
22   // Prints photo (width 4 inci, height depends on
23   // height/width ratio of photo)
24   int h = Convert.ToInt32(
25       150 * picStudent.Image.Height / picStudent.Image.Width);
26   e.Graphics.DrawImage(picStudent.Image,
27       e.MarginBounds.X, y, 150, h);
28
29   int slideRight = 175;
30
31   // Prints text information
32   myFont = new Font("Arial", 12, FontStyle.Regular);
33   e.Graphics.DrawString("Student ID:", myFont, Brushes.Black,
34       e.MarginBounds.X + slideRight, y);
35   e.Graphics.DrawString(txtStudentID.Text, myFont, Brushes.Black,
36       e.MarginBounds.X + slideRight + slideRight, y);
37   y += Convert.ToInt32(myFont.GetHeight(e.Graphics));
38
39   e.Graphics.DrawString("Student Name:", myFont, Brushes.Black,
40       e.MarginBounds.X + slideRight, y);
41   e.Graphics.DrawString(txtFirstName.Text + txtLastName.Text,
42       myFont, Brushes.Black, e.MarginBounds.X + 2*slideRight, y);
43   y += Convert.ToInt32(myFont.GetHeight(e.Graphics));
44
45   e.Graphics.DrawString("Parent Name:", myFont, Brushes.Black,
46       e.MarginBounds.X + slideRight, y);
47   e.Graphics.DrawString(cboParent.Text,
48       myFont, Brushes.Black, e.MarginBounds.X + 2*slideRight, y);
49   y += Convert.ToInt32(myFont.GetHeight(e.Graphics));
50
51   e.Graphics.DrawString("Gender:", myFont, Brushes.Black,
52       e.MarginBounds.X + slideRight, y);
53   e.Graphics.DrawString(cboGender.Text, myFont, Brushes.Black,
```

```
54        e.MarginBounds.X + 2 * slideRight, y);
55      y += Convert.ToInt32(myFont.GetHeight(e.Graphics));
56
57      e.Graphics.DrawString("Birth Date:", myFont, Brushes.Black,
58        e.MarginBounds.X + slideRight, y);
59      e.Graphics.DrawString(dtpBirthDate.Text, myFont, Brushes.Black,
60        e.MarginBounds.X + 2 * slideRight, y);
61      y += Convert.ToInt32(myFont.GetHeight(e.Graphics));
62
63      e.Graphics.DrawString("Phone:", myFont, Brushes.Black,
64        e.MarginBounds.X + slideRight, y);
65      e.Graphics.DrawString(txtPhone.Text, myFont, Brushes.Black,
66        e.MarginBounds.X + 2* slideRight, y);
67      y += Convert.ToInt32(myFont.GetHeight(e.Graphics));
68
69      e.Graphics.DrawString("Mobile:", myFont, Brushes.Black,
70        e.MarginBounds.X + slideRight, y);
71      e.Graphics.DrawString(txtMobile.Text, myFont,
72        Brushes.Black, e.MarginBounds.X + 2 * slideRight, y);
73      y += Convert.ToInt32(myFont.GetHeight(e.Graphics));
74
75      e.Graphics.DrawString("Status:", myFont, Brushes.Black,
76        e.MarginBounds.X + slideRight, y);
77      e.Graphics.DrawString(chkStatus.Text, myFont, Brushes.Black,
78        e.MarginBounds.X + 2 * slideRight, y);
79      y += Convert.ToInt32(myFont.GetHeight(e.Graphics));
80
81      e.Graphics.DrawString("Ethnicity:", myFont, Brushes.Black,
82        e.MarginBounds.X + slideRight, y);
83      e.Graphics.DrawString(cboEthnicity.Text, myFont, Brushes.Black,
84        e.MarginBounds.X + 2 * slideRight, y);
85      y += Convert.ToInt32(myFont.GetHeight(e.Graphics));
86
87      e.Graphics.DrawString("Nationality:", myFont, Brushes.Black,
88        e.MarginBounds.X + slideRight, y);
89      e.Graphics.DrawString(cboNationality.Text, myFont,
90        Brushes.Black, e.MarginBounds.X + 2 * slideRight, y);
91      y += Convert.ToInt32(myFont.GetHeight(e.Graphics));
92
93      e.Graphics.DrawString("Religion:", myFont, Brushes.Black,
94        e.MarginBounds.X + slideRight, y);
95      e.Graphics.DrawString(cboReligion.Text, myFont, Brushes.Black,
96        e.MarginBounds.X + 2 * slideRight, y);
97      y += Convert.ToInt32(myFont.GetHeight(e.Graphics));
98
99      Font myFont2 = new Font("Arial", 14, FontStyle.Bold);
100     e.Graphics.DrawString("****************************
101       *****************************", myFont2, Brushes.Black,
102       e.MarginBounds.X, y);
103
104     pageNumber++;
```

```
105        if (pageNumber <= managerStudent.Count)
106            e.HasMorePages = true;
107        else
108        {
109            e.HasMorePages = false;
110            pageNumber = 1;
111        }
112 }
```

On each page, a header is printed along with the data fields and student's photo.

Step 6   Save and run the application. Click on the **Print** button. The print preview control will be displayed on all student pages, as shown in Figure 5.38.

TUTORIAL 6
BALIGE ACADEMY
DATABASE PROJECT: PART 2

6.1 Tutorial Steps of Creating Form for Teacher Table: Interface

Step 1   In this tutorial, you will build such a form for **Teacher** table. This table has fourteen fields: **TeacherID**, **RegNumber**, **FirstName**, **LastName**, **BirthDate**, **Rank**, **Status**, **Ethnicity**, **Nationality**, **Mobile**, **Phone**, **Religion**, **Gender**, and **PhotoFile**).

You need an input form so that user can edit existing records, delete records, or add new records. The form will also have the capability of navigating from one record to another. The steps that need to be done are as follows.

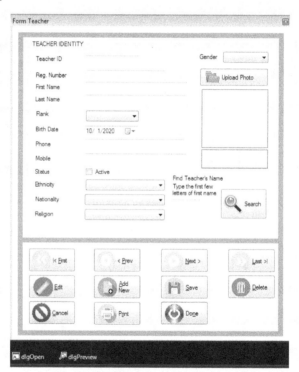

Figure 6.1 Design of parent form

Start a new Visual C# application. You need fifteen label controls, one picture box, seven text boxes, five comboxes, one check box, one date time picker, one openfiledialog, and one printpreviewdialog. You also need four buttons for navigation, six buttons for controlling editing features, one button for searching member's name, and one button to upload member's photo. Place these controls on the form. The complete form looks as shown in Figure 6.1.

Step 2   Set the properties of each control as follows:

Form1 Control	
Name	FormTeacher
BackColor	Control
FormBorderStyle	FixedSingle
StartPosition	CenterScreen
Text	Form Teacher

label1 Control	
Text	Teacher ID

textBox1 Control	
Name	txtTeacherID
ReadOnly	True

label2 Control	
Text	Gender

combobox1 Control	
Text	cboGender
BackColor	White
Items	{Male, Female}

label3 Control	
Text	First Name

textBox2 Control	
Name	txtFirstName

label4 Control	
Text	Last Name

textBox3 Control	
Name	txtLastName

label5 Control	
Text	Birth Date

dateTimePicker1 Control	
Name	dtpBirthDate
Format	short

label6 Control	
Text	Phone

textBox4 Control	

Name	txtPhone

label7 Control	
Text	Mobile

textBox5 Control	
Name	txtMobile

label8 Control	
Text	Status

checkbox1 Control	
Name	chkStatus
Text	Active

label9 Control	
Text	Ethnicity

combobox2 Control	
Name	cboEthnicity
Items	{Jawa, Sasak, Sunda, Batak, Betawi, Minang, Papua Bima, Melayu}

label10 Control	
Text	Nationality

combobox3 Control	
Name	cboNationality
Items	{Indonesia, Inggris Jepang, Amerika Korea Selatan, Malaysia, Singapur Vietnam}

label11 Control	
Text	Religion

combobox4 Control	
Name	cboReligion
Items	{ Islam, Kristen Protestan, Kristen Katolik, Buddha, Hindu, Konguchu, Kepercayaan}

label12 Control	
Name	lblPhotoFile

pictureBox1 Control

Name	picTeacher
SizeMode	StretchImage

label13 Control

Text	Type the first few letters of first name

textBox6 Control

Name	txtFind

label14 Control

Text	Reg. Number

textBox7 Control

Name	txtRegNumber
ReadOnly	True

label15 Control

Text	Rank

combobox5 Control

Name	cboRank
Items	{3A, 3B, 3C, 3D, 4A, 4B, 4C, 4D, 4E}

button1 Control

Name	btnFirst
Text	|< First

button2 Control

Name	btnPrev
Text	< Prev

button3 Control

Name	btnNext
Text	Next >

button4 Control

Name	btnLast
Text	Last >|

button5 Control

Name	btnSearch
Text	Search

button6 Control

Name	btnEdit
Text	&Edit

button7 Control

Name	btnSave
Text	&Save

button8 Control	
Name	btnCancel
Text	&Cancel

button9 Control	
Name	btnAddNew
Text	&Add New

button10 Control	
Name	btnDelete
Text	&Delete

button11 Control	
Name	btnDone
Text	Do&ne

button12 Control	
Name	btnUpload
Text	&Upload Photo

button13 Control	
Name	btnPrint
Text	&Print

openFileDialog1 Control	
Name	dlgOpen

printPreviewDialog1 Control	
Name	dlgPreview

Step 3   You will add features to this teacher form gradually. At this point, you will add code
to construct the data table and to navigate the records in the **Teacher** table. Add these
lines of code at the top of the window:

```
1   using System.Data.SqlClient;
2   using System.IO;
3   using System.Drawing.Printing;
```

Step 4   Write the following form-level declarations for creating data objects:

```
1   SqlConnection connBook;
2   SqlCommand commandTeacher;
3   SqlDataAdapter adapterTeacher;
4   DataTable tableTeacher;
5   CurrencyManager managerTeacher;
```

Step 5   Add the following code to the **FormTeacher_Load** event method:

```
1   private void FormTeacher_Load(object sender, EventArgs e)
2   {
3       try
4       {
```

```
5    // Connects to database
6    connBook = new SqlConnection("Data Source=.\\SQLEXPRESS;
7        AttachDbFilename=D:\\Database\\DBMS.mdf;
8        Integrated Security = True; Connect Timeout = 30;
9        User Instance = True");
10
11   // Opens connection
12   connBook.Open();
13
14   // Creates Command object
15   commandTeacher = new SqlCommand(
16       "SELECT * FROM Teacher ORDER BY FirstName", connBook);
17
18   // Creates DataAdapter/DataTable objects
19   adapterTeacher = new SqlDataAdapter();
20   adapterTeacher.SelectCommand = commandTeacher;
21   tableTeacher = new DataTable();
22   adapterTeacher.Fill(tableTeacher);
23
24   // Binds controls to data table
25   txtTeacherID.DataBindings.Add("Text",
26       tableTeacher, "TeacherID");
27   txtRegNumber.DataBindings.Add("Text",
28       tableTeacher, "RegNumber");
29   cboRank.DataBindings.Add("Text", tableTeacher, "Rank");
30   txtFirstName.DataBindings.Add("Text",
31       tableTeacher, "FirstName");
32   txtLastName.DataBindings.Add("Text",
33       tableTeacher, "LastName");
34   dtpBirthDate.DataBindings.Add("Text",
35       tableTeacher, "BirthDate");
36   lblPhotoFile.DataBindings.Add("Text",
37       tableTeacher, "PhotoFile");
38   txtPhone.DataBindings.Add("Text", tableTeacher, "Phone");
39   txtMobile.DataBindings.Add("Text", tableTeacher, "Mobile");
40   chkStatus.DataBindings.Add("Checked",
41       tableTeacher, "Status");
42   cboEthnicity.DataBindings.Add("Text",
43       tableTeacher, "Ethnicity");
44   cboNationality.DataBindings.Add("Text",
45       tableTeacher, "Nationality");
46   cboReligion.DataBindings.Add("Text",
47       tableTeacher, "Religion");
48   cboGender.DataBindings.Add("Text", tableTeacher, "Gender");
49
50   // Creates data update
51   managerTeacher =
52       (CurrencyManager)BindingContext[tableTeacher];
53
54   SetText();
55
```

```
56          DisplayPhoto();
57          this.Show();
58      }
59      catch (Exception ex)
60      {
61          MessageBox.Show(ex.Message,
62            "Error in reading Parent table.",
63            MessageBoxButtons.OK, MessageBoxIcon.Error);
64          return;
65      }
66  }
```

The code above creates the data objects needed to open the database and construct the
Teacher table (includes all fields). The code above then binds the controls with the
update manager object (**CurrencyManager**).

Step 6   Define **DisplayPhoto** to display teacher's photo in **picTeacher**:

```
1   private void DisplayPhoto()
2   {
3       // Displays photo
4       if (!lblPhotoFile.Text.Equals(""))
5       {
6           try
7           {
8               picTeacher.Image = Image.FromFile(lblPhotoFile.Text);
9           }
10          catch (Exception ex)
11          {
12              MessageBox.Show(ex.Message, "Error Loading Photo File",
13                  MessageBoxButtons.OK, MessageBoxIcon.Error);
14          }
15      }
16      else
17      {
18          string dir =
19              Path.GetDirectoryName(Application.ExecutablePath);
20          string filename = Path.Combine(dir, @"teacher.png");
21          picTeacher.Image = Image.FromFile(filename);
22      }
23  }
```

Step 7   Define **SetText** method to display description in title bar of form:

```
1   private void SetText()
2   {
3       this.Text = "Form Teacher - Record " +
4           (managerTeacher.Position + 1).ToString() + " of " +
5           managerTeacher.Count.ToString() + " Records";
6   }
```

Step 8   Add the following code to **FormTeacher_FormClosing** event method to close the
database connection:

```
1   private void FormTeacher_FormClosing(object sender,
2   FormClosingEventArgs e)
3   {
4       // Closes connection to database
5       connBook.Close();
6
7       // Deletes objects
8       connBook.Dispose();
9       commandTeacher.Dispose();
10      adapterTeacher.Dispose();
11  }
```

Step 9   Write the following code for the **Click** event of the four navigation buttons:

```
1   private void btnPrev_Click(object sender, EventArgs e)
2   {
3       if (managerTeacher.Position == 0)
4       {
5           Console.Beep();
6       }
7       managerTeacher.Position--;
8       DisplayPhoto();
9       SetText();
10  }
11
12  private void btnNext_Click(object sender, EventArgs e)
13  {
14      if (managerTeacher.Position == managerTeacher.Count - 1)
15      {
16          Console.Beep();
17      }
18      managerTeacher.Position++;
19      DisplayPhoto();
20      SetText();
21  }
22
23  private void btnFirst_Click(object sender, EventArgs e)
24  {
25      managerTeacher.Position = 0;
26      DisplayPhoto();
27      SetText();
28  }
29
30  private void btnLast_Click(object sender, EventArgs e)
31  {
32      managerTeacher.Position = managerTeacher.Count - 1;
```

```
33    DisplayPhoto();
34    SetText();
35  }
```

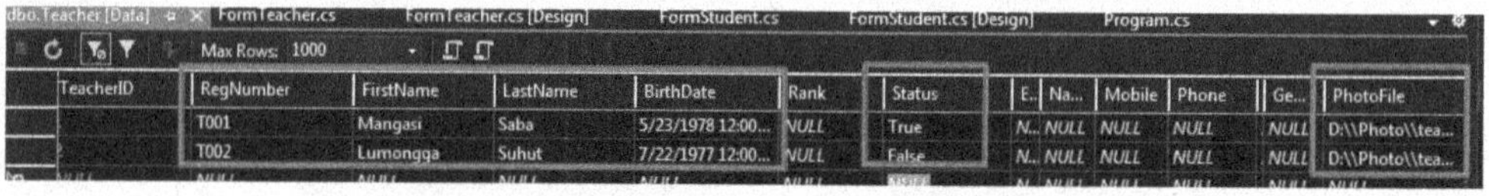

Figure 6.2 Inserting some data into **Teacher** table

Figure 6.3 Teacher form when it first runs

Step 10   Insert some data into **Teacher** table as shown in Figure 6.2.

Step 11   Save and run the application. What is displayed first is the first record in **Teacher** table. Click on four navigation buttons to prove the result.

Figure 6.4 The result when user clicks **Last >|** button

6.2 Tutorial Steps of Creating Form for Student Table: Message Box

Step 1   There are two places where you can use the message box in **Student** table input form. One message box is provided after saving updates to let the user know that the save was successful and another message box is related to record deletion.

Use the following code in **btnSave_Click** event method:

```
1  private void btnSave_Click(object sender, EventArgs e)
2  {
3      MessageBox.Show("Records successfully saved", "Save",
4          MessageBoxButtons.OK, MessageBoxIcon.Information);
5  }
```

There will be more code in this event. The code implements only message box.

Step 2   Use this code on **btnDelete_Click** event method:

```
1  private void btnDelete_Click(object sender, EventArgs e)
2  {
3      DialogResult response;
4      response = MessageBox.Show("Dou you really want to delete this record?",
5          "Delete", MessageBoxButtons.YesNo, MessageBoxIcon.Question,
6          MessageBoxDefaultButton.Button2);
7  }
```

Step 3   Save the application and run it. Click on **Delete** button to see as shown in Figure 6.5.

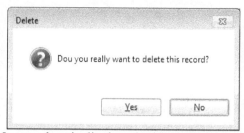

Figure 6.5 Message box is displayed when user clicks **Delete** button

6.3 Tutorial Steps of Creating Form for Teacher Table: Application State

Step 1   The **Teacher** form operates in one of three states: **View** state, **Add** state, or **Edit** state. In the **View** state, user can navigate one record to another, user can switch to **Edit** state, user can add and/or delete records, or user can exit the application.

In **Add** and **Edit** state, no navigation is made possible, data can be updated, and user can have access to **Save** and **Cancel** operations. Each of these steps can be implemented using the **Enabled** property of the button and the **ReadOnly** property of the text box. You use **TabIndex** (and **TabOrder**) to shift focus on the text box controls. You will use a method of moving from one state to another.

Clear all tab ordering for the ten buttons by setting the **TabStop** property to **False**. Additionally, set the **TabStop** property to **False** for the **Teacher ID** text box.

Step 2   Add a method named **SetState** as follows:

```
1   private void SetState(string stateStr) {
2       switch (stateStr)
3       {
4           case "View":
5               txtTeacherID.BackColor = Color.Red;
6               txtTeacherID.ForeColor = Color.Black;
7               txtFirstName.ReadOnly = true;
8               txtLastName.ReadOnly = true;
9               dtpBirthDate.Enabled = false;
10              txtPhone.ReadOnly = true;
11              txtMobile.ReadOnly = true;
12              txtRegNumber.ReadOnly = true;
13              chkStatus.Enabled = false;
14              cboEthnicity.Enabled = false;
15              cboNationality.Enabled = false;
16              cboReligion.Enabled = false;
17              cboGender.Enabled = false;
```

```csharp
            cboRank.Enabled = false;
            btnUpload.Enabled = false;
            btnFirst.Enabled = true;
            btnPrev.Enabled = true;
            btnNext.Enabled = true;
            btnLast.Enabled = true;
            btnAddNew.Enabled = true;
            btnSave.Enabled = false;
            btnDelete.Enabled = true;
            btnCancel.Enabled = false;
            btnEdit.Enabled = true;
            btnDone.Enabled = true;
            btnPrint.Enabled = true;
            txtFirstName.Focus();
            break;

        case "Edit": // Edit
            txtTeacherID.ReadOnly = true;
            txtTeacherID.BackColor = Color.Red;
            txtTeacherID.ForeColor = Color.Black;
            txtFirstName.ReadOnly = false;
            txtLastName.ReadOnly = false;
            txtRegNumber.ReadOnly = false;
            dtpBirthDate.Enabled = true;
            txtPhone.ReadOnly = false;
            txtMobile.ReadOnly = false;
            chkStatus.Enabled = true;
            cboEthnicity.Enabled = true;
            cboNationality.Enabled = true;
            cboReligion.Enabled = true;
            cboGender.Enabled = true;
            btnUpload.Enabled = true;
            btnFirst.Enabled = false;
            btnPrev.Enabled = false;
            btnNext.Enabled = false;
            btnLast.Enabled = false;
            btnAddNew.Enabled = false;
            btnSave.Enabled = true;
            btnDelete.Enabled = false;
            btnCancel.Enabled = true;
            btnEdit.Enabled = false;
            btnDone.Enabled = false;
            btnPrint.Enabled = false;
            cboRank.Enabled = true;
            txtFirstName.Focus();
            break;

        case "Add":
            txtTeacherID.ReadOnly = false;
            txtTeacherID.BackColor = Color.Red;
            txtTeacherID.ForeColor = Color.Black;
```

```
69          txtFirstName.ReadOnly = false;
70          txtLastName.ReadOnly = false;
71          txtRegNumber.ReadOnly = false;
72          dtpBirthDate.Enabled = true;
73          dtpBirthDate.Value = DateTime.Now;
74          txtPhone.ReadOnly = false;
75          txtMobile.ReadOnly = false;
76          chkStatus.Enabled = true;
77          cboEthnicity.Enabled = true;
78          cboEthnicity.DataBindings.Clear();
79          cboEthnicity.SelectedIndex = -1;
80          cboNationality.Enabled = true;
81          cboNationality.DataBindings.Clear();
82          cboNationality.SelectedIndex = -1;
83          cboReligion.Enabled = true;
84          cboReligion.DataBindings.Clear();
85          cboReligion.SelectedIndex = -1;
86          cboGender.Enabled = true;
87          cboGender.DataBindings.Clear();
88          cboGender.SelectedIndex = -1;
89          cboRank.Enabled = true;
90          cboRank.DataBindings.Clear();
91          cboRank.SelectedIndex = -1;
92          btnUpload.Enabled = true;
93          btnFirst.Enabled = false;
94          btnPrev.Enabled = false;
95          btnNext.Enabled = false;
96          btnLast.Enabled = false;
97          btnAddNew.Enabled = false;
98          btnSave.Enabled = true;
99          btnDelete.Enabled = false;
100         btnCancel.Enabled = true;
101         btnEdit.Enabled = false;
102         btnDone.Enabled = false;
103         btnPrint.Enabled = false;
104         lblPhotoFile.Text = "";
105         txtFirstName.Focus();
106         break;
107     }
108 }
```

The code above specifies **View**, **Add**, or **Edit** state for the application. Pay attention to which buttons are available and which are not. Note that **Teacher ID** text box is given red back color if it is in **Add** or **Edit** state to indicate that it cannot be changed.

Step 3   Set the **View** state when the application first runs. Add the following code in line 58 to **FormTeacher_Load** event method:

```
1   private void FormTeacher_Load(object sender, EventArgs e)
2   {
```

```
3      try
4      {
5          // Connects to database
6          connBook = new SqlConnection("Data Source=.\\SQLEXPRESS;
7              AttachDbFilename=D:\\Database\\DBMS.mdf;
8              Integrated Security = True; Connect Timeout = 30;
9              User Instance = True");
10
11         // Opens connection
12         connBook.Open();
13
14         // Creates Command object
15         commandTeacher = new SqlCommand(
16             "SELECT * FROM Teacher ORDER BY FirstName", connBook);
17
18         // Creates DataAdapter/DataTable objects
19         adapterTeacher = new SqlDataAdapter();
20         adapterTeacher.SelectCommand = commandTeacher;
21         tableTeacher = new DataTable();
22         adapterTeacher.Fill(tableTeacher);
23
24         // Binds controls to data table
25         txtTeacherID.DataBindings.Add("Text",
26             tableTeacher, "TeacherID");
27         txtRegNumber.DataBindings.Add("Text",
28             tableTeacher, "RegNumber");
29         cboRank.DataBindings.Add("Text", tableTeacher, "Rank");
30         txtFirstName.DataBindings.Add("Text",
31             tableTeacher, "FirstName");
32         txtLastName.DataBindings.Add("Text",
33             tableTeacher, "LastName");
34         dtpBirthDate.DataBindings.Add("Text",
35             tableTeacher, "BirthDate");
36         lblPhotoFile.DataBindings.Add("Text",
37             tableTeacher, "PhotoFile");
38         txtPhone.DataBindings.Add("Text", tableTeacher, "Phone");
39         txtMobile.DataBindings.Add("Text", tableTeacher, "Mobile");
40         chkStatus.DataBindings.Add("Checked",
41             tableTeacher, "Status");
42         cboEthnicity.DataBindings.Add("Text",
43             tableTeacher, "Ethnicity");
44         cboNationality.DataBindings.Add("Text",
45             tableTeacher, "Nationality");
46         cboReligion.DataBindings.Add("Text",
47             tableTeacher, "Religion");
48         cboGender.DataBindings.Add("Text", tableTeacher, "Gender");
49
50         // Creates data update
51         managerTeacher =
52             (CurrencyManager)BindingContext[tableTeacher];
53
```

```
54
55          SetText();
56          DisplayPhoto();
57          this.Show();
58          SetState("View");
59      }
60      catch (Exception ex)
61      {
62          MessageBox.Show(ex.Message,
63            "Error in reading Parent table.",
64            MessageBoxButtons.OK, MessageBoxIcon.Error);
65          return;
66      }
67  }
```

Step 4   When **Add New** button is clicked, you need to switch to **Add** state. Add the following
          code to **btnAddNew_Click** event method:

```
1   private void btnAddNew_Click(object sender, EventArgs e)
2   {
3       SetState("Add");
4   }
```

Step 5   When **Edit** button is clicked, the application will be switched to **Edit** state. Add the
          following code to **btnEdit_Click** event method:

```
1   private void btnEdit_Click(object sender, EventArgs e)
2   {
3       SetState("Edit");
4   }
```

Step 6   When **Cancel** or **Save** button is clicked (in **Add** or **Edit** state), application will return
          to the **View** state. Put this line of code in **btnCancel_Click** and **btnSave_Click** event
          methods:

```
1   private void btnCancel_Click(object sender, EventArgs e)
2   {
3       SetState("View");
4   }
5
6   private void btnSave_Click(object sender, EventArgs e)
7   {
8       SetState("View");
9   }
```

Step 7   Save and run the application. You will see the application in its initial state (**View**
          state) as shown in Figure 6.6.

Figure 6.6 Teacher form is in **View** state when it first runs

When user clicks the **Edit** button, you will see what is shown in Figure 6.7.

Figure 6.7 Teacher form is in **Edit** state

When user clicks the **Add New** button, you will see what is shown in Figure 6.8.

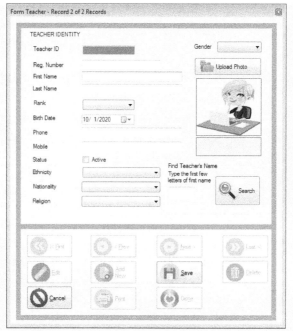

Figure 6.8 Teacher form is in **Add** state

6.4 Tutorial Steps of Creating Form for Teacher Table: Error Trapping

Step 1   Modify **btnAddNew_Click**, **btnSave_Click**, and **btnDelete_Click** event methods to
handle error trapping:

```
 1   private void btnAddNew_Click(object sender, EventArgs e)
 2   {
 3       try
 4       {
 5           SetState("Add");
 6       }
 7       catch (Exception ex)
 8       {
 9           MessageBox.Show("Error adding new record.", "Error",
10               MessageBoxButtons.OK, MessageBoxIcon.Error);
11       }
12   }
```

```
 1   private void btnSave_Click(object sender, EventArgs e)
 2   {
 3       try
 4       {
 5           MessageBox.Show("Record successfully saved", "Save",
 6           MessageBoxButtons.OK, MessageBoxIcon.Information);
 7           SetState("View");
 8       }
```

```
9        catch (Exception ex)
10       {
11           MessageBox.Show("Error saving record.", "Error",
12               MessageBoxButtons.OK, MessageBoxIcon.Error);
13       }
14   }
```

```
1    private void btnDelete_Click(object sender, EventArgs e)
2    {
3        DialogResult response;
4        response = MessageBox.Show("Dou you really want to delete this record?",
5            "Delete", MessageBoxButtons.YesNo, MessageBoxIcon.Question,
6            MessageBoxDefaultButton.Button2);
7        if (response == DialogResult.No)
8        {
9            return;
10       }
11
12       try
13       {
14
15       }
16       catch (Exception ex)
17       {
18           MessageBox.Show("Error deleting record.", "Error",
19               MessageBoxButtons.OK, MessageBoxIcon.Error);
20       }
21   }
```

6.5 Tutorial Steps of Creating Form for Teacher Table: Editing Record

Step 1   You will now add editing capability and other related capabilities to save and/or cancel edits. Before saving update into database, you need to validate data entered by user. In this case, you need to validate teacher name and year range of birth date. Define a method named **ValidateData** to validate data entered by user:

```
1    private bool ValidateData()
2    {
3        string message = "";
4        int yearInput, yearNow;
5        bool allOK = true;
6
7        // Checks name in txtRegNumber, txtFirstName and txtLastName
8        if (txtRegNumber.Text.Trim().Equals("")  ||
9            txtFirstName.Text.Trim().Equals("") ||
10           txtLastName.Text.Trim().Equals(""))    {
11           message = "You should enter first and last name." + "\r\n";
12           txtFirstName.Focus();
13           allOK = false;
```

```
14
15        }
16
17        // Checks birth date range
18        yearInput = dtpBirthDate.Value.Year;
19        yearNow = DateTime.Now.Year;
20
21        if (yearInput > yearNow || yearInput < yearNow - 150)
22        {
23            message += "Year should be between " +
24                (yearNow - 150).ToString() +
25                " and " + yearNow.ToString();
26            dtpBirthDate.Focus();
27            allOK = false;
28        }
29
30        if (!allOK)
31        {
32            MessageBox.Show(message, "Validation Error",
33                MessageBoxButtons.OK, MessageBoxIcon.Information);
34        }
35
36        return (allOK);
37 }
```

Step 2   Add a **KeyPress** event for the **txtFirstName** and **txtLastName** text boxes to accept only letters:

```
1   private void txtFirstName_KeyPress(object sender, KeyPressEventArgs e)
2   {
3       if ((e.KeyChar >= 'a' && e.KeyChar <= 'z') ||
4           (e.KeyChar >= 'A' && e.KeyChar <= 'Z') ||
5           (int)e.KeyChar == 8 || (int)e.KeyChar == 32)
6       {
7           // Key can be accepted
8           e.Handled = false;
9       }
10      else
11      {
12          e.Handled = true;
13          Console.Beep();
14      }
15
16      if ((int)e.KeyChar == 13)
17          txtLastName.Focus();
18  }
```

```
1   private void txtLastName_KeyPress(object sender, KeyPressEventArgs e)
2   {
3       if ((e.KeyChar >= 'a' && e.KeyChar <= 'z') ||
```

```
 4            (e.KeyChar >= 'A' && e.KeyChar <= 'Z') ||
 5            (int)e.KeyChar == 8 || (int)e.KeyChar == 32)
 6        {
 7            // Key can be accepted
 8            e.Handled = false;
 9        }
10        else
11        {
12            e.Handled = true;
13            Console.Beep();
14        }
15
16        if ((int)e.KeyChar == 13)
17            dtpBirthDate.Focus();
18    }
```

Step 3   Add a **KeyPress** event for the **txtMobile** and **txtPhone** text boxes to accept only digits:

```
 1    private void txtMobile_KeyPress(object sender, KeyPressEventArgs e)
 2    {
 3        e.Handled = !char.IsDigit(e.KeyChar) &&
 4            !char.IsControl(e.KeyChar);
 5
 6        if ((int)e.KeyChar == 13)
 7            chkStatus.Focus();
 8    }
 9
10    private void txtPhone_KeyPress(object sender, KeyPressEventArgs e)
11    {
12        e.Handled = !char.IsDigit(e.KeyChar) &&
13            !char.IsControl(e.KeyChar);
14
15        if ((int)e.KeyChar == 13)
16            txtMobile.Focus();
17    }
```

Step 4   Add a **KeyPress** event for other controls to move to the next control:

```
 1    private void txtRegNumber_KeyPress(object sender, KeyPressEventArgs e)
 2    {
 3        if ((int)e.KeyChar == 13)
 4            txtFirstName.Focus();
 5    }
 6
 7    private void dtpBirthDate_KeyPress(object sender, KeyPressEventArgs e)
 8    {
 9        if ((int)e.KeyChar == 13)
10            txtPhone.Focus();
11    }
12
13    private void chkStatus_KeyPress(object sender, KeyPressEventArgs e)
```

```
14    {
15        if ((int)e.KeyChar == 13)
16            cboEthnicity.Focus();
17    }
18
19    private void cboEthnicity_KeyPress(object sender, KeyPressEventArgs e)
20    {
21        if ((int)e.KeyChar == 13)
22            cboNationality.Focus();
23    }
24
25    private void cboNationality_KeyPress(object sender, KeyPressEventArgs e)
26    {
27        if ((int)e.KeyChar == 13)
28            cboReligion.Focus();
29    }
30
31    private void cboReligion_KeyPress(object sender, KeyPressEventArgs e)
32    {
33        if ((int)e.KeyChar == 13)
34            txtFirstName.Focus();
35    }
```

Step 5   Add the following line of code to the form-level declaration:

```
1    string appState;
```

step 6   Add this code in line 2 to **SetState** method:

```
1    private void SetState(string stateStr) {
2        appState = stateStr;
3
4        switch (stateStr)
5        {
6            case "View":
7                txtTeacherID.BackColor = Color.Red;
8                txtTeacherID.ForeColor = Color.Black;
9                txtFirstName.ReadOnly = true;
10               txtLastName.ReadOnly = true;
11               dtpBirthDate.Enabled = false;
12               txtPhone.ReadOnly = true;
13               txtMobile.ReadOnly = true;
14               txtRegNumber.ReadOnly = true;
15               chkStatus.Enabled = false;
16               cboEthnicity.Enabled = false;
17               cboNationality.Enabled = false;
18               cboReligion.Enabled = false;
19               cboGender.Enabled = false;
20               cboRank.Enabled = false;
21               btnUpload.Enabled = false;
```

```
22          btnFirst.Enabled = true;
23          btnPrev.Enabled = true;
24          btnNext.Enabled = true;
25          btnLast.Enabled = true;
26          btnAddNew.Enabled = true;
27          btnSave.Enabled = false;
28          btnDelete.Enabled = true;
29          btnCancel.Enabled = false;
30          btnEdit.Enabled = true;
31          btnDone.Enabled = true;
32          btnPrint.Enabled = true;
33          txtFirstName.Focus();
34          break;
35
36      case "Edit": // Edit
37          txtTeacherID.ReadOnly = true;
38          txtTeacherID.BackColor = Color.Red;
39          txtTeacherID.ForeColor = Color.Black;
40          txtFirstName.ReadOnly = false;
41          txtLastName.ReadOnly = false;
42          txtRegNumber.ReadOnly = false;
43          dtpBirthDate.Enabled = true;
44          txtPhone.ReadOnly = false;
45          txtMobile.ReadOnly = false;
46          chkStatus.Enabled = true;
47          cboEthnicity.Enabled = true;
48          cboNationality.Enabled = true;
49          cboReligion.Enabled = true;
50          cboGender.Enabled = true;
51          btnUpload.Enabled = true;
52          btnFirst.Enabled = false;
53          btnPrev.Enabled = false;
54          btnNext.Enabled = false;
55          btnLast.Enabled = false;
56          btnAddNew.Enabled = false;
57          btnSave.Enabled = true;
58          btnDelete.Enabled = false;
59          btnCancel.Enabled = true;
60          btnEdit.Enabled = false;
61          btnDone.Enabled = false;
62          btnPrint.Enabled = false;
63          cboRank.Enabled = true;
64          txtFirstName.Focus();
65          break;
66
67      case "Add":
68          txtTeacherID.ReadOnly = false;
69          txtTeacherID.BackColor = Color.Red;
70          txtTeacherID.ForeColor = Color.Black;
71          txtFirstName.ReadOnly = false;
72          txtLastName.ReadOnly = false;
```

```
73              txtRegNumber.ReadOnly = false;
74              dtpBirthDate.Enabled = true;
75              dtpBirthDate.Value = DateTime.Now;
76              txtPhone.ReadOnly = false;
77              txtMobile.ReadOnly = false;
78              chkStatus.Enabled = true;
79              cboEthnicity.Enabled = true;
80              cboEthnicity.DataBindings.Clear();
81              cboEthnicity.SelectedIndex = -1;
82              cboNationality.Enabled = true;
83              cboNationality.DataBindings.Clear();
84              cboNationality.SelectedIndex = -1;
85              cboReligion.Enabled = true;
86              cboReligion.DataBindings.Clear();
87              cboReligion.SelectedIndex = -1;
88              cboGender.Enabled = true;
89              cboGender.DataBindings.Clear();
90              cboGender.SelectedIndex = -1;
91              cboRank.Enabled = true;
92              cboRank.DataBindings.Clear();
93              cboRank.SelectedIndex = -1;
94              btnUpload.Enabled = true;
95              btnFirst.Enabled = false;
96              btnPrev.Enabled = false;
97              btnNext.Enabled = false;
98              btnLast.Enabled = false;
99              btnAddNew.Enabled = false;
100             btnSave.Enabled = true;
101             btnDelete.Enabled = false;
102             btnCancel.Enabled = true;
103             btnEdit.Enabled = false;
104             btnDone.Enabled = false;
105             btnPrint.Enabled = false;
106             lblPhotoFile.Text = "";
107             txtFirstName.Focus();
108             break;
109         }
110 }
111
```

Step 7   Modify **btnSave_Click** event method to save the change and reposition the pointer to
the record just edited:

```
1   private void btnSave_Click(object sender, EventArgs e)
2   {
3       if (!ValidateData())
4       {
5           return;
6       }
7
8       string nameSaved = txtFirstName.Text;
```

```
 9    int rowSaved;
10
11    try
12    {
13        managerTeacher.EndCurrentEdit();
14
15        if (appState.Equals("Add"))
16        {
17            tableTeacher.Rows[managerTeacher.Count - 1]["Status"] =
18                chkStatus.Checked;
19            chkStatus.DataBindings.Add("Checked",
20                tableTeacher, "Status");
21        }
22
23        tableTeacher.DefaultView.Sort = "FirstName";
24        rowSaved = tableTeacher.DefaultView.Find(nameSaved);
25        managerTeacher.Position = rowSaved;
26
27        // Saves changes into database
28        SqlCommandBuilder teacherAdapterCommand = new
29            SqlCommandBuilder(adapterTeacher);
30        adapterTeacher.Update(tableTeacher);
31
32        MessageBox.Show("Records successfully saved", "Save",
33            MessageBoxButtons.OK, MessageBoxIcon.Information);
34
35        SetState("View");
36    }
37    catch (Exception ex)
38    {
39        MessageBox.Show("Error saving record.", "Error",
40            MessageBoxButtons.OK, MessageBoxIcon.Error);
41    }
42 }
43
```

Step 8   Modify **btnCancel_Click** event method to restore controls if the edit is canceled:

```
1    private void btnCancel_Click(object sender, EventArgs e)
2    {
3        managerTeacher.CancelCurrentEdit();
4
5        SetState("View");
6        DisplayPhoto();
7    }
```

Step 9   Add the following code in line to the **FormTeacher_FormClosing** method to save
any changes to the database file:

```
1   private void FormTeacher_FormClosing(object sender,
2   FormClosingEventArgs e)
3   {
4       try
5       {
6           // Saves changes into database
7           SqlCommandBuilder teacherAdapterCommand =
8               new SqlCommandBuilder(adapterTeacher);
9           adapterTeacher.Update(tableTeacher);
10      }
11      catch (Exception ex)
12      {
13          MessageBox.Show("Error saving database into file: \r\n" +
14              ex.Message, "Saving Error", MessageBoxButtons.OK,
15              MessageBoxIcon.Error);
16      }
17
18      // Closes connection to database
19      connBook.Close();
20
21      // Deletes objects
22      connBook.Dispose();
23      commandTeacher.Dispose();
24      adapterTeacher.Dispose();
25  }
```

Figure 6.9 Editing operation is successfully performed

Step 10   Define Click event of **btnUpload** as follows:

```
1   private void btnUpload_Click(object sender, EventArgs e)
2   {
3       try
4       {
5           if (dlgOpen.ShowDialog() == DialogResult.OK)
6           {
7               lblPhotoFile.Text = dlgOpen.FileName;
8               DisplayPhoto();
9           }
10      }
11      catch (Exception ex)
12      {
13          MessageBox.Show(ex.Message, "Error in loading photo",
14              MessageBoxButtons.OK, MessageBoxIcon.Error);
15      }
16  }
```

Step 11   Save and run the application. Make sure Edit feature is working properly. Try filling
other fields. Make sure the **Cancel** button is working properly. This is shown in Figure
6.9.

6.6 Tutorial Steps of Creating Form for Teacher Table: Adding New Record

Step 1   You now implement the capability on the form to add new records to the database.
Add the following line of code to the form-level declaration:

```
1   int myBookmark;
```

Step 2   Modify **btnAddNew_Click** event method to add a new record by adding code in line
6-13:

```
1   private void btnAddNew_Click(object sender, EventArgs e)
2   {
3       try
4       {
5           // Deletes binding from checkbox chkStatus
6           chkStatus.DataBindings.Clear();
7           chkStatus.Checked = false;
8
9           lblPhotoFile.Text = "";
10          DisplayPhoto();
11
12          myBookmark = managerTeacher.Position;
13          managerTeacher.AddNew();
14          SetState("Add");
15      }
```

```
16    catch (Exception ex)
17    {
18        MessageBox.Show("Error adding new record.", "Error",
19            MessageBoxButtons.OK, MessageBoxIcon.Error);
20    }
21  }
```

Figure 6.10 The new record has been successfully saved into the database

Step 3   Modify **btnCancel_Click** event method to differentiate between cancellation during **Edit** mode and **Add** mode by adding code in line 5-10:

```
1   private void btnCancel_Click(object sender, EventArgs e)
2   {
3       managerTeacher.CancelCurrentEdit();
4
5       if (appState.Equals("Add"))
6       {
7           managerTeacher.Position = myBookmark;
8           chkStatus.DataBindings.Add("Checked",
9               tableTeacher, "Status");
10      }
11      SetState("View");
12      DisplayPhoto();
13  }
```

Step 4   Save and run the application. Click **Add New** button. Note that all text boxes are blank (including **teacher ID** text box. Fill registration number, first name, last name, and other fields, then click **Save**. New record has been successfully saved as shown in Figure 6.10.

6.7 Tutorial Steps of Creating Form for Teacher Table: Deleting Record

Step 1   You will now add the capability to delete records from **Teacher** table. Modify the **btnDelete_Click** event method by adding code in line 14 to delete records if the user responds to **Yes** in the message box:

```
1   private void btnDelete_Click(object sender, EventArgs e)
2   {
3       DialogResult response;
4       response = MessageBox.Show("Dou you really want to delete this record?",
5           "Delete", MessageBoxButtons.YesNo, MessageBoxIcon.Question,
6           MessageBoxDefaultButton.Button2);
7       if (response == DialogResult.No)
8       {
9           return;
10      }
11
12      try
13      {
14          managerTeacher.RemoveAt(managerTeacher.Position);
15      }
16      catch (Exception ex)
17      {
18          MessageBox.Show("Error deleting record.", "Error",
19              MessageBoxButtons.OK, MessageBoxIcon.Error);
20      }
21  }
```

Step 2   Save the application and run it. Make sure the **Yes** and **No** responses in the message box give correct results. Delete only those records you added using **Add New** button.

6.8 Tutorial Steps of Creating Form for Parent Table: Stopping Application

Step 1   Add the following code in line 4-12 and line 34 to **FormTeacher_FormClosing** event method to ensure user doesn't close the application during **Edit** or **Add** mode:

```
1   private void FormTeacher_FormClosing(object sender,
2   FormClosingEventArgs e)
3   {
4       if (appState.Equals("Edit") || appState.Equals("Add"))
5       {
6           MessageBox.Show(
```

```
7           "You should finish editing before closing application.",
8              "", MessageBoxButtons.OK, MessageBoxIcon.Information);
9          e.Cancel = true;
10     }
11     else
12     {
13         try
14         {
15             // Saves changes into
16             SqlCommandBuilder teacherAdapterCommand =
17                 new SqlCommandBuilder(adapterTeacher);
18             adapterTeacher.Update(tableTeacher);
19         }
20         catch (Exception ex)
21         {
22             MessageBox.Show("Error saving database into file: \r\n" +
23                 ex.Message, "Error Saving", MessageBoxButtons.OK,
24                 MessageBoxIcon.Error);
25         }
26
27         // Closes connection to database
28         connBook.Close();
29
30         // Deletes objects
31         connBook.Dispose();
32         commandTeacher.Dispose();
33         adapterTeacher.Dispose();
34     }
35 }
```

Step 2   Put this code in **btnDone_Click** event method:

```
1 private void btnDone_Click(object sender, EventArgs e)
2 {
3     this.Close();
4 }
```

Step 3   Save and run the application. Make sure the **Done** button is working properly. Make
sure the user cannot close the application in **Edit** or **Add** mode.

6.9 Tutorial Steps of Searching Capability

Step 1   In the **SetState** method, enable group box control in **View** mode and disable it in **Add**
and **Edit** mode. Use its **Enabled** property.

Figure 6.11 Teacher's name search feature added

Step 3   Add the following code to **btnSearch_Click** event method:

```csharp
private void btnSearch_Click(object sender, EventArgs e)
{
    if (txtFind.Text.Equals(""))
    {
        return;
    }

    int rowSaved = managerTeacher.Position;
    DataRow[] rowFound;
    tableTeacher.DefaultView.Sort = "FirstName";
    rowFound = tableTeacher.Select("FirstName LIKE '" +
        txtFind.Text + "*'");

    if (rowFound.Length == 0)
    {
        managerTeacher.Position = rowSaved;
    }
    else
    {
        managerTeacher.Position =
            tableTeacher.DefaultView.Find(rowFound[0]["FirstName"]);
        DisplayPhoto();
    }
}
```

Step 4   Save and run the application. Try searching by providing the first or two letters of the parent's name, as shown in Figure 6.11.

6.10 Tutorial Steps of Adding Search Buttons

Step 1   Add a button control on the form. Set its **Name** property as **btnAll** and its **Text** poperty as **Show All Parents**. You add another **DataGridView** control and set its **Name** property as **grdParent**. You also need to add a label and set its **Text** property as **Number of Records:**. Then add a textbox on the form. Set its **Name** property as **txtNumberRecord**. The resulting form is shown in Figure 6.12.

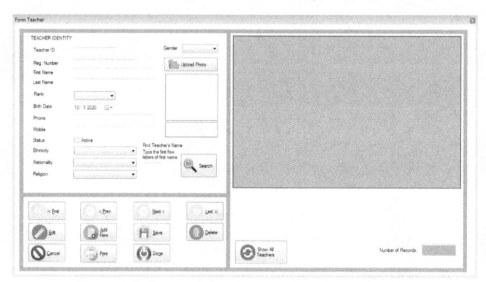

Figure 6.12 Teacher form after a number of controls added

Step 2   Add the following form-level declarations:

```
1  String SQLAll = "SELECT * FROM Teacher ";
2  Button[] buttonArr = new Button[26];
```

SQLAll is a variable that contains the default SQL statements, while **buttonArr** is an array containing the search buttons.

Step 3   Define a new method named **createSearchButton()** as follows:

```
1  private void createSearchButton()
2  {
3      // Creates search buttons
4      int w, lStart, l, t;
5      int btnHeight = 35; // by trial and error
6
```

```
7      // Search buttons
8      // Button width - 13 buttons in a row
9      w = Convert.ToInt32(grdTeacher.Width / 13);
10
11     // Aligns buttons
12     lStart = Convert.ToInt32((grdTeacher.Width))-20;
13     l = lStart; t = grdTeacher.Top + grdTeacher.Height + 10;
14
15     // Creates and positions 26 buttons
16     for (int i = 0; i < 26; i++)
17     {
18         // Creates push button
19         buttonArr[i] = new Button();
20         buttonArr[i].TabStop = false;
21
22         // Sets Text property
23         buttonArr[i].Text = ((char)(65 + i)).ToString();
24         buttonArr[i].Font = new Font(buttonArr[i].Font.FontFamily,
25             9, FontStyle.Bold);
26
27         // Positions buttons
28         buttonArr[i].Width = w;
29         buttonArr[i].Height = btnHeight;
30         buttonArr[i].Left = l;
31         buttonArr[i].Top = t;
32
33         // Gives color
34         buttonArr[i].BackColor = Color.Red;
35         buttonArr[i].ForeColor = Color.White;
36
37         // Adds each button on form
38         this.Controls.Add(buttonArr[i]);
39
40         // Adds event handler
41         buttonArr[i].Click +=
42             new System.EventHandler(this.btnSQL_Click);
43         l += w+1;
44
45         if (i == 12)
46         {
47             // Next row
48             l = lStart; t += btnHeight;
49         }
50     }
51 }
```

This method creates search buttons A through Z using **buttonArrr** array. The code above then specifies the width of the button and places it on the form. Finally, the resulting records are displayed by programmatically clicking **btnSQL** button.

Step 4   Write the code for **btnSQL_Click** event method (handle **Click** event for all search buttons) as follows:

```
private void btnSQL_Click(object sender, EventArgs e)
{
    SqlCommand commResult = null;
    SqlDataAdapter adapterResult = new SqlDataAdapter();
    DataTable tableResult = new DataTable();
    String StatementSQL;

    // Determines which button is clicked and creates SQL statement
    Button buttonClicked = (Button)sender;
    switch (buttonClicked.Text)
    {
        case "Show All Teachers":
            StatementSQL = SQLAll;
            break;
        case "Z":
            // Z button is clicked
            // Appends at SQLAll to limit records upto for item Z
            StatementSQL = SQLAll + " WHERE FirstName > 'Z' ";
            break;
        default:
            // Letter keys except Z
            // Appends at SQLAll to limit records
            // for letter that is clicked
            int idx = (int)(Convert.ToChar(buttonClicked.Text)) - 65;
            StatementSQL = SQLAll + " WHERE FirstName > '" +
            buttonArr[idx].Text + " ' ";
            StatementSQL += " AND FirstName < '" +
                    buttonArr[idx + 1].Text + " ' ";

            // Binds to controls
            int rowSaved = managerTeacher.Position;
            DataRow[] rowFound;
            tableTeacher.DefaultView.Sort = "FirstName";
            rowFound = tableTeacher.Select("FirstName LIKE '" +
                buttonArr[idx].Text + "*'");

            if (rowFound.Length == 0)
            {
                managerTeacher.Position = rowSaved;
            }
            else
            {
                managerTeacher.Position =
                    tableTeacher.DefaultView.Find(
                        rowFound[0]["FirstName"]);
                DisplayPhoto();
            }
```

```
48              break;
49          }
50      StatementSQL += " ORDER BY FirstName";
51
52      // Applies SQL statement
53      try
54      {
55          // Creates Command and DataAdapater objects
56          commResult = new SqlCommand(StatementSQL, connBook);
57          adapterResult.SelectCommand = commResult;
58          adapterResult.Fill(tableResult);
59
60          // Binds DataGridView with data table
61          grdTeacher.DataSource = tableResult;
62          txtNumberRecord.Text = tableResult.Rows.Count.ToString();
63      }
64
65      catch (Exception ex)
66      {
67          MessageBox.Show(ex.Message, "Error Processing SQL",
68              MessageBoxButtons.OK, MessageBoxIcon.Error);
69      }
70      commResult.Dispose();
71      adapterResult.Dispose();
72      tableResult.Dispose();
73  }
```

This method determines which button is clicked and forms an SQL statement. If the button with the **Text** property of the button is **"Show All Teachers"** is clicked, then all records will be displayed. When a key letter is clicked, the code determines which letter the user clicks on and attaches an additional test (using **AND**) to the **WHERE** field in the default SQL statement.

Step 5   Add the following code in line 60-64 to **FormTeacher_Load** event method. The code creates search buttons and perform **Click** event of **btnAll** programmatically:

```
1   private void FormTeacher_Load(object sender, EventArgs e)
2   {
3       try
4       {
5           // Connects to database
6           connBook = new SqlConnection("Data Source=.\\SQLEXPRESS;
7               AttachDbFilename=D:\\Database\\DBMS.mdf;
8               Integrated Security = True; Connect Timeout = 30;
9               User Instance = True");
10
11          // Opens connection
12          connBook.Open();
13
14          // Creates Command object
```

```
15    commandTeacher = new SqlCommand(
16        "SELECT * FROM Teacher ORDER BY FirstName", connBook);
17
18    // Creates DataAdapter/DataTable objects
19    adapterTeacher = new SqlDataAdapter();
20    adapterTeacher.SelectCommand = commandTeacher;
21    tableTeacher = new DataTable();
22    adapterTeacher.Fill(tableTeacher);
23
24    // Binds controls to data table
25    txtTeacherID.DataBindings.Add("Text",
26        tableTeacher, "TeacherID");
27    txtRegNumber.DataBindings.Add("Text",
28        tableTeacher, "RegNumber");
29    cboRank.DataBindings.Add("Text", tableTeacher, "Rank");
30    txtFirstName.DataBindings.Add("Text",
31        tableTeacher, "FirstName");
32    txtLastName.DataBindings.Add("Text",
33        tableTeacher, "LastName");
34    dtpBirthDate.DataBindings.Add("Text",
35        tableTeacher, "BirthDate");
36    lblPhotoFile.DataBindings.Add("Text",
37        tableTeacher, "PhotoFile");
38    txtPhone.DataBindings.Add("Text", tableTeacher, "Phone");
39    txtMobile.DataBindings.Add("Text", tableTeacher, "Mobile");
40    chkStatus.DataBindings.Add("Checked",
41        tableTeacher, "Status");
42    cboEthnicity.DataBindings.Add("Text",
43        tableTeacher, "Ethnicity");
44    cboNationality.DataBindings.Add("Text",
45        tableTeacher, "Nationality");
46    cboReligion.DataBindings.Add("Text",
47        tableTeacher, "Religion");
48    cboGender.DataBindings.Add("Text", tableTeacher, "Gender");
49
50    // Creates data update
51    managerTeacher =
52        (CurrencyManager)BindingContext[tableTeacher];
53
54    SetText();
55    DisplayPhoto();
56    this.Show();
57    SetState("View");
58
59    //Creates 26 search buttons
60    createSearchButton();
61
62    // Clicks all records when form starts
63    btnAll.Click += new System.EventHandler(this.btnSQL_Click);
64    btnAll.PerformClick();
65
```

```
66      }
67      catch (Exception ex)
68      {
69          MessageBox.Show(ex.Message,
70              "Error in reading Parent table.",
71              MessageBoxButtons.OK, MessageBoxIcon.Error);
72          return;
73      }
74  }
```

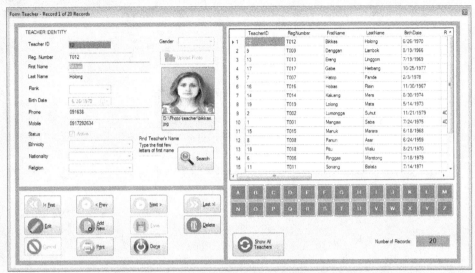

Figure 6.13 The application when it first runs

Step 6   Define **RowPostPaint** event of **grdParent** control to give it a row numbering:

```
1   private void grdParent_RowPostPaint(object sender,
2   DataGridViewRowPostPaintEventArgs e)
3   {
4       var grid = sender as DataGridView;
5       var rowIdx = (e.RowIndex + 1).ToString();
6
7       var centerFormat = new StringFormat()
8       {
9           // Aligns to middle
10          Alignment = StringAlignment.Center,
11          LineAlignment = StringAlignment.Center
12      };
13
14      var headerBounds = new Rectangle(e.RowBounds.Left,
15          e.RowBounds.Top, grid.RowHeadersWidth, e.RowBounds.Height);
16      e.Graphics.DrawString(rowIdx, this.Font,
17          SystemBrushes.ControlText, headerBounds, centerFormat);
18  }
```

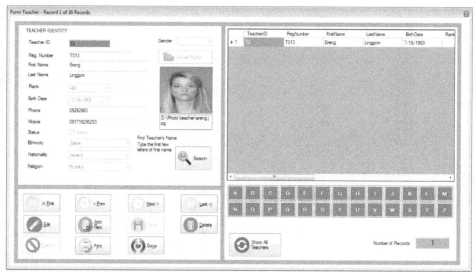

Figure 6.14 The results when the 'E' button is clicked

Step 7   Define **Refresh_DGV** to refresh data grid view, **grdTeacher**, as follows:

```
1   private void Refresh_DGV()
2   {
3       // Connects to database
4       connBook = new SqlConnection("Data Source=.\\SQLEXPRESS;
5           AttachDbFilename=D:\\Database\\DBMS.mdf;
6           Integrated Security = True; Connect Timeout = 30;
7           User Instance = True");
8       connBook.Open();
9
10      // Save changes to database
11      SqlCommandBuilder teacherAdapterCommand = new
12          SqlCommandBuilder(adapterTeacher);
13      adapterTeacher.Update(tableTeacher);
14
15      SqlCommand commandResult = null;
16      SqlDataAdapter adapterResult = new SqlDataAdapter();
17      DataTable tableResult = new DataTable();
18
19      try
20      {
21          // Creates Command and DataAdapter objects
22          commandResult = new SqlCommand(SQLAll, connBook);
23          adapterResult.SelectCommand = commandResult;
24          tableResult.Clear();
25          adapterResult.Fill(tableResult);
26
27          // Binds grid view to data table
28          grdTeacher.DataSource = tableResult;
29          txtNumberRecord.Text = tableResult.Rows.Count.ToString();
```

```
30        }
31
32        catch (Exception ex)
33        {
34            MessageBox.Show(ex.Message, "Error in processing SQL",
35                MessageBoxButtons.OK, MessageBoxIcon.Error);
36        }
37
38        commandResult.Dispose();
39        adapterResult.Dispose();
40        tableResult.Dispose();
41 }
```

Step 8   Call **Refresh_DGV** from **Click** event of **btnAll** as follows:

```
1    private void btnAll_Click(object sender, EventArgs e)
2    {
3        Refresh_DGV();
4    }
```

Step 9   Save and run the application. The result is shown in Figure 6.13. Notice how the search
buttons are created. Also note that all records are displayed initially. Click on one of
the search buttons. Only records with the teacher's initial matching the letter in the
clicked button will be displayed. Figure 6.14 is the query result when the 'E' button is
clicked.

6.11 Tutorial Steps of Selecting Gender

Step 1   You can add a feature to select teacher's gender. Add a label and a combo box on form.
Set **Text** property of the label **"Choose Gender"** and set **Name** property of combo
box as **cboSelectGender**. Define **SelectedIndexChanged** event of combo box as
follows:

```
1    private void cboSelectGender_SelectedIndexChanged(object sender,
2    EventArgs e)
3    {
4        // Connects to database
5        connBook = new SqlConnection("Data Source=.\\SQLEXPRESS;
6            AttachDbFilename=D:\\Database\\DBMS.mdf;
7            Integrated Security = True; Connect Timeout = 30;
8            User Instance = True");
9        connBook.Open();
10
11       // Creates data objects
12       SqlDataAdapter adapterResult = new SqlDataAdapter();
13       DataTable tableResult = new DataTable();
14       SqlCommand commandResult;
```

```
15
16      try
17      {
18          if (cboSelectGender.SelectedItem != null)
19          {
20              // Creates command and data adapter objects
21              string SQLAll = "SELECT * FROM Teacher ";
22
23              SQLAll += "WHERE Gender = '" +
24                  cboSelectGender.SelectedItem.ToString() +
25                  "' ORDER BY FirstName";
26
27              commandResult = new SqlCommand(SQLAll, connBook);
28              adapterResult.SelectCommand = commandResult;
29              adapterResult.Fill(tableResult);
30
31              // binds DataGridView to data table
32              grdTeacher.DataSource = tableResult;
33              txtNumberRecord.Text =
34                  tableResult.Rows.Count.ToString();
35          }
36
37      }
38      catch (Exception ex)
39      {
40          MessageBox.Show(ex.Message, "Error in processing SQL",
41              MessageBoxButtons.OK, MessageBoxIcon.Error);
42      }
}
```

Step 2   Run the application. Choose gender as shown in Figure 6.15 and Figure 6.16.

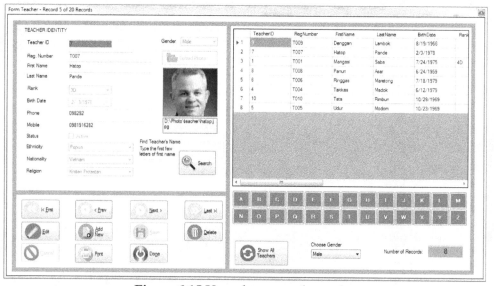

Figure 6.15 User chooses male gender

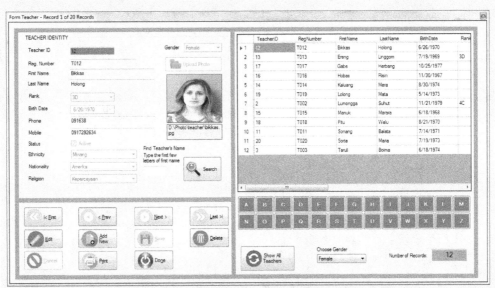

Figure 6.16 User chooses female gender

6.12 Tutorial Steps of Reporting Teachers

Step 1
Now, you will add a feature to read all the data in the database. You need a database report. The report is quite simple. For each record, the data from each field will be displayed.

Add this line of code at the top of the code window:

```
1   using System.Drawing.Printing;
```

Step 2
Add the page number variable to the form level declaration:

```
1   int pageNumber;
```

Step 3
In the **SetState** method, set **Enabled** property of **btnPrint** to **true** in **View** mode and **false** in **Add/Edit** mode.

Step 4
Add the following code to **btnPrint_Click** event method:

```
1   private void btnPrint_Click(object sender, EventArgs e)
2   {
3       // Declares document
4       PrintDocument docTeacher;
5
6       // Creates document and gives it a name
7       docTeacher = new PrintDocument();
8       docTeacher.DocumentName = "Parent Data";
```

```
9
10      // Adds code handler
11      docTeacher.PrintPage += new
12          PrintPageEventHandler(this.PrintTeacher);
13
14      // Prints document in preview control
15      pageNumber = 1;
16      int positionSaved = managerTeacher.Position;
17      dlgPreview.Document = docTeacher;
18      dlgPreview.ShowDialog();
19
20      // Deletes document when finished printing
21      docTeacher.Dispose();
22      managerTeacher.Position = positionSaved;
23
24      DisplayPhoto();
25  }
```

Step 5   Add the following code to **PrintTeacher** method:

```
1   private void PrintTeacher(object sender, PrintPageEventArgs e)
2   {
3       // Tracks every record, prints every record
4       managerTeacher.Position = pageNumber - 1;
5       DisplayPhoto();
6
7       Font myFont = new Font("Arial", 14, FontStyle.Bold);
8       int y = e.MarginBounds.Top + 50;
9
10      // Prints Header
11      e.Graphics.DrawString("Teacher Data (" +
12          DateTime.Now.ToShortDateString() + ") - Page " +
13          pageNumber.ToString(), myFont, Brushes.Black,
14          e.MarginBounds.Left, y);
15      y += 2 * Convert.ToInt32(myFont.GetHeight(e.Graphics));
16
17      e.Graphics.DrawString("*****************************
18          ***************************", myFont, Brushes.Black,
19          e.MarginBounds.X, y);
20      y += Convert.ToInt32(myFont.GetHeight(e.Graphics));
21
22      // Prints photo (width 4 inci, height depends on
23      // height/width ratio of photo)
24      int h = Convert.ToInt32(
25          150 * picTeacher.Image.Height / picTeacher.Image.Width);
26      e.Graphics.DrawImage(picTeacher.Image,
27          e.MarginBounds.X, y, 150, h);
28
29      int slideRight = 175;
30
```

```
31    // Prints text information
32    myFont = new Font("Arial", 12, FontStyle.Regular);
33    e.Graphics.DrawString("Teacher ID:", myFont, Brushes.Black,
34        e.MarginBounds.X + slideRight, y);
35    e.Graphics.DrawString(txtTeacherID.Text, myFont, Brushes.Black,
36        e.MarginBounds.X + slideRight + slideRight, y);
37    y += Convert.ToInt32(myFont.GetHeight(e.Graphics));
38
39    e.Graphics.DrawString("Reg. Number:", myFont, Brushes.Black,
40        e.MarginBounds.X + slideRight, y);
41    e.Graphics.DrawString(txtRegNumber.Text, myFont, Brushes.Black,
42        e.MarginBounds.X + slideRight + slideRight, y);
43    y += Convert.ToInt32(myFont.GetHeight(e.Graphics));
44
45    e.Graphics.DrawString("Full Name:", myFont, Brushes.Black,
46        e.MarginBounds.X + slideRight, y);
47    e.Graphics.DrawString(txtFirstName.Text +" "+txtLastName.Text,
48        myFont, Brushes.Black, e.MarginBounds.X + 2*slideRight, y);
49    y += Convert.ToInt32(myFont.GetHeight(e.Graphics));
50
51    e.Graphics.DrawString("Rank:", myFont, Brushes.Black,
52        e.MarginBounds.X + slideRight, y);
53    e.Graphics.DrawString(cboRank.Text, myFont, Brushes.Black,
54        e.MarginBounds.X + slideRight + slideRight, y);
55    y += Convert.ToInt32(myFont.GetHeight(e.Graphics));
56
57
58    e.Graphics.DrawString("Gender:", myFont, Brushes.Black,
59        e.MarginBounds.X + slideRight, y);
60    e.Graphics.DrawString(cboGender.Text, myFont, Brushes.Black,
61        e.MarginBounds.X + 2 * slideRight, y);
62    y += Convert.ToInt32(myFont.GetHeight(e.Graphics));
63
64    e.Graphics.DrawString("Birth Date:", myFont, Brushes.Black,
65        e.MarginBounds.X + slideRight, y);
66    e.Graphics.DrawString(dtpBirthDate.Text, myFont, Brushes.Black,
67        e.MarginBounds.X + 2 * slideRight, y);
68    y += Convert.ToInt32(myFont.GetHeight(e.Graphics));
69
70    e.Graphics.DrawString("Phone:", myFont, Brushes.Black,
71        e.MarginBounds.X + slideRight, y);
72    e.Graphics.DrawString(txtPhone.Text, myFont, Brushes.Black,
73        e.MarginBounds.X + 2* slideRight, y);
74    y += Convert.ToInt32(myFont.GetHeight(e.Graphics));
75
76    e.Graphics.DrawString("Mobile:", myFont, Brushes.Black,
77        e.MarginBounds.X + slideRight, y);
78    e.Graphics.DrawString(txtMobile.Text, myFont,
79        Brushes.Black, e.MarginBounds.X + 2 * slideRight, y);
80    y += Convert.ToInt32(myFont.GetHeight(e.Graphics));
81
```

```
82      e.Graphics.DrawString("Status:", myFont, Brushes.Black,
83          e.MarginBounds.X + slideRight, y);
84      e.Graphics.DrawString(chkStatus.Text, myFont, Brushes.Black,
85          e.MarginBounds.X + 2 * slideRight, y);
86      y += Convert.ToInt32(myFont.GetHeight(e.Graphics));
87
88      e.Graphics.DrawString("Ethnicity:", myFont, Brushes.Black,
89          e.MarginBounds.X + slideRight, y);
90      e.Graphics.DrawString(cboEthnicity.Text, myFont, Brushes.Black,
91          e.MarginBounds.X + 2 * slideRight, y);
92      y += Convert.ToInt32(myFont.GetHeight(e.Graphics));
93
94      e.Graphics.DrawString("Nationality:", myFont, Brushes.Black,
95          e.MarginBounds.X + slideRight, y);
96      e.Graphics.DrawString(cboNationality.Text, myFont,
97          Brushes.Black, e.MarginBounds.X + 2 * slideRight, y);
98      y += Convert.ToInt32(myFont.GetHeight(e.Graphics));
99
100     e.Graphics.DrawString("Religion:", myFont, Brushes.Black,
101         e.MarginBounds.X + slideRight, y);
102     e.Graphics.DrawString(cboReligion.Text, myFont, Brushes.Black,
103         e.MarginBounds.X + 2 * slideRight, y);
104     y += Convert.ToInt32(myFont.GetHeight(e.Graphics));
105
106     Font myFont2 = new Font("Arial", 14, FontStyle.Bold);
107     e.Graphics.DrawString("***************************
108         ***************************", myFont2, Brushes.Black,
109         e.MarginBounds.X, y);
110
111     pageNumber++;
112     if (pageNumber <= managerTeacher.Count)
113         e.HasMorePages = true;
114     else
115     {
116         e.HasMorePages = false;
117         pageNumber = 1;
118     }
119 }
```

On each page, a header is printed along with the data fields and teacher's photo.

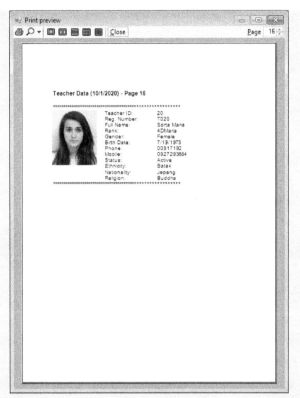

Figure 6.17 Each record in the table can now be printed

Step 6 Save and run the application. Click on the **Print** button. The print preview control will be displayed on all parent pages, as shown in Figure 6.17.

6.12 Tutorial Steps of Creating Form for Subject Table: Interface

Step 1 In this tutorial, you will build such a form for **Subject** table. This table has only three fields: **SubjectID**, **Name**, and **Description**.

You need an input form so that user can edit existing records, delete records, or add new records. The form will also have the capability of navigating from one record to another. The steps that need to be done are as follows.

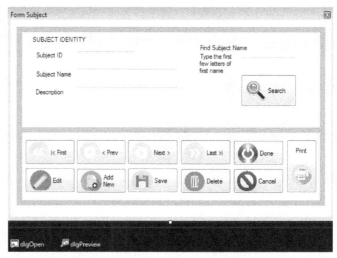

Figure 6.18 Design of subject form

Start a new Visual C# application. You need four label controls, four text boxes, one openfiledialog, and one printpreviewdialog. You also need four buttons for navigation, secen buttons for utilities, and one button for searching subject name. Place these controls on the form. The complete form looks as shown in Figure 6.18.

Step 2   Set the properties of each control as follows:

Form1 Control	
Name	FormSubject
BackColor	Control
FormBorderStyle	FixedSingle
StartPosition	CenterScreen
Text	Form Subject

label1 Control	
Text	Subject ID

textBox1 Control	
Name	txtSubjectID
ReadOnly	True

label2 Control	
Text	Subject Name

textBox2 Control	
Text	txtName

label3 Control	
Text	Description

textBox3 Control	
Name	txtDescription

label4 Control	

Text	Type the first few letters of first name

textBox4 Control	
Name	txtFind

button1 Control	
Name	btnFirst
Text	|< First

button2 Control	
Name	btnPrev
Text	< Prev

button3 Control	
Name	btnNext
Text	Next >

button4 Control	
Name	btnLast
Text	Last >|

button5 Control	
Name	btnSearch
Text	Search

button6 Control	
Name	btnEdit
Text	&Edit

button7 Control	
Name	btnSave
Text	&Save

button8 Control	
Name	btnCancel
Text	&Cancel

button9 Control	
Name	btnAddNew
Text	&Add New

button10 Control	
Name	btnDelete
Text	&Delete

button11 Control	
Name	btnDone
Text	Do&ne

button12 Control	
Name	btnPrint
Text	&Print

openFileDialog1 Control	
Name	dlgOpen

printPreviewDialog1 Control	

Name   dlgPreview

Step 3   You will add features to this subject form gradually. At this point, you will add code
to construct the data table and to navigate the records in the **Subject** table. Add these
lines of code at the top of the window:

```
1   using System.Data.SqlClient;
2   using System.IO;
3   using System.Drawing.Printing;
```

Step 4   Write the following form-level declarations for creating data objects:

```
1   SqlConnection connBook;
2   SqlCommand commandSubject;
3   SqlDataAdapter adapterSubject;
4   DataTable tableSubject;
5   CurrencyManager managerSubject;
```

Step 5   Add the following code to the **FormSubject_Load** event method:

```
1    private void FormSubject_Load(object sender, EventArgs e)
2    {
3        try
4        {
5            // Connects to database
6            connBook = new SqlConnection("Data Source=.\\SQLEXPRESS;
7                AttachDbFilename=D:\\Database\\DBMS.mdf;
8                Integrated Security = True; Connect Timeout = 30;
9                User Instance = True");
10
11           // Opens connection
12           connBook.Open();
13
14           // Creates Command object
15           commandSubject = new SqlCommand(
16               "SELECT * FROM Subject ORDER BY Name", connBook);
17
18           // Creates DataAdapter/DataTable objects
19           adapterSubject = new SqlDataAdapter();
20           adapterSubject.SelectCommand = commandSubject;
21           tableSubject = new DataTable();
22           adapterSubject.Fill(tableSubject);
23
24           // Binds controls to data table
25           txtSubjectID.DataBindings.Add("Text",
26               tableSubject, "SubjectID");
27           txtName.DataBindings.Add("Text", tableSubject, "Name");
28           txtDescription.DataBindings.Add("Text",
29               tableSubject, "Description");
30
```

```
31        // Creates data update
32        managerSubject =
33            (CurrencyManager)BindingContext[tableSubject];
34
35        SetText();
36        this.Show();
37    }
38    catch (Exception ex)
39    {
40        MessageBox.Show(ex.Message,
41          "Error in reading Subject table.",
42          MessageBoxButtons.OK, MessageBoxIcon.Error);
43        return;
44    }
}
```

The code above creates the data objects needed to open the database and construct the **Subject** table (includes all fields). The code above then binds the controls with the update manager object (**CurrencyManager**).

Step 6   Define **SetText** method to display description in title bar of form:

```
1    private void SetText()
2    {
3        this.Text = "Form Subject - Record " +
4            (managerSubject.Position + 1).ToString() + " of " +
5            managerSubject.Count.ToString() + " Records";
6    }
```

Step 7   Add the following code to **FormSubject_FormClosing** event method to close the database connection:

```
1    private void FormSubject_FormClosing(object sender,
2    FormClosingEventArgs e)
3    {
4        // Closes connection to database
5        connBook.Close();
6
7        // Deletes objects
8        connBook.Dispose();
9        commandSubject.Dispose();
10       adapterSubject.Dispose();
11   }
```

Step 8   Write the following code for the **Click** event of the four navigation buttons:

```
1    private void btnPrev_Click(object sender, EventArgs e)
2    {
3        if (managerSubject.Position == 0)
4        {
5            Console.Beep();
```

```
6            }
7        managerSubject.Position--;
8        SetText();
9    }
10
11   private void btnNext_Click(object sender, EventArgs e)
12   {
13       if (managerSubject.Position == managerSubject.Count - 1)
14       {
15           Console.Beep();
16       }
17       managerSubject.Position++;
18       SetText();
19   }
20
21   private void btnFirst_Click(object sender, EventArgs e)
22   {
23       managerSubject.Position = 0;
24       SetText();
25   }
26
27   private void btnLast_Click(object sender, EventArgs e)
28   {
29       managerSubject.Position = managerSubject.Count - 1;
30       SetText();
31   }
```

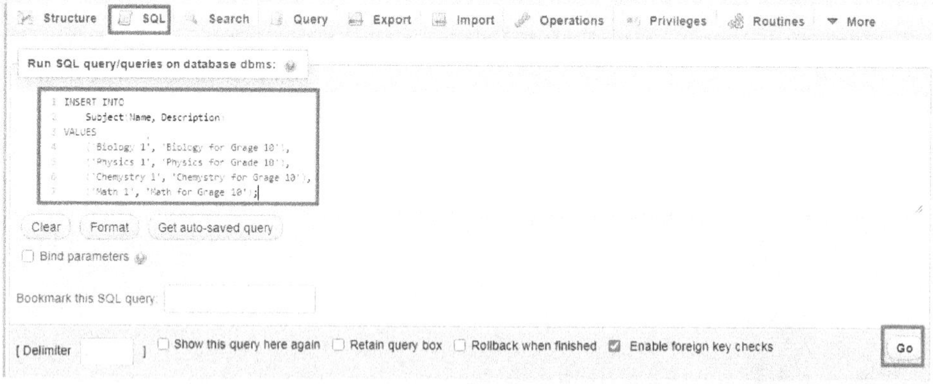

Figure 6.19 Inserting some data into **Subject** table

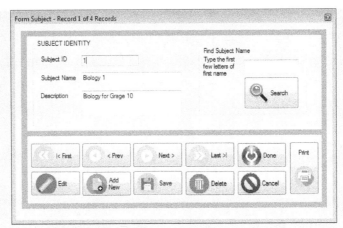

Figure 6.20 Subject form when it first runs

Step 9   Insert some data into **Subject** table as shown in Figure 6.19.

Step 10   Save and run the application. What is displayed first is the first record in **Subject** table.
             Click on four navigation buttons to prove the result.

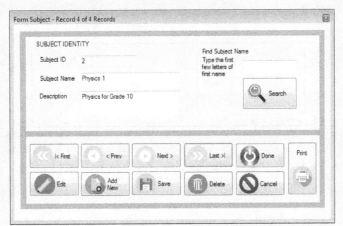

Figure 6.21 The result when user clicks **Last >|** button

6.13 Tutorial Steps of Creating Form for Student Table: Message Box

Step 1   There are two places where you can use the message box in **Student** table input form.
             One message box is provided after saving updates to let the user know that the save
             was successful and another message box is related to record deletion.

             Use the following code in **btnSave_Click** event method:

```
1   private void btnSave_Click(object sender, EventArgs e)
2   {
3       MessageBox.Show("Record is successfully saved", "Save",
```

```
4        MessageBoxButtons.OK, MessageBoxIcon.Information);
5    }
```

There will be more code in this event. The code implements only message box.

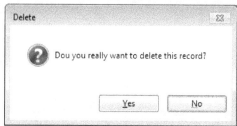

Figure 6.22 Message box is displayed when user clicks **Delete** button

Step 2   Use this code on **btnDelete_Click** event method:

```
1    private void btnDelete_Click(object sender, EventArgs e)
2    {
3        DialogResult response;
4        response = MessageBox.Show("Dou you really want to delete this record?",
5            "Delete", MessageBoxButtons.YesNo, MessageBoxIcon.Question,
6            MessageBoxDefaultButton.Button2);
7    }
```

Step 3   Save the application and run it. Click on **Delete** button to see as shown in Figure 6.20.

6.14 Tutorial Steps of Creating Form for Subject Table: Application State

Step 1   The **Subject** form operates in one of three states: **View** state, **Add** state, or **Edit** state. In the **View** state, user can navigate one record to another, user can switch to **Edit** state, user can add and/or delete records, or user can exit the application.

In **Add** and **Edit** state, no navigation is made possible, data can be updated, and user can have access to **Save** and **Cancel** operations. Each of these steps can be implemented using the **Enabled** property of the button and the **ReadOnly** property of the text box. You use **TabIndex** (and **TabOrder**) to shift focus on the text box controls. You will use a method of moving from one state to another.

Clear all tab ordering for the ten buttons by setting the **TabStop** property to **False**. Additionally, set the **TabStop** property to **False** for the **Subject ID** text box.

Step 2   Add a method named **SetState** as follows:

```
1    private void SetState(string stateStr) {
2        switch (stateStr)
3        {
4            case "View":
```

```
5        txtSubjectID.BackColor = Color.Red;
6        txtSubjectID.ForeColor = Color.Black;
7        txtName.ReadOnly = true;
8        txtDescription.ReadOnly = true;
9        btnFirst.Enabled = true;
10       btnPrev.Enabled = true;
11       btnNext.Enabled = true;
12       btnLast.Enabled = true;
13       btnAddNew.Enabled = true;
14       btnSave.Enabled = false;
15       btnDelete.Enabled = true;
16       btnCancel.Enabled = false;
17       btnEdit.Enabled = true;
18       btnDone.Enabled = true;
19       btnPrint.Enabled = true;
20       txtName.Focus();
21       break;
22
23    default: // Edit or Add
24       txtSubjectID.ReadOnly = true;
25       txtSubjectID.BackColor = Color.Red;
26       txtSubjectID.ForeColor = Color.Black;
27       txtName.ReadOnly = false;
28       txtDescription.ReadOnly = false;
29       btnFirst.Enabled = false;
30       btnPrev.Enabled = false;
31       btnNext.Enabled = false;
32       btnLast.Enabled = false;
33       btnAddNew.Enabled = false;
34       btnSave.Enabled = true;
35       btnDelete.Enabled = false;
36       btnCancel.Enabled = true;
37       btnEdit.Enabled = false;
38       btnDone.Enabled = false;
39       btnPrint.Enabled = false;
40       txtName.Focus();
41       break;
42    }
43 }
```

The code above specifies **View**, **Add**, or **Edit** state for the application. Pay attention
to which buttons are available and which are not. Note that **Subject ID** text box is
given red back color if it is in **Add** or **Edit** state to indicate that it cannot be changed.

Step 3   Set the **View** state when the application first runs. Add the following code in line 37
to **FormSubject_Load** event method:

```
1  private void FormSubject_Load(object sender, EventArgs e)
2  {
3      try
```

```
4    {
5        // Connects to database
6        connBook = new SqlConnection("Data Source=.\\SQLEXPRESS;
7            AttachDbFilename=D:\\Database\\DBMS.mdf;
8            Integrated Security = True; Connect Timeout = 30;
9            User Instance = True");
10
11        // Opens connection
12        connBook.Open();
13
14        // Creates Command object
15        commandSubject = new SqlCommand(
16            "SELECT * FROM Subject ORDER BY Name", connBook);
17
18        // Creates DataAdapter/DataTable objects
19        adapterSubject = new SqlDataAdapter();
20        adapterSubject.SelectCommand = commandSubject;
21        tableSubject = new DataTable();
22        adapterSubject.Fill(tableSubject);
23
24        // Binds controls to data table
25        txtSubjectID.DataBindings.Add("Text",
26            tableSubject, "SubjectID");
27        txtName.DataBindings.Add("Text", tableSubject, "Name");
28        txtDescription.DataBindings.Add("Text",
29            tableSubject, "Description");
30
31        // Creates data update
32        managerSubject =
33            (CurrencyManager)BindingContext[tableSubject];
34
35        SetText();
36        this.Show();
37        SetState("View");
38    }
39    catch (Exception ex)
40    {
41        MessageBox.Show(ex.Message,
42          "Error in reading Subject table.",
43          MessageBoxButtons.OK, MessageBoxIcon.Error);
44        return;
45    }
46 }
```

Step 4   When **Add New** button is clicked, you need to switch to **Add** state. Add the following code to **btnAddNew_Click** event method:

```
1    private void btnAddNew_Click(object sender, EventArgs e)
2    {
3        SetState("Add");
```

```
4    }
```

Step 5   When **Edit** button is clicked, the application will be switched to **Edit** state. Add the following code to **btnEdit_Click** event method:

```
1  private void btnEdit_Click(object sender, EventArgs e)
2  {
3      SetState("Edit");
4  }
```

Step 6   When **Cancel** or **Save** button is clicked (in **Add** or **Edit** state), application will return to the **View** state. Put this line of code in **btnCancel_Click** and **btnSave_Click** event methods:

```
1  private void btnCancel_Click(object sender, EventArgs e)
2  {
3      SetState("View");
4  }
5
6  private void btnSave_Click(object sender, EventArgs e)
7  {
8      SetState("View");
9  }
```

Step 7   Save and run the application. You will see the application in its initial state (**View** state) as shown in Figure 6.23.

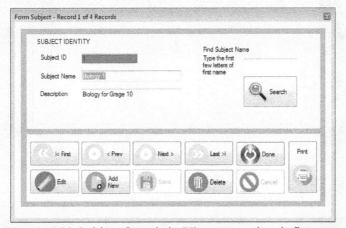

Figure 6.23 Subject form is in **View** state when it first runs

When user clicks the **Edit/Add New** button, you will see what is shown in Figure 6.24.

Figure 6.24 Subject form is in **Edit** or **Add** state

6.15 Tutorial Steps of Creating Form for Subject Table: Error Trapping

Step 1   Modify **btnAddNew_Click**, **btnSave_Click**, and **btnDelete_Click** event methods to handle error trapping:

```
1   private void btnAddNew_Click(object sender, EventArgs e)
2   {
3       try
4       {
5           SetState("Add");
6       }
7       catch (Exception ex)
8       {
9           MessageBox.Show("Error adding new record.", "Error",
10              MessageBoxButtons.OK, MessageBoxIcon.Error);
11      }
12  }
```

```
1   private void btnSave_Click(object sender, EventArgs e)
2   {
3       try
4       {
5           MessageBox.Show("Record successfully saved", "Save",
6           MessageBoxButtons.OK, MessageBoxIcon.Information);
7           SetState("View");
8       }
9       catch (Exception ex)
10      {
11          MessageBox.Show("Error saving record.", "Error",
12              MessageBoxButtons.OK, MessageBoxIcon.Error);
13      }
14  }
```

```
1   private void btnDelete_Click(object sender, EventArgs e)
2   {
3       DialogResult response;
4       response = MessageBox.Show("Dou you really want to delete this record?",
5           "Delete", MessageBoxButtons.YesNo, MessageBoxIcon.Question,
6           MessageBoxDefaultButton.Button2);
7       if (response == DialogResult.No)
8       {
9           return;
10      }
11
12      try
13      {
14
15      }
16      catch (Exception ex)
17      {
18          MessageBox.Show("Error deleting record.", "Error",
19              MessageBoxButtons.OK, MessageBoxIcon.Error);
20      }
21  }
```

6.16 Tutorial Steps of Creating Form for Subject Table: Editing Record

Step 1   You will now add editing capability and other related capabilities to save and/or cancel
edits. Before saving update into database, you need to validate data entered by user. In
this case, you need to validate subject name. Define a method named **ValidateData** to
validate data entered by user:

```
1   private bool ValidateData()
2   {
3       string message = "";
4       bool allOK = true;
5
6       // Checks name of subject
7       if (txtName.Text.Trim().Equals(""))
8       {
9           message = "You should enter subject name." + "\r\n";
10          txtName.Focus();
11          allOK = false;
12      }
13
14      if (!allOK)
15      {
16          MessageBox.Show(message, "Validation Error",
17              MessageBoxButtons.OK, MessageBoxIcon.Information);
18      }
19      return (allOK);
```

```
20  }
```

Step 2   Add a **KeyPress** event for the **txtName** and **txtDescription** text boxes to move to
another control:

```
1   private void txtName_KeyPress(object sender, KeyPressEventArgs e)
2   {
3       if ((int)e.KeyChar == 13)
4           txtDescription.Focus();
5   }
6
7   private void txtDescription_KeyPress(object sender,
8   KeyPressEventArgs e)
9   {
10      if ((int)e.KeyChar == 13)
11          txtFind.Focus();
12  }
```

Step 3   Add the following line of code to the form-level declaration:

```
1   string appState;
```

Step 4   Add this code in line 2 to **SetState** method:

```
1   private void SetState(string stateStr) {
2       appState = stateStr;
3       switch (stateStr)
4       {
5           case "View":
6               txtSubjectID.BackColor = Color.Red;
7               txtSubjectID.ForeColor = Color.Black;
8               txtName.ReadOnly = true;
9               txtDescription.ReadOnly = true;
10              btnFirst.Enabled = true;
11              btnPrev.Enabled = true;
12              btnNext.Enabled = true;
13              btnLast.Enabled = true;
14              btnAddNew.Enabled = true;
15              btnSave.Enabled = false;
16              btnDelete.Enabled = true;
17              btnCancel.Enabled = false;
18              btnEdit.Enabled = true;
19              btnDone.Enabled = true;
20              btnPrint.Enabled = true;
21              txtName.Focus();
22              break;
23
24          default: // Edit or Add
25              txtSubjectID.ReadOnly = true;
26              txtSubjectID.BackColor = Color.Red;
```

```
27          txtSubjectID.ForeColor = Color.Black;
28          txtName.ReadOnly = false;
29          txtDescription.ReadOnly = false;
30          btnFirst.Enabled = false;
31          btnPrev.Enabled = false;
32          btnNext.Enabled = false;
33          btnLast.Enabled = false;
34          btnAddNew.Enabled = false;
35          btnSave.Enabled = true;
36          btnDelete.Enabled = false;
37          btnCancel.Enabled = true;
38          btnEdit.Enabled = false;
39          btnDone.Enabled = false;
40          btnPrint.Enabled = false;
41          txtName.Focus();
42          break;
43      }
}
```

Step 5   Modify **btnSave_Click** event method to save the change and reposition the pointer to
the record just edited:

```
1   private void btnSave_Click(object sender, EventArgs e)
2   {
3       if (!ValidateData())
4       {
5           return;
6       }
7
8       string nameSaved = txtName.Text;
9       int rowSaved;
10
11      try
12      {
13          managerSubject.EndCurrentEdit();
14          tableSubject.DefaultView.Sort = "Name";
15          rowSaved = tableSubject.DefaultView.Find(nameSaved);
16          managerSubject.Position = rowSaved;
17
18          // Saves changes into database
19          SqlCommandBuilder subjectAdapterCommand = new
20              SqlCommandBuilder(adapterSubject);
21          adapterSubject.Update(tableSubject);
22
23          MessageBox.Show("Records successfully saved", "Save",
24              MessageBoxButtons.OK, MessageBoxIcon.Information);
25
26          SetState("View");
27      }
28      catch (Exception ex)
29
```

```
30    {
31            MessageBox.Show("Error saving record.", "Error",
32                MessageBoxButtons.OK, MessageBoxIcon.Error);
33    }
   }
```

Step 6   Modify **btnCancel_Click** event method to restore controls if the edit is canceled:

```
1    private void btnCancel_Click(object sender, EventArgs e)
2    {
3        managerSubject.CancelCurrentEdit();
4        SetState("View");
5    }
```

Step 7   Add the following code in line to the **FormSubject_FormClosing** method to save any changes to the database file:

```
1    private void FormSubject_FormClosing(object sender,
2    FormClosingEventArgs e)
3    {
4        try
5        {
6            // Saves changes into database
7            SqlCommandBuilder subjectAdapterCommand =
8                new SqlCommandBuilder(adapterTeacher);
9            adapterTeacher.Update(tableSubject);
10        }
11        catch (Exception ex)
12        {
13            MessageBox.Show("Error saving database into file: \r\n" +
14                ex.Message, "Saving Error", MessageBoxButtons.OK,
15                MessageBoxIcon.Error);
16        }
17
18        // Closes connection to database
19        connBook.Close();
20
21        // Deletes objects
22        connBook.Dispose();
23        commandSubject.Dispose();
24        adapterSubject.Dispose();
25    }
```

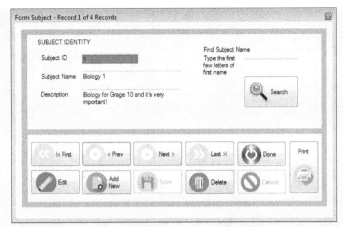

Figure 6.25 Editing operation is successfully performed

Step 8   Save and run the application. Make sure Edit feature is working properly. Make sure the **Cancel** button is working properly. This is shown in Figure 6.25.

6.17 Tutorial Steps of Creating Form for Subject Table: Adding New Record

Step 1   You now implement the capability on the form to add new records to the database. Add the following line of code to the form-level declaration:

```
1   int myBookmark;
```

Step 2   Modify **btnAddNew_Click** event method to add a new record by adding code in line 6-13:

```
1   private void btnAddNew_Click(object sender, EventArgs e)
2   {
3       try
4       {
5           myBookmark = managerSubject.Position;
6           managerSubject.AddNew();
7           SetState("Add");
8       }
9       catch (Exception ex)
10      {
11          MessageBox.Show("Error adding new record.", "Error",
12              MessageBoxButtons.OK, MessageBoxIcon.Error);
13      }
14  }
```

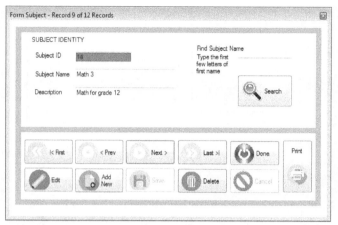

Figure 6.26 The new record has been successfully saved into the database

Step 3   Modify **btnCancel_Click** event method to differentiate between cancellation during
Edit mode and **Add** mode by adding code in line 5-8:

```
1   private void btnCancel_Click(object sender, EventArgs e)
2   {
3       managerSubject.CancelCurrentEdit();
4
5       if (appState.Equals("Add"))
6       {
7           managerSubject.Position = myBookmark;
8       }
9       SetState("View");
10  }
```

Step 4   Save and run the application. Click **Add New** button. Note that all text boxes are blank
(including **Subject ID** text box. Fill in all fields, then click **Save**. New record has been
successfully saved as shown in Figure 6.26.

6.18 Tutorial Steps of Creating Form for Subject Table: Deleting Record

Step 1   You will now add the capability to delete records from **Subject** table. Modify the
btnDelete_Click event method by adding code in line 14 to delete records if the user
responds to **Yes** in the message box:

```
1   private void btnDelete_Click(object sender, EventArgs e)
2   {
3       DialogResult response;
4       response = MessageBox.Show("Dou you really want to delete this record?",
5           "Delete", MessageBoxButtons.YesNo, MessageBoxIcon.Question,
6           MessageBoxDefaultButton.Button2);
7       if (response == DialogResult.No)
8       {
```

```
 9          return;
10      }
11
12      try
13      {
14          managerSubject.RemoveAt(managerSubject.Position);
15      }
16      catch (Exception ex)
17      {
18          MessageBox.Show("Error deleting record.", "Error",
19              MessageBoxButtons.OK, MessageBoxIcon.Error);
20      }
21  }
```

Step 2   Save the application and run it. Make sure the **Yes** and **No** responses in the message box give correct results. Delete only those records you added using **Add New** button.

6.19 Tutorial Steps of Creating Form for Subject Table: Stopping Application

Step 1   Add the following code in line 4-12 and line 34 to **FormSubject_FormClosing** event method to ensure user doesn't close the application during **Edit** or **Add** mode:

```
 1  private void FormSubject_FormClosing(object sender,
 2  FormClosingEventArgs e)
 3  {
 4      if (appState.Equals("Edit") || appState.Equals("Add"))
 5      {
 6          MessageBox.Show(
 7              "You should finish editing before closing application.",
 8              "", MessageBoxButtons.OK, MessageBoxIcon.Information);
 9          e.Cancel = true;
10      }
11      else
12      {
13          try
14          {
15              // Saves changes into
16              SqlCommandBuilder subjectAdapterCommand =
17                  new SqlCommandBuilder(adapterSubject);
18              adapterSubject.Update(tableSubject);
19          }
20          catch (Exception ex)
21          {
22              MessageBox.Show("Error saving database into file: \r\n" +
23                  ex.Message, "Error Saving", MessageBoxButtons.OK,
24                  MessageBoxIcon.Error);
25          }
26
```

```
27      // Closes connection to database
28      connBook.Close();
29
30      // Deletes objects
31      connBook.Dispose();
32      commandSubject.Dispose();
33      adapterSubject.Dispose();
34    }
35  }
```

Step 2   Put this code in **btnDone_Click** event method:

```
1   private void btnDone_Click(object sender, EventArgs e)
2   {
3       this.Close();
4   }
```

Step 3   Save and run the application. Make sure the **Done** button is working properly. Make sure the user cannot close the application in **Edit** or **Add** mode.

6.20 Tutorial Steps of Searching Capability

Step 1   In the **SetState** method, enable group box control in **View** mode and disable it in **Add** and **Edit** mode. Use its **Enabled** property.

Step 3   Add the following code to **btnSearch_Click** event method:

```
1   private void btnSearch_Click(object sender, EventArgs e)
2   {
3       if (txtFind.Text.Equals(""))
4       {
5           return;
6       }
7
8       int rowSaved = managerSubject.Position;
9       DataRow[] rowFound;
10      tableSubject.DefaultView.Sort = "Name";
11      rowFound = tableSubject.Select("LIKE '" +
12          txtFind.Text + "*'");
13
14      if (rowFound.Length == 0)
15      {
16          managerSubject.Position = rowSaved;
17      }
18      else
19      {
20          managerSubject.Position =
21              tableSubject.DefaultView.Find(rowFound[0]["Name"]);
```

```
22    }
23 }
```

Step 4   Save and run the application. Try searching by providing the first or two letters of the parent's name, as shown in Figure 6.27.

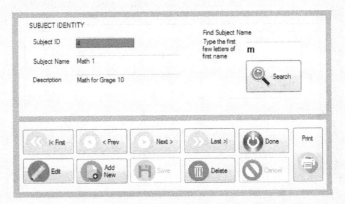

Figure 6.27 Subject's name search feature added

6.21 Tutorial Steps of Adding Search Buttons

Step 1   Add a button control on the form. Set its **Name** property as **btnAll** and its **Text** poperty as **Show All Subjects**. You add another **DataGridView** control and set its **Name** property as **grdSubject**. You also need to add a label and set its **Text** property as **Number of Records:**. Then add a textbox on the form. Set its **Name** property as **txtNumberRecord**. The resulting form is shown in Figure 6.28.

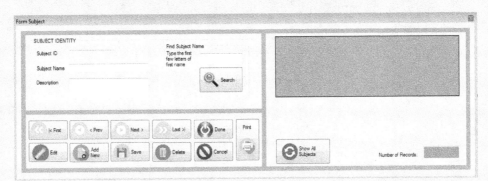

Figure 6.28 Subject form after a number of controls added

Step 2   Add the following form-level declarations:

```
1  String SQLAll = "SELECT * FROM Subject ";
2  Button[] buttonArr = new Button[26];
```

SQLAll is a variable that contains the default SQL statements, while **buttonArr** is an array containing the search buttons.

Step 3   Define a new method named **createSearchButton()** as follows:

```
1   private void createSearchButton()
2   {
3       // Creates search buttons
4       int w, lStart, l, t;
5       int btnHeight = 35; // by trial and error
6
7       // Search buttons
8       // Button width - 13 buttons in a row
9       w = Convert.ToInt32(grdSubject.Width / 13);
10
11      // Aligns buttons
12      lStart = Convert.ToInt32((grdSubject.Width))-20;
13      l = lStart; t = grdSubject.Top + grdSubject.Height + 10;
14
15      // Creates and positions 26 buttons
16      for (int i = 0; i < 26; i++)
17      {
18          // Creates push button
19          buttonArr[i] = new Button();
20          buttonArr[i].TabStop = false;
21
22          // Sets Text property
23          buttonArr[i].Text = ((char)(65 + i)).ToString();
24          buttonArr[i].Font = new Font(buttonArr[i].Font.FontFamily,
25              9, FontStyle.Bold);
26
27          // Positions buttons
28          buttonArr[i].Width = w;
29          buttonArr[i].Height = btnHeight;
30          buttonArr[i].Left = l;
31          buttonArr[i].Top = t;
32
33          // Gives color
34          buttonArr[i].BackColor = Color.Red;
35          buttonArr[i].ForeColor = Color.White;
36
37          // Adds each button on form
38          this.Controls.Add(buttonArr[i]);
39
40          // Adds event handler
41          buttonArr[i].Click +=
42              new System.EventHandler(this.btnSQL_Click);
43          l += w+1;
44
45          if (i == 12)
```

```
46    {
47          // Next row
48          l = lStart; t += btnHeight;
49    }
50  }
51 }
```

This method creates search buttons A through Z using **buttonArrr** array. The code above then specifies the width of the button and places it on the form. Finally, the resulting records are displayed by programmatically clicking **btnSQL** button.

Step 4   Write the code for **btnSQL_Click** event method (handle **Click** event for all search buttons) as follows:

```
1  private void btnSQL_Click(object sender, EventArgs e)
2  {
3      SqlCommand commResult = null;
4      SqlDataAdapter adapterResult = new SqlDataAdapter();
5      DataTable tableResult = new DataTable();
6      String StatementSQL;
7
8      // Determines which button is clicked and creates SQL statement
9      Button buttonClicked = (Button)sender;
10     switch (buttonClicked.Text)
11     {
12         case "Show All Members":
13             StatementSQL = SQLAll;
14             break;
15         case "Z":
16             // Z button is clicked
17             // Appends at SQLAll to limit records upto for item Z
18             StatementSQL = SQLAll + " WHERE Name > 'Z' ";
19             break;
20         default:
21             // Letter keys except Z
22             // Appends at SQLAll to limit records
23             // for letter that is clicked
24             int idx = (int)(Convert.ToChar(buttonClicked.Text)) - 65;
25             StatementSQL = SQLAll + " WHERE Name > '" +
26             buttonArr[idx].Text + " ' ";
27             StatementSQL += " AND Name < '" +
28                     buttonArr[idx + 1].Text + " ' ";
29
30             // Binds to controls
31             int rowSaved = managerSubject.Position;
32             DataRow[] rowFound;
33             tableSubject.DefaultView.Sort = "Name";
34             rowFound = tableSubject.Select("Name LIKE '" +
35                 buttonArr[idx].Text + "*'");
36
```

```
37          if (rowFound.Length == 0)
38          {
39              managerSubject.Position = rowSaved;
40          }
41          else
42          {
43              managerSubject.Position =
44                  tableSubject.DefaultView.Find(
45                      rowFound[0]["Name"]);
46          }
47          break;
48      }
49      StatementSQL += " ORDER BY Name";
50
51      // Applies SQL statement
52      try
53      {
54          // Creates Command and DataAdapater objects
55          commResult = new SqlCommand(StatementSQL, connBook);
56          adapterResult.SelectCommand = commResult;
57          adapterResult.Fill(tableResult);
58
59          // Binds DataGridView with data table
60          grdSubject.DataSource = tableResult;
61          txtNumberRecord.Text = tableResult.Rows.Count.ToString();
62      }
63
64      catch (Exception ex)
65      {
66          MessageBox.Show(ex.Message, "Error Processing SQL",
67              MessageBoxButtons.OK, MessageBoxIcon.Error);
68      }
69      commResult.Dispose();
70      adapterResult.Dispose();
71      tableResult.Dispose();
72  }
73
```

This method determines which button is clicked and forms an SQL statement. If the button with the **Text** property of the button is **"Show All Subjects"** is clicked, then all records will be displayed. When a key letter is clicked, the code determines which letter the user clicks on and attaches an additional test (using **AND**) to the **WHERE** field in the default SQL statement.

Step 5   Add the following code in line 40-44 to **FormSubject_Load** event method. The code creates search buttons and perform **Click** event of **btnAll** programmatically:

```
1   private void FormSubject_Load(object sender, EventArgs e)
2   {
```

```csharp
3    try
4    {
5        // Connects to database
6        connBook = new SqlConnection("Data Source=.\\SQLEXPRESS;
7            AttachDbFilename=D:\\Database\\DBMS.mdf;
8            Integrated Security = True; Connect Timeout = 30;
9            User Instance = True");
10
11        // Opens connection
12        connBook.Open();
13
14        // Creates Command object
15        commandSubject = new SqlCommand(
16            "SELECT * FROM Subject ORDER BY Name", connBook);
17
18        // Creates DataAdapter/DataTable objects
19        adapterSubject = new SqlDataAdapter();
20        adapterSubject.SelectCommand = commandSubject;
21        tableSubject = new DataTable();
22        adapterSubject.Fill(tableSubject);
23
24        // Binds controls to data table
25        txtSubjectID.DataBindings.Add("Text",
26            tableSubject, "SubjectID");
27        txtName.DataBindings.Add("Text", tableSubject, "Name");
28        txtDescription.DataBindings.Add("Text",
29            tableSubject, "Description");
30
31        // Creates data update
32        managerSubject =
33            (CurrencyManager)BindingContext[tableSubject];
34
35        SetText();
36        this.Show();
37        SetState("View");
38
39        //Creates 26 search buttons
40        createSearchButton();
41
42        // Clicks all records when form starts
43        btnAll.Click += new System.EventHandler(this.btnSQL_Click);
44        btnAll.PerformClick();
45    }
46    catch (Exception ex)
47    {
48        MessageBox.Show(ex.Message,
49            "Error in reading Subject table.",
50            MessageBoxButtons.OK, MessageBoxIcon.Error);
51        return;
52    }
```

}

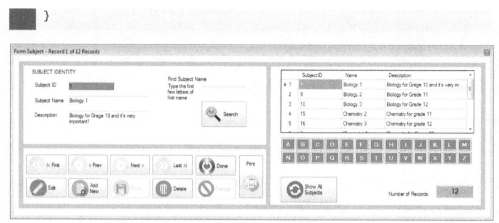

Figure 6.29 The application when it first runs

Step 6   Define **RowPostPaint** event of **grdSubject** control to give it a row numbering:

```
1   private void grdSubject_RowPostPaint(object sender,
2   DataGridViewRowPostPaintEventArgs e)
3   {
4       var grid = sender as DataGridView;
5       var rowIdx = (e.RowIndex + 1).ToString();
6
7       var centerFormat = new StringFormat()
8       {
9           // Aligns to middle
10          Alignment = StringAlignment.Center,
11          LineAlignment = StringAlignment.Center
12      };
13
14      var headerBounds = new Rectangle(e.RowBounds.Left,
15          e.RowBounds.Top, grid.RowHeadersWidth, e.RowBounds.Height);
16      e.Graphics.DrawString(rowIdx, this.Font,
17          SystemBrushes.ControlText, headerBounds, centerFormat);
18  }
```

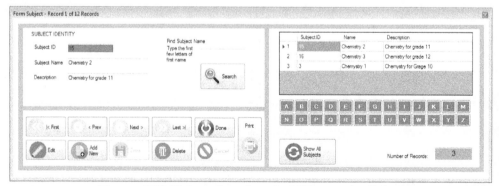

Figure 6.30 The results when the 'C' button is clicked

Step 7   Define **Refresh_DGV** to refresh data grid view, **grdSubject**, as follows:

```csharp
private void Refresh_DGV()
{
    // Connects to database
    connBook = new SqlConnection("Data Source=.\\SQLEXPRESS;
        AttachDbFilename=D:\\Database\\DBMS.mdf;
        Integrated Security = True; Connect Timeout = 30;
        User Instance = True");
    connBook.Open();

    // Save changes to database
    SqlCommandBuilder subjectAdapterCommand = new
        SqlCommandBuilder(adapterSubject);
    adapterSubject.Update(tableSubject);

    SqlCommand commandResult = null;
    SqlDataAdapter adapterResult = new SqlDataAdapter();
    DataTable tableResult = new DataTable();

    try
    {
        // Creates Command and DataAdapter objects
        commandResult = new SqlCommand(SQLAll, connBook);
        adapterResult.SelectCommand = commandResult;
        tableResult.Clear();
        adapterResult.Fill(tableResult);

        // Binds grid view to data table
        grdSubject.DataSource = tableResult;
        txtNumberRecord.Text = tableResult.Rows.Count.ToString();
    }

    catch (Exception ex)
    {
        MessageBox.Show(ex.Message, "Error in processing SQL",
            MessageBoxButtons.OK, MessageBoxIcon.Error);
    }

    commandResult.Dispose();
    adapterResult.Dispose();
    tableResult.Dispose();
}
```

Step 8   Call **Refresh_DGV** from **Click** event of **btnAll** as follows:

```csharp
private void btnAll_Click(object sender, EventArgs e)
{
    Refresh_DGV();
}
```

Step 9   Save and run the application. The result is shown in Figure 6.29. Notice how the search buttons are created. Also note that all records are displayed initially. Click on one of the search buttons. Only records with the subject's initial matching the letter in the clicked button will be displayed. Figure 6.30 is the query result when the 'C' button is clicked.

6.22 Tutorial Steps of Reporting Subjects

Step 1   Now, you will add a feature to read all the data in the database. You need a database report. The report is quite simple. For each record, the data from each field will be displayed.

Add this line of code at the top of the code window:

```
1    using System.Drawing.Printing;
```

Step 2   Add the page number and subject per page variables to the form level declaration:

```
1    int pageNumber;
2    int subjectPerPage = 20;
```

Step 3   In the **SetState** method, set **Enabled** property of **btnPrint** to **true** in **View** mode and **false** in **Add/Edit** mode.

Step 4   Add the following code to **btnPrint_Click** event method:

```
1    private void btnPrint_Click(object sender, EventArgs e)
2    {
3        // Declares document
4        PrintDocument docSubject;
5
6        // Creates document and gives it a name
7        docSubject = new PrintDocument();
8        docSubject.DocumentName = "Subject Data";
9
10       // Adds code handler
11       docSubject.PrintPage += new
12           PrintPageEventHandler(this.PrintSubject);
13
14       // Prints document in preview control
15       pageNumber = 1;
16       int positionSaved = managerSubject.Position;
17       dlgPreview.Document = docSubject;
18       dlgPreview.ShowDialog();
19
20       // Deletes document when finished printing
21       docSubject.Dispose();
```

```
22      managerSubject.Position = positionSaved;
23  }
```

Step 5   Add the following code to **PrintSubject** method:

```
1   private void PrintSubject(object sender, PrintPageEventArgs e)
2   {
3       // For every page
4       // Prints header
5       Font myFont = new Font("Courier New", 14, FontStyle.Bold);
6       e.Graphics.DrawString("Subject - Page " +
7           pageNumber.ToString(), myFont, Brushes.Black,
8           e.MarginBounds.Left, e.MarginBounds.Top);
9
10      myFont = new Font("Courier New", 12, FontStyle.Underline);
11      int y = Convert.ToInt32(e.MarginBounds.Top + 50);
12      e.Graphics.DrawString("Subject ID", myFont, Brushes.Black,
13          e.MarginBounds.Left, y);
14      e.Graphics.DrawString("Name", myFont, Brushes.Black,
15          e.MarginBounds.Left + Convert.ToInt32(0.6 *
16          (e.MarginBounds.Width)), y);
17
18      y += Convert.ToInt32(2 * myFont.GetHeight());
19      myFont = new Font("Courier New", 12, FontStyle.Regular);
20      int iLast = subjectPerPage * pageNumber;
21
22      if (iLast > tableSubject.Rows.Count)
23      {
24          iLast = tableSubject.Rows.Count;
25          e.HasMorePages = false;
26      }
27      else
28      {
29          e.HasMorePages = true;
30      }
31
32      for (int i = 1 + subjectPerPage * (pageNumber - 1); i <= iLast; i++)
33      {
34          // Moves to all records
35          if (txtSubjectID.Text.Length < 35)
36          {
37              e.Graphics.DrawString(txtSubjectID.Text, myFont,
38                  Brushes.Black, e.MarginBounds.Left, y);
39          }
40          else
41          {
42              e.Graphics.DrawString(
43                  txtSubjectID.Text.Substring(0, 35), myFont,
44                  Brushes.Black, e.MarginBounds.Left, y);
45          }
46          if (txtName.Text.Length < 35)
```

```
47    {
48        e.Graphics.DrawString(txtName.Text, myFont,
49            Brushes.Black, e.MarginBounds.Left +
50            Convert.ToInt32(0.6 * (e.MarginBounds.Width)), y);
51    }
52    else
53    {
54        e.Graphics.DrawString(txtName.Text.Substring(0, 20),
55            myFont, Brushes.Black, e.MarginBounds.Left +
56            Convert.ToInt32(0.6 * (e.MarginBounds.Width)), y);
57    }
58
59    btnNext.PerformClick();
60    y += Convert.ToInt32(myFont.GetHeight());
61    }
62
63    if (e.HasMorePages)
64        pageNumber++;
65    else
66        pageNumber = 1;
67 }
```

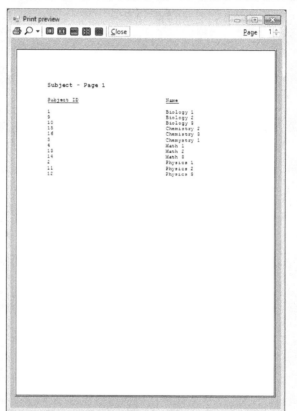

Figure 6.31 List of all subject ids and names

Step 6   Save and run the application. Click on the **Print** button. The print preview control will
list all subject ids and names, as shown in Figure 6.31.

TUTORIAL 7
BALIGE ACADEMY
DATABASE PROJECT: PART 3

7.1 Tutorial Steps of Creating Form for Grade: Interface

Step 1   In this tutorial, you will build such a form for **Grade** table. This table has seven fields: **GradeID**, **Name**, **SubjectID**, **TeacherID**, **SchoolYear**, **TimaStart**, and **TimeFinish**.

You need an input form so that user can edit existing records, delete records, or add new records. The form will also have the capability of navigating from one record to another. The steps that need to be done are as follows.

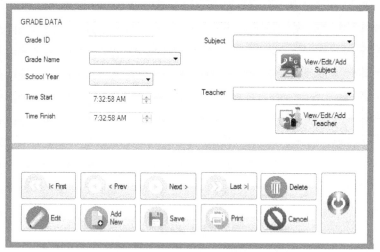

Figure 7.1 Design of grade form

Start a new Visual C# application. You need seven label controls, one text box, four comboxes, and two date time pickers. You also need four buttons for navigation, seven buttons for controlling editing features, one button to open subject form, and one button to open teacher form. Place these controls on the form. The complete form looks as shown in Figure 7.1.

Step 2   Set the properties of each control as follows:

Form1 Control	
Name	FormGrade

BackColor	Control
FormBorderStyle	FixedSingle
StartPosition	CenterScreen
Text	Form Grade

label1 Control

Text	Grade ID

textBox1 Control

Name	txtGradeID
ReadOnly	True

label2 Control

Text	Grade Name

comboBox1 Control

Text	cboGrade
Items	{Grade 10, Grade 11, Grade 12}

label3 Control

Text	School Year

comboBox2 Control

Name	cboSchoolYear
Items	{2020,2021,2022, 2023,2024,2025, 2026,2027,2028, 2029,2030}

label4 Control

Text	Time Start

dateTimePicker1 Control

Name	dtpStart
Format	Time

label5 Control

Text	Time Finish

dateTimePicker2 Control

Name	dtpFinish
Format	Custom
CustomFormat	HH:mm

label6 Control

Text	Subject

comboBox3 Control

Name	cboSubject

label7 Control

Text	Teacher

comboBox4 Control	
Name	cboTeacher

button1 Control	
Name	btnFirst
Text	|< First

button2 Control	
Name	btnPrev
Text	< Prev

button3 Control	
Name	btnNext
Text	Next >

button4 Control	
Name	btnLast
Text	Last >|

button5 Control	
Name	btnSearch
Text	Search

button6 Control	
Name	btnEdit
Text	&Edit

button7 Control	
Name	btnSave
Text	&Save

button8 Control	
Name	btnCancel
Text	&Cancel

button9 Control	
Name	btnAddNew
Text	&Add New

button10 Control	
Name	btnDelete
Text	&Delete

button11 Control	
Name	btnDone
Text	Do&ne

button12 Control	
Name	btnPrint
Text	&Print

button13 Control	
Name	btnFormSubject
Text	View/Edit/Add Subject

button14 Control	
Name	btnFormTeacher
Text	View/Edit/Add Teacher

printPreviewDialog1 Control	
Name	dlgPreview

Step 3   You will add features to this parent form gradually. At this point, you will add code to construct the data table and to navigate the records in the **Grade** table. Add these lines of code at the top of the window:

```
1  using System.Data.SqlClient;
2  using System.IO;
3  using System.Drawing.Printing;
```

Step 4   Write the following form-level declarations for creating data objects:

```
1   SqlConnection connBook;
2   SqlCommand commandGrade;
3   SqlDataAdapter adapterGrade;
4   DataTable tableGrade;
5   CurrencyManager managerGrade;
6
7   SqlCommand commandSubject;
8   SqlDataAdapter adapterSubject;
9   DataTable tabelSubject;
10
11  SqlCommand commandTeacher;
12  SqlDataAdapter adapterTeacher;
13  DataTable tableTeacher;
```

Step 5   Add the following code to the **FormGrade_Load** event method:

```
1   private void FormGrade_Load(object sender, EventArgs e)
2   {
3       try
4       {
5           // Connects to database
6           connBook = new SqlConnection("Data Source=.\\SQLEXPRESS;
7               AttachDbFilename=D:\\Database\\DBMS.mdf;
8               Integrated Security = True; Connect Timeout = 30;
9               User Instance = True");
10
11          // Opens connection
12          connBook.Open();
13
14          // Creates Command object
15          commandGrade = new SqlCommand(
16              "SELECT * FROM Grade ORDER BY Name", connBook);
17
```

```
18      // Creates DataAdapter/DataTable objects
19      adapterGrade = new SqlDataAdapter();
20      adapterGrade.SelectCommand = commandGrade;
21      tableGrade = new DataTable();
22      adapterGrade.Fill(tableGrade);
23
24      // Binds controls to data table
25      txtGradeID.DataBindings.Add("Text", tableGrade, "GradeID");
26      cboGrade.DataBindings.Add("Text", tableGrade, "Name");
27      cboSchoolYear.DataBindings.Add("Text", tableGrade, "SchoolYear");
28      dtpStart.DataBindings.Add("Text", tableGrade, "TimeStart");
29      dtpFinish.DataBindings.Add("Text", tableGrade, "TimeFinish");
30
31      // Populates cboSubject
32      commandSubject = new SqlCommand(
33          "SELECT * FROM Subject ORDER BY Name", connBook);
34      adapterSubject = new SqlDataAdapter();
35      adapterSubject.SelectCommand = commandSubject;
36      tabelSubject = new DataTable();
37      adapterSubject.Fill(tabelSubject);
38      cboSubject.DataSource = tabelSubject;
39      cboSubject.DisplayMember = "Name";
40      cboSubject.ValueMember = "SubjectID";
41      cboSubject.DataBindings.Add("SelectedValue",
42          tableGrade, "SubjectID");
43
44      // Populates cboTeacher
45      commandTeacher = new SqlCommand(
46          "SELECT * FROM Teacher ORDER BY FirstName", connBook);
47      adapterTeacher = new SqlDataAdapter();
48      adapterTeacher.SelectCommand = commandTeacher;
49      tableTeacher = new DataTable();
50      adapterTeacher.Fill(tableTeacher);
51      cboTeacher.DataSource = tableTeacher;
52      cboTeacher.DisplayMember = "FirstName";
53      cboTeacher.ValueMember = "TeacherID";
54      cboTeacher.DataBindings.Add("SelectedValue",
55          tableGrade, "TeacherID");
56
57      // Creates data update manager
58      managerGrade = (CurrencyManager)BindingContext[tableGrade];
59
60      SetText();
61      this.Show();
62  }
63  catch (Exception ex)
64  {
65      MessageBox.Show(ex.Message, "Error reading table.",
66          MessageBoxButtons.OK, MessageBoxIcon.Error);
67      return;
68  }
```

}

The code above creates the data objects needed to open the database and construct the **Grade** table (includes all fields). The code above then binds the controls with the update manager object (**CurrencyManager**). It also populates **cboTeacher** and **cboSubject**.

Step 6   Add the following code to **FormGrade_FormClosing** event method to close the database connection:

```
1   private void FormGrade_FormClosing(object sender,
2   FormClosingEventArgs e)
3   {
4       // Closes connection to database
5       connBook.Close();
6
7       // Deletes objects
8       connBook.Dispose();
9       commandGrade.Dispose();
10      adapterGrade.Dispose();
11      commandSubject.Dispose();
12      adapterSubject.Dispose();
13      tabelSubject.Dispose();
14      commandTeacher.Dispose();
15      adapterTeacher.Dispose();
16      tableTeacher.Dispose();
17  }
```

Step 7   Define **SetText** method to give description on title bar as follows:

```
1   private void SetText()
2   {
3       this.Text = "Grade Data - Record " +
4           (managerGrade.Position + 1).ToString() + " of " +
5           managerGrade.Count.ToString() + " Records";
6   }
```

Step 8   Write the following code for the **Click** event of the four navigation buttons:

```
1   private void btnPrev_Click(object sender, EventArgs e)
2   {
3       if (managerGrade.Position == 0)
4       {
5           Console.Beep();
6       }
7       managerGrade.Position--;
8       SetText();
9   }
10
11  private void btnNext_Click(object sender, EventArgs e)
```

```
12  {
13      if (managerGrade.Position == managerGrade.Count - 1)
14      {
15          Console.Beep();
16      }
17      managerGrade.Position++;
18      SetText();
19  }
20
21  private void btnFirst_Click(object sender, EventArgs e)
22  {
23      managerGrade.Position = 0;
24      SetText();
25  }
26
27  private void btnLast_Click(object sender, EventArgs e)
28  {
29      managerGrade.Position = managerGrade.Count - 1;
30      SetText();
31  }
```

Figure 7.2 Inserting some data into **Grade** table

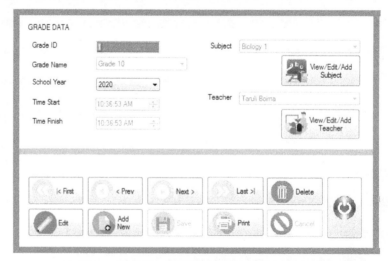

Figure 7.3 Grade form when it first runs

Step 9   Insert some data into **Grade** table as shown in Figure 7.4.

Step 10   Save and run the application. What is displayed first is the first record in **Grade** table.
          Click on four navigation buttons to prove the result.

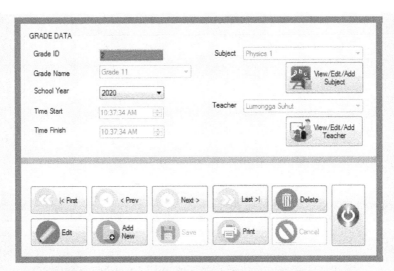

Figure 7.4 The result when user clicks **Last >|** button

7.2 Tutorial Steps of Creating Form for Grade Table: Message Box

Step 1   There are two places where you can use the message box in **Grade** table input form. One message box is provided after saving updates to let the user know that the save was successful and another message box is related to record deletion.

Use the following code in **btnSave_Click** event method:

```
private void btnSave_Click(object sender, EventArgs e)
{
    MessageBox.Show("Record is successfully saved", "Save",
        MessageBoxButtons.OK, MessageBoxIcon.Information);
}
```

There will be more code in this event. The code implements only message box.

Step 2   Use this code on **btnDelete_Click** event method:

```
private void btnDelete_Click(object sender, EventArgs e)
{
    DialogResult response;
    response = MessageBox.Show("Dou you really want to delete this record?",
        "Delete", MessageBoxButtons.YesNo, MessageBoxIcon.Question,
        MessageBoxDefaultButton.Button2);
}
```

Step 3   Save the application and run it. Click on **Delete** button to see as shown in Figure 7.5.

Figure 7.5 Message box is displayed when user clicks **Delete** button

7.3 Tutorial Steps of Creating Form for Grade Table: Application State

Step 1   The **Grade** form operates in one of three states: **View** state, **Add** state, or **Edit** state. In the **View** state, user can navigate one record to another, user can switch to **Edit** state, user can add and/or delete records, or user can exit the application.

In **Add** and **Edit** state, no navigation is made possible, data can be updated, and user can have access to **Save** and **Cancel** operations. Each of these steps can be implemented using the **Enabled** property of the button and the **ReadOnly** property of the text box. You use **TabIndex** (and **TabOrder**) to shift focus on the text box controls. You will use a method of moving from one state to another.

Clear all tab ordering for the ten buttons by setting the **TabStop** property to **False**. Additionally, set the **TabStop** property to **False** for the **Grade ID** text box.

Step 2   Add a method named **SetState** as follows:

```
1   private void SetState(string stateStr) {
2       switch (stateStr)
3       {
4           case "View":
5               txtGradeID.BackColor = Color.Red;
6               txtGradeID.ForeColor = Color.Black;
7               cboGrade.Enabled = false;
8               cboSchoolYear.Enabled = false;
9               cboSubject.Enabled = false;
10              cboTeacher.Enabled = false;
11              dtpStart.Enabled = false;
12              dtpFinish.Enabled = false;
13              btnFormSubject.Enabled = false;
14              btnFormTeacher.Enabled = false;
15              btnFirst.Enabled = true;
16              btnPrev.Enabled = true;
17              btnNext.Enabled = true;
18              btnLast.Enabled = true;
19              btnAddNew.Enabled = true;
20              btnSave.Enabled = false;
```

```csharp
21            btnDelete.Enabled = true;
22            btnCancel.Enabled = false;
23            btnEdit.Enabled = true;
24            btnDone.Enabled = true;
25            break;
26
27        case "Edit": // Edit
28            txtGradeID.ReadOnly = true;
29            txtGradeID.BackColor = Color.Red;
30            txtGradeID.ForeColor = Color.Black;
31            cboGrade.Enabled = true;
32            cboSchoolYear.Enabled = true;
33            cboSubject.Enabled = true;
34            cboTeacher.Enabled = true;
35            dtpStart.Enabled = true;
36            dtpFinish.Enabled = true;
37            btnFormSubject.Enabled = true;
38            btnFormTeacher.Enabled = true;
39            btnFirst.Enabled = false;
40            btnPrev.Enabled = false;
41            btnNext.Enabled = false;
42            btnLast.Enabled = false;
43            btnAddNew.Enabled = false;
44            btnSave.Enabled = true;
45            btnDelete.Enabled = false;
46            btnCancel.Enabled = true;
47            btnEdit.Enabled = false;
48            btnDone.Enabled = false;
49            btnPrint.Enabled = false;
50            break;
51
52        case "Add":
53            txtGradeID.ReadOnly = false;
54            txtGradeID.BackColor = Color.Red;
55            txtGradeID.ForeColor = Color.Black;
56            cboGrade.Enabled = true;
57            cboGrade.SelectedIndex = -1;
58            cboSchoolYear.Enabled = true;
59            cboSchoolYear.SelectedIndex = -1;
60            cboSubject.Enabled = true;
61            cboTeacher.Enabled = true;
62            dtpStart.Enabled = true;
63            dtpStart.Value = DateTime.Now;
64            dtpFinish.Enabled = true;
65            dtpFinish.Value = DateTime.Now;
66            btnFormSubject.Enabled = true;
67            btnFormTeacher.Enabled = true;
68            btnFirst.Enabled = false;
69            btnPrev.Enabled = false;
70            btnNext.Enabled = false;
71            btnLast.Enabled = false;
```

```
72          btnAddNew.Enabled = false;
73          btnSave.Enabled = true;
74          btnDelete.Enabled = false;
75          btnCancel.Enabled = true;
76          btnEdit.Enabled = false;
77          btnDone.Enabled = false;
78          btnPrint.Enabled = false;
79          break;
80      }
81  }
```

The code above specifies **View**, **Add**, or **Edit** state for the application. Pay attention
to which buttons are available and which are not. Note that **Grade ID** text box is given
red back color if it is in **Add** or **Edit** state to indicate that it cannot be changed.

Step 3   Set the **View** state when the application first runs. Add the following code in line 61
to **FormGrade_Load** event method:

```
1   private void FormGrade_Load(object sender, EventArgs e)
2   {
3       try
4       {
5           // Connects to database
6           connBook = new SqlConnection("Data Source=.\\SQLEXPRESS;
7               AttachDbFilename=D:\\Database\\DBMS.mdf;
8               Integrated Security = True; Connect Timeout = 30;
9               User Instance = True");
10
11          // Opens connection
12          connBook.Open();
13
14          // Creates Command object
15          commandGrade = new SqlCommand(
16              "SELECT * FROM Grade ORDER BY Name", connBook);
17
18          // Creates DataAdapter/DataTable objects
19          adapterGrade = new SqlDataAdapter();
20          adapterGrade.SelectCommand = commandGrade;
21          tableGrade = new DataTable();
22          adapterGrade.Fill(tableGrade);
23
24          // Binds controls to data table
25          txtGradeID.DataBindings.Add("Text", tableGrade, "GradeID");
26          cboGrade.DataBindings.Add("Text", tableGrade, "Name");
27          cboSchoolYear.DataBindings.Add("Text", tableGrade, "SchoolYear");
28          dtpStart.DataBindings.Add("Text", tableGrade, "TimeStart");
29          dtpFinish.DataBindings.Add("Text", tableGrade, "TimeFinish");
30
31          // Populates cboSubject
32          commandSubject = new SqlCommand(
```

```
33          "SELECT * FROM Subject ORDER BY Name", connBook);
34      adapterSubject = new SqlDataAdapter();
35      adapterSubject.SelectCommand = commandSubject;
36      tabelSubject = new DataTable();
37      adapterSubject.Fill(tabelSubject);
38      cboSubject.DataSource = tabelSubject;
39      cboSubject.DisplayMember = "Name";
40      cboSubject.ValueMember = "SubjectID";
41      cboSubject.DataBindings.Add("SelectedValue",
42          tableGrade, "SubjectID");
43
44      // Populates cboTeacher
45      commandTeacher = new SqlCommand(
46          "SELECT * FROM Teacher ORDER BY FirstName", connBook);
47      adapterTeacher = new SqlDataAdapter();
48      adapterTeacher.SelectCommand = commandTeacher;
49      tableTeacher = new DataTable();
50      adapterTeacher.Fill(tableTeacher);
51      cboTeacher.DataSource = tableTeacher;
52      cboTeacher.DisplayMember = "FirstName";
53      cboTeacher.ValueMember = "TeacherID";
54      cboTeacher.DataBindings.Add("SelectedValue",
55          tableGrade, "TeacherID");
56
57      // Creates data update manager
58      managerGrade = (CurrencyManager)BindingContext[tableGrade];
59
60      SetText();
61      this.Show();
62      SetState("View");
63      }
64  catch (Exception ex)
65  {
66      MessageBox.Show(ex.Message, "Error reading table.",
67          MessageBoxButtons.OK, MessageBoxIcon.Error);
68      return;
69      }
    }
```

Step 4 When **Add New** button is clicked, you need to switch to **Add** state. Add the following code to **btnAddNew_Click** event method:

```
1   private void btnAddNew_Click(object sender, EventArgs e)
2   {
3       SetState("Add");
4   }
```

Step 5 When **Edit** button is clicked, the application will be switched to **Edit** state. Add the following code to **btnEdit_Click** event method:

```
1   private void btnEdit_Click(object sender, EventArgs e)
2   {
3       SetState("Edit");
4   }
```

Step 6   When **Cancel** or **Save** button is clicked (in **Add** or **Edit** state), application will return
to the **View** state. Put this line of code in **btnCancel_Click** and **btnSave_Click** event
methods:

```
1   private void btnCancel_Click(object sender, EventArgs e)
2   {
3       SetState("View");
4   }
5
6   private void btnSave_Click(object sender, EventArgs e)
7   {
8       SetState("View");
9   }
```

Step 7   Save and run the application. You will see the application in its initial state (**View**
state) as shown in Figure 7.6.

Figure 7.6 Grade form is in **View** state when it first runs

When user clicks the **Edit** or **Add New** button, you will see what is shown in Figure
7.7 and 7.8.

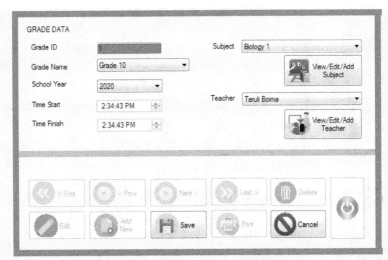

Figure 7.7 Grade form is in **Edit** state

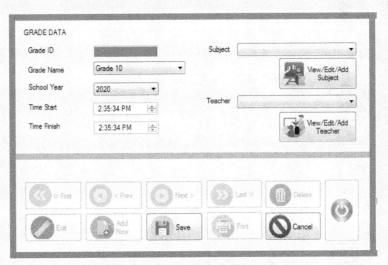

Figure 7.8 Grade form is in **Add** state

7.4 Tutorial Steps of Creating Form for Grade Table: Error Trapping

Step 1   Modify **btnAddNew_Click**, **btnSave_Click**, and **btnDelete_Click** event methods to
handle error trapping:

```
1   private void btnAddNew_Click(object sender, EventArgs e)
2   {
3       try
4       {
5           SetState("Add");
6       }
7   catch (Exception ex)
```

```
8      {
9          MessageBox.Show("Error adding new record.", "Error",
10             MessageBoxButtons.OK, MessageBoxIcon.Error);
11     }
12 }
```

```
1  private void btnSave_Click(object sender, EventArgs e)
2  {
3      try
4      {
5          MessageBox.Show("Record successfully saved", "Save",
6          MessageBoxButtons.OK, MessageBoxIcon.Information);
7          SetState("View");
8      }
9      catch (Exception ex)
10     {
11         MessageBox.Show("Error saving record.", "Error",
12             MessageBoxButtons.OK, MessageBoxIcon.Error);
13     }
14 }
```

```
1  private void btnDelete_Click(object sender, EventArgs e)
2  {
3      DialogResult response;
4      response = MessageBox.Show("Dou you really want to delete this record?",
5          "Delete", MessageBoxButtons.YesNo, MessageBoxIcon.Question,
6          MessageBoxDefaultButton.Button2);
7      if (response == DialogResult.No)
8      {
9          return;
10     }
11
12     try
13     {
14
15     }
16     catch (Exception ex)
17     {
18         MessageBox.Show("Error deleting record.", "Error",
19             MessageBoxButtons.OK, MessageBoxIcon.Error);
20     }
21 }
```

7.5 Tutorial Step of Creating Form for Grade Table: Opening Subject and Teacher Form

Step 1   Define Click event of **btnFormSubject** and **btnFormTeacher** as follows:

```
1  private void btnFormTeacher_Click(object sender, EventArgs e)
```

```
2    {
3        FormTeacher frmteacher = new FormTeacher();
4        frmteacher.Show();
5    }
6
7    private void btnFormSubject_Click(object sender, EventArgs e)
8    {
9        FormSubject frmsubject = new FormSubject();
10       frmsubject.Show();
11   }
```

7.6 Tutorial Steps of Creating Form for Grade Table: Editing Record

Step 1   Add the following line of code to the form-level declaration:

```
1    string appState;
```

step 2   Add this code in line 2 to **SetState** method:

```
1    private void SetState(string stateStr) {
2        appState = stateStr;
3        switch (stateStr)
4        {
5            case "View":
6                txtGradeID.BackColor = Color.Red;
7                txtGradeID.ForeColor = Color.Black;
8                cboGrade.Enabled = false;
9                cboSchoolYear.Enabled = false;
10               cboSubject.Enabled = false;
11               cboTeacher.Enabled = false;
12               dtpStart.Enabled = false;
13               dtpFinish.Enabled = false;
14               btnFormSubject.Enabled = false;
15               btnFormTeacher.Enabled = false;
16               btnFirst.Enabled = true;
17               btnPrev.Enabled = true;
18               btnNext.Enabled = true;
19               btnLast.Enabled = true;
20               btnAddNew.Enabled = true;
21               btnSave.Enabled = false;
22               btnDelete.Enabled = true;
23               btnCancel.Enabled = false;
24               btnEdit.Enabled = true;
25               btnDone.Enabled = true;
26               break;
27
28           case "Edit": // Edit
29               txtGradeID.ReadOnly = true;
```

```
30          txtGradeID.BackColor = Color.Red;
31          txtGradeID.ForeColor = Color.Black;
32          cboGrade.Enabled = true;
33          cboSchoolYear.Enabled = true;
34          cboSubject.Enabled = true;
35          cboTeacher.Enabled = true;
36          dtpStart.Enabled = true;
37          dtpFinish.Enabled = true;
38          btnFormSubject.Enabled = true;
39          btnFormTeacher.Enabled = true;
40          btnFirst.Enabled = false;
41          btnPrev.Enabled = false;
42          btnNext.Enabled = false;
43          btnLast.Enabled = false;
44          btnAddNew.Enabled = false;
45          btnSave.Enabled = true;
46          btnDelete.Enabled = false;
47          btnCancel.Enabled = true;
48          btnEdit.Enabled = false;
49          btnDone.Enabled = false;
50          btnPrint.Enabled = false;
51          break;
52
53      case "Add":
54          txtGradeID.ReadOnly = false;
55          txtGradeID.BackColor = Color.Red;
56          txtGradeID.ForeColor = Color.Black;
57          cboGrade.Enabled = true;
58          cboGrade.SelectedIndex = -1;
59          cboSchoolYear.Enabled = true;
60          cboSchoolYear.SelectedIndex = -1;
61          cboSubject.Enabled = true;
62          cboTeacher.Enabled = true;
63          dtpStart.Enabled = true;
64          dtpStart.Value = DateTime.Now;
65          dtpFinish.Enabled = true;
66          dtpFinish.Value = DateTime.Now;
67          btnFormSubject.Enabled = true;
68          btnFormTeacher.Enabled = true;
69          btnFirst.Enabled = false;
70          btnPrev.Enabled = false;
71          btnNext.Enabled = false;
72          btnLast.Enabled = false;
73          btnAddNew.Enabled = false;
74          btnSave.Enabled = true;
75          btnDelete.Enabled = false;
76          btnCancel.Enabled = true;
77          btnEdit.Enabled = false;
78          btnDone.Enabled = false;
79          btnPrint.Enabled = false;
80          break;
```

```
81          }
82      }
```

Step 3   Modify **btnSave_Click** event method to save the change and reposition the pointer to the record just edited:

```
1    private void btnSave_Click(object sender, EventArgs e)
2    {
3        if (cboGrade.SelectedIndex == -1 ||
4            cboSubject.SelectedIndex == -1 ||
5            cboTeacher.SelectedIndex == -1)
6        {
7            return;
8        }
9
10       string nameSaved = cboGrade.SelectedItem.ToString();
11       int rowSaved;
12
13       try
14       {
15           managerGrade.EndCurrentEdit();
16           tableGrade.DefaultView.Sort = "Name";
17           rowSaved = tableGrade.DefaultView.Find(nameSaved);
18           managerGrade.Position = rowSaved;
19
20           // Saves changes into database
21           SqlCommandBuilder graderAdapterCommand = new
22               SqlCommandBuilder(adapterGrade);
23           adapterGrade.Update(tableGrade);
24
25           MessageBox.Show("Record is successfully saved", "Save",
26               MessageBoxButtons.OK, MessageBoxIcon.Information);
27           SetState("View");
28       }
29       catch (Exception ex)
30       {
31           MessageBox.Show("Error in saving record.", "Error",
32               MessageBoxButtons.OK, MessageBoxIcon.Error);
33       }
34   }
```

Step 4   Modify **btnCancel_Click** event method to restore controls if the edit is canceled:

```
1    private void btnCancel_Click(object sender, EventArgs e)
2    {
3        managerGrade.CancelCurrentEdit();
4
5        SetState("View");
6    }
```

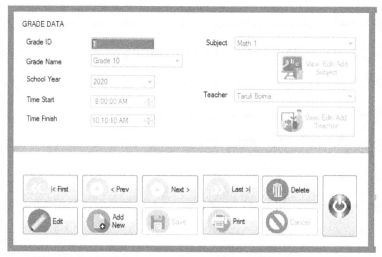

Figure 7.9 Editing operation is successfully performed

Step 5   Add the following code in line to the **FormGrade_FormClosing** method to save any changes to the database file:

```
private void FormGrade_FormClosing(object sender,
FormClosingEventArgs e)
{
    try
    {
        // Saves changes into database
        SqlCommandBuilder gradeAdapterCommand =
            new SqlCommandBuilder(adapterGrade);
        adapterGrade.Update(tableGrade);
    }
    catch (Exception ex)
    {
        MessageBox.Show("Error saving database into file: \r\n" +
            ex.Message, "Saving Error", MessageBoxButtons.OK,
            MessageBoxIcon.Error);
    }

    // Closes connection to database
    connBook.Close();

    // Deletes objects
    connBook.Dispose();
    commandGrade.Dispose();
    adapterGrade.Dispose();
    commandSubject.Dispose();
    adapterSubject.Dispose();
    tabelSubject.Dispose();
    commandTeacher.Dispose();
    adapterTeacher.Dispose();
    tableTeacher.Dispose();
```

```
30  }
```

Step 6   Save and run the application. Make sure Edit feature is working properly. Make sure the **Cancel** button is working properly. This is shown in Figure 7.9.

7.7 Tutorial Steps of Creating Form for Grade Table: Adding New Record

Step 1   You now implement the capability on the form to add new records to the database. Add the following line of code to the form-level declaration:

```
1  int myBookmark;
```

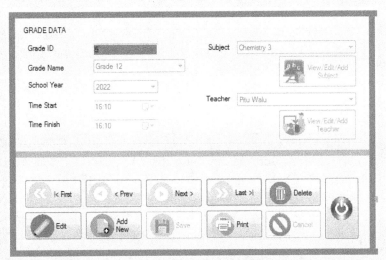

Figure 7.10 The new record has been successfully saved into the database

Step 2   Modify **btnAddNew_Click** event method to add a new record by adding code in line 5-6:

```
1   private void btnAddNew_Click(object sender, EventArgs e)
2   {
3       try
4       {
5           myBookmark = managerGrade.Position;
6           managerGrade.AddNew();
7           SetState("Add");
8       }
9       catch (Exception ex)
10      {
11          MessageBox.Show("Error adding new record.", "Error",
12              MessageBoxButtons.OK, MessageBoxIcon.Error);
13      }
14  }
```

Step 3   Modify **btnCancel_Click** event method to differentiate between cancellation during
Edit mode and **Add** mode by adding code in line 5-10:

```
1   private void btnCancel_Click(object sender, EventArgs e)
2   {
3       managerGrade.CancelCurrentEdit();
4
5       if (appState.Equals("Add"))
6       {
7           managerGrade.Position = myBookmark;
8       }
9       SetState("View");
10      DisplayPhoto();
11  }
```

Step 4   Save and run the application. Click **Add New** button. Note that all text boxes are blank
(including **Grade ID** text box. Fill first name, last name, and other fields, then click
Save. New record has been successfully saved as shown in Figure 7.10.

7.8 Tutorial Steps of Creating Form for Grade Table: Deleting Record

Step 1   You will now add the capability to delete records from **Grade** table. Modify the
btnDelete_Click event method by adding code in line 14 to delete records if the user
responds to **Yes** in the message box:

```
1   private void btnDelete_Click(object sender, EventArgs e)
2   {
3       DialogResult response;
4       response = MessageBox.Show("Dou you really want to delete this record?",
5           "Delete", MessageBoxButtons.YesNo, MessageBoxIcon.Question,
6           MessageBoxDefaultButton.Button2);
7       if (response == DialogResult.No)
8       {
9           return;
10      }
11
12      try
13      {
14          managerGrade.RemoveAt(managerGrade.Position);
15      }
16      catch (Exception ex)
17      {
18          MessageBox.Show("Error deleting record.", "Error",
19              MessageBoxButtons.OK, MessageBoxIcon.Error);
20      }
21  }
```

Step 2   Save the application and run it. Make sure the **Yes** and **No** responses in the message box give correct results. Delete only those records you added using **Add New** button.

7.9 Tutorial Steps of Creating Form for Grade Table: Stopping Application

Step 1   Add the following code in line 4-12 and line 39 to **FormGrade_FormClosing** event method to ensure user doesn't close the application during **Edit** or **Add** mode:

```
1  private void FormGrade_FormClosing(object sender,
2  FormClosingEventArgs e)
3  {
4      if (appState.Equals("Edit") || appState.Equals("Add"))
5      {
6          MessageBox.Show(
7              "You should finish editing before closing application.",
8              "", MessageBoxButtons.OK, MessageBoxIcon.Information);
9          e.Cancel = true;
10     }
11     else
12     {
13         try
14         {
15             // Saves changes into database
16             SqlCommandBuilder gradeAdapterCommand =
17                 new SqlCommandBuilder(adapterGrade);
18             adapterGrade.Update(tableGrade);
19         }
20         catch (Exception ex)
21         {
22             MessageBox.Show("Error saving database into file: \r\n" +
23                 ex.Message, "Error Saving", MessageBoxButtons.OK,
24                 MessageBoxIcon.Error);
25         }
26
27         // Closes connection to database
28         connBook.Close();
29
30         // Deletes objects
31         connBook.Dispose();
32         commandGrade.Dispose();
33         adapterGrade.Dispose();
34         commandSubject.Dispose();
35         adapterSubject.Dispose();
36         tabelSubject.Dispose();
37         commandTeacher.Dispose();
38         adapterTeacher.Dispose();
39         tableTeacher.Dispose();
40     }
41  }
```

Step 2   Put this code in **btnDone_Click** event method:

```
1   private void btnDone_Click(object sender, EventArgs e)
2   {
3       this.Close();
4   }
```

Step 3   Save and run the application. Make sure the **Done** button is working properly. Make sure the user cannot close the application in **Edit** or **Add** mode.

7.10 Tutorial Steps of Adding Search Buttons

Step 1   Add a button control on the form. Set its **Name** property as **btnAll** and its **Text** poperty as **Show All Grades**. You add another **DataGridView** control and set its **Name** property as **grdGrade**. You alse need to add a label and set its **Text** property as **Number of Records:**. Then add a textbox on the form. Set its **Name** property as **txtNumberRecord**. The resulting form is shown in Figure 7.11.

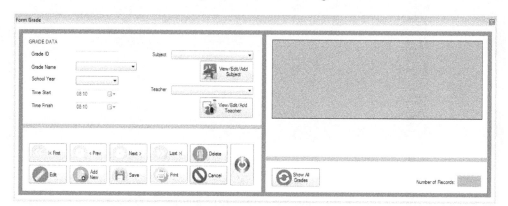

Figure 7.11 Grade form after a number of controls added

Step 2   Add the following form-level declarations:

```
1   Button[] buttonArr = new Button[26];
```

Variable **buttonArr** is an array containing the search buttons.

Step 3   Define a new method named **createSearchButton()** as follows:

```
1   private void createSearchButton()
2   {
3       // Creates search buttons
4       int w, lStart, l, t;
5       int btnHeight = 40; // by trial and error
6
```

```
7      // Search buttons
8      // Button width - 13 buttons in a row
9      w = Convert.ToInt32(grdGrade.Width / 13);
10
11     // Aligns buttons
12     lStart = Convert.ToInt32((grdGrade.Width))+120;
13     l = lStart; t = grdGrade.Top + grdGrade.Height + 10;
14
15     // Creates and positions 26 buttons
16     for (int i = 0; i < 26; i++)
17     {
18         // Creates push button
19         buttonArr[i] = new Button();
20         buttonArr[i].TabStop = false;
21
22         // Sets Text property
23         buttonArr[i].Text = ((char)(65 + i)).ToString();
24         buttonArr[i].Font = new Font(buttonArr[i].Font.FontFamily,
25             9, FontStyle.Bold);
26
27         // Positions buttons
28         buttonArr[i].Width = w;
29         buttonArr[i].Height = btnHeight;
30         buttonArr[i].Left = l;
31         buttonArr[i].Top = t;
32
33         // Gives color
34         buttonArr[i].BackColor = Color.Red;
35         buttonArr[i].ForeColor = Color.White;
36
37         // Adds each button on form
38         this.Controls.Add(buttonArr[i]);
39
40         // Adds event handler
41         buttonArr[i].Click +=
42             new System.EventHandler(this.btnSQL_Click);
43         l += w+1;
44
45         if (i == 12)
46         {
47             // Next row
48             l = lStart; t += btnHeight;
49         }
50     }
51 }
```

This method creates search buttons A through Z using **buttonArrr** array. The code above then specifies the width of the button and places it on the form. Finally, the resulting records are displayed by programmatically clicking **btnSQL** button.

Step 4   Define **createSQLStatement** method as follows:

```
1   private string createSQLStatement()
2   {
3       // Create SQL Statement
4       string SqlString = null;
5       SqlString += "SELECT Grade.Name, Subject.Name,
6          Subject.Description, ";
7       SqlString += "CONCAT(Teacher.FirstName, ' ', Teacher.LastName)
8          AS Teacher_Name, ";
9       SqlString += "Grade.SchoolYear, Grade.TimeStart,
10         Grade.TimeFinish ";
11      SqlString += "FROM Grade, Subject, Teacher ";
12      SqlString += "WHERE Grade.SubjectID = Subject.SubjectID ";
13      SqlString += "AND Grade.TeacherID = Teacher.TeacherID ";
14
15      return SqlString;
16  }
```

Step 5   Write the code for **btnSQL_Click** event method (handle **Click** event for all search buttons) as follows:

```
1   private void btnSQL_Click(object sender, EventArgs e)
2   {
3       SqlCommand commResult = null;
4       SqlDataAdapter adapterResult = new SqlDataAdapter();
5       DataTable tableResult = new DataTable();
6       String StatementSQL;
7
8        string SQLAll = createSQLStatement();
9
10      // Determines which button is clicked and creates SQL statement
11      Button buttonClicked = (Button)sender;
12      switch (buttonClicked.Text)
13      {
14          case "Show All Grades":
15              StatementSQL = SQLAll;
16              break;
17          case "Z":
18              // Z button is clicked
19              // Appends at SQLAll to limit records upto for item Z
20              StatementSQL = SQLAll + " AND Teacher.FirstName > 'Z' ";
21              break;
22          default:
23              // Letter keys except Z
24              // Appends at SQLAll to limit records
25              // for letter that is clicked
26              int idx = (int)(Convert.ToChar(buttonClicked.Text)) - 65;
27              StatementSQL = SQLAll + " AND Teacher.FirstName > '" +
28              buttonArr[idx].Text + " ' ";
```

```
29          StatementSQL += " AND Teacher.FirstName < '" +
30                  buttonArr[idx + 1].Text + " ' ";
31          break;
32      }
33      StatementSQL += " ORDER BY Grade.Name";
34
35      // Applies SQL statement
36      try
37      {
38          // Creates Command and DataAdapater objects
39          commResult = new SqlCommand(StatementSQL, connBook);
40          adapterResult.SelectCommand = commResult;
41          adapterResult.Fill(tableResult);
42
43          // Binds DataGridView with data table
44          grdGrade.DataSource = tableResult;
45          txtNumberRecord.Text = tableResult.Rows.Count.ToString();
46
47          // Colors DGV
48          setRowColor(grdGrade);
49      }
50
51      catch (Exception ex)
52      {
53          MessageBox.Show(ex.Message, "Error Processing SQL",
54              MessageBoxButtons.OK, MessageBoxIcon.Error);
55      }
56      commResult.Dispose();
57      adapterResult.Dispose();
58      tableResult.Dispose();
59  }
```

This method determines which button is clicked and forms an SQL statement. If the
button with the **Text** property of the button is **"Show All Grades"** is clicked, then all
records will be displayed. When a key letter is clicked, the code determines which
letter the user clicks on and attaches an additional test (using **AND**) to the **WHERE**
field in the default SQL statement.

Step 6   Add the following code in line 64-68 to **FormGrade_Load** event method. The code
creates search buttons and perform **Click** event of **btnAll** programmatically:

```
1  private void FormGrade_Load(object sender, EventArgs e)
2  {
3      try
4      {
5          // Connects to database
6          connBook = new SqlConnection("Data Source=.\\SQLEXPRESS;
7              AttachDbFilename=D:\\Database\\DBMS.mdf;
8              Integrated Security = True; Connect Timeout = 30;
9              User Instance = True");
```

```
10
11      // Opens connection
12      connBook.Open();
13
14      // Creates Command object
15      commandGrade = new SqlCommand(
16          "SELECT * FROM Grade ORDER BY Name", connBook);
17
18      // Creates DataAdapter/DataTable objects
19      adapterGrade = new SqlDataAdapter();
20      adapterGrade.SelectCommand = commandGrade;
21      tableGrade = new DataTable();
22      adapterGrade.Fill(tableGrade);
23
24      // Binds controls to data table
25      txtGradeID.DataBindings.Add("Text", tableGrade, "GradeID");
26      cboGrade.DataBindings.Add("Text", tableGrade, "Name");
27      cboSchoolYear.DataBindings.Add("Text", tableGrade, "SchoolYear");
28      dtpStart.DataBindings.Add("Text", tableGrade, "TimeStart");
29      dtpFinish.DataBindings.Add("Text", tableGrade, "TimeFinish");
30
31      // Populates cboSubject
32      commandSubject = new SqlCommand(
33          "SELECT * FROM Subject ORDER BY Name", connBook);
34      adapterSubject = new SqlDataAdapter();
35      adapterSubject.SelectCommand = commandSubject;
36      tabelSubject = new DataTable();
37      adapterSubject.Fill(tabelSubject);
38      cboSubject.DataSource = tabelSubject;
39      cboSubject.DisplayMember = "Name";
40      cboSubject.ValueMember = "SubjectID";
41      cboSubject.DataBindings.Add("SelectedValue",
42          tableGrade, "SubjectID");
43
44      // Populates cboTeacher
45      commandTeacher = new SqlCommand(
46          "SELECT * FROM Teacher ORDER BY FirstName", connBook);
47      adapterTeacher = new SqlDataAdapter();
48      adapterTeacher.SelectCommand = commandTeacher;
49      tableTeacher = new DataTable();
50      adapterTeacher.Fill(tableTeacher);
51      cboTeacher.DataSource = tableTeacher;
52      cboTeacher.DisplayMember = "FirstName";
53      cboTeacher.ValueMember = "TeacherID";
54      cboTeacher.DataBindings.Add("SelectedValue",
55          tableGrade, "TeacherID");
56
57      // Creates data update manager
58      managerGrade = (CurrencyManager)BindingContext[tableGrade];
59
60      SetText();
```

```
61        this.Show();
62        SetState("View");
63
64        createSearchButton();
65
66        // Clicks all records when form starts
67        btnAll.Click += new System.EventHandler(this.btnSQL_Click);
68        btnAll.PerformClick();
69    }
70    catch (Exception ex)
71    {
72        MessageBox.Show(ex.Message, "Error reading table.",
73            MessageBoxButtons.OK, MessageBoxIcon.Error);
74        return;
75    }
76 }
```

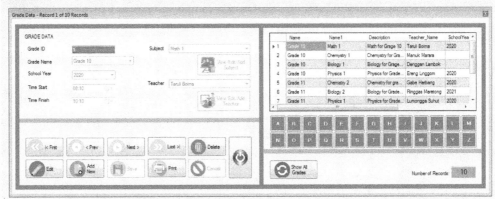

Figure 7.12 The grade form when it first runs

Step 7   Define **RowPostPaint** event of **grdGrade** control to give it a row numbering:

```
1   private void grdGrade_RowPostPaint(object sender,
2   DataGridViewRowPostPaintEventArgs e)
3   {
4       var grid = sender as DataGridView;
5       var rowIdx = (e.RowIndex + 1).ToString();
6
7       var centerFormat = new StringFormat()
8       {
9           // Aligns to middle
10          Alignment = StringAlignment.Center,
11          LineAlignment = StringAlignment.Center
12      };
13
14      var headerBounds = new Rectangle(e.RowBounds.Left,
15          e.RowBounds.Top, grid.RowHeadersWidth, e.RowBounds.Height);
16      e.Graphics.DrawString(rowIdx, this.Font,
17          SystemBrushes.ControlText, headerBounds, centerFormat);
```

```
18  }
```

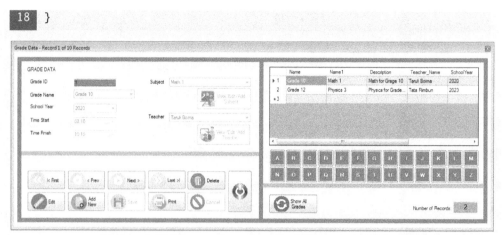

Figure 7.13 The results when the 'T' button is clicked

Step 8   Define **setRowColor** method to alternately give color to rows of **grdStudent**. This
method is called from **btnSQL_Click**:

```
1   // Altenately colors row
2   private void setRowColor(DataGridView dgv)
3   {
4       for (int i = 0; i < dgv.Rows.Count; i++)
5       {
6           if (i % 2 == 0)
7           {
8               for (int j = 0; j < dgv.Columns.Count; j++ )
9                   dgv.Rows[i].Cells[j].Style.BackColor =
10                      System.Drawing.Color.LightGreen;
11          }
12          else
13          {
14              for (int j = 0; j < dgv.Columns.Count; j++)
15                  dgv.Rows[i].Cells[j].Style.BackColor =
16                      System.Drawing.Color.LightYellow;
17          }
18      }
19  }
```

Step 9   Define **Refresh_DGV** to refresh data grid view, **grdGrade**, as follows:

```
1   private void Refresh_DGV()
2   {
3       // Connects to database
4       connBook = new SqlConnection("Data Source=.\\SQLEXPRESS;
5           AttachDbFilename=D:\\Database\\DBMS.mdf;
6           Integrated Security = True; Connect Timeout = 30;
7           User Instance = True");
8       connBook.Open();
9
```

```
10      // Save changes to database
11      SqlCommandBuilder gradeAdapterCommand = new
12          SqlCommandBuilder(adapterGrade);
13      adapterGrade.Update(tableGrade);
14
15      SqlCommand commandResult = null;
16      SqlDataAdapter adapterResult = new SqlDataAdapter();
17      DataTable tableResult = new DataTable();
18      string SQLAll = createSQLStatement();
19
20      try
21      {
22          // Creates Command and DataAdapter objects
23          commandResult = new SqlCommand(SQLAll, connBook);
24          adapterResult.SelectCommand = commandResult;
25          tableResult.Clear();
26          adapterResult.Fill(tableResult);
27
28          // Binds grid view to data table
29          grdGrade.DataSource = tableResult;
30          txtNumberRecord.Text = tableResult.Rows.Count.ToString();
31      }
32
33      catch (Exception ex)
34      {
35          MessageBox.Show(ex.Message, "Error in processing SQL",
36              MessageBoxButtons.OK, MessageBoxIcon.Error);
37      }
38
39      commandResult.Dispose();
40      adapterResult.Dispose();
41      tableResult.Dispose();
}
```

Step 10   Call **Refresh_DGV** from **Click** event of **btnAll** as follows:

```
1   private void btnAll_Click(object sender, EventArgs e)
2   {
3       Refresh_DGV();
4   }
```

Step 11   Save and run the application. The result is shown in Figure 7.12. Notice how the search buttons are created. Also note that all records are displayed initially. Click on one of the search buttons. Only records with the teacher's initial matching the letter in the clicked button will be displayed. Figure 7.13 is the query result when the 'T' button is clicked.

7.11 Tutorial Steps of Reporting Grades

Step 1   Now, you will add a feature to read all the data in the database. You need a database report. The report is quite simple. For each record, the data from each field will be displayed.

Add this line of code at the top of the code window:

```
1   using System.Drawing.Printing;
```

Step 2   Add the page number variable to the form level declaration:

```
1   int pageNumber;
2   int subjectPerPage = 30;
```

Step 3   In **SetState** method, set **Enabled** property of **btnPrint** to **true** in **View** mode and **false** in **Add/Edit** mode.

Step 4   Add the following code to **btnPrint_Click** event method:

```
1    private void btnPrint_Click(object sender, EventArgs e)
2    {
3        // Declares document
4        PrintDocument docGrade;
5
6        // Creates document and gives it a name
7        docGrade = new PrintDocument();
8        docGrade.DocumentName = "Grade Data";
9
10       // Adds code handler
11       docGrade.PrintPage += new
12           PrintPageEventHandler(this.PrintGrade);
13
14       // Prints document in preview control
15       pageNumber = 1;
16       int positionSaved = managerGrade.Position;
17       dlgPreview.Document = docGrade;
18       dlgPreview.ShowDialog();
19
20       // Deletes document when finished printing
21       docGrade.Dispose();
22       managerGrade.Position = positionSaved;
23   }
```

Step 5   Add the following code to **PrintGrade** method:

```
1    private void PrintGrade(object sender, PrintPageEventArgs e)
2    {
3        // For every page
4        // Prints header
```

```
5      Font myFont = new Font("Courier New", 14, FontStyle.Bold);
6      e.Graphics.DrawString("Grade - Page " +
7          pageNumber.ToString(), myFont, Brushes.Black,
8          e.MarginBounds.Left, e.MarginBounds.Top);
9
10     myFont = new Font("Courier New", 12, FontStyle.Underline);
11     int y = Convert.ToInt32(e.MarginBounds.Top + 50);
12         e.Graphics.DrawString("Grade Name", myFont, Brushes.Black,
13         e.MarginBounds.Left, y);
14
15     e.Graphics.DrawString("Subject", myFont, Brushes.Black,
16         e.MarginBounds.Left +
17         Convert.ToInt32(0.3 *(e.MarginBounds.Width)), y);
18
19     e.Graphics.DrawString("Teacher", myFont, Brushes.Black,
20         e.MarginBounds.Left +
21         Convert.ToInt32(0.6 * (e.MarginBounds.Width)), y);
22
23     y += Convert.ToInt32(2 * myFont.GetHeight());
24     myFont = new Font("Courier New", 12, FontStyle.Regular);
25     int iLast = subjectPerPage * pageNumber;
26
27     if (iLast > tableGrade.Rows.Count)
28     {
29         iLast = tableGrade.Rows.Count;
30         e.HasMorePages = false;
31     }
32     else
33     {
34         e.HasMorePages = true;
35     }
36
37     for (int i = 1 + subjectPerPage * (pageNumber - 1); i <= iLast; i++)
38     {
39         // Moves to all records
40         if (cboGrade.Text.Length < 25)
41         {
42             e.Graphics.DrawString(cboGrade.Text, myFont,
43                 Brushes.Black, e.MarginBounds.Left, y);
44         }
45         else
46         {
47             e.Graphics.DrawString(
48                 cboGrade.Text.Substring(0, 15), myFont,
49                 Brushes.Black, e.MarginBounds.Left, y);
50         }
51         if (cboSubject.Text.Length < 25)
52         {
53             e.Graphics.DrawString(cboSubject.Text, myFont,
54                 Brushes.Black, e.MarginBounds.Left +
55                 Convert.ToInt32(0.3 * (e.MarginBounds.Width)), y);
```

```
56      }
57      else
58      {
59          e.Graphics.DrawString(
60              cboTeacher.Text.Substring(0, 20),
61              myFont, Brushes.Black, e.MarginBounds.Left +
62              Convert.ToInt32(0.3 * (e.MarginBounds.Width)), y);
63      }
64      if (cboTeacher.Text.Length < 25)
65      {
66          e.Graphics.DrawString(cboTeacher.Text, myFont,
67              Brushes.Black, e.MarginBounds.Left +
68              Convert.ToInt32(0.6 * (e.MarginBounds.Width)), y);
69      }
70      else
71      {
72          e.Graphics.DrawString(
73              cboTeacher.Text.Substring(0, 20),
74              myFont, Brushes.Black, e.MarginBounds.Left +
75              Convert.ToInt32(0.6 * (e.MarginBounds.Width)), y);
76      }
77
78      btnNext.PerformClick();
79      y += Convert.ToInt32(myFont.GetHeight());
80  }
81
82  if (e.HasMorePages)
83      pageNumber++;
84  else
85      pageNumber = 1;
86 }
```

On each page, a header is printed along with the data fields.

Step 6   Save and run the application. Click on the **Print** button. The print preview control will be displayed with all grades, as shown in Figure 7.14.

```
Grade - Page 1

Grade Name          Subject            Teacher

Grade 10            Math 1             Taruli Boima
Grade 10            Chemystry 1        Manuk Marara
Grade 10            Biology 1          Denggan Lambok
Grade 10            Physics 1          Ereng Linggom
Grade 11            Chemistry 2        Gabe Herbang
Grade 11            Biology 2          Ringgas Maretong
Grade 11            Physics 1          Lumongga Suhut
Grade 12            Chemistry 3        Pitu Walu
Grade 12            Math 3             Mangasi Saba
Grade 12            Physics 3          Tata Rimbun
```

Figure 7.14 Each record in the table can now be printed

7.12 Tutorial Steps of Creating Form for Grade_Student: Interface

Step 1   In this tutorial, you will build such a form for **Grade_Student** table. This table has only three fields: **Grade_StudentID**, **GradeID**, and **StudentID**.

You need an input form so that user can edit existing records, delete records, or add new records. The form will also have the capability of navigating from one record to another. The steps that need to be done are as follows.

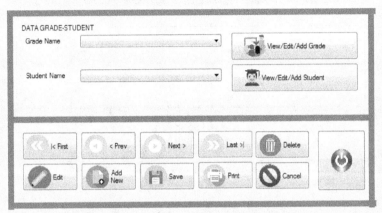

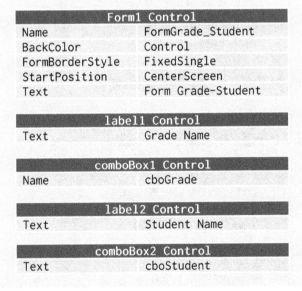

Figure 7.15 Design of grade-student form

Start a new Visual C# application. You need two label controls and two comboxes. You also need four buttons for navigation, seven buttons for controlling editing features, one button to open grade form, and one button to open student form. Place these controls on the form. The complete form looks as shown in Figure 7.15.

Step 2   Set the properties of each control as follows:

Form1 Control	
Name	FormGrade_Student
BackColor	Control
FormBorderStyle	FixedSingle
StartPosition	CenterScreen
Text	Form Grade-Student

label1 Control	
Text	Grade Name

comboBox1 Control	
Name	cboGrade

label2 Control	
Text	Student Name

comboBox2 Control	
Text	cboStudent

button1 Control	
Name	btnFirst
Text	|< First

button2 Control	
Name	btnPrev
Text	< Prev

button3 Control	
Name	btnNext
Text	Next >

button4 Control	
Name	btnLast
Text	Last >|

button5 Control	
Name	btnSearch
Text	Search

button6 Control	
Name	btnEdit
Text	&Edit

button7 Control	
Name	btnSave
Text	&Save

button8 Control	
Name	btnCancel
Text	&Cancel

button9 Control	
Name	btnAddNew
Text	&Add New

button10 Control	
Name	btnDelete
Text	&Delete

button11 Control	
Name	btnDone
Text	Do&ne

button12 Control	
Name	btnPrint
Text	&Print

button13 Control	
Name	btnFormGrade
Text	View/Edit/Add Grade

button14 Control	
Name	btnFormStudent
Text	View/Edit/Add Student

printPreviewDialog1 Control	
Name	dlgPreview

Step 3   You will add features to this parent form gradually. At this point, you will add code to construct the data table and to navigate the records in the **Grade_Student** table. Add these lines of code at the top of the window:

```
1  using System.Data.SqlClient;
2  using System.IO;
3  using System.Drawing.Printing;
```

Step 4   Write the following form-level declarations for creating data objects:

```
1   SqlConnection connBook;
2   SqlCommand commandGradeStudent;
3   SqlDataAdapter adapterGradeStudent;
4   DataTable tableGradeStudent;
5   CurrencyManager managerGradeStudent;
6
7   SqlCommand commandGrade;
8   SqlDataAdapter adapterGrade;
9   DataTable tableGrade;
10
11  SqlCommand commandStudent;
12  SqlDataAdapter adapterStudent;
13  DataTable tabelStudent;
```

Step 5   Add the following code to the **FormGrade_Student_Load** event method:

```
1   private void FormGrade_Student_Load(object sender, EventArgs e)
2   {
3       try
4       {
5           // Connects to database
6           connBook = new SqlConnection("Data Source=.\\SQLEXPRESS;
7               AttachDbFilename=D:\\Database\\DBMS.mdf;
8               Integrated Security = True; Connect Timeout = 30;
9               User Instance = True");
10
11          // Opens connection
12          connBook.Open();
13
14          // Creates Command object
15          string StatementSQL =
16              "SELECT * FROM Grade_Student ORDER BY GradeID";
17          commandGradeStudent = new SqlCommand(
18              StatementSQL, connBook);
19
20          // Creates DataAdapter/DataTable objects
21          adapterGradeStudent = new SqlDataAdapter();
```

```
22      adapterGradeStudent.SelectCommand = commandGradeStudent;
23      tableGradeStudent = new DataTable();
24      adapterGradeStudent.Fill(tableGradeStudent);
25
26      // Binds controls to data table
27      cboGrade.DataBindings.Add("Text",
28          tableGradeStudent, "GradeID");
29      cboStudent.DataBindings.Add("Text",
30          tableGradeStudent, "StudentID");
31
32      // Populates cboGrade
33      commandGrade = new SqlCommand(
34          "SELECT GradeID, Name FROM Grade ORDER BY Name",
35          connBook);
36      adapterGrade = new SqlDataAdapter();
37      adapterGrade.SelectCommand = commandGrade;
38      tableGrade = new DataTable();
39      adapterGrade.Fill(tableGrade);
40      cboGrade.DataSource = tableGrade;
41      cboGrade.DisplayMember = "Name";
42      cboGrade.ValueMember = "GradeID";
43      cboGrade.DataBindings.Add("SelectedValue",
44          tableGradeStudent, "GradeID");
45
46      // Populates cboStudent
47      commandStudent = new SqlCommand("SELECT StudentID,
48          CONCAT(FirstName, ' ', LASTNAME) AS Name
49          FROM Student ORDER BY FirstName", connBook);
50      adapterStudent = new SqlDataAdapter();
51      adapterStudent.SelectCommand = commandStudent;
52      tabelStudent = new DataTable();
53      adapterStudent.Fill(tabelStudent);
54      cboStudent.DataSource = tabelStudent;
55      cboStudent.DisplayMember = "Name";
56      cboStudent.ValueMember = "StudentID";
57      cboStudent.DataBindings.Add("SelectedValue",
58          tableGradeStudent, "StudentID");
59
60      // Creates CurrencyManager object
61      managerGradeStudent =
62          (CurrencyManager)BindingContext[tableGradeStudent];
63
64      SetText();
65      this.Show();
66  }
67  catch (Exception ex)
68  {
69      MessageBox.Show(ex.Message, "Error in reading table",
70          MessageBoxButtons.OK, MessageBoxIcon.Error);
71      return;
72  }
```

}

The code above creates the data objects needed to open the database and construct the
Grade_Student table (includes all fields). The code above then binds the controls with
the update manager object (**CurrencyManager**). It also populates **cboGrade** and
cboSubject.

Step 6   Add the following code to **FormGrade_Student_FormClosing** event method to close
the database connection:

```csharp
private void FormGrade_Student_FormClosing(object sender,
FormClosingEventArgs e)
{
    // Closes connection to database
    connBook.Close();

    // Deletes objects
    connBook.Dispose();
    commandGradeStudent.Dispose();
    adapterGradeStudent.Dispose();
    commandGrade.Dispose();
    adapterGrade.Dispose();
    tableGrade.Dispose();
    commandStudent.Dispose();
    adapterStudent.Dispose();
    tabelStudent.Dispose();
}
```

Step 7   Define **SetText** method to give description on title bar as follows:

```csharp
private void SetText()
{
    this.Text = "Grade - Student Data - Record " +
        (managerGrade.Position + 1).ToString() + " of " +
        managerGrade.Count.ToString() + " Records";
}
```

Step 8   Write the following code for the **Click** event of the four navigation buttons:

```csharp
private void btnPrev_Click(object sender, EventArgs e)
{
    if (managerGradeStudent.Position == 0)
    {
        Console.Beep();
    }
    managerGradeStudent.Position--;
    SetText();
}

private void btnNext_Click(object sender, EventArgs e)
```

```
12   {
13       if (managerGradeStudent.Position == managerGradeStudent.Count - 1)
14       {
15           Console.Beep();
16       }
17       managerGradeStudent.Position++;
18       SetText();
19   }
20
21   private void btnFirst_Click(object sender, EventArgs e)
22   {
23       managerGradeStudent.Position = 0;
24       SetText();
25   }
26
27   private void btnLast_Click(object sender, EventArgs e)
28   {
29       managerGradeStudent.Position = managerGrade.Count - 1;
30       SetText();
31   }
```

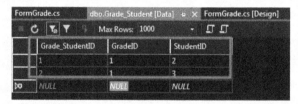

Figure 7.15 Inserting some data into **Grade_Student** table

Figure 7.16 The **Grade_Student** form when it first runs

Step 9   Insert some data into **Grade_Student** table as shown in Figure 7.15.

Step 10   Save and run the application. What is displayed first is the first record in **Grade** table. Click on four navigation buttons to prove the result.

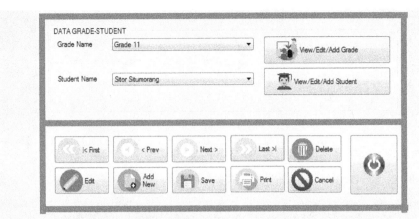

Figure 7.17 The result when user clicks **Last >|** button

7.13 Tutorial Steps of Creating Form for Grade_Student Table: Message Box

Step 1   There are two places where you can use the message box in **Grade_Student** form.
One message box is provided after saving updates to let the user know that the save
was successful and another message box is related to record deletion.

Use the following code in **btnSave_Click** event method:

```
private void btnSave_Click(object sender, EventArgs e)
{
    MessageBox.Show("Record is successfully saved", "Save",
        MessageBoxButtons.OK, MessageBoxIcon.Information);
}
```

There will be more code in this event. The code implements only message box.

Step 2   Use this code on **btnDelete_Click** event method:

```
private void btnDelete_Click(object sender, EventArgs e)
{
    DialogResult response;
    response = MessageBox.Show("Dou you really want to delete this record?",
        "Delete", MessageBoxButtons.YesNo, MessageBoxIcon.Question,
        MessageBoxDefaultButton.Button2);
}
```

Step 3   Save the application and run it. Click on **Delete** button to see as shown in Figure 7.18.

Figure 7.18 Message box is displayed when user clicks **Delete** button

7.14 Tutorial Steps of Creating Form for Grade_Student Table: Application State

Step 1   The **Grade_Student** form operates in one of three states: **View** state, **Add** state, or **Edit** state. In the **View** state, user can navigate one record to another, user can switch to **Edit** state, user can add and/or delete records, or user can exit the application.

        In **Add** and **Edit** state, no navigation is made possible, data can be updated, and user can have access to **Save** and **Cancel** operations. Each of these steps can be implemented using the **Enabled** property of the button and the **ReadOnly** property of the text box.

Step 2   Add a method named **SetState** as follows:

```
1   private void SetState(string stateStr) {
2       switch (stateStr)
3       {
4           case "View":
5               btnFirst.Enabled = true;
6               btnPrev.Enabled = true;
7               btnNext.Enabled = true;
8               btnLast.Enabled = true;
9               btnAddNew.Enabled = true;
10              btnSave.Enabled = false;
11              btnDelete.Enabled = true;
12              btnCancel.Enabled = false;
13              btnEdit.Enabled = true;
14              btnDone.Enabled = true;
15              cboGrade.Enabled = false;
16              cboStudent.Enabled = false;
17              btnFormGrade.Enabled = false;
18              btnFormStudent.Enabled = false;
19              break;
20
21          default: // Edit or Add
22              cboGrade.Enabled = true;
23              cboStudent.Enabled = true;
24              btnFirst.Enabled = false;
```

```
25        btnPrev.Enabled = false;
26        btnNext.Enabled = false;
27        btnLast.Enabled = false;
28        btnAddNew.Enabled = false;
29        btnSave.Enabled = true;
30        btnDelete.Enabled = false;
31        btnCancel.Enabled = true;
32        btnEdit.Enabled = false;
33        btnDone.Enabled = false;
34        btnPrint.Enabled = false;
35        btnFormGrade.Enabled = true;
36        btnFormStudent.Enabled = true;
37        break;
38    }
39 }
```

The code above specifies **View**, **Add**, or **Edit** state for the application. Pay attention to which buttons are available and which are not.

Step 3   Set the **View** state when the application first runs. Add the following code in line 65 to **FormGrade_Student_Load** event method:

```
1  private void FormGrade_Student_Load(object sender, EventArgs e)
2  {
3      try
4      {
5          // Connects to database
6          connBook = new SqlConnection("Data Source=.\\SQLEXPRESS;
7              AttachDbFilename=D:\\Database\\DBMS.mdf;
8              Integrated Security = True; Connect Timeout = 30;
9              User Instance = True");
10
11         // Opens connection
12         connBook.Open();
13
14         // Creates Command object
15         string StatementSQL =
16             "SELECT * FROM Grade_Student ORDER BY GradeID";
17         commandGradeStudent = new SqlCommand(
18             StatementSQL, connBook);
19
20         // Creates DataAdapter/DataTable objects
21         adapterGradeStudent = new SqlDataAdapter();
22         adapterGradeStudent.SelectCommand = commandGradeStudent;
23         tableGradeStudent = new DataTable();
24         adapterGradeStudent.Fill(tableGradeStudent);
25
26         // Binds controls to data table
27         cboGrade.DataBindings.Add("Text",
28             tableGradeStudent, "GradeID");
```

```
29      cboStudent.DataBindings.Add("Text",
30          tableGradeStudent, "StudentID");
31
32      // Populates cboGrade
33      commandGrade = new SqlCommand(
34          "SELECT GradeID, Name FROM Grade ORDER BY Name",
35          connBook);
36      adapterGrade = new SqlDataAdapter();
37      adapterGrade.SelectCommand = commandGrade;
38      tableGrade = new DataTable();
39      adapterGrade.Fill(tableGrade);
40      cboGrade.DataSource = tableGrade;
41      cboGrade.DisplayMember = "Name";
42      cboGrade.ValueMember = "GradeID";
43      cboGrade.DataBindings.Add("SelectedValue",
44          tableGradeStudent, "GradeID");
45
46      // Populates cboStudent
47      commandStudent = new SqlCommand("SELECT StudentID,
48          CONCAT(FirstName, ' ', LASTNAME) AS Name
49          FROM Student ORDER BY FirstName", connBook);
50      adapterStudent = new SqlDataAdapter();
51      adapterStudent.SelectCommand = commandStudent;
52      tabelStudent = new DataTable();
53      adapterStudent.Fill(tabelStudent);
54      cboStudent.DataSource = tabelStudent;
55      cboStudent.DisplayMember = "Name";
56      cboStudent.ValueMember = "StudentID";
57      cboStudent.DataBindings.Add("SelectedValue",
58          tableGradeStudent, "StudentID");
59
60      // Creates CurrencyManager object
61      managerGradeStudent =
62          (CurrencyManager)BindingContext[tableGradeStudent];
63
64      SetText();
65      SetState("View");
66      this.Show();
67  }
68  catch (Exception ex)
69  {
70      MessageBox.Show(ex.Message, "Error in reading table",
71          MessageBoxButtons.OK, MessageBoxIcon.Error);
72      return;
73  }
74 }
```

Step 4   When **Add New** button is clicked, you need to switch to **Add** state. Add the following code to **btnAddNew_Click** event method:

```
1  private void btnAddNew_Click(object sender, EventArgs e)
2  {
3      SetState("Add");
4  }
```

Step 5   When **Edit** button is clicked, the application will be switched to **Edit** state. Add the following code to **btnEdit_Click** event method:

```
1  private void btnEdit_Click(object sender, EventArgs e)
2  {
3      SetState("Edit");
4  }
```

Step 6   When **Cancel** or **Save** button is clicked (in **Add** or **Edit** state), application will return to the **View** state. Put this line of code in **btnCancel_Click** and **btnSave_Click** event methods:

```
1  private void btnCancel_Click(object sender, EventArgs e)
2  {
3      SetState("View");
4  }
5
6  private void btnSave_Click(object sender, EventArgs e)
7  {
8      SetState("View");
9  }
```

Step 7   Save and run the application. You will see the application in its initial state (**View** state) as shown in Figure 7.19.

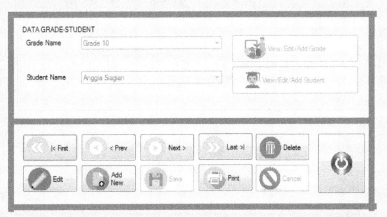

Figure 7.19 Grade_Student form is in **View** state when it first runs

When user clicks the **Edit** and **Add New** button, you will see what is shown in Figure 7.20 and 7.21.

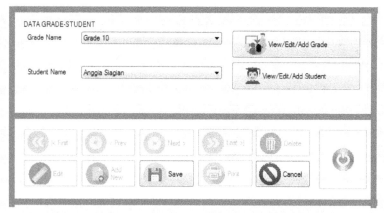

Figure 7.20 Grade_Student form is in **Edit** state

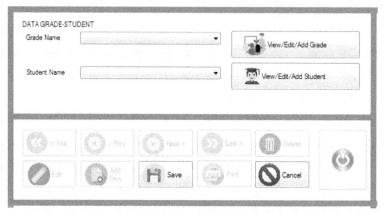

Figure 7.21 Grade_Student form is in **Add** state

7.15 Tutorial Steps of Creating Form for Grade_Student Table: Error Trapping

Step 1   Modify **btnAddNew_Click**, **btnSave_Click**, and **btnDelete_Click** event methods to
handle error trapping:

```
1   private void btnAddNew_Click(object sender, EventArgs e)
2   {
3       try
4       {
5           SetState("Add");
6       }
7       catch (Exception ex)
8       {
9           MessageBox.Show("Error adding new record.", "Error",
10              MessageBoxButtons.OK, MessageBoxIcon.Error);
11      }
12  }
```

```csharp
private void btnSave_Click(object sender, EventArgs e)
{
    try
    {
        MessageBox.Show("Record successfully saved", "Save",
        MessageBoxButtons.OK, MessageBoxIcon.Information);
        SetState("View");
    }
    catch (Exception ex)
    {
        MessageBox.Show("Error saving record.", "Error",
            MessageBoxButtons.OK, MessageBoxIcon.Error);
    }
}
```

```csharp
private void btnDelete_Click(object sender, EventArgs e)
{
    DialogResult response;
    response = MessageBox.Show("Dou you really want to delete this record?",
        "Delete", MessageBoxButtons.YesNo, MessageBoxIcon.Question,
        MessageBoxDefaultButton.Button2);
    if (response == DialogResult.No)
    {
        return;
    }

    try
    {

    }
    catch (Exception ex)
    {
        MessageBox.Show("Error deleting record.", "Error",
            MessageBoxButtons.OK, MessageBoxIcon.Error);
    }
}
```

7.16 Tutorial Step of Creating Form for Grade_Student Table: Opening Grade and Student Form

Step 1   Define Click event of **btnFormGrade** and **btnFormStudent** as follows:

```csharp
private void btnFormGrade_Click(object sender, EventArgs e)
{
    FormGrade frm = new FormGrade ();
    frm.Show();
}

private void btnFormStudent_Click(object sender, EventArgs e)
```

```
8    {
9        FormStudent frm = new FormStudent();
10       frm.Show();
11   }
```

7.17 Tutorial Steps of Creating Form for Grade_Student Table: Editing Record

Step 1   Add the following line of code to the form-level declaration:

```
1    string appState;
```

step 2   Add this code in line 2 to **SetState** method:

```
1    private void SetState(string stateStr) {
2        appState = stateStr;
3        switch (stateStr)
4        {
5            case "View":
6                btnFirst.Enabled = true;
7                btnPrev.Enabled = true;
8                btnNext.Enabled = true;
9                btnLast.Enabled = true;
10               btnAddNew.Enabled = true;
11               btnSave.Enabled = false;
12               btnDelete.Enabled = true;
13               btnCancel.Enabled = false;
14               btnEdit.Enabled = true;
15               btnDone.Enabled = true;
16               cboGrade.Enabled = false;
17               cboStudent.Enabled = false;
18               btnFormGrade.Enabled = false;
19               btnFormStudent.Enabled = false;
20               break;
21
22           default: // Edit or Add
23               cboGrade.Enabled = true;
24               cboStudent.Enabled = true;
25               btnFirst.Enabled = false;
26               btnPrev.Enabled = false;
27               btnNext.Enabled = false;
28               btnLast.Enabled = false;
29               btnAddNew.Enabled = false;
30               btnSave.Enabled = true;
31               btnDelete.Enabled = false;
32               btnCancel.Enabled = true;
33               btnEdit.Enabled = false;
34               btnDone.Enabled = false;
35               btnPrint.Enabled = false;
```

```
36          btnFormGrade.Enabled = true;
37          btnFormStudent.Enabled = true;
38          break;
39      }
40  }
```

Step 3   Modify **btnSave_Click** event method to save the change and reposition the pointer to the record just edited:

```
1   private void btnSave_Click(object sender, EventArgs e)
2   {
3       if (cboGrade.SelectedIndex == -1 || cboStudent.SelectedIndex == -1)
4       {
5           MessageBox.Show(
6           "You need to choose grade and subject names", "Information",
7           MessageBoxButtons.OK, MessageBoxIcon.Information);
8           return;
9       }
10
11      string nameSaved = cboStudent.SelectedValue.ToString();
12      int rowSaved;
13
14      try
15      {
16          managerGradeStudent.EndCurrentEdit();
17          tableGradeStudent.DefaultView.Sort = "StudentID";
18          rowSaved = tableGradeStudent.DefaultView.Find(nameSaved);
19          managerGradeStudent.Position = rowSaved;
20
21          // Saves changes into database
22          SqlCommandBuilder GSAdapterCommand = new
23              SqlCommandBuilder(adapterGradeStudent);
24          adapterGradeStudent.Update(tableGradeStudent);
25
26          MessageBox.Show("Record is successfully saved", "Save",
27              MessageBoxButtons.OK, MessageBoxIcon.Information);
28          SetState("View");
29      }
30      catch (Exception ex)
31      {
32          MessageBox.Show("Error in saving record.", "Error",
33              MessageBoxButtons.OK, MessageBoxIcon.Error);
34      }
35  }
```

Step 4   Modify **btnCancel_Click** event method to restore controls if the edit is canceled:

```
1   private void btnCancel_Click(object sender, EventArgs e)
2   {
3       managerGradeStudent.CancelCurrentEdit();
4
```

```
5      SetState("View");
6  }
```

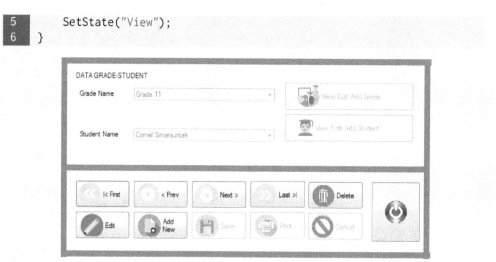

Figure 7.22 Editing operation is successfully performed

Step 5   Add the following code in line to the **FormGrade_Student_FormClosing** method to save any changes to the database file:

```
1   private void FormGrade_Student_FormClosing(object sender,
2   FormClosingEventArgs e)
3   {
4       try
5       {
6           // Saves changes into database
7           SqlCommandBuilder GSAdapterCommand =
8               new SqlCommandBuilder(adapterGradeStudent);
9           adapterGradeStudent.Update(tableGradeStudent);
10      }
11      catch (Exception ex)
12      {
13          MessageBox.Show("Error saving database into file: \r\n" +
14              ex.Message, "Saving Error", MessageBoxButtons.OK,
15              MessageBoxIcon.Error);
16      }
17
18      // Closes connection to database
19      connBook.Close();
20
21      // Deletes objects
22      connBook.Dispose();
23      commandGradeStudent.Dispose();
24      adapterGradeStudent.Dispose();
25      commandGrade.Dispose();
26      adapterGrade.Dispose();
27      tableGrade.Dispose();
28      commandStudent.Dispose();
29      adapterStudent.Dispose();
```

```
30    tabelStudent.Dispose();
31  }
```

Step 6   Save and run the application. Make sure Edit feature is working properly. Make sure the **Cancel** button is working properly. This is shown in Figure 7.22.

7.18 Tutorial Steps of Creating Form for Grade_Student Table: Adding New Record

Step 1   You now implement the capability on the form to add new records to the database. Add the following line of code to the form-level declaration:

```
1  int myBookmark;
```

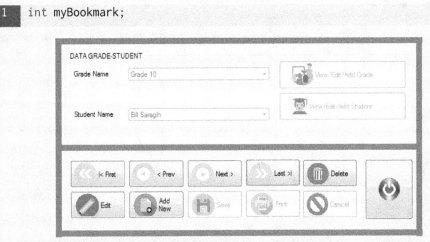

Figure 7.23 The new record has been successfully saved into the database

Step 2   Modify **btnAddNew_Click** event method to add a new record by adding code in line 5-6:

```
1  private void btnAddNew_Click(object sender, EventArgs e)
2  {
3      try
4      {
5          myBookmark = managerGradeStudent.Position;
6          managerGradeStudent.AddNew();
7          SetState("Add");
8      }
9      catch (Exception ex)
10     {
11         MessageBox.Show("Error adding new record.", "Error",
12             MessageBoxButtons.OK, MessageBoxIcon.Error);
13     }
14 }
```

Step 3   Modify **btnCancel_Click** event method to differentiate between cancellation during
Edit mode and **Add** mode by adding code in line 5-8:

```
1   private void btnCancel_Click(object sender, EventArgs e)
2   {
3       managerGradeStudent.CancelCurrentEdit();
4
5       if (appState.Equals("Add"))
6       {
7           managerGradeStudent.Position = myBookmark;
8       }
9       SetState("View");
10  }
```

Step 4   Save and run the application. Click **Add New** button. New record has been
successfully saved as shown in Figure 7.23.

7.19 Tutorial Steps of Creating Form for Grade_Student Table: Deleting Record

Step 1   You will now add the capability to delete records from **Grade_Student** table. Modify
the **btnDelete_Click** event method by adding code in line 14 to delete records if the
user responds to **Yes** in the message box:

```
1   private void btnDelete_Click(object sender, EventArgs e)
2   {
3       DialogResult response;
4       response = MessageBox.Show("Dou you really want to delete this record?",
5           "Delete", MessageBoxButtons.YesNo, MessageBoxIcon.Question,
6           MessageBoxDefaultButton.Button2);
7       if (response == DialogResult.No)
8       {
9           return;
10      }
11
12      try
13      {
14          managerGradeStudent.RemoveAt(managerGradeStudent.Position);
15      }
16      catch (Exception ex)
17      {
18          MessageBox.Show("Error deleting record.", "Error",
19              MessageBoxButtons.OK, MessageBoxIcon.Error);
20      }
21  }
```

Step 2   Save the application and run it. Make sure the **Yes** and **No** responses in the message
box give correct results. Delete only those records you added using **Add New** button.

7.20 Tutorial Steps of Creating Form for Grade_Student Table: Stopping Application

Step 1   Add the following code in line 4-12 and line 39 to **FormGrade_Student_FormClosing** event method to ensure user doesn't close the application during **Edit** or **Add** mode:

```
1   private void FormGrade_FormClosing(object sender,
2   FormClosingEventArgs e)
3   {
4       if (appState.Equals("Edit") || appState.Equals("Add"))
5       {
6           MessageBox.Show(
7               "You should finish editing before closing application.",
8               "", MessageBoxButtons.OK, MessageBoxIcon.Information);
9           e.Cancel = true;
10      }
11      else
12      {
13          try
14          {
15              // Saves changes into database
16              SqlCommandBuilder GSdapterCommand =
17                  new SqlCommandBuilder(adapterGradeStudent);
18              adapterGradeStudent.Update(tableGradeStudent);
19          }
20          catch (Exception ex)
21          {
22              MessageBox.Show("Error saving database into file: \r\n" +
23                  ex.Message, "Error Saving", MessageBoxButtons.OK,
24                  MessageBoxIcon.Error);
25          }
26
27          // Closes connection to database
28          connBook.Close();
29
30          // Deletes objects
31          connBook.Dispose();
32          commandGradeStudent.Dispose();
33          adapterGradeStudent.Dispose();
34          commandGrade.Dispose();
35          adapterGrade.Dispose();
36          tableGrade.Dispose();
37          commandStudent.Dispose();
38          adapterStudent.Dispose();
39          tabelStudent.Dispose();
40      }
41  }
```

Step 2   Put this code in **btnDone_Click** event method:

```
1   private void btnDone_Click(object sender, EventArgs e)
2   {
3       this.Close();
4   }
```

Step 3   Save and run the application. Make sure the **Done** button is working properly. Make sure the user cannot close the application in **Edit** or **Add** mode.

7.21 Tutorial Steps of Selecting Students Based on Grade

Step 1   Add a button control on the form. Set its **Name** property as **btnRefreshGrade** and its **Text** poperty as **Refresh**. You add a **DataGridView** control and set its **Name** property as **grdGrade**.

You also need to add a label and set its **Text** property as **Number of Records:**. Add a textbox on the form. Set its **Name** property as **txtRecordGrade**.

Then add another label and set its **Text** property as **Choose Grade**. Finally, add a combobox and set its Name property as **cboChooseGrade**.
The resulting form is shown in Figure 7.24.

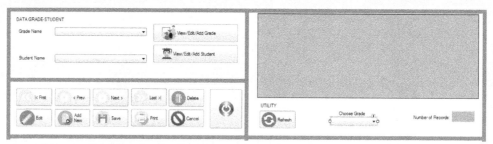

Figure 7.24 Grade_Student form after a number of new controls added

Step 2   Define createStatementSQL as follows:

```
1    private string createStatementSQL()
2    {
3        string StatementSQL = "";
4        StatementSQL = "SELECT Grade.Name, Grade.SchoolYear, 
5            Subject.Name AS Subject_Name, ";
6        StatementSQL += "CONCAT(Teacher.FirstName, ' ', 
7            Teacher.LastName) AS Teacher_Name, ";
8        StatementSQL += "CONCAT(Student.FirstName, ' ', 
9            Student.LastName) AS Student_Name, ";
10       StatementSQL += "Subject.Description, ";
11       StatementSQL += "Grade.TimeStart, Grade.TimeFinish ";
12       StatementSQL += "FROM ((((Student INNER JOIN Grade_Student ON 
13           Student.StudentID = Grade_Student.StudentID) ";
```

```
14    StatementSQL += "INNER JOIN Grade ON Grade_Student.GradeID =
15        Grade.GradeID) ";
16    StatementSQL += "INNER JOIN Subject ON Grade.SubjectID =
17        Subject.SubjectID) ";
18    StatementSQL += "INNER JOIN Teacher ON Grade.TeacherID =
19        Teacher.TeacherID) ";
20
21    return StatementSQL;
22 }
```

Step 3   Define a new method named **Refresh_DGV** as follows:

```
1    private void Refresh_DGV(DataGridView dgv, string StatementSQL,
2    TextBox txt1)
3    {
4        // Connects to database
5        connBook = new SqlConnection("Data Source=.\\SQLEXPRESS;
6            AttachDbFilename=D:\\Database\\DBMS.mdf;
7            Integrated Security = True; Connect Timeout = 30;
8            User Instance = True");
9        connBook.Open();
10
11        SqlCommand commandResult = null;
12        SqlDataAdapter adapterResult = new SqlDataAdapter();
13        DataTable tabelResult = new DataTable();
14
15        try
16        {
17            // Creates Command and DataAdapater objects
18            commandResult = new SqlCommand(StatementSQL, connBook);
19            adapterResult.SelectCommand = commandResult;
20            adapterResult.Fill(tabelResult);
21
22            // Binds DataGridView to data table
23            dgv.DataSource = tabelResult;
24            txt1.Text = tabelResult.Rows.Count.ToString();
25
26            // Colors rows in DGV
27            setRowColor(dgv);
28        }
29        catch (Exception ex)
30        {
31            MessageBox.Show(ex.Message, "Error Processing SQL",
32            MessageBoxButtons.OK, MessageBoxIcon.Error);
33        }
34
35        // Updates database
36        SqlCommandBuilder GSAdapterCommand = new
37            SqlCommandBuilder(adapterGradeStudent);
38        adapterGradeStudent.Update(tableGradeStudent);
```

```
39
40      commandResult.Dispose();
41      adapterResult.Dispose();
42      tabelResult.Dispose();
    }
```

Step 4   Define **Click** event of **btnRefreshGrade** as follows:

```
1   private void btnRefreshGrade_Click(object sender, EventArgs e)
2   {
3       string StatementSQL = createStatementSQL();
4       Refresh_DGV(grdGrade, StatementSQL, txtRecordGrade);
5   }
```

Step 5   Then define **populatecboChooseGrade** method to populate **cboChooseGrade** as follows:

```
1   private void populatecboChooseGrade()
2   {
3       commandCombo1 = new SqlCommand(
4           "SELECT DISTINCT(Name) FROM Grade ORDER BY Name", connBook);
5       adapterCombo1 = new SqlDataAdapter();
6       adapterCombo1.SelectCommand = commandCombo1;
7       tabelCombo1 = new DataTable();
8       adapterCombo1.Fill(tabelCombo1);
9       cboChooseGrade.DataSource = tabelCombo1;
10      cboChooseGrade.DisplayMember = "Name";
11  }
```

Step 6   Define **SelectedIndexChanged** event of **cboChooseGrade** as follows:

```
1   private void cboChooseGrade_SelectedIndexChanged(object sender,
2   EventArgs e)
3   {
4       // Connects to database
5       connBook = new SqlConnection("Data Source=.\\SQLEXPRESS;
6           AttachDbFilename=D:\\Database\\DBMS.mdf;
7           Integrated Security = True; Connect Timeout = 30;
8           User Instance = True");
9       connBook.Open();
10
11      SqlDataAdapter adapterResult = new SqlDataAdapter();
12      DataTable tableResult = new DataTable();
13      SqlCommand commandResult;
14      string gradeName;
15
16      try
17      {
18          if (cboChooseGrade.SelectedItem != null)
19          {
```

```
20    DataRow rowSelected =
21        ((DataRowView)cboChooseGrade.SelectedValue).Row;
22    gradeName = rowSelected["Name"].ToString();
23
24    string StatementSQL = createStatementSQL();
25    StatementSQL += "WHERE Grade.Name = '" +
26        gradeName + "' ORDER BY Grade.Name";
27
28    commandResult = new SqlCommand(StatementSQL, connBook);
29    adapterResult.SelectCommand = commandResult;
30    adapterResult.Fill(tableResult);
31
32    // Binds DataGridView to data table
33    grdGrade.DataSource = tableResult;
34    txtRecordGrade.Text = tableResult.Rows.Count.ToString();
35
36    // Colors rows in DGV
37    setRowColor(grdGrade);
38    }
39    }
40    catch (Exception ex)
41    {
42        MessageBox.Show(ex.Message, "Error Processing SQL",
43            MessageBoxButtons.OK, MessageBoxIcon.Error);
44    }
}
```

Step 7   Add the following code in line 66-67 to **FormGrade_Student_Load** event method.

```
1    private void FormGrade_Student_Load(object sender, EventArgs e)
2    {
3        try
4        {
5            // Connects to database
6            connBook = new SqlConnection("Data Source=.\\SQLEXPRESS;
7                AttachDbFilename=D:\\Database\\DBMS.mdf;
8                Integrated Security = True; Connect Timeout = 30;
9                User Instance = True");
10
11           // Opens connection
12           connBook.Open();
13
14           // Creates Command object
15           string StatementSQL =
16               "SELECT * FROM Grade_Student ORDER BY GradeID";
17           commandGradeStudent = new SqlCommand(
18               StatementSQL, connBook);
19
20           // Creates DataAdapter/DataTable objects
21           adapterGradeStudent = new SqlDataAdapter();
22           adapterGradeStudent.SelectCommand = commandGradeStudent;
```

```
23        tableGradeStudent = new DataTable();
24        adapterGradeStudent.Fill(tableGradeStudent);
25
26        // Binds controls to data table
27        cboGrade.DataBindings.Add("Text",
28            tableGradeStudent, "GradeID");
29        cboStudent.DataBindings.Add("Text",
30            tableGradeStudent, "StudentID");
31
32        // Populates cboGrade
33        commandGrade = new SqlCommand(
34            "SELECT GradeID, Name FROM Grade ORDER BY Name",
35            connBook);
36        adapterGrade = new SqlDataAdapter();
37        adapterGrade.SelectCommand = commandGrade;
38        tableGrade = new DataTable();
39        adapterGrade.Fill(tableGrade);
40        cboGrade.DataSource = tableGrade;
41        cboGrade.DisplayMember = "Name";
42        cboGrade.ValueMember = "GradeID";
43        cboGrade.DataBindings.Add("SelectedValue",
44            tableGradeStudent, "GradeID");
45
46        // Populates cboStudent
47        commandStudent = new SqlCommand("SELECT StudentID,
48            CONCAT(FirstName, ' ', LASTNAME) AS Name
49            FROM Student ORDER BY FirstName", connBook);
50        adapterStudent = new SqlDataAdapter();
51        adapterStudent.SelectCommand = commandStudent;
52        tabelStudent = new DataTable();
53        adapterStudent.Fill(tabelStudent);
54        cboStudent.DataSource = tabelStudent;
55        cboStudent.DisplayMember = "Name";
56        cboStudent.ValueMember = "StudentID";
57        cboStudent.DataBindings.Add("SelectedValue",
58            tableGradeStudent, "StudentID");
59
60        // Creates CurrencyManager object
61        managerGradeStudent =
62            (CurrencyManager)BindingContext[tableGradeStudent];
63
64        SetText();
65        SetState("View");
66        this.Show();
67        populatecboChooseGrade();
68        btnRefreshGrade.PerformClick();
69    }
70    catch (Exception ex)
71    {
72        MessageBox.Show(ex.Message, "Error in reading table",
73            MessageBoxButtons.OK, MessageBoxIcon.Error);
```

```
74          return;
75      }
    }
```

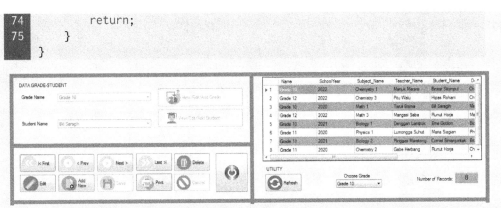

Figure 7.25 The grade_student form when it first runs

Step 8   Define **RowPostPaint** event of **grdGrade** control to give it a row numbering:

```
1  private void grdGrade_RowPostPaint(object sender,
2  DataGridViewRowPostPaintEventArgs e)
3  {
4      var grid = sender as DataGridView;
5      var rowIdx = (e.RowIndex + 1).ToString();
6
7      var centerFormat = new StringFormat()
8      {
9          // Aligns to middle
10         Alignment = StringAlignment.Center,
11         LineAlignment = StringAlignment.Center
12     };
13
14     var headerBounds = new Rectangle(e.RowBounds.Left,
15         e.RowBounds.Top, grid.RowHeadersWidth, e.RowBounds.Height);
16     e.Graphics.DrawString(rowIdx, this.Font,
17         SystemBrushes.ControlText, headerBounds, centerFormat);
18 }
```

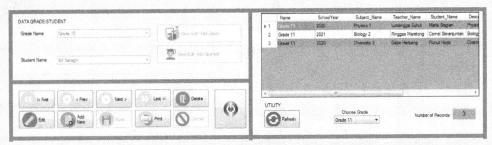

Figure 7.26 The results when user chooses Grade 11

Step 9   Define **setRowColor** method to alternately give color to rows of DGV control as
follows:

```
1  // Altenately colors row
```

```
2    private void setRowColor(DataGridView dgv)
3    {
4        for (int i = 0; i < dgv.Rows.Count; i++)
5        {
6            if (i % 2 == 0)
7            {
8                for (int j = 0; j < dgv.Columns.Count; j++ )
9                    dgv.Rows[i].Cells[j].Style.BackColor =
10                       System.Drawing.Color.LightGreen;
11           }
12           else
13           {
14               for (int j = 0; j < dgv.Columns.Count; j++)
15                   dgv.Rows[i].Cells[j].Style.BackColor =
16                       System.Drawing.Color.LightYellow;
17           }
18       }
19   }
```

Step 10   Save and run the application. The result is shown in Figure 7.25. Figure 7.26 is the
query result when user chooses Grade 11.

Figure 7.27 The results when user chooses one of teachers.

Step 11   You can add another combo box and set its Name property as **cboChooseTeacher**.
Define **populatecboChooseTeacher** method as follows:

```
1    private void populatecboChooseTeacher()
2    {
3        commandCombo1 = new SqlCommand(
4            "SELECT FirstName FROM Teacher ORDER BY FirstName",
5            connBook);
6        adapterCombo1 = new SqlDataAdapter();
7        adapterCombo1.SelectCommand = commandCombo1;
8        tabelCombo1 = new DataTable();
9        adapterCombo1.Fill(tabelCombo1);
10       cboChooseTeacher.DataSource = tabelCombo1;
11       cboChooseTeacher.DisplayMember = "FirstName";
12   }
```

Step 12   Then define **SelectedIndexChanged** of **cboChooseTeacher** as follows:

```csharp
private void cboChooseTeacher_SelectedIndexChanged(object sender,
EventArgs e)
{
    // Connects to database
    connBook = new SqlConnection("Data Source=.\\SQLEXPRESS;
        AttachDbFilename=D:\\Database\\DBMS.mdf;
        Integrated Security = True; Connect Timeout = 30;
        User Instance = True");
    connBook.Open();
    SqlDataAdapter adapterResult = new SqlDataAdapter();
    DataTable tableResult = new DataTable();
    SqlCommand commandResult;
    string teacherName;

    try
    {
        if (cboChooseTeacher.SelectedItem != null)
        {
            DataRow rowSelected =
                ((DataRowView) cboChooseTeacher.SelectedValue).Row;
            teacherName = rowSelected["FirstName"].ToString();

            string StatementSQL = createStatementSQL();
            StatementSQL += "WHERE Teacher.FirstName = '" +
                teacherName + "' ORDER BY Teacher.FirstName";

            commandResult = new SqlCommand(StatementSQL, connBook);
            adapterResult.SelectCommand = commandResult;
            adapterResult.Fill(tableResult);

            // Binds DataGridView to data table
            grdGrade.DataSource = tableResult;
            txtRecordGrade.Text = tableResult.Rows.Count.ToString();

            // Colors rows in DGV
            setRowColor(grdGrade);
        }
    }
    catch (Exception ex)
    {
        MessageBox.Show(ex.Message, "Error Processing SQL",
            MessageBoxButtons.OK, MessageBoxIcon.Error);
    }
}
```

Step 13   Save and run the application. Figure 7.27 is the query result when user chooses one of teachers.